THE ECONOMICS OF ALFRED MARSHALL

Also Published in

Reprints of Economic Classics

BY HERERT J. DAVENPORT

VALUE AND DISTRIBUTION [1908]

THE ECONOMICS OF
ALFRED MARSHALL

BY

H. J. DAVENPORT
LATE PROFESSOR OF ECONOMICS IN
CORNELL UNIVERSITY

REPRINTS OF ECONOMIC CLASSICS

Augustus M. Kelley, Bookseller
New York 1965

Original edition *1935.*   Reprinted *1965* by arrangement with
Cornell University Press.

Library of Congress Catalogue Card Number
65 - 19648

KEPT WELL KNOW

PRINTED IN THE UNITED STATES OF AMERICA
by SENTRY PRESS, NEW YORK, N. Y. 10019

FOREWORD

FOR many years in classroom and seminar Professor Davenport's primary concern was with criticism and constructive amendment of the doctrinal content of the classical and neo-classical economics. His attitude toward systematic economic theory was never that of the iconoclast. He was indeed a jealous guardian of the economic discipline, and thought of himself as contributing to the perpetuation of an improved body of economic doctrine. Professor Davenport's own contributions to economic theory were frequently couched in the form of more or less controversial comment upon the doctrines of other economists. In his own thinking and in his teaching Marshall especially was a perennial point of reference. The present study, though mainly written in the two years following Professor Davenport's retirement from active academic duties, is therefore the product of more than thirty years' preoccupation with Marshall's economics.

The book is in one sense a finished product and in another it is not. It covers all the ground which Professor Davenport intended to cover and says on all points substantially what he wished to say. His death, however, prevented completion of the final revising and polishing which was under way, and to this fact may be attributed much unevenness of quality.

The book has been prepared for publication by a committee of the department of economics of Cornell University consisting of Paul T. Homan and M. Slade Kendrick, in collaboration with Margaret F. Milliken, formerly of the department of economics of Stanford University. The members of the committee decided that the manuscript had reached a stage which made it unwise to attempt editorial improvement even of the less perfect parts. It is therefore published almost exactly as it was left. A few obvious errors have been corrected, and a number of repetitive quotations have been removed. Special mention must be made of the services rendered by Miss Milliken who assisted Professor Davenport in the preparation of the manuscript at all stages.

CONTENTS

THE ECONOMICS OF ALFRED MARSHALL

Chapter I

INTRODUCTION

THE LAST edition of Alfred Marshall's *Principles of Economics* appeared in 1920, his final presentation of a course of thought of which successive editions during four decades had recorded the widening and deepening process. The very fact that a difficult treatise in systematic economics, a volume of 858 pages, totaling not far short of 400,000 words, could have arrived at an eighth edition, sufficiently attests the wide acceptance and un-exampled influence of Marshall's thought. It is probably well within the truth to assert that the authority of Marshall has been for several decades, and still remains, supreme among the economists of the English-speaking world. This Eighth Edition reports, then, not only the latest but the most authoritative rendering of the school of thought known as the Classical Economics. The position of leading economist of the leading school of economic thought in the world at large could probably, though less securely, be ascribed to Marshall. For many years, in any case, he has ranked as the dean of English economic writers and thinkers. He still so ranks.

The successive editions remained in a surprising degree faithful to the positions which were central to Marshall's earlier published work. Growth there doubtless was—but mainly in the details and the amplitude of statement and development. Both his starting point and his point of arrival were—and were avowedly—at essentially classical positions.

It is especially, then, as representative of this classical body of doctrine, and as the latest authoritative presentation of it in systematic form, that this work of Marshall's is here chosen for interpretation and criticism. This is to assume, doubtless, some common point of view or some unity of doctrine in this so-called school —an assumption that must a little await its justification. This, however, is not intended to deny that in the large, and still more emphatically in particulars, there was a considerable volume of

1

dissenting thought. But in the main these differences refer to issues lying well within the large outlines of the system. Not only is it true, then, that the classical economists outrun both in number and in doctrinal authoritativeness the economists of systematic dissent, but that still more decisive in numbers and in weight would be these majorities with regard to particular and specific issues of doctrine. Most, indeed, of the views, even of the avowed opponents of classical thought, have put in issue nothing that classical thinking would be seriously concerned to deny. It is true merely that the classical writers did not hold these views. But easily they might have, without violence to the rest of their thought. This holds especially, for example, as it seems to me, of the entire marginal-utility analysis. Nothing in it puts at issue anything that is essential to the classical scheme of thought.

Marshall in this regard makes his own thought[1] entirely clear:

. . . there is a widely spread belief that it [Ricardo's theory of cost of production in relation to value] has needed to be reconstructed. . . . Cause is shown . . . for not accepting this opinion; and for holding on the contrary that the foundations of the theory as they were left by Ricardo remain intact; that much has been added to them, and that very much has been built upon them, but that little has been taken from them . . . he knew that demand played an essential part in governing value, but . . . regarded its action as less obscure than that of cost of production, and therefore passed it lightly over in the notes which he made for the use of his friends, and himself; for he never essayed to write a formal treatise: . . . he regarded cost of production as dependent—not as Marx asserted him to have done on the mere quantity of labour used up in production, but—on the quality as well as quantity of that labour; together with the amount of stored up capital needed to aid labour, and the length of time during which such aid was invoked.

Marshall saw his task not as the instituting of a new point of view or method of approach in economic analysis, and not in the

---

[1] Alfred Marshall, *Principles of Economics* (8th ed., London, 1920), p. 503. All quotations are from this edition, unless otherwise specifically noted. Hereafter, Marshall references will be indicated by page numbers only, without more formal footnote citation. In the interests of space and of the clearer definition of the specific issues under examination many dangerously extensive elisions have been ventured—always, it is hoped, with due care against misinterpretation or misreport. Antecedent nouns for relative pronouns have been inserted in brackets as needed.

development of essentially new lines of generalization, but rather in the defense and reinforcement of the old; more sympathetic and more secure interpretations; supplementary and supporting rather than modifying doctrine; extensions of generalizations at some points and limitations at others; rectification of overstatement or of inaccuracies incident to an inadequate terminology—faults of the letter rather than of the spirit; a closer articulation of doctrines to a wider factual inclusiveness.

Never inhospitable to new truth for the supplementation and extension of classical generalizations, and zealous always to incorporate into the classical system whatever in later thought could best be made to serve the purposes of enrichment or of better articulation, he remained steadfastly convinced of the essential validity and finality of the classical body of doctrine. With him further to improve was merely the better to defend.

Actually, then, at any rate—and rightly also as I think—Marshall's *Principles* stands as the most systematic and most authoritative presentation of the classical point of view and of the classical body of doctrine. Thus far both advocates and opponents of classical theory agree. His work continues the system of thought that, developing through the contributions of a series of brilliant and masterly thinkers from Ricardo down to the present time, and exercising a controlling influence in the field of social doctrine and outlook as well as of political and economic policy, still holds its world-wide primacy in all of these fields. It is in this emphasis, then, that a study of Marshall as first among the neo-classical writers in economics is undertaken.

And it is thus that the lines of distinction between what was implicitly part of the classical doctrine and what was essentially Marshall's thought, are almost impossible to draw. In Marshall's thought, indeed, any lines of this sort could hardly have existed. And even had any been possible of drawing, he would have been first in protest against the attempt. Nor, in the main, will any effort in this emphasis be made here. Whencesoever any particular doctrines of his may have been derived, the purpose will be merely to examine those that appear to be central and important in his thought—as implicit in the classical view and as pivotal for theoretical issues. The present purpose is not primarily that of a study of Marshall, but rather of an examination of the main doctrines of the classical economics.[2]

The writer with whom classical thought first arrived at systematic form, the writer also whose views have turned out to fix in the main the later lines of doctrinal development, was Ricardo. Quite

---

[2] Perhaps here as well as elsewhere it may be said that Marshall's familiarity with the factual aspects of business and industry, his concreteness in factual discussions, his wealth of detail, are nothing short of astounding. Rarely does he offer a generalization that is not profusely and illuminatingly illustrated in the descriptive-factual field. In this regard he has, it may safely be asserted, no equal among English-speaking economists. It is also fairly to be said that he equally surpasses all of them in his prodigality of space—rarely, however, permitting himself a superfluous word. Nevertheless he is a leisurely writer, watchful never to permit either condensation of thought or brevity of statement to overburden the reader's attention or effort; and occasionally prolix.

In point, however, of precision of terms or of statement, something may later need be said. Moreover, it has been sometimes urged—and perhaps with some degree of truth—that his prodigality of descriptive materials and factual illustration may occasionally confuse or obscure the generalization which it is intended to support, or may occasionally leave it incomplete or even forgotten—the forest sometimes unseen for the nearness and multiplicity of the trees. That the houses may not hide the town may require the more distant outlook from the hilltop or the airplane. One may be too closely a part of the scrimmage to see the battle—as it is proverbially the onlooker who sees the most of the game.

Marshall is, however, always mindful that the facts are his subject matter to be systematized—not the air, but the ground, that ultimately must be mapped. Only a wisdom of compromise is possible in adjusting the claims of the close-up as against the remote point of observation. To stand too far away may mean that many things of importance are not seen at all, or are seen wrongly; while the eye that is close to the earth does not see much, and may see nothing in its proper perspective. Neither the minute accuracy of the Dutch school of painters, depicting the fly that you are tempted—but forbidden—to brush away, nor the large strokes of the drop curtain that fall to a mere daub at close inspection, but only observation adequate for the purpose in hand—just being near enough—is the safe prescription.

Subject, then, to these limitations, the man of science must be the servant of his factual materials. For even if science be taken to have to do with more than the analysis and generalization of its factual subject matter, its primary duty, nevertheless, and its first task, must be with the facts.

This factual material, at any rate, Marshall has in abundance, and presents with accuracy. Whatever later may be our issues with him, if any rightly there are, will be those of analysis and of derivative generalization. It is, as Marshall himself makes clear, the facts and the generalization of them that are our subject matter. He says (p. 53) that "as to the exact places in which some at least of the lines of definition should be drawn . . . questions at issue must in general be solved by judgments as to the practical convenience of different courses . . . there must remain a margin of debatable ground. But there is no such margin in the analysis itself: if two people differ with regard to that, they cannot both be right."

clearly this is Marshall's view, as also it is the consensus of opinion with economists at large. The sequence thus beginning, and including Senior, J. S. Mill and Cairnes, terminates, for the present at least, with Marshall. There were, to be sure, numerous other writers belonging to the same general body of thinking and significant in many respects, but of lesser eminence or of smaller influence in doctrinal aspects. Mainly because of his time, but somewhat also on account of the quality of his thought, Adam Smith was not a systematizer; instead he was a catholic commentator, to whom very nearly all doctrines in modern economics, and still more clearly all schools of doctrine, trace their beginnings. Doctrinally Malthus was mainly a dissenter, an annotator also rather than a systematizer, but none the less a thinker of extraordinary insight, whose influence was mostly lost in the sweeping Ricardian ascendancy. Similarly with Say. Jevons also belonged, for better or worse, to a divergent emphasis and trend. In the main, then, we are committed to a study of Ricardian economics in the Marshall interpretations, supplementations and extensions. What, then, in broad outlines is the classical economics—first, as Marshall found it, and second, as Marshall left it?

The Classical System

Central in classical thinking and characteristic of it, is the principle that relative prices are determined by relative labor costs of production. Accurately, however, this labor theory is not one but two: (a) the labor-wage theory, and (b) the labor-discomfort or protest theory. In either division, however, this labor theory purports to explain only the relative prices of those things that come about in part or entirely through human effort, and are also, as the earlier economists phrased it, "freely reproducible"—things that derive from competitive production and are competitively—in the sense of non-monopolistically—produced. Not only does each of these two views stress cost of production as determinative of each particular price—with the explanatory emphasis on the supply rather than on the demand side of the price equation, and with relative prices determined by relative costs of production—but these costs are traced ultimately to the labor or effort aspects of cost.

It is not, however, peculiar to classical doctrine that its central problem is the problem of relative prices; or that each several price is taken to find its determination at the equating point between demand and supply; or even that the influences effective for price changes are, in point both of difficulty of analysis and of causal significance, mainly to be sought on the supply side of the price equation; or that relative prices are determined by relative costs of production—either directly in terms of money costs or indirectly in terms of feeling costs, through the determination of the money costs by the effort costs; but in strictness solely that each particular price is held to be the equating point between the pleasures (or gratifications, or satisfactions, or utilities) of consumption, as over against the stress, or strain, or feeling protest (the discomfort, or dissatisfaction, or disutility) of production. The price is taken to report an equality ratio between utilities and disutilities, a one-to-one ratio. Impliedly also relative prices are traced back to the same ultimate principle. That a unit of commodity A buys a unit of commodity B is explained by the (marginal) equality of the two consumption satisfactions and the two production dissatisfactions. That one item of A buys five items of B, or commands five times the price, indicates not only the equality of the marginal satisfactions of each item to its marginal dissatisfactions in production, but also that the production and consumption of a marginal unit of A involves five times the dissatisfaction and five times the satisfaction attending the production and consumption of a marginal unit of B.

Thus, while, no doubt, the classical system of price analysis is a demand and supply analysis, and an analysis stressing especially the supply side of price-determining influences—in terms of costs of production—it is still something further and more than this: the costs of production with which it has to do are resolved into (a) human effort as the ultimate and decisive producing agency— the real-cost level of explanation, or (b) the money hires of effort as the ultimate influence of price-determining effectiveness—the money-cost level. In this money-wage cost view, the money costs of that enterpriser last in the time series are made up of his own labor, as reported in terms of the attendant money resistances, plus those sums paid out by him as compensations to earlier enterprisers, as recouping them in turn for their real costs translated into money terms, along also with their money advances to the enterprisers one stage back in the time regress—a combined money and real-cost regress.

In the real-cost emphasis, these relative money-cost charges are at the margin taken to find their ultimate explanation in relative real costs at the margin—these relative feeling resistances being appealed to as explaining the relative money debits in the productive process. Equally in the real-cost and in the money-cost view, all outlays or debits attaching to land uses in the productive process are taken to have no price-causal bearing on marginal items of product. The hires of the non-land auxiliaries in production—perhaps as incorporating earlier real or money costs, or possibly as not submitted to exclusion by the same marginal analysis—are on the other hand held to be causal in their relation to prices.

In either interpretation of costs, however, these relative costs are taken to explain the relative prices of such products solely as are of the class of "freely reproducible goods."

Not only, then, does the classical school stress cost of production as the determinant of each particular price—with the explanatory emphasis on the supply rather than on the demand side of the price equation, and with relative prices determined by relative costs of production—but also determining money costs are traced back in turn for explanation to their real-cost backgrounds.

As descriptive of the price processes of competitive-employer producers, there is doubtless merit in the labor-wage point of view. But as either causally or logically ultimate, its merits have never strongly appealed to classical thinkers. It purports to explain product prices by costs that also are themselves mere prices. As an attempt to arrive at more nearly fundamental explanations, the labor-discomfort theory of relative prices, appealing ultimately to real costs —the feeling items rather than the mere money items in the industrial processes of producing things—has come to be common to practically all classical analysis—not necessarily, however, as displacing the labor-wage theory, but rather as providing for it an underlying level of explanation.

It is thus that, mainly through Ricardo, a basis of harmony was reached between the labor-wage and the labor-pain theories of relative prices. True, Ricardo argued, the relative prices are as the relative wages, and true it is also that the prices are as the relative irksomenesses of the absorbed labor. But inasmuch as the wages are as are the irksomenesses, the superficially contrasting views are harmonized. The prices of the cost things are obviously never the causes of the products, either priced or unpriced. Only things may cause things. But in the sense of stimulus and response, prices may induce the making of a thing that has a price—the prices the motive for the doing of the thing. Solely in this pecuniary and incentive and adventuring sense can price-cost things be the causes of price-product things. One line of procedure would, then, suffice for both of these lines of explanation—if, and when, however, the precise meaning to be attributed to labor-pain were satisfactorily ascertained.

In terms of what, then, was it possible to speak of labor as a cost in other than the mere wage-outlay sense? For purposes of protest-resistance, of discomfort or irksomeness, neither the time allotted nor the effort put forth could bear more than indirectly on the degree of the indisposition or the irksomeness. The protest or discomfort fact—the real cost as a feeling debit attendant on the putting forth of an effort, the fact of the undergoing rather than of the mere doing—was the ultimate thing in labor cost in this real-cost sense. To appeal to the indisposition to make wage outlays—the toothaches of parting with money, or the foregoing of having some good by purchase—would be to get upon a different level of explanation—to talk about the payer of the wages rather than the doer of the work, and to return to the circuity of explaining some prices by other prices—to abandon the truly causal sequence and to confuse the logical movement of the analysis. Labor cost and money cost must be kept rigorously distinct in thought in order that the two levels of analysis be not confused and that the logic be faultless.

In similar fashion also would logical procedure be violated if the discomfort attending the labor were interpreted to include the foregoing of some alternative money income by the worker. Resistance of this sort is, of course, commonplace enough; but it is not a resistance attaching as a discomfort to the mere performance of the process itself from which the alternative price results are to be had. These foregone money returns are for explanatory purposes like wage-outlay costs. They belong strictly to the pecuniary level—to the first floor and not to the basement level of explanation. As explanation of money costs they are infect by circuity.

Certain further steps in the classical analysis were, however, possible without the clear necessity of any distinction between real and money costs. As against bare hands or even a spear, a fish-pole helps the day's intake of fish. Similarly, per unit of labor or of wage outlay, good agricultural equipment will achieve, say, two bushels of result as against the one bushel possible with none. These bushels are assumed to be per unit interchangeable in quality and price. But one of them is achieved at half the labor absorbed by the other.

In reply, however, the classical analysis runs that the machinery is merely stored-up labor, labor indirectly applied; or is *capital*— the capitalist merely a laborer gone to seed. Taking account, then, of both the direct and the indirect applications of the labor, or of the wage outlay, the proportionality of price products with costs of production remains unimpaired.

But forthwith a further difficulty, though of not very dissimilar character, had to be met. How about the fact that to a given application of labor or of wage outlay, a high-grade tract of land responds, say, with two bushels of grain, whereas a poorer tract may return only one bushel—divergent labor costs for products interchangeable in price?

The offered solution did not, and logically could not, stress the possible view that the higher rents on the better land are merely the derivatives of their betterness, leaving unchanged the per-bushel price costs. Instead, by a familiar classical analysis, the appeal was made to production at the margin of cultivation. All of the different bushels, from no matter what grades of land, sell, to be sure, at one price. But it was argued, prices are fixed by the price-determining, land-margin costs. All the lands, then, have the same marginal —and thereby the same price-determining—costs. On each piece of crop-land, production is carried to the intensive margin, the point at which the selling price in prospect is barely sufficient to indemnify the costs attending the final increment of output; a cost, therefore, into which no rent charges can enter—the privilege of producing these price-determining final bushels of product being worth nothing, and therefore getting nothing—the labor and other non-land costs absorbing the entire selling price of the product. Rent is therefore presented as the result of a price that the labor and capital costs have caused, and thus as deriving from a price for which the labor and capital charges have solely accounted.

This method, which will be for brevity called "marginal isolation," appeals, it is to be noted, not merely to marginal costs of production as explanatory of price, and not merely to costs on the land margin as the price-determining marginal costs; but assumes also that the supra-marginal bushels—for the privilege of producing which the rent is paid—are low-cost bushels, thereby enjoying in rent the benefits of a price determined by the higher-cost marginal bushels.

It is, moreover, worthy of note that this analysis of agricultural production, with its reference to a price-determining, intensive-margin land cost of production, introduces a principle that the foregoing capital-hire analysis did not include—the marginal-isolation principle, the instrument marginal reference. The capital analysis made no reference to any intensive-marginal, and therefore value-less, use of the instrument, but turned solely on the costlessness of land in point of origins, the while the machines, as items of stored-up labor, impose indirect labor hires. Nothing was made of the fact that, equally with machinery as with land, the marginal-isolation analysis is open—always, with either, a point arriving at which, in view of the prices of products, it is not worth while to use the instrument of production more intensively—an increment of product finally arrived at that is barely worth achieving, in view of the other cost items involved—an item of product the privilege of producing which, being worth nothing, gets nothing.

This resort in classical analysis to a price-determining land-margin cost of production at which the non-land costs of production are presented as the causes of the prices, of which, in turn, the land hires are the results—interest cause, rent result—this division of enterprisers' money resistances into price-determining and price-determined parts, made inevitable a distinction fundamental in classical thought, that of land from capital, property in land from property in other cost goods. It was a distinction tying up with the explanation of money costs through their underlying real costs; the exclusion of land hires from price-determining standing because of the non-labor origin of land; its place a free gift of nature or bounty of Providence—an outstanding example of the employee-regress type of analysis as supplementary to the employer-outlay type, or as somehow articulated with it, or it may be, as ultimately, on occasion, displacing it.

Something, however, was still lacking to the rounding out of the classical system. A real-cost basis of wage payments seemed obvious enough, as also for interest outlays taken as mere installments of payment against earlier accrued wage rights. But interest as a rate of return on a principal sum? For with passing time these interest payments must come to total indefinitely more than a numerical equality with the wages as summed up into the price of the capital-goods item.

The difficulty with this indirect-wage view is that interest returns arrive at an end only by the cancellation of the principal through payment of it in full—but never by the wearing down of it through interest payment. A full legal title amounts to the right to a never-ending series of incomes—a theoretical immortality attaching to interest returns from a capital holding. The interest fact is an aspect of capital as viewed in its time dimension. It is hire for a period—for a time-slice, cut off for the borrower's benefit, from the full eternity of the ownership right. An eternity can never suffer any diminution—a truth mysterious to some of us. But always there will be as long a time and as many interest payments ahead as ever in any earlier time there were. Interest is not a series of installments applying to the discharge of a capital sum. Capital is a fund; interest a flow from, but not out of, the fund. The principal is the subject matter of one contract in the loan relation, the contract for the discharge of the principal sum in a deferred-payment undertaking. Interest in its very nature manifests itself only in this relation—with its basis in the postponed discharge of the very obligation that the deferred payment discharges. It is a surplus above the sum returned as deferred payment, and is a surplus paid precisely because the payment is deferred, a time charge, a rate per cent per dollar per period: deferred payment, the postponement of a money obligation; interest, a payment, on the basis of a dollar-time unit, for the postponement.

Whereby, obviously, money costs of production, price-determining or other, include more than raw-material outlays, labor hires, land rents, and capital-goods rents; there is also a time hire or a time discount charge on the entire operating and investment fund. Not only must the materials count as costs with some allowance for the time at which they are paid for, but equally so for the wage outlays, and the rents of different sorts. An interest charge must be computed on each, precisely as it would be on the funds borrowed to meet them. The pay-roll, for example, employs funds that would earn if loaned out, and that cost if borrowed.

Obviously, then, interest is a cost along with the raw-material, labor and equipment charges. But what about the real costs underlying these capital-hire costs? That efforts carry real costs with them is easy enough; labor imposes discomforts; or if not always so, yet it does so at the margin; or, if not always even there is it irksome, always still it must displace pleasant recreation or interfere with quiet or sleep.

But are there real costs attaching to that mere not-having that is implicit in the fact of lending? What discomfort or grief is in this? Displaced money gains are plainly not admissable in this connection; they belong not to the real-cost level. But displaced leisure? True, it is not a discomfort or an irksome thing in its own right. But it is a debit on the feeling level. But the mere postponement of a satisfaction, an exercised preference for the later rather than the immediate gratification?

It was at this point that Senior made his great doctrinal contribution. He invoked the painfulness or the discomfort or the irksomeness of *abstinence*—that sort of protest sometimes called *impatience* —the unwelcome thing that, along-side of *effort costs,* Marshall indicates as *waiting costs.*

Such, then, in large lines is the classical movement of economic analysis. Money costs are price-explaining, but ultimately so only as accounted for in terms of the underlying real costs; prices proportional with money costs, and money costs proportional with real costs—always, of course, at the determinant margins.

And still, it must be noted, money costs are in their very nature homogeneous, made up of interchangeable money units. If, then, unit by unit they are to be accounted for, or even in some average sort accounted for, they must be accounted for in terms of some homogeneous underlying influence. But is it true that the wages that are paid to different men of different aptitudes, lines and degrees of training, intelligence, strength, industriousness, and feeling reactions to their occupations, can be—as a homogeneous total of money-unit costs, received as wages—accounted for in terms of homogeneous units of laborers' real costs? Take this to be possible —as tacitly it was taken. Can a similar homogeneity of abstaining or waiting costs be predicated to parallel the receipt of homogeneous money units of interest by the different lenders or investors of funds: widows, orphans, Rockefellers, commercial banks, savings banks, life insurance companies, middle-class bond buyers? Take this also to be possible—as actually it was taken. Enterpriser costs are a homogeneous money total of labor and capital hires, together with time charges on capital funds or on banking accommodations. Can a correspondingly homogeneous background of real costs, behind this money-cost total, be credibly affirmed? Labor irksomenesses purport, as we have seen, to be totaled. Waiting costs also have been assumed to make up somehow a homogeneous fund. Is it also possible to combine into an aggregate of homogeneous units the two separately arrived-at homogeneities of labor costs and waiting costs? The classical analysis required all this; and thereupon, without examination or analysis or evidence, assumed it.

Chapter II

NEO-CLASSICAL SYSTEM OUTLINED

MARSHALL'S restatement of classical doctrine is far more difficult of summary, even in its most general form, than the Ricardian analysis. Most of it, indeed, must await the setting of later discussions to become possible of presentation within practicable limits of space.

Along with his predecessors, Marshall is a price economist, a demand-and-supply economist, and, in principle and emphasis, a supply and cost-of-production economist. The demand aspects of his analysis are, without serious difficulty, to be articulated with the little that classical doctrine had to say in this regard.

Mainly, in classical thinking, demand was taken for granted. Having *utility,* a thing must be limited in volume relative to the desires for it in order to take on a price; no one will pay for what he does not want; or pay for what he wants unless he has to. Goods may be so plentiful relative to the desires for them as to be free; not that they are not *goods,* that they have no utility—but, as later thought would have it, that they have no marginal utility. Classical thinking, however, was innocent of these utility refinements. Money demands were objectively evident; mainly they were taken as self-explanatory. People buy with their money the things that they want at their prices—in view, of course, of other things at their prices. So much was by mere inspection plain—too plain to need stressing. Demands take on the form of offers of money units. As such, these demands were translatable into a schedule of the various volumes of goods purchasable at the respective price ordinates on the demand curve or schedule. That market price reports a ratio of exchange between price-thing and priced-thing was, to be sure, a mere commonplace. But money *quantities,* not *ratios* of money to things, were on the demand side of the ratio. In the lack of careful analysis, or even of any pressing occasion for it, it was easy to think of a

15

money total of demands—as the sum, for example, of the following five price offers for hats:

9 dollars for 1 hat; 8 dollars for 1 hat; 7 dollars for 1 hat; 6 dollars for 1 hat; 5 dollars for 1 hat; totaling, however, somehow, not into 35 dollars for 5 hats, but only into 25 dollars for 5 hats.

But there did nevertheless appear to be a total, though there was manifestly something amiss about the mathematics of it. But plainly five hats could find buyers on the basis of five dollars per hat. At this price the total of the five payments deriving from the five quite disparate demand ratios, was easily, though loosely, taken to make up into one *money-demand* total, whereas accurately there was merely a *purchase-price* total. The paradox in the attempt to add together different *ratios* escaped attention—precise thinking entangled in an inadequate terminology—as for that matter it still is. It is indeed difficult enough to total a series of identical ratios. Try it; 2:1, plus 2:1, plus 2:1—total into 6:3—just another two-to-one ratio.

Comfortably, and in the main safely, these classical folk got along with utility without any marginal utility derivative, and found it to suffice that each one of us with his money buys the thing that at its price he prefers to anything else at its price. A hat bought at 5 that, if I must, I should have paid 9 to get, has attractiveness— I have a desire for it? Yes, obviously. In the ratio sense also? To be sure—if you insist—let it go at that. A buyer's surplus, then, of 4, through the divergence of my price-offer ratio from the market-exchange ratio? Yes, I admit it—never earlier having thought of it, and not being keen about it now: but what is the use?

There was, however, implicit in the naïve classical view of demand the obvious fact of deciding to offer money for a good, or the willingness to take it, up to a certain price limit—implicit, therefore, the essential facts in all these utility and marginal utility refinements; and finally, therewith, the fact that a maximum price offer presumes a choice of one marginal utility, at its price, as against any alternative marginal utility, at its price, and therefore specifically against the ranking alternative marginal utility.

As later we shall strongly emphasize, Marshall, in harmony with the Austrian analysis, goes far in these directions of detail toward conclusions at which his classical predecessors might readily have arrived, but did not; and perhaps would not have thought especially worth while; but for which, nevertheless, they would have found no difficulty—so far as they were correct—in making room.

But Marshall, further in harmony with the Austrians, interprets the price offer of an individual for a good—his maximum price of taking it—in two different and contradictory senses: (1) as deriving from and reporting a choice between alternative marginal utilities; and (2) as deriving from and reporting the marginal utility of the good for which the price is offered. In sense (1) the bid reporting an equality ratio between competing marginal utilities, each of indeterminate quantity; and, in sense (2), reporting not a ratio fact but a quantity fact—not the desiredness of the thing relative to something else, but the desiredness of it quantitatively and unrelatedly. And, as also it will later be necessary to stress greatly, there are far-reaching and important issues turning on which of these two positions is deserving of acceptance. Marshall's final position, in the sense of his working doctrine in later discussions, is position (2). But it will suffice for the present to recognize that not both of these positions can be defended; that they are fundamentally contradictory; that if (2) is right, (1) must be wrong; and that Marshall in accepting (2) for use in later analyses has tacitly repudiated the (1) to which he earlier committed himself.

But it is equally clear that, with reference strictly to the interpretation of money demands and to their derivation, classical analysis had committed itself to practically nothing. Neither (1) nor (2) was explicitly adopted. With the choice aspect plainly implicit in price offers, the conscious acceptance of view (1) was close in the offing. But the quantitative interpretation of demand, and the assumed possibility of arriving at money totals of different individual items of it, pointed clearly in the direction of (2). And, moreover, if price is the equating point between money demands and money costs of production, with utility as the background and explanation of money demand, with discomfort the explanation of money costs, and with prices therefore finally the equating point between utilities on the demand side and real costs on the supply side—the pleasure-pain theory of values as the ultimate classical thesis in the labor theory of value—it is plain that (2) becomes imperative. And this second view Marshall ended finally by adopting, despite the fact that earlier he had set forth and supported the antithetical view.

So much for the present, then, for Marshall's demand analysis and its ultimate commitments. The supply side of his discussions must here be most inadequately set forth. Mainly it is a cost-of-production analysis: what cost of production means; how it is made up; the place of real and of money costs in it; how it bears on prices—and when, and why. With Marshall, as with most other economists, cost of production absorbs the main share of attention, and presents the main occasions of doctrinal disagreement.

In line with the real-cost explanation of relative prices, Marshall follows classical authority in excluding land rents from price-determining costs—this with Marshall, however, not because of the labor-free origins of land, the classical position, but because of the inflexibility of land stocks; whereby comes the necessity of distinguishing between land and capital, and whereby also becomes necessary the inclusion of the fertility aspects of land within the capital classification. Similarly, fertility rents fall under the quasi-rent analysis rather than under the land-rent analysis. Not origins but inelasticity of stocks is the ultimate line of distinction between land and capital, no matter what havoc this view may finally work with the real-cost explanation of money costs. Cost-free fertility of land comes now to be treated as on a level with interest or wages, with reference to price determination. The analysis, nevertheless, by which Marshall, at this point in his argument, excludes land rents from price-determining costs is the marginal-isolation analysis—a method not only entirely irrelevant to the question of origins, or to the flexibility of stocks, but a method also which is elsewhere admitted to be equally applicable to equipment rents in general. In the short run, during the production period of a cost-produced capital good, the hire of it is held by Marshall to be price-determined—as are permanently the hires of the positional aspects of land.

Marshall's analysis of the relation of money costs to prices, and of real costs to money costs, follows Ricardo. But, with Marshall, real costs include *waiting costs* along with *effort costs*. The theory thereby comes to be a total-discomfort theory of values rather than a pure labor-discomfort theory. In this respect Marshall incorporates Senior's supplementation of the Ricardian view.

Moreover, in Marshall's view, it is not at all times, but only at the times that he calls *normal,* that prices are determined by money costs, or money costs found proportional with real costs.

It is, in fact, a commonplace that the hires of equipment goods may greatly diverge from the expected returns on the original money investment, as also from the going rates of return on this original investment. These hires may, then, be either greater or less than the return on the expectation of which the providing of the equipment goods was conditioned. The hires at the present time are determined by the current enterpriser demands for the control of such equipment goods as there are now. And the prices of the final products are also determined by the conditions of the time in point of demand and supply, in view of the actual stocks of equipment goods.

But the prices of these equipment goods are held by Marshall to derive also from the prices of the products, the hires of the goods not the causes but the results of the prices. At these times, then, only prime costs are regarded by Marshall as causal with relation to price. Moreover, it is not even true that the prime costs are always and necessarily commensurate with the prices of the products into which they enter; rarely in fact are they so.

It must, nevertheless, be objected that these quasi-rents as distributive shares, are covered by the prices of the products; as also are the land rents. The wages, it seems clear, are among the prime costs, though these wages are in most respects indistinguishable from quasi-rents. The prime costs do in some cases, doubtless, account for the product prices in their entirety; but commonly the equipment goods contribute something toward the price outcome, in the sense, at any rate, that they are competitively assigned some distributive part of it—ranking still, Marshall insists, not as causal facts with relation to the product prices, but only as results.

In fact, then, Marshall appears to hold that at all non-normal times the prices of products are not fixed by costs, but only by *the general conditions of demand and supply*—an explanation valid always, it seems, but actually invoked solely in cases of this sort. Nor are these prices fixed by or commensurate with the *prime* costs. Only, therefore, in normal situations are prices derived from money costs, or are money costs proportional with real costs.

Normal times, then, are times when the prices of products are such as to award to the equipment goods, and presumably to each and all of them, hires commensurate with those expectations of investors on which the maintenance of the normal stocks of equipment goods is conditioned. It is through the investors' forecasts and expectations of satisfactory investment returns that the various stocks of equipment goods are maintained, whereby the investors' terms of maintenance become the long-run cost determinants of the prices of goods. Only when the enterprisers' outlay costs for equipment goods are neither more nor less than sufficient to attract adequate maintenance investments, are prices commensurate, as Marshall holds, with enterpriser costs, or enterpriser costs commensurate with the investors' requirements for the maintenance of stocks. Only then do money costs account for prices; only then are money costs proportionate with real costs; or prices proportionate with real costs. Not, then, very often, if ever actually.

The connection, therefore, between market prices and money costs, and through money costs with real costs, is not in Marshall's view a constant relation. In the Ricardian view, however, the causal bearing of costs at any one time was the causal bearing at all times. Whatever the costs at any time actually are, these costs, in the Ricardian view, explain the prices of the products, in the sense and in the degree that costs ever explain prices. The returns on equipment goods—cost-produced goods always, in the classical view—may be higher or lower than adequate investment returns; but such as they are, they are the price-determining costs for the time. In whatever sense the prices of raw materials, whether above or below an adequate return to their producers, are price-determining, so equally are machine hires. Or in whatever sense the hires of labor —which may or may not be high enough to stimulate marriages or birth rates, or to justify the rearing and training costs of children —are costs, these equipment rents are also costs. It is true merely that the raw materials and the laborers have a much greater mobility among industries than have commonly most of the equipment goods, and have, therefore, a wider range of elasticity in hires.

Doubtless also, we note, changes in the prices of products do not occur, in point of time, strictly with changes in costs. There are lags all around the circle. But this belongs to the way in which costs affect prices. It is an ex-post-facto sort of process, through the response of output to enterprisers' gains. Cost affects price only through affecting the volume of product. With prices above costs the output expands to reinstate the parity; and with prices below costs, the output contracts, with prices responding. Never are prices commensurate with costs, excepting in the sense that, as fluctuating back and forth across the cost line, there must be instants of equality. That prices are continually away in one direction or the other from this line, with an ultimate shaking down toward it, does not in the traditional classical view deny the fixational bearing of costs on prices.

Always, also, with Marshall, there is recognized this trend toward a moving or stable price equilibrium; and always also the trend of cost prices to their equilibrium points. But only when these stable product and cost prices are present—or perhaps when there is a situation to which these stable prices are appropriate—are the prices of the products taken to be fixed by costs—the costs, that is to say, price-determining. Then only are the prices held to be in harmony with their appropriate levels of investment returns, or, through these investment returns, proportionate to real costs. During the intermediate, non-normal, periods, all of the hires of equipment goods, and possibly of labor, and even, it may be, the prices of raw material goods, fall under Marshall's quasi-rent principle—are price-determined rather than price-determining facts. For most of the time, therefore, the enterpriser cost process, even in the superficial sense appropriate to it, does not afford an explanation of price.[1]

Implicit, of course, in the explanation of price costs by real costs, for whatever times the explanation is taken to be valid, is Marshall's assumption that the real costs of individuals are, at their respective margins, quantitatively measurable facts in the respective individual experiences as doubtless they are; that prices carry the measure function; and that price costs can be made to measure real costs, not merely for any one individual but inter-individually.

[1] I am well aware that this is a questionable interpretation. Many students of Marshall would put it promptly in issue. I do not feel secure in it. I grant that there are many passages in Marshall's work inconsistent with it. But also, I am sure, there are, in words and in the articulation of doctrinal positions, still more that can not be reconciled with any other interpretation. It is merely the best that I can do. Many of the issues to come are also of this sort—the fundamental question that of what precisely is in issue. Not rarely, indeed, the most difficult task will be precisely this one of secure interpretation—the discussion of the tenability of a particular doctrine modified accordingly as the reasonable interpretation of it may seem to be this or that. For further examples: the notion of *norms;* the concept of a *representative firm;* the meaning of *sacrifice* as a cost category; the ratio as against the quantity view of price offer, goods offer, and market price, together with the possibility of measuring, by money or price, either values, or utilities, or real costs; the significance of *waiting* as a real cost; the ultimate resolution of investment costs—either of equipment goods or of their uses—into real costs; the attempt to apply to human beings, and to the incomes from their efforts, the money-cost or the real-cost analysis; the rent elements in labor compensations in their price-fixing relations; the place of enterpriser efforts and their money returns in real and money costs; the various standpoints in the cost analysis—the long-run views and the short-time views, as, shading off into each other, they undergo functional transformations; the shifting of types of cost and price analysis between the "basement" level of stocks of factors, and the enterpriser-cost level of expended or displaced hires; in the regress emphasis, the discomfort costs of the employed labor or its price resistances deriving from alternative openings; the price and the real costs of that enterpriser next back in the regress series who provides the particular enterpriser with his raw materials and equipment goods; the indefinite regress to the price costs or the real costs of the investors most remote in the series, either in acquiring the capital funds or in the investing-waiting applications of them; the various laws of return as mere product laws, and as collective or social laws; the meaning of the term *capital* in the interest problem, and the functions by which incomes accrue on it and interest *rates* are attached to it.

I have, then, found it impossible to indicate the relations of Marshall's positions to the traditional doctrines of the classical school in other than the broadest of strokes; and impossible, even then, to avoid interpretations of which I myself feel insecure. At any rate, I can do no better here—the space even to explain my doubts being unavailable.

In his price analysis Marshall, like all economists classical or other, recognizes the concrete business fact of enterpriser money costs; and of the affiliations of these costs, either as causes or as results, with market prices—the employer point of view in the interpretation of price costs. He has also an employee version of costs: (1) as the discomfort costs—the real costs—of the employed laborers, together with the waiting costs of the lenders of the capital goods or funds; or (2) the *money* costs of that enterpriser (or of those enterprisers) providing the cost goods for that enterpriser whose own costs are in question. This is the enterpriser money-cost view pushed one step back in the enterpriser series— *the regress analysis.*

And Marshall has also a further, a third, view of costs: this regress procedure carried back to the original-investor situation, as indicative of the returns that must be received by these investors, and must be borne as outlay costs by the enterpriser producers last in the production series, if the stocks of equipment goods and of raw materials—and equally, it may be, of laborers—in the particular lines of production are to be maintained. These investor costs, as ultimate money costs, are traced back in turn to their real cost determinants in the production and saving processes. And these determining costs, in turn—as decisive of the stocks of industrial goods which any particular line of production may hire—are all presented as *real*-cost facts setting the resistance limits on particular stocks of indirect goods; these real costs getting applied in those directions promising best in point of monetary returns to investors. That the price resistance faced by any particular investor in providing himself with any particular sort of equipment goods is not, or may not be, decisively that of the discomforts of effort and waiting, but, instead, of the resistance of alternative openings for gainful investment—opportunity costs—Marshall does not take into account, otherwise than as instances under the general *law of substitution.* Or if in any way he recognizes these alternative openings as limiting and resisting influences, it is not in their aspect of money costs, but only as somehow effective to limit the various stocks of indirect (equipment) goods, and marginally thereby, to attach to them higher rents or higher purchase prices. These limiting costs become, then, in Marshall's view composites of the real costs earlier involved in producing, along with the real costs currently involved in waiting.

Finally, moreover, Marshall has another line of analysis in the explanation of prices and of their relations to one another, an explanation that is not accurately a cost of production analysis of any sort, but is rather a repudiation of it or a substitute for it. On the supply side of the problem, Marshall turns not rarely, on the "basement" level of explanation, to appeal not to the hires of things as explaining, through the cost mechanism, the terms on which the production of goods is conditioned—the necessary indemnities that the sales prices of the products must cover—but instead to direct attention immediately and solely to the existing stock of indirect goods available now, or later to become available, for the particular line of production: not, for example, the relatively high wage of the hired labor, but the relatively limited volume of it, is taken to explain the relatively limited volume of product, the relatively high price of it, and thus finally the relatively high compensation deriving as distributive share from its price product.

Not rarely then, as we shall later see, Marshall appears to solve a point of difficulty in the cost-of-production analysis by shifting entirely out of that level of analysis. Thus, for example, when he deduces his explanation for the prices of products from the stocks of indirect goods and not from the hires of them. Sometimes he denies that the hire of a productive good is one of the cost-causes of the price of the product, insisting instead that not even the prospect of the hires bears, through costs, on prices, but solely that these hires that are now in prospect are effective now to determine what stocks of indirect goods there will later be; thereby what volumes of products there will later be; thereby what prices for the products there will later be; and thereby finally what prices received for the services of the indirect goods there will later be. So viewed, then, these hires emerge only at the end of the causal sequence; they are not causal links in the chain but the terms of result that close it.

Viewed in the large, then, Marshall seems to interpret cost of production as never ultimately an explanation of price. Instead, the explanation must be sought in the determining influences of an underlying situation; and, on the cost side, therefore, in the relative stocks of the various agents of production. These are the sole influences that are *determining* influences. The cost derivatives are merely representative facts. They, therefore, merely *govern*. Accurately speaking, they neither *fix* nor *determine*.

The initial term in the causal sequence ending in the making of the prices of products is the investment policies of the dispensers of capital funds—savers presumably, but borrowers possibly. These investors scan carefully the outlook near and remote for its prospects of gain. As directed by these prospects, they are induced to finance the provision of raw material and equipment goods for later uses. Prospects of both demand and supply are theirs narrowly to watch, appraising always as best as they can all future trends and changes.

But as long as modifications in fundamental conditions of demand and supply continue, no stable equilibrium is possible of attainment. Nor presumably will these investors look forward to any equilibrium, in more than some general approximation. They are operating, therefore, in a continuous process of tentative, forward-looking adjustment to continuously, though ordinarily slowly, changing fundamental conditions—changes, however, that, in the main, permit of intelligent forecast.

With time enough, therefore, the adjustment to stable fundamental conditions would become complete. Always, then, there are certain approximately final adjustments possible, in the sense of approximate adjustments to any particular set of existing conditions—a short-time *normal* as distinguished from a true, long-time, normal equilibrium.

Investment policies have in view, sometimes a period of years; again, of decades; or even of life-times; and have to be undertaken in face of the certainty of many, and not rarely, of almost incalculable changes. Let us assume, however, that the fundamental conditions remain fixed long enough for investment to have fully adjusted itself to these conditions—the factors essential to the right provision of investment properties being clearly defined and well recognized. Abstract, then, from the length of time envisaged in these forward-looking investment policies. For simplicity, take the period to be merely a day. The flow of investment funds into the the various lines of equipment goods—expansion here, contraction there—will bring tomorrow equalized investment rates of return and a definite system of product prices—stable investment policies in view of stable conditions and returns. Always normal prices mean the prices appropriate to any given situation, if and when it has had time to mill itself out.

It is not true, then, that there are no normal prices, excepting, in the sense that in a changing world they can never get realized. There are prices that, in the conceptual sort, are normal to any given situation; the prices into which that situation would work itself out, if only it had the time—if only it remained long enough unchanged to permit of the readjustments implicit in it. The terminal facts in such a movement are, at the beginning, the investors, with their flexible policies in the directing of funds; at the end, the costs of enterprisers—costs undergone in the process of the evening-up of prices, to the outcome that no further changes, anywhere open, would be gainful to anybody.

The inevitable time facts in any such process are now to be reinstated. They are, however, mere time facts—that have concretely to be recognized in what is logically a timeless process. Normal price situations are those in which the volume of investment funds, in their relative applications, at the beginning of the process, and the enterprisers and consumers at the end of it, have arrived at a completely harmonious adjustment—on all the intersecting lines that a full adjustment requires—investors with other investors; investors with later producers; later producers with one another; and all with consumers.

The prices appropriate to this normal adjustment are always the prices toward which, under no matter what current conditions, each particular price is gravitating, and toward which as a price system all prices are tending. *On the supply side* of the price equation with any one commodity—as with all commodities—all price changes derive from changes in volume of agents of production, both absolutely and relatively to one another. These changes, it is obvious, can take place only with respect to things the volume of which can be modified by changes in investment policies—only with factors that are not *fixed,* that are *responsive.* Land capital does not in this sense change in volume. All price changes, therefore, in the sort under examination, result from the flow of investment funds into other than land-capital lines. True, investors can invest in land; but that is merely to redistribute the investment funds and the lands—not to change the quantity of land.

Such is the ultimate meaning of the assertion that rents are price-determined—or price-governed. Land and the rents of it take no part in the great stream of price change. Prices modify rents, not rents prices. Doubtless land stocks have to do with prices. And in this sense also, rents have to do with prices. But changes in prices derive from changes in the things that can be changed; and these prices are the active facts in modifying rents. We have here to do with an on-going process. *In this process* land and its rents are passive. But quasi-rent things are active. And the labor and wages of human beings are also active, since—as in Marshall's view—they come about mainly or entirely as directed and determined by investment policies. Men and wages, then, like equipment goods—and unlike land—are items in the stream of change.

Is this, so far, a correct interpretation? I am not sure. But further, as I understand the position, save when prices at the "terminal end" of the process are adjusted to investment policies at the "terminal initiation" of it—save, that is, as prices are *normal*—cost of production does not determine or govern prices. In all interim times, all costs, excepting prime costs—all of the hires of supplementary-cost goods, of quasi-rent goods and, of course, of land capital—are price-determined hires. Some or all, also, of the hires of labor—of that labor, in any event, that being cost-acquired by investment policy, belongs to the quasi-rent class of productive factors—receives price-determined hires. Such labor, or such a human being that labors, is a supplementary-cost good; it may or it may not turn out a good investment—like other quasi-rent goods. In this interim period, only prime costs are price-determining costs.

Does Marshall say this? So I believe—am convinced—that he does. If so, then, where is the explanation of these interim prices to be sought? In the *general conditions of demand and supply;* but not this in the meaning that would make the explanation merely farcical—an almost empty formula, or a renunciation. This explanation is merely retreating to the "basement" level, and is invoking the fundamental and directive situation of the particular time, in point of the stocks of productive factors, as over against the desires for products. It appeals to human desires in all their variety on the demand side and to the absolute and relative stocks of the wide variety of productive agents—inclusive of human productive abilities in all their sorts and degrees—on the supply side. Is this what Marshall really means? I think so, but am not certain.

The primary difficulty is that this underlying, this *basement,* situation, that always must be the ultimately explanatory fact, and as such must include all of the relevant facts, is also equally explanatory of all of the factor hires of any time—interim or normal. It does not, then, for a particular time—on the cost-of-production level—displace these factor hires as explanations, in whatever sense they could in any normal time serve as explanations. They are price-determining, or price-governing at any interim time, if they are at any other time. Exclusion at one time is exclusion for all times.

Moreover, always, in the very nature of the initiatory investment policies, the various investment openings limit one another in their absorption of funds. The great principle of *substitution* presides over these choices—a system of inter-resistance—in other words, of opportunity costs. Wherefore it seems to be true that the limit on investment in any one direction can rarely be a real-cost limit, but instead a *sacrifice*—a substitution—limit, precisely as in the purchasing field the limit on the buying of one thing is commonly set by the going-without of other things. The real-cost limit to the production of goods is parallel in error to the marginal-utility limit in the purchase of goods.

But we appear to be getting over into the emphasis of discussing positions rather than merely of presenting them. But sometimes the making of a position clear involves the indication of how far it goes.

Does Marshall really hold real costs to set the limit on the investment funds directed to the provision of each particular line of producers' goods? Or does he hold real costs to set the limit in the aggregate? Both of these positions he must hold, if relative real costs are to explain relative price costs. But perhaps he holds only that real costs *as a whole* set the limit on investment volumes as a whole. This solely, however, would not suffice for the purpose of explaining relative prices—or, for that matter, any one price.

I am not sure; and, so far as I can make out, it does not matter for the purposes of any functional distinction at any time between rent costs and other costs. Land volumes affect the volumes of agricultural products relatively to other products, and thereby their relative prices. Particular land volumes affect the relative volumes of the various agricultural products. Relative rent costs are therefore to the point in the making up of those relative costs of production that at normal times—even if at no other—must affect the relative prices of products.

Note on Sphere and Definition

Specialization in both industry and business characterizes the actual competitive society—precisely as, though differently organized, specialization in industry and industrial supervision must characterize any credible form of either anarchism or collectivism. Because actual society is individualistic in its gainful specializations of activity, it must achieve through trade its individual allocations of income and of goods for consumption. And having trade, it is practically inevitable that it have intermediates in trade—one medium or various media of exchange. For a barter society, as we shall later see, would not be lacking intermediates in its exchange processes. In its very term it would be a trading society. By the fact, indeed, that it was specialized in its industrial activities it must be a trading society. A conventional medium of exchange is a method, not of avoiding intermediates, but of avoiding the complexities that must attend the lack of coincidence of trading dispositions. Money obviates trading about, the multiplication of intermediates that—were there ever a pure barter society—must attend the systematic barter process. A money society—and therefore a price society—is one in which the intermediate function is mainly centered in one commodity. What ultimate quid-pro-quo one gets for what he has to sell turns in the first instance on the amount of money into which he can convert what he has to sell. And this first stage in the exchange process is commonly the step of the larger difficulty.

In recognition of the fact that a society specialized and competitive in its productive activities must be a price society, Marshall says (p. 22) that " 'money' or 'general purchasing power' or 'command over material wealth,' is the center around which economic science clusters. . . ." Similarly he says elsewhere: ". . . the problems, which are grouped as economic, because they relate specially to man's conduct under the influence of motives that are measurable by a money price, are found to make a fairly homogeneous group. . . ." (p. 27)

And at the opening of his chapter describing the subject matter of economics: "Economics is a study of men as they live and move and think in the ordinary business of life. But it concerns itself chiefly with those motives which affect, most powerfully and most steadily, man's conduct in the business part of his life . . . the steadiest motive to ordinary business work is the desire for the pay which is the *material* reward of work . . . the motive is supplied by a definite amount of money. . . ." (p. 14)[2]

In a later summary Marshall says: ". . . economics is, on the one side, a Science of Wealth; and, on the other, that part of the Social Science of man's action in society, which deals with his Efforts to satisfy his Wants, in so far as the efforts and wants are capable of being measured in terms of wealth, or its general representative, *i.e.*, money. . . ." (p. 49)

The emphasis here is neither obviously collective nor obviously competitive. In the main, however, Marshall's analysis directs itself to the competitive aspects of the economic process. His is a price economics. Rightly, therefore, such aggregate or collective aspects of the process as require attention must be presented—as seemingly is Marshall's view—through an inventory or an appraisal of the large outcomes of situations that are in process purely individualistic and competitive. And rightly also Marshall is, in the main, talking about business as distinguished from industry. All competitive industry is primarily business; but not all business is industry.

And what does Marshall mean by "the pay which is the *material*

---

[2] Excepting where indications to the contrary are given, the italicizing of words or phrases in these passages from the *Principles* may be safely taken to be not Marshall's, but my own. Occasionally, however, where it quite clearly cannot matter whose they are, Marshall's italics will be reproduced without warning that they are his, instead of mine—a practice that appears to permit, on the whole, a minimum of annoyance to the reader.

reward of work"? Perhaps *objective,* or *exterior,* or *impersonal.* It is at all events clear that Marshall does not restrict the subject matter of economics to material existences. Nor does he so delimit *productivity.* In his discussion of wealth he says (pp. 54-55): "A man's *non-material* goods fall into two classes. One consists of his own qualities and faculties for action and for enjoyment . . . called *internal.* The second class are called *external* . . . relations beneficial to him with other people . . . the chief instances . . . now-a-days . . . the good will and business connection of traders and professional men." In fact one important category of capital with Marshall is *organization.* He might also have included patents, copyrights and franchises; and probably would do so without demur. In further evidence of his point of view, we find: ". . . the most systematic part of people's lives is generally that by which they earn their living . . . and numerical estimates can be framed as to the amount of money or general purchasing power that is required to supply a sufficient motive for them." (p. 21)

The best proof, however, that Marshall is a price economist is to be found in the general movement of his discussion and analysis. In the large, as is true of most economists, he is busy with these different influences in their different aspects that bear on market prices—not rarely, it is true, termed market *values.*

It is not, however, altogether so clear that either in interest or procedure is Marshall nothing more than a price economist. Not rarely, in fact, he discusses along with the conditions of price fixation, the bearing of the prices on human welfare. Often he seems to say that these welfare bearings are a part of the science rather than of the practical applications of it:

"Economics has then as its purpose firstly to acquire knowledge for its own sake, and secondly to throw light on practical issues. But . . . we should not plan out our work with direct reference to them. . . .

"Scientific inquiries are to be arranged with reference not to the practical aims which they subserve, but to the nature of the subjects with which they are concerned.

". . . The practical uses of economic studies should never be out of the mind of the economist, but his special business is to study and interpret facts and to find out what are the effects of different causes acting singly and in combination." (pp. 39-40, including marginal caption)

But the better view—as also the prevailing view with men of science —takes as the sole purpose of science that which Marshall appears to regard as merely the leading purpose.[3]

[3] See Ralph Barton Perry, *Present Philosophical Tendencies* (New York, 1912): ". . . science expresses itself in neutral or indifferent terms, the interests at stake being eliminated and the application being held in reserve. . . ." (p. 25)

Purely by the test of efficiency, at any rate, the wiser plan seems to be to observe the principle of the division of labor—to leave to the men of science the exclusive following of their lines of special competency, with no responsibility for any issues of *what to do about it*—the first step, at least, being obviously to find out, so far as may be possible, what *it* is. The *fire, and then inquire,* of frontier practice may have its frontier merit, but logically and practically in orderly procedures the *what* has priority over the *how.* These practical issues, moreover, are rarely, if ever, solved out of the contributions of any one field of science. These men of science are competent beyond the rest of us for particular problems, only as they are in especial degree informed about the facts of their particular fields. Were men's sole interest doing rather than knowing, meteorology and even mathematics could not have far developed. We shall continue to do little about the weather. The density of Betelgeuse is too slight for it to matter much just how slight it is. How hot is the interior of it or of any other star? Even the astronomers, we may believe, are mostly lacking in remedial programs.

Directly and in their own right, however, these issues of the function of science are not important for the purposes of our later discussions. Present significance attaches to the inclusion of welfare considerations within the field of economic analysis, only so far as, through welfare preoccupations, the generalizations and terminology of economics have been blurred or distorted by the introduction of categories of appreciation or of appraisal. It is fundamental to clear thinking to realize that the process facts in a competitive economic order cannot be organized on welfare lines. To describe in appraisal terms is perforce to misdescribe— the bases of generalization as various as are the individuals to make them—like the law when administered according to the length of the chancellor's foot. What is waste, or parasitism, or crime to you—may be wisdom, or merit or social service to me. How about war, face-powder,

---

". . . it is the mark of developed science that these properties and configurations are recorded without reference to the sequel, and in terms purged of the comment of passion." (p. 27)

"It has come to be the recognized aim of science to formulate what happens, whether for better or for worse; leaving out of account, as an extra-scientific concern, whatever bearing it may have on interest." (p. 54)

"Scientific description, then, is governed by two motives, on the one hand, unity, parsimony, or simplicity, the reduction of variety and change to as few terms as possible; and, on the other hand, exact formulation. When a scientific description satisfying these conditions is experimentally verified, it is said to be a law." (p. 55)

". . . the motive of science . . . is simply to describe and record, with special reference to their unity and constancy, the actual changes. . . ." (p. 62)

". . . science does not deal with value, but with the *quantitative constancies exhibited in natural processes.*" (p. 87)

coffee, beer, and vegetarianism? To conceive of *productivity,* not by the test of *gain* or *proceeds,* but by whatever you or I may hold to be good or wholesome in all this vain life that we spend as a shadow, is to get us nowhere with our task of accounting for the rate of interest, or for rent, or salaries, or profits. It is to organize our factual subject matter, not in accordance with its objective processes, but only by how we severally feel about it—German, Jap or bible-belter. Obviously chemistry or physics or biology will not organize after this fashion. That you do not warmly approve of the coal, or oil, or water-power situation; or of navies, and wars, and munition factories; and only dubiously of dives, and stews, and rum-running, and bootlegging, may infer much for your high ethical standards—but does not certify your economic competency. It was thirst with Omar rather than economic interest that prompted him to "wonder what the vintners buy one-half so precious as the stuff they sell." This ill solicitude, however, need not have declared him—when he was sober—as any the worse economist. The competent man of science may default in his laundry dues or renig on his bets; the excellent citizen may be weak in value theory.

Nothing, however, decrees that the social philosopher must know no economics, or that the economist may not be also a social philosopher—always a wise guide and counsellor in most or in all problems both of individual and social policy. But the economist who is more or other or better than mere economist does not, with his excursions into other fields, carry along his field with him, or reduce the new territory to the economic jurisdiction. There is no requirement that economists be not also human beings.

Not, therefore, their interest outside the field of economic science, but solely their non-scientific procedure within the field, is the point in criticism of the so-called welfare economists—not their welfare preoccupations, nor even their welfare finalities, but their employment of their ethical pronouncements for the scientific organization of factual materials —their attempt at a descriptive-causal account of competitive economic processes in terms of welfare appraisals. If only, therefore—as is not always the case—never were their procedure, their terminology or their systematized thought subjected to these welfare preoccupations; were always their scientific generalizations rigorously guarded from all inter-mixture of appraisal or appreciation elements, all occasion of dissent or criticism would disappear. But like the other sciences, economics would prosper not through the high character or the right ethical attitudes of its disciples, but through their ability to observe accurately and to think straight.

But, be it repeated, for the issues ahead of us, nothing in all this greatly matters. It may go without saying that Marshall's frequent discussions—

or more accurately pronouncements—on welfare topics are in the main—
or so they seem to me—temperate, well-informed, wise and wholesome.
But were they not so, or even also were his theology bad, his economic
analyses and generalizations need not thereby be the worse. It may be,
however, that he is occasionally a bit pontifical on these issues, or that he
is prone to find over-many things "somehow good," an optimism appropriate to upper-class Victorianism, and especially fitting in view of the
classical economic tradition. But not everywhere, nevertheless, does he
arrive at assuming the coincidence of private gain with the general welfare. He says (pp. 596-97) that "the struggle for survival tends to make
those methods of organization prevail, which are best fitted to *thrive in*
their environment; but not necessarily those best fitted to *benefit* their
environment. . . ."

Marshall's thought here, to be sure, is not precisely that unsocial
activities often pay, but only that, among the many that would be socially
desirable, some fail of performance because they do not individually pay.
It is, however, elsewhere said (p. 244): "The fact that there is an
economic demand for the services of Jewish and Armenian money-dealers
in Eastern Europe and Asia, or for Chinese labour in California, is not by
itself a proof . . . that such arrangements tend to raise the quality of
human life as a whole." But robbery, adulteration, bribery, fraud, lying
and cheating are, nevertheless, in the main outside of Marshall's view—
perhaps as not normal.

It is then enough for all present purposes that always Marshall's appeal
in economic analysis is to price, and that implicitly productivity almost
always connotes money gain. It is, therefore—you and I may hold
inaccurately—but still in an approximately acceptable sense, that he says
(p. 139): "The growth of mankind in numbers, in health and strength,
in knowledge, ability, and in richness of character is the end of all our
studies . . ."—adding, however, that, "it is an aim to which economics
can do no more than contribute some important elements." Substantially
then, he puts economics in its art aspect in its proper place. And again
(p. 42): "One of the justifications of science, though not its subject
matter, is the practical serviceability of it." In this sense, then, we may
agree that (p. 42): "the aims of the study are to gain knowledge for its
own sake, and to obtain guidance in the practical conduct of life. . . ."
So much, to be sure, may be said for most of the sciences. Such, at all
events is the high faith of science—though not the principle of its
motivation.

Nor more does it concern the issues which we are set to examine that
Marshall makes what appears to be an untenable distinction between
science in its theoretical aspect and science in its practical applications.
"Some parts," he says (p. 37, note) "of economics are relatively abstract

or *pure,* because they are concerned mainly with broad general propositions. . . . Other parts are relatively *applied,* because they deal with narrower questions more in detail . . . they consider economic conditions in fuller and closer relation to other conditions of life." (Italics Marshall's)

This distinction between pure and applied economics is obviously that commonly stressed between *science* and *art.* Neither the distinction nor the importance of it needs here to be brought in question. But to Marshall's further and equally significant distinction between *breadth* and *detail* in the treatment and organization of the factual material of any science, the terms *pure* and *applied* seem inappropriate. Irrespective of the terms appropriate to the distinction, particularization, it is true, is neither the more nor the less scientific than generalization in greater detail. Precisely here is the excuse and the necessity for the subdivision of general economics into its various and subordinate fields of Money and Banking, Finance, Transportation, Labor, and so on. It is only generalization in the sense of broad lines—of large strokes of the brush—that the ordinary general treatise can cover. The painting effective and realistically adequate for the beholder at a distance becomes a daub under close inspection. Things can not be seen at one glance both in the large and in the microscopic. Objectivity and realism, loyalty to fact, command acceptance as the primary scientific requirements. Scientific issues are always, therefore, issues of fidelity to the objective facts. As aforetime the ant to the sluggard, so strongly is your errant adversary admonished to betake himself to the facts—a field, seemingly, of the especial preemption of any one of us—wherein new light will shine on every wanderer. But this wholesome admonition—not the less so for its manifest smugness—does not ordain that all the facts be accounted for to their utmost of minute detail; else no treatise could run at less than fifty-seven volumes, with fortnightly revisions. To see things in the whole, as well as sanely, is of necessity to see things in the large—the town not shut off by the houses, or the forest beyond seeing for the trees.

Such at all events is in substance Marshall's position. His prodigality of factual material is in the main a prodigality of illustration in the illumination of generalizations that are never in purpose particularizations, but are presented solely in the broad lines of the large picture. It is, then, in the conviction that solely in this emphasis is any doctrinal discussion or criticism worth while, that the doctrinal system of classical economics in Marshall's particular rendering of it is here intended to be examined—and attacked.

Chapter III

DEMAND AND SUPPLY MECHANICS

THAT with Marshall the price point of view delimits the economic field, does not precisely commit him to the demand-and-supply approach in price analysis. He is, however, a demand-and-supply economist. This, to be sure, is not much to say. All economists are so, no matter what they may accept, or purport to accept, as the principle, or the problem, or the group of problems, defining the economic field. Always and everywhere with all economists, price is the point of equilibrium or adjustment or equilibration between demand and supply. It is, then, safe as far as it goes—but always in the sense of the commonplace or the obvious—to announce that price is determined by demand and supply. It is merely an oracular way of asserting an undisputed thing. Knowing not even so much as the question propounded, one may always refer the solution to demand and supply. Never is the argument thereby advanced excepting, perhaps, in the sense of a formal indication of a desirable or necessary line of procedure. No influence that does not report itself in demand or in supply terms, or in both, is relevant to price determination. The *demand-and-supply* expression is merely a formula of the sign-board sort pointing to the terms to which all economic analyses must finally get reduced. Difficulties appear only with the attempt to trace out the various influences that finally report themselves in demand and in supply terms—to render an account of these underlying and explanatory facts and processes.

Wherefore, according to Marshall, the first step in economic reasoning is the following:

. . . to examine the general relations of demand and supply; especially those which are connected with that adjustment of price, by which they are maintained in "equilibrium."

. . . .

... it is not descriptive, nor does it deal constructively with real problems. But it sets out the theoretical backbone of our knowledge of the causes which govern value [price], and thus prepares the way for the construction which is to begin in the following Book. It aims not so much at the attainment of knowledge, as at the power to obtain and arrange knowledge with regard to two opposing sets of forces, those which impel man to economic efforts and sacrifices, and those which hold him back. (pp. 323-24)

It may later become significant that Marshall's sole analysis of the process of adjustment of demand with supply concerns itself with middlemen buyers and producer sellers. Nowhere is there discussion of trading processes in which the buying is consumer buying. For the present, in any case, this need not seriously matter. The immediate analysis is to proceed on the sheer assumption of a price-offer and a goods-offer situation, with no slightest attempt to account for either. It is the mere mechanics of price adjustment that is to be examined. In its main essentials, the early part of the analysis here offered will be in harmony with that of Marshall, as also with the analysis of practically all economists. It is so far wholly a procedure analysis. The terms that are commonly employed in it are entirely familiar. But there is nevertheless need for the critical examination of them in point of their precise meanings and connotations, and especially with reference to Marshall's particular employment of them, the consistency of his use of them, and the logical movement of his analysis in their use.

It is obvious that for barter trading the demand and supply terminology must be extremely awkward or entirely inappropriate. If, in the exchanging of plums against peaches, either is to be called demand as against the other, it must be entirely indifferent which; nor could either make good as against the other its claim to the position of supply. There are merely reciprocal stocks or supplies or demands for goods for advancement of trading terms. Because there must be assumed on each side the disposition to trade—on the one side plums for peaches, and on the other side peaches for plums—*reciprocal demands* is perhaps the best descriptive term. When an exchange is concluded, every item among the transferred goods has achieved a quid-pro-quo standing, the goods on each side serving essentially as the price-goods of those on the other side. The case was on one side that of peaches offered for plums, on the other side, that of plums offered for peaches. Even the German terms *Angebot* and *Nachfrage,* excellent in some aspects, report distinctions that here are patently nonexistent, or that attach solely to the choice of point of view. The plain fact is that the offer of plums is a demand for peaches; the seller of peaches is a buyer of plums.

It is only with exchanges of ordinary commodities against the money commodity that occasion arrives for the conventional antithesis between demand and supply. The rôle of demand is attributed to the money—money-for-shoes. The shoes-for-money side is called the supply side. On the face of the case, to be sure, this still suggests the merely arbitrary or conventional. Grant, however, that there are no compelling reasons for it; there still appear to be no decisive objections to it. Moreover, it conforms to a somehow established popular and business usage.

But there is a better justification. Prevailingly now—whatever may or may not have been the earlier fact—trades occur, not in the barter form of goods against goods, but in the money-goods form. The trading takes place through an intermediate commodity, money; and the terminology of trade has practically so to report it. Ours is a pecuniary society. It belongs to our specialization of productive activity and to the development of the middleman function that there are a large number of individuals in possession severally of a wide variety of products, most of which call to get exchanged into other products. It attaches to the function of a medium, an intermediate, of exchange that actually, and almost by necessity, whatever possessors of various goods there are who prefer, say, shoes in place of their respective goods, must first by severally selling their holdings of goods place themselves in possession of exchange media wherewith to buy shoes.

Assuming then that the terms *demand* and *supply* are to be retained, there is no decisive reason why the offers of money against goods could not be indicated by *supply*. But the offers of goods against money could not workably be called *demand*. These offers do not present themselves in mass, but in particular groups, each to arrive at a separate price adjustment. There is one money quantum directed toward shoes; another toward butter, etc. In descriptive fidelity to the market facts, there is no one process of price fixation for all of the groups taken together. No demands schedule or curve could be constructed that could inclusively set goods offers over against any one money-offer group. Goods-offer *demand* is applicable only to particular price-offer groups.

In principle, however, it still holds true that the shoes are as much demand for money, as is the money for the shoes. The general money total does divide into particular sub-totals. And as soon, in turn, as the shoes-offer people have come into their several money receipts for their shoes, these money holdings get distributed into sub-groups of price-offers over against the wide range of commodities.

Against the background of the actual on-going of things, there is, then, justification for a more specific terminology, than that appropriate to barter transactions. In money trading the antithesis indicated under the prevailing demand and supply usage is actual. Nor, for purposes of popular and business use, is there any imperative call for a new terminology, even were it credibly possible to get it adopted. Tested, however, by the requirements of technical analysis, the current terminology is unfortunate, or even indefensible. Attending it are too many ambiguities both of immediate use and of connotation, too many logical inadequacies, too many invitations to error. Moreover, terms easily understandable for general use, and not misleading for technical purposes, are easily available —not, it is true, terms ideal by every test or in all connections, but intelligible and unambiguous everywhere.

Angebot and *Nachfrage,* were they workably translatable, would make a strong, though not a perfect, case. More nearly meeting all the needs would be *price-offer* as against *goods-offer.*

Implicit in the construction of any price-offer or goods-offer schedule or curve is always the notion of a limit offer attaching to each unit—an upper limit to each price-offer unit, a lower limit to each goods-offer unit. It has, however, sometimes been supposed that goods may actually be on sale, free altogether of price-limit conditions; offered on terms of whatever they will bring; a situation to be represented graphically only by a vertical line. The situation is here conceived as one in which the price is to be arrived at merely by counting down on the price-offer curve. But rarely, if ever—and practically never—does the factual situation so run. It is doubtless possible that goods be offered for sale at whatever sacrifice terms the market may be credibly forecasted to impose—distress stocks, the reservation limits on which are exceptionally low—so low, indeed, that they do not need to be specifically indicated. At higher, certainly, than the actual limit the goods are safe to sell.

But this does not rightly infer that such goods will be let go for nothing, but only that no one of them is held at a price higher than the market is likely to accord anyway. Were it, however, true that in the ordinary horse trade, or in the ordinary money bargaining for a horse, no selling limit were actual, the exchange terms could have no lower limit; and if there were no limit on either side, the terms of the exchange would be entirely indeterminate—depending solely on the skill and guile of the traders.

But never on either side is the situation thus extreme. Always there is something else to buy with the money. Even if the issue were one of life and death, there must be more than one need of this degree of stress. Always also the holder of goods can find some alternative opportunity of sale, or, if not, can better hold for a later sale, or for his own slightly pressing present or prospective need. Never in truth does theoretical analysis need to assume the literal absence of reservation prices, but only reservation prices so low as securely to lack significance in the outcome. Where goods-offer limits do not exist, price offers at any level must presumably also be lacking—no one likely to want at a price what no holder would make any price sacrifice to keep. The thing in question would then be a no-good, an unwanted thing; or possibly the two curves for a wanted thing may be thought of as intersecting at lower than the zero point of price—the stock of it so great that any unit of it is a surplus item. Both price-offer and goods-offer curves have, then, in the factual emphasis their points of starting and their points of ending. The goods-offer curve could obviously be indefinitely extended to the right within the limits of available stocks. But neither curve requires carrying beyond the point of credible bearing on the price outcome—this point, when once located, discovering and reporting the causal irrelevancy of all unit offers to the right.

The falling scale of price offers for increasing purchases of any good was an economic commonplace long before the law of satiation and the derivative marginal-utility analysis arrived at general recognition. In the large, to sell more must mean to sell cheaper. Each consumer has his particular declining scale of demands—a series of price offers now reported graphically by the familiar curve declining to the right. The summation of these individual curves gives the market demands curve. That back of each of these individual price curves, and somehow causally related to them, are individual utility curves, need not concern the present discussion.

In Marshall's first account of this market price-offer curve it is presented as a curve of consumers' money offers. No reference is called for at that stage of the analysis to the make-up of the goods-offer curve, whether from producer or middleman or speculative selling dispositions. Even the existence of any goods for sale is avowed only by implication. But his later account of the full demand and supply adjustment of price presents the demand side of the case as one of middlemen's price offers, and the supply side as one of producers' selling dispositions. The implicit equating of present price offers against past producers' costs somewhat detracts from the logical quality of the analysis, though not from its schematic and illustrative adequacy for the mechanics of price fixation. Where, however, the price offers are those of consumers, it would be preferable to have the supply side of the situation refer to the middlemen's terms of providing the stocks. The Marshall view, as we shall later see, presents price as the equating point between consumer gratifications and producer discomforts. But middlemen are one kind of producers with their appropriate costs. The point, therefore, at which Marshall should find his "real" costs at balance against consumer gratifications should be with the exchange process between retailers and consumers; not in a rural-town market in which producers of corn are making sales to grain merchants, whether wholesale or retail. This issue will later take on some importance. It has none at present. It therefore suffices now to note that irrespective of his later procedure Marshall's early account of the relation of utility to price offer presents these price demands as consumer demands—so far, then, the traditional approach. He says (p. 109) that "a list of demand prices represents the changes in the price at which a commodity can be sold consequent on changes in the amount offered for sale, *other things being equal. . . .*" (Italics Marshall's).

Repeatedly, as is characteristic of Marshall's masterly employment of graphs to report his thought, he both admits and stresses the list, or schedule, quality of demand in the analysis of price determination; similarly also with the supply side. We get, however, at this point our first glimpse of the dangerous ambiguities in Marshall's terminology—which is also the prevailing terminology. Precisely as it is misleading to interpret demand in the sense of one money total of the various price offers, so, in even greater degree, is it to invite error to regard supply as *amount offered for sale.* Make for yourself the effort to draw a goods-offer curve in terms of "an amount offered for sale." Both the price-offer and the goods-offer schedules contain price affirmations. The *demands* assert a succession of *Nachfragen* for successive units of the commodity. The *Angebot* side of the case, presented as a curve inclining upward to the right, reports increments of goods offers at successively higher holding prices. There is no price resultant possibly to be deduced from the mere notion of money offered against goods as over against a quantity of goods offered against money. The *supplies* schedule or list, as reduced to graphical expression, predicates a succession of minimum sales prices, precisely as does the *demands* curve affirm a succession of maximum paying prices. The supply curve at each point is quantitative in the unit-of-stock sense, but with reservation, or refusal, prices reported at each several point upon it. And thus it would be possible, with unchanged offer prices and an unchanged stock of offered goods, to have higher prices, if only the reservation prices moved upward;

or even to have higher prices rather than lower, if increases "in the amount offered for sale" were attended by reservation prices sufficiently advanced. From changes that are merely changes in quantity of offered goods, nothing can be inferred.

May not just this, however, be the meaning of the phrase, "other things being equal"? Presumably not; and even if it were, the situation would not be greatly improved. The increased volume signified by increments on the upper reaches of the goods-offer curve would have nothing to say for the market price.

In most connections, though clearly not in all, Marshall's use of *demand* presents no serious difficulties of interpretation or of analysis. Not so, however, with further usages of *supply*. Often, and indeed commonly, this term means *output* or *product* or *existing stock*. Excepting in discussions in near-by association with his graphical presentations, Marshall's use of *supply* rarely carries with it any connotation of holding prices—reservation terms, conditions attaching to successive releases of units of stock. Occasionally, indeed, important doctrinal issues will later be found to turn on Marshall's assumption of *a one* demand price, or of *the* long- or short-run supply price, or of an imputed relation between *the* demand price and *the* supply price.

Solely in the sense of list or schedule is it safe to speak either of *demand* or of *supply*. As test of this, attempt to present mentally to yourself a price-offer curve. Note the connotations. It presents the falling price-offer conditions at which successive increments of commodity are desired. Accurately it is not a *demand* but a *demands* curve. Only in the emphasis of an inventory of the different price offers is it to be thought of in the group sense. And even then, as we shall see, it is not a sum of anything. Even with an individual's price-offer schedule this holds; it is only an account of his price-offer units for respective items of commodity—his unit-buying schedule for respective units of the goods. These enter as units into the aggregate account of price offers, according to the individual's position in regard to how many units he is disposed to buy, and on terms of what limit price offers for each respective unit.

Doubtless, however, an aggregate price-offer curve at any unit point downward along it may be interpreted cumulatively in the quantitative sense of a group of potential price offers and purchases; but as reporting neither any one price offer, nor any sum of price offers as distinguished from a sum of potential price purchases.[1] Such a curve indicates only how many units of goods the various price offers will together absorb at each particular price point— with this absorption of goods totaled neither as one price offer nor as one purchase, but only as a total of units to be purchased at a total purchase outlay. Precisely because the curve connotes the sum of all the goods to be purchased at the same unit price for all, it cannot report the sum of the unit price offers; else it must implicitly deny any buyers' price surpluses, either for any particular individual or for individuals in the aggregate. At any particular point, then, down to zero the curve reports the number of units of goods and the potential total money payment for them at the one price per unit common to all. And if it were a curve of the equilateral hyperbola type, the determination of a total of all possible sales and their total of purchase outlays represented by the entire area under the curve would involve the use of the integral calculus. But not the curve in its entirety nor any one point along it can carry the significance of *a demand at the price,* but only of a total of the several money payments at any one point. As a curve, a schedule, a list, it connotes only a series of separate unit-buying attitudes, any mathematical summing-up of which no market could ever make possible or any economist ever be concerned to compute.

To thus much, either explicitly or implicitly, is Marshall definitely and irrevocably committed through his adoption of the curve or schedule or list conception of the demand and supply categories. In no sense, however, is this committal to be taken in the sense of admission or concession, or of anything short of definite and in-

[1] To revert to the illustration on p. 16, a total payment of twenty-five dollars for five hats may be derived from five quite disparate price offers, and may be represented by the co-ordinates of a particular point on a price-offer curve. No point on such a curve can connote, however, a total of the different price-offer ratios.

tentional advocacy. It is with him a forthright, clear, and un-equivocal position. It may be asserted that never anywhere by Marshall is it questioned or qualified or modified—still less abandoned. And especially in this emphasis is his meaning clear in some of his accounts of the relation of utility to the price offers of individuals. And thus it is against the background of this position—clearly, and as I hold both rightly and inevitably, taken by Marshall—that certain of his later analyses must be both examined and questioned. Not yet, however, have we finished with some of the near-by implications in his terminology and analysis of these demands and supplies curves:

. . . We cannot express a person's demand for a thing by the "amount he is willing to buy," or by the "intensity of his eagerness to buy a certain amount," without reference to the prices at which he would buy that amount and other amounts. We can represent it exactly only by lists of the prices at which he is willing to buy different amounts.
. . . A general increase in his demand is an increase throughout the whole list of prices at which he is willing to purchase different amounts of it, and not merely that he is willing to buy more of it at the current prices. (pp. 96-97)

And further, in a note on the same pages: "Then $p_1 \, p_2 \cdots p_8$ are points on his demand curve for tea; . . . " And thus that he will buy 10 pounds at a total payment of 20 shillings does not express any money sum of his different price-paying dispositions. Plotting the curve will suffice to make this entirely clear. On the 20 shillings terms of purchase, there are buyer's surpluses of which the 20 shillings make no report or suggestion. No less is this the case where there are an indefinitely large number of separate bidders and buyers. And similarly for the total utility under a utility curve—not a price-offer curve, note—declining toward zero. The total utility is not the marginal utility times the number of items. Total utility is an area of the triangular sort—or, more accurately, the trapezoid: not a parallelogram with the number of items as base and with marginal utility as height:

. . . we cannot trust the marginal utility of a commodity to indicate its total utility. . . . of salt . . . every one buys so much of it that an additional pound would bring him little additional satisfaction: the total utility of salt to him is very great indeed, and yet its marginal utility is low. . . . (p. 129)

Graphically represented, price, as we have seen, is indicated by the point of intersection of the price-offer and goods-offer curves. And it has been noted that never does either curve require extension to include all actual or possible items. There is no one of us but presumably would buy a car—of the right make and model, and with an adequate endowment attached—if only it could be had at, say, a dollar and a half. At some point also, every one of us would sell all the family pictures or plates or bibles, it being only price offers high enough that are lacking. All existing items in the various stocks of goods are to be included in the supply, only that the reservation prices on most of them are so high as to leave them without significance in the actual fixation of prices. Only, then, a small share of the price offers and of the goods offers require inclusion in the schedules, or attention in the analysis.

Moreover, the price is actually influenced by only a part of the items that at the outset required recognition. The rest stand as mere potentials or might-have-beens. And further, each unit in the price-offer schedule that has influenced the price outcome at all has had an influence interchangeable in point of degree with every other. Similarly also with the goods-offer schedule. The notion that the so-called marginal items in the exchange do the price-determining or have some special degree of influence or of strategic bearing is error. In this regard Marshall rightly says (p. 410): "Of course the withdrawal of (say) iron from any of its necessary uses would have just the same influence on its value as its withdrawal from its marginal uses; . . . " The marginal item on each side is significant beyond other items only as indicating the degree of influence on the actual price that has attached to any one item.

It should then be clear that to define *demand* as the volume of goods that will be bought at any particular price, or at the particular price reported by the intersection point, or arrived at through the market adjustment, is to define only one point on the curve, or to arrive at a definition which accurately amounts to the summation of a multitude of definitions. And similarly of *supply*. And further, to select for particular definition of either demand or supply only that point on either curve at which it intersects the other, is to define both supply and demand by reference to the particular price point that the demand and the supply are together invoked to explain. It is bad logical procedure, ex-post-facto legislation, a next-day-after-the-fair exhibit. It derives a price from nowhere, and then defines demand and supply—as explanations of it—by reference to it, and as derivatives from it. Previous to the determination there were no determinants. It is the magician's device of fixing up his hat to fit his magic. In no analysis is it defensible as determinative of the price outcome or as derivative from it. *The* supply price of any volume of competitively produced goods—some one price—whether the connotation be that of the mathematical summation of many and various goods-offers of intending sellers, or the various cost-of-production terms of many producers, is plain error, pointing both backward and forward to associated errors.

Both of these curves that speak for the conditions of a particular time and place have, be it repeated, for present purposes, no concern with causes. They are given—taken by assumption—like the figures in geometry, presenting generalized conditions for examination. It is, then, not to the point to urge that no prospective buyer ever knows just how high he would go in price payment for any one item out of a particular stock of interchangeable goods. He expects to talk things over with others before he makes up his mind, or may first shop around a good bit; and may several times meanwhile change his mind—assuming that ever he gets so far as to have one—before he arrives finally at a clear notion of how high he will go. Or, the very contacts and processes of the market itself may be the necessary conditions to his arrival at a bid. Or, he may just put in an order *at the market*. Or, definitely wanting a pound and a half of lamb chops, he may at the outset intend to buy them at whatever turns out to be their price—it being not likely to run at, say, over two dollars per chop. In short, most buyers are supramarginal in their price offers, and think little—and in most cases both know and care less—about any price limits on their purchases.

The wife has said to *buy chops*. They get heads-in at the butcher's only far enough to put in a *send-chops* order. The bargain hunter even, or the indifferent marginal participant, is guiltless of any such precision of purpose as these price-offer schedules imply.

Doubtless so. Precisely what you might pay or may actually consent to pay for a chop you probably do not know. But there is a price to which you know that you would not go; and a general price area at some point in which you would draw your line—a line which, to be sure, you have never had to make precise, but which you could be pushed into making so. That for you, say with bananas or with cars, there is a limit is evident by the fact that you do somewhere stop buying. To get near to marginality is to approach this limit of stopping.

But nothing in all this is accurately to the point anyway. The limits set here are limits by sheer assumption, solely for illustrative purposes. Nowhere in book or on blackboard was there ever a perfect square or equilateral triangle. Neither pencil nor chalk can ever have traced a line of only one dimension or have formed a point of none. But even a spade may stand for a stream in which Ophelia drowned herself. All that is needed is an assumption that is logically adequate. The price offers with which we start, we simply start with.

Possibly also one purchaser is buying ahead of using; or is instead waiting for a fall in price; and so bids low or buys little. Or again he may be hurrying his purchases to get early under the wire; or he will use none of the commodity till Christmas. But we are not now concerned with any factual issues of how these price-offer items came about, or with the bearing of futurity on them. In fact, they didn't come about. We simply assumed them. Nor is it to the present purpose to inquire whether Marshall or the Austrian economists can be justified in asserting or denying that a market price measures utility or marginal utility, or is determined by either; or whether even any one price offer can do thus much; or what may be the relation of the reservation price to the cost of production of the goods that are being offered; or how the reservation price may be affected by the utility or marginal utility of the goods that the reservation price might alternatively buy.

All these issues we set outside the present discussion. We have now solely to get clear the mechanism of the price process, and to arrive at secure and definite meanings of the terms and relations involved in it.

The ratio aspect of both price offer and goods offer is obvious. It is money-for-goods and goods-for-money—*a* for *b, b* for *a*. In the nature of these ratios, they are ratios of unit values—1 : 1, or 1/1. Limits are reported on the terms acceptable by the different individuals as exchange parities for them. These individual parities underlie and explain the resultant market exchange parity—that exchange ratio of price-good to commodity-good that is effective for all the actual traders. It belongs always, as we have seen, to the use of an intermediate, that in market exchanges one of the offer schedules is a money schedule. The many different and separate market adjustments—all of the particular prices—together constitute a price system, each of the different exchange relations being reported as its particular price relation. Each of the different goods units arrives in terms of money units at its particular market standing. Therewith the exchange relations of the different commodities to one another appear as their relative prices.

These different commodity ratios of exchange to the money unit may, to be sure, be interpreted over into a report not of the ratio of each good unit to its particular number of money units, but instead into the exchange ratios of the money unit to each one of the different goods—a dollar, that is to say, as buying ten pounds of sugar, three and a half pounds of cheese, a quarter of a pair of shoes, two-thirds of a bushel of wheat, a fiftieth part of a radio set, or the thousandth part of a piano. Therefrom, doubtless, it is possible by computation to deduce the exchange relations of the different goods to one another. But only by exception do the actual market exchanges run in these terms. Practically they cannot in general so run; though dollar days, ten-cent and ninety-nine cent shops are familiar exceptions. Exchanges in the retail shops, and still more clearly in the wholesale markets, cannot usually so run, and the maximum of convenience in arriving at the exchange relations of goods to one another is found in the pricing of all goods units in money. To report these various relations in terms of the exchange relations of the money unit against the different numbers of goods units, in all of the different exchanges of money for goods would be greatly to impair the convenience attaching to the standard function of money.

But in any case, even if convenience could be made consistent with exchanges in either this money-unit form or in this money-unit type of report, the established habits of exchange prescribe the contrary line of procedure. And this is enough for most purposes. And even did they not so prescribe, the fact that the actual society is a trading society and a society trading through a conventional intermediate, would still leave inevitable the opposing categories of price offer and goods offer in every particular market exchange. Price per goods-unit is, not only the convenient and practicable, but the actual, outcome. The process also is readily amenable to clear and adequate analysis.

But it is nevertheless true that the very commonplaceness of the process in its actual setting offers the constant temptation to interpretation in quantitative rather than in ratio terms. Never in any significant aspect are its data quantitative. Essentially always they are ratios between quantities. On no matter what terms of time and effort, this must become clear. It is fundamental to all unambiguous thinking in the field of exchange relations. Partly in this emphasis the price-*offer* and goods-*offer* terminology has been urged. Each offer on the demand side of the market setting means a money quantity against a goods quantity, a bidding ratio—money for, say, shoes. Each item on the supply side equally affirms a readiness for exchange between money and shoes, but it is formulated in antithetical emphasis on the one side, *a*-to-*b;* on the other side, *b*-to-*a*. Only thus are the items of the market process to be represented in curves available for intersection. Only thus does the notion of adjustment by equilibrium or equation become appropriate. The point of intersection represents the point of price adjustment.

No criticism, or even suggestion, of unreality or artificiality is in-

tended here, other than that attaching to the convenient artificiality
attendant on the presence of a medium of exchange. Price-offer and
goods-offer schedules and curves are adequately descriptive of the
process facts. Even the sharp antithesis of the curves is descriptively faithful to these facts. In certain important analytical aspects
nevertheless, the antithesis does not hold. Instead, there is an
underlying harmony, or even identity. These essential similarities
the antithetical form of presentation is adapted rather to obscure
or hide than to report and emphasize. The ultimate relations are
masked in the mere commonplaceness of the process facts. And
especially are the ratio connotations thereby ignored, or even impliedly denied. The fact is that money is never offered against
shoes, or shoes against money; but solely a quantity of money
against a quantity of shoes, or a quantity of shoes against a quantity
of money. The price offer is not an *a* offer, but only an *a*-to-*b*
offer; the goods-offer not a *b* offer, but only a *b*-to-*a* offer—definite
quantities of particular things being necessary in both terms of a
ratio expression.

But, not merely is the ratio aspect common to both of the schedules, but also the primary condition to an exchange is a ratio
relation. In this aspect there is no essential distinction between a
demand and a supply item. This is easily made manifest by reversing
the antithetical formulation of *a*-to-*b* and *b*-to-*a* into a first and
a second *a*-to-*b*—from the usual report of money-for-good and
good-for-money into a form presenting the fundamental identity
of the ratios—an identity implicit in the very nature of a money
offer for a hat and a hat offer for money. But first it is necessary
that the two schedules be divested of their seemingly quantitative
emphasis. They must not be interpreted as a demand schedule of
6, 5, and 4 of money, as over against a supply schedule of 4, 5,
and 6, with an equilibrating point of 5. Presenting them in such
form as to disclose clearly the one ratio aspect of both, we have—

price offers:	goods offers:
A, 6 of money for 1 hat	X, one hat for 6 of money
B, 5 of money for 1 hat	Y, one hat for 5 of money
C, 4 of money for 1 hat	Z, one hat for 4 of money

But still the ratio relation runs on one side in the *a*-to-*b* form, and on the other in the reverse, the *b*-to-*a* form. All may, however, be reduced to the *a*-to-*b* form as follows:

A limits his sacrifice to 6 to get   one hat
X limits his sacrifice to 6 to keep one hat
B limits his sacrifice to 5 to get   one hat
Y limits his sacrifice to 5 to keep one hat
C limits his sacrifice to 4 to get   one hat
Z limits his sacrifice to 4 to keep one hat

But to be allocated among these six individuals there are still only three hats. With which among these six individuals are the several hats finally to rest, and at what price for those of the hats that get transferred? Were these price offers of 6, 6, 5, 5, 4, 4, the offers of any one individual, it is clear that at price 6 he would buy only one hat; and at price 5 two hats; at price 4 three hats. To arrive at the price in this present setting that reports in the *a*-to-*b* form all this individual readinesses to sacrifice money for hats, we count down along the declining curve or schedule of price offers—a mere process so far of matching offers and goods. But the price can obviously not be above 5, there being only two individuals with a sacrifice limit of more than 5, and three individuals A, X and B, disposed if necessary to sacrifice as much as 5 for a single hat; Y being not even clearly of a buying readiness as high as 5, but merely indisposed to sell at less than 5; and there being three hats for allocation. The price cannot be less than 5, there being at this point four individuals at as high a sacrifice limit as this, and only three hats for them—two candidates therefore for the third hat. The price must then be 5 without possibility of shading in either direction.

This method leaves obviously no place for contrasted curves or schedules, or for any point of reported intersection. Not that it is thereby any the better or the worse. It has, to be sure, demerits— later to be recognized—but equally securely it has its peculiar merits. It stresses the essential ratio aspect of all of these exchange readiness attitudes and their essential unity of principle. For it is not ultimately the fact that some of the offers are mere money attitudes and some mere goods attitudes. All are equally money-for-goods attitudes, and all equally goods-for-money attitudes. It brings also into clear definition that all these goods-for-money offers on the supply side at their respective money minima embody also price-offer attitudes towards goods—not those of seekers of goods, but those of individuals already in possession.

With these aspects of principle in mind, it becomes obviously an outlawed question to inquire which of the two, demand or supply, has the more to do with price, or is primary with regard to it. The goods-offer items hide demand functions. Nor longer could any economist attribute market price solely to the handful of exchanges in some trading center like London or Chicago—a mere frothy activity on the surface of deep waters—turning then to speculate on what price collapse must attend the emergence for sale of all the remaining world stocks. Reservation prices everywhere are as much a part of the market setting as are the commodity stocks or the buying dispositions. To ask what would happen to prices if all the holders of money lost their price orientations toward the commodity is to make the problem over into a nonsense problem. Almost as radical a reformulation of it is involved in asking what would happen if all the holders of stocks should lose their commodity orientations toward money.

Obviously, then, a reservation price, as reporting in turn what utmost money sacrifice a holder of a good will make to retain it, is therefore, so far, the precise correlative of the price offer of a seeker of goods. A reservation price cannot, however, without some shading, be set over into the price-offer schedule along with the original price offers. To revert to our earlier hat case, as representative of what Z, Y, and X would pay in order to get a unit of the commodity, rather than what they would severally require to let go a unit already in hand, these reservation prices must run not at 4, 5, and 6, but at, say, 3.9, 4.9, and 5.9. Our reformed price-offer schedule runs then at

A 6
X 5.9

B 5
Y 4.9
C 4
Z 3.9

The allocation of the three items of stock becomes now entirely unambiguous. A, X, and B emerge with hats. Only A and B become vendees; only Y and Z vendors; X has insisted on too much money to achieve a sale; C on too much for his money to arrive at a purchase.

The main purpose of this chapter thus far has been to emphasize the ratio aspect of all of the data under examination. The issue is both crucial and far reaching. Each price offer reports a ratio limit, a money-offer limit, at beyond which the good fails to offer the stronger appeal; as also, on the goods-offer side, each corresponding gesture indicates a point of approximate indifference between having and not having the money instead of the good. The traders that are marginal at the declared price are the traders that are at or near the indifference ratio—a unit ratio, an equality of appeal between having and not having. The price arrived at, the equating or equilibrating price, is the market or exchange ratio between the pricing and the priced good.

Along, then, with all other exchanges, the exchanges of money against goods fall under the principle of reciprocal demand. Not quantities, but ratios between quantities, are the subject matter of these schedules or curves. Only in the sense that ratios are always relations between quantities, can quantities be involved—the terms between which a ratio exists being necessarily quantitative terms. The market adjustment merely declares the ratio at which all traders get a quantity of one thing for a quantity of another thing—a this-for-that adjustment. To talk of *quantities demanded* or of *the quantity supplied* is therefore to misinterpret the facts and to confuse the analysis—to the point, indeed, of cancelling anything to analyze. Both the price offers and the goods offers are goods-quantity-to-medium-quantity facts, ratios between quantities. There is no distinction in principle between the trading of money for peaches and the trading of plums for peaches.

With the ratio aspect of both demand and supply schedules held firmly in mind, the impossibility of any quantitative totaling of either becomes manifest. Ratios cannot be added together; or, more precisely, can be added together only when identical in the ratio aspect; and then they arrive at the same ratio as before, with quantitative changes solely in the terms—the same ratio, but between larger quantities. It must, then, be clearly recognized that even a single price offer in any individual schedule—e.g., three-cents-for-one-banana—is not a quantity.

That I, for one banana, would pay three cents, while you would pay five cents, can permit of no one point in the price curve predicating eight cents for two bananas. If finally both you and I buy at two cents, instead of at the three of my price offer or at the five of yours, neither one of these two-cent outlays can enter into any summed-up or compound *demand,* but only into a sum of two two-cent *payments.* My three-cent price offer is now accounted for by two cents of outlay and one cent of buyer's surplus; your five-cent offer by two cents of payment and three cents of surplus.

But does it, after all, matter? A firm grasp of the fact that none of these schedules speaks for quantities, but only for ratios, does fundamentally matter. Consider the eminence of error in the brief expression: *increased supply increases demand.* In any significant sense there is no more adding together of any of these ratios than there is of adding cousinships or of points on the compass. Nor can there be any totaling even of any individual's several price offers. Not, then, *supply,* but only *stock* or *product,* can change in *volume.* On the price-offer side of the case accuracy is doubtless less difficult, and inaccuracy less serious. No change in the supplies schedule can affect the demands schedule; nor, in the demands schedule, the supplies schedule. Changes in either schedule may affect the price—if only they are rightly placed. And changes in the number of transfers must always go along with—are merely one aspect of—these processes of price change.

With both demand and supply reduced to ratio relations reported in terms of lists or schedules or curves, a further error to which the conventional terminology leads becomes clear; the notion that either demand or supply, in that strict sense applicable to one particular time and place, can manifest *elasticity*. Thinking in terms of a price-offer curve, try to attribute elasticity to the curve as a whole, or especially an elasticity in response to changing conditions of goods offer. When consumers' price-offer schedules are in question, nothing more can be meant than that a falling price induces more buying or consuming. But that a change in the goods-offer side will not be met by a change in the price-offer side is itself the sole warrant for this assertion. What is it that changes? By assumption, in the first instance, at any rate, it is the goods-offer side. Plot such a change. There is neither occasion nor room for retracing the price-offer schedule. The change, as a change solely on the goods-offer side, involves a new point of intersection with a price-offer curve that has not changed. This is merely a repetition of the earlier assertion that there is merely a change, so far as the price-offer curve is concerned, in the number of transfers effected. Hence it is only the buying or the consuming that responds to changing prices. The *elasticity* is in buying or consuming, if any-where; but this is an elasticity already implicit in the nature of the original price-offer curve.

But with changing times and conditions, new curves of price offer and of goods offer are inevitable. Doubtless there will also be changes in the cost-of-production curve. But, even so, only in the sense that there must be new curves. Output or stocks may become larger or smaller. New reservation prices may attach. The demands situation may change. Either production or consumption may evince elasticity; but if no more than that is meant, it would conduce to clarity in both the expression and the communication of thought to say nothing more. Consumption does show modifiability with changing times, places and conditions. But that does not say that the demands schedule of any time holds over to another time, only with its curve retraced. It says merely that there is a new curve for the new time. Marshall puts it (p. 462) that "such a change as any of these [substantive changes in conditions of demand and supply] . . . may render it necessary to make out a new demand schedule or a new supply schedule, or both of them."

Costs of production stagnate or change; but nothing seems to be added to this assertion by calling them inelastic or elastic. The response of habits of consumption to changing opportunities, the modifiability of standards of living, the reaction of costs to changing markets, are perhaps as accurately described by calling them *modifiable* as elastic. In its ordinary employment, at any rate, the term *elasticity* is not only an offense against clear thinking, but carries with it the evidence of previous unclear thinking. For this, however, the demand and supply terminology is mainly at fault.[2]

And traders' surpluses? They are prone to be interpreted as surpluses of utility. But the difference between what one would pay if he had to and what he actually has to pay—between what one would produce or sell for and what one actually receives—all these are price surpluses.

Doubtless the purchasing power set free for other things will buy goods that must else be gone without, but this argument holds for incomes in general. The volume of utility surpluses derives from the volume of price surpluses. The intermediate thing does not become the end thing, merely because the one buys the other —money becoming a pair of shoes, or a sheep, or a box of cigars, by the mere fact that any one of them may be bought with the money. The difference must be recognized precisely because the amount of the one turns on the amount of the other. A steer is not a radio set by the mere fact that the money from selling the steer will go into the purchase of such a set. The aggregate of traders' surpluses for any individual or for society at large will later become an important issue. In some connections Marshall will recognize that these surpluses are price facts, and yet will find them to amount for each individual to more than his entire income, and for society to more than the social dividend. This problem, however, is neither presented nor solved by any of the terminological issues connected with *demand* and *supply*.

But again, does it matter? And how? These issues of producers', consumers' and traders' surpluses have serious significance for the

---

[2] See Note on Demand and Supply Terminology, p. 61.

larger problems of tax policy and for the analysis of the incidence of taxes—questions, however, which will neither directly nor greatly concern our later discussions. Elasticities of demand or of supply likewise concern us at present only as minor or illustrative aspects of a careless and ambiguous terminology of demand and supply. In entirely different connections, however, these ambiguous uses are to become of transcendant and even crucial significance for issues central to economic theory. Some of these further connections may well be shortly indicated here.

In general, no doubt, Marshall's meaning in particular uses of *demand* and *supply* is clear. In most of the cases of ambiguity, also, nothing of especial importance turns on the choice of alternatives. But it does matter seriously and fundamentally when the talk is of *a* supply price, or of *the* supply price; and similarly with demand. Explanations of price adjustment are not rarely then implied that are, not only misleading, but often plainly incorrect. The one supply price that is indicated must be that supply price that is presented as equating against one particular demand price—else there is nothing to the point and no price can be reached. But there are, in fact, numerous different supply prices and numerous different demand prices, even for any particular individual; and the isolation of any one item of demand or of any one item of supply, as an item that is prospectively to be the significant or decisive one on its side of the price adjustment, is plainly without justification. Which one among all the supply items is going to be the one to equate as *the* supply item, against which one among all the demand items?

And especially when we arrive at *the* normal supply item or *the* normal demand item, as implying that in a normal-price situation there are not schedules on both sides of the account, the invitation to error is patent. And when also we meet *the* representative firm, with its single supply price—derived perhaps from *the* respective particular supply prices of several different representative firms— set over against *the* demand price of a representative middleman or consumer, there must be still worse confusion.

And particularly must this be the case, if all of these representative firms are to be identified solely through the fact that their respective prices, whether of demand or of supply, turn out somehow to be equal to the actual market price. For each of these representative firms must obviously have its different demand price and its different supply price for its different volumes of commodity—else each would so far not be representative, but instead incredibly peculiar.

Something further, however, remains to be said of the process of price fixation where the price-offer schedules are constructed in other than the consumer sense and emphasis. Doubtless it is in general true that a smaller output of goods will carry with it higher asking prices on the part of sellers, a higher market-price adjustment, and thereby a diminished buying and consuming. It is true also that the prospect of a light crop, say of wheat, will report itself in higher prices and in a diminished rate of consumption, in advance of the time when the restricted output will itself become manifest in market stocks. In such an event buying, however, will be promptly stimulated rather than restricted—the fact that prices must later advance recording itself immediately in the activities of speculators and middlemen, and measurably also in the forward ordering or buying of consumers. The principle holds also and especially clearly with stock-exchange securities. Actually it is characteristic of all long-time commitments. Either rising or risen prices make, doubtless, for restricted consumption, and are prompt in exerting their influence. Commonly, however, rising prices exert the contrary influence on the purchasing of durable goods, either direct or indirect. Never are speculators or investors keen for stocks or lands by virtue of an actual or prospective decline in their prices. Never are manufacturers replenishing their stocks of raw materials or expanding their other inventories, and never are middlemen filling their warehouses or their shelves, through the lure of lower prices in prospect. The housewife buys a barrel of sugar for her later purposes of canning or preserving with the prospect, not of lower, but of higher, prices. Doubtless she may plan a larger buying and consuming when once the prices have dropped, or may even, in this prospect, forthwith increase her consumption. Not immediate buying, however, but only postponed buying is her present line of strategy. With perishable goods of daily consumption, to be sure, falling or fallen prices will forthwith expand both buying and consuming. But in the short run, with durable goods of either the direct or the indirect sort, changing prices—as distinguished from changed prices—affect buying in one direction and consumption in the reverse direction.

It is especially in this aspect that Marshall's selection of middle-men-buyer markets as illustrative of the more simple and fundamental processes of price fixation is unfortunate. Instead, an analysis of the very sort of situation that is least likely to come under observation—that of consumer traders on both sides of the process of price adjustment—offers the best illustration of the fundamental principles of demand and supply analysis. That of consumer with retailer is next in order of preference—consumers accounting thus for one, but for only one, side of the process. Marshall's choice of retailer with producer is a poor third.[3]

[3] But promptly the inevitable and recurrent question—does it matter? Is all this absorption with terms, and all this insistence on precision in their use, to the point for our present task? Take it, if you will, that never with technical terms should there be two things for one word or two words for one thing; our concern remains nevertheless solely to interpret and then to examine Marshall's positions for the criticism and appraisal of them. What then we need to know is what he means, and not what better terms he might have chosen for saying it. To get outside of this purpose is mere finicking, fluster, irrelevancy or nagging. Only when, in its setting of subject matter and context, the meaning is in doubt, is there occasion for all this touchiness as to inaccuracies or confusion of terms.

Quite so—or so it may easily be. Only with the issues and the discussions ahead can it come to be clear what importance may attach to these multiple and shifting meanings of terms. That it is, for example, error to talk of demand in any other sense than of list or schedule or curve; or of either demand or supply as a quantity; or of the demands of different individuals, or even of any one individual, as making up into one demand sum; or of demand or supply or price as a measurable thing; or of price offer or goods offer or market price as measuring demand or supply or utility or marginal utility, or discomfort, or real costs; or of demand or any price offer or market price as interchangeable with any one of them, or as measured by any one of them; or of demand or of supply—being lists or schedules—as elastic to changing prices; or to talk of *a* demand price, or of *the* demand price, or of *a* supply price, or of *the* supply price, or of any one of them, or all of them, as accounting for the market-price adjustment—all this I believe to be the fact, in total and in detail. But that any one of these things, taken to be error, must thereby lead later with Marshall to any erroneous and important doctrinal position, does not follow. For all that the argument has thus far shown, such may not be the fact. Or, I submit, it may be.

My justification for all this current concern with terminology is precisely that

Note on Demand and Supply Terminology

In the following quotations Marshall correctly presents demand and supply in the sense of *list,* or *schedule,* or *curve:*

". . . such a change [substantive change in conditions of demand and supply] . . . may render it necessary to make out a new demand schedule or a new supply schedule, or both of them. . . .

"An increase of normal demand for a commodity involves an increase in the price at which each several amount can find purchasers; or, which is the same thing, an increase of the quantity which can find purchasers at any price. . . . Similarly an increase of normal supply means an increase of the amounts that can be supplied at each several price, and a diminution of the price at which each separate amount can be supplied." (pp. 462-63)

"The demand schedule for gas remains the same as it would be if gas were a freely-produced commodity; it specifies the price per thousand feet at which consumers in the town will among them use any given number of feet. But the supply schedule must represent the normal expenses of production of each several amount supplied. . . ." (pp. 478-79)

On the following pages demand and supply are presented as curves intersecting at the point of price: 384, 388, 389-91, 479 note.

On the following pages demand is presented as a curve: 98, 100, 104, 105, 109, 342, 467, 469; also, sometimes with supply, in the list or schedule or curve sense, 368, 382-84, 388-89, 462-69, 483.

Chapter IV of Book III in discussing the relation of wants to demand, treats demand in the *schedule* emphasis, with many illustrative curves— not, however, without some confusion between *demand* and *purchasing* as also between *demand* and *want,* along with further confusions between *supplies* as over against *output* and *stocks:*

". . . a person's desire for a commodity . . . diminishes, other things being equal, with every increase in his *supply* of that commodity. . . . If it [this diminution] is slow the price that he will give . . . will not fall much in consequence of a considerable increase in his *supply* of it; and a small fall in price will cause a comparatively large increase in his *purchases.* But if it is rapid, a small fall in price will cause only a very small increase in his purchases. In the former case *his willingness to*

I hold these uses of terms to be erroneous in such sort as to lead actually and inevitably into later errors, each of which concerns and underlies in important ways Marshall's later analyses and generalizations. In fact practically every later position of Marshall is to stand or fall by the test of the issues in some one or more of the discussions that here, I fully admit, may have the present seeming of mere logomachies.

purchase the thing stretches itself out a great deal under the action of a small inducement: the elasticity of his *wants*, we may say, is great. In the latter case the extra inducement given by the fall in price causes hardly any extension of his *desire* to purchase: the *elasticity* of his demand is small.... That is when the *demand is elastic* for a fall in price, it is elastic also for a rise. (Italics the present author's.)

". . . so with that of a whole market. . . . The *elasticity* (or *responsiveness*) *of demand* . . . is great or small according as the amount demanded increases much or little for a given fall in price, and diminishes much or little for a given rise in price." (p. 102; italics Marshall's)

"The current prices of meat, milk and butter . . . are such that every variation in price makes a great change in the *consumption* . . . by the working classes . . . In other words, the direct demand . . . is very elastic . . ." (p. 105)

But in a note on page 105 it is said that "the character of the demand schedule for any commodity depends in a great measure on whether the prices of its rivals are taken to be fixed or to alter with it."

". . . At moderate prices the *demand* for it [water] is very elastic. . . ." (p. 107)

". . . Part of the demand for the more expensive kinds of food is really a demand for the means of obtaining social distinction, and is almost insatiable." (p. 106)

But later in the chapter Marshall returns to the conception of demand in the list or schedule sense:

". . . of the difficulties of getting exact lists of demand prices . . . The first which we have to consider arises from the element of *time*. . . .

"Thus while a list of demand prices represents the changes in the price at which a commodity can be sold consequent on changes in the *amount* offered for sale, *other things being equal;* yet *other things* seldom are equal. . . .

". . . allowance must be made for changes in fashion, and taste and habit. . . . For time is required to enable a rise in the price of a commodity to exert its full influence. . . .

". . . there are many *purchases* which can easily be put off for a short time. . . .

". . . A rise of prices tends to check *consumption;* but if the rise is expected to continue, it will . . . lead dealers to increase their *stocks.*" (pp. 109-12)

Demand and supply are presented not as list or schedule or curve, but as *quantity* in the following passages:

". . . An increase in *the* price offered by purchasers does indeed always increase supply: . . . a similar increase in the demand for a hand-made commodity might call forth quickly a great increase in supply. . . ." (p. 456; see also pp. 99, 236, 368, 573)

". . . the extra inducement given by the fall in price causes hardly any extension of his desire to purchase: the elasticity of his demand is small. . . ." (p. 102)

". . . the supply of anything available for use in making any commodity is apt to be greatly influenced by the demand for that thing derived from its uses in making other commodities: and so on. . . ." (p. 403)

". . . if the supply is increased, the thing will be applied to uses for which it is less needed. . . ." (p. 526)

". . . the case of *joint products: i.e.* of things which cannot easily be produced separately; but are joined in a common origin . . . may therefore be said to have a *joint supply.* . . . This case corresponds to that of things which have a *joint demand,* and it may be discussed almost in the same words, by merely substituting 'demand' for 'supply,' and *vice versa.* . . . The single *supply* of the common origin is split up into so many derived supplies . . ." (p. 388)

Ambiguous uses are found on pages 370, 379, 383, 384, 427.

Elasticity, not of buying or selling, but of demand or supply, in the quantitative, not in the list, schedule or curve sense is connoted in the following:

". . . There will not be any uniform relation between the fall in price and the increase of demand. . . ." (p. 99)

"The current prices of wall-fruit, . . . are such as to make the consumption of them by the middle class increase much with every fall in price; in other words, the middle class demand for them is very elastic. . . ." (p. 105)

". . . A fall in the price, at which a commodity is offered, acts on demand always in one direction. The amount of the commodity demanded may increase much or little according as the demand is elastic or inelastic. . . .

". . . an increase in *the* price offered for its products may have no perceptible effect in increasing the output for some considerable time: while a similar increase in *the* demand for a hand-made commodity might call forth quickly a great increase in supply. . . ." (pp. 455-56)

Especially for certain of their bearings on later issues, some of these uses of terms call for further examination—especially those terms that seem to assert that there is one particular demand price for a commodity, *the* demand price for it, normal or other; or that there belongs to a commodity one particular supply volume, with its particular attaching supply price; or that it has its one appropriate and particular cost or expense of production, normal or other. But, if in the individualized nature of price offer and of goods offer, as also of costs and of expenses of production, no one of these things can possibly be—so much being implicit in the very nature of the schedule notion of demands and of supplies—and if, further, each item in every one of these schedules is essentially a ratio fact rather than ultimately a quantity fact, there are certain devastating things to follow for not a few of Marshall's positions.

With Marshall, as with classical usage at large, value as technically defined is clearly a ratio, and not a quantity, fact:

"The value, that is the exchange value, of one thing in terms of another at any place and time, is the amount of that second thing which can be got there and then in exchange for the first. Thus the term value is relative, and expresses the relation between two things at a particular place and time.

". . . expressing the values . . . in terms of money . . . [we] call the value of each thing thus expressed its *price*. If we know that a ton of lead will exchange for fifteen sovereigns at any place and time, while a ton of tin will exchange for ninety sovereigns, we say that their prices then and there are £15 and £90 respectively, and we know that the value of a ton of tin in terms of lead is six tons then and there." (pp. 61-62)

In the following passages, demand is as need: as one price offer, adequate to call forth a particular volume of product, or particular situation; as efficient; as that demand adequate for articulating with some particular quantitative supply:

". . . the distribution of that dividend . . . will be unequal. It will be governed by the demand of the people themselves. The share of those in any industrial compartment will be the higher, the more extensive and urgent the *needs* which they are able to satisfy on the part of those who are themselves drawing large shares of the national income." (p. 514)

". . . the demand for any industrial arrangement is not certain to call forth a supply, unless it is something more than a mere desire . . . or a need. . . . It must be an efficient demand; that is, it must take effect by offering adequate payment . . ." (p. 242)

". . . The circumstances which govern this price for any given *amount* of the commodity vary in character from one problem to another; but in every case the more of a thing is offered for sale [on what ratio terms?] in a market the lower is the price at which it will find *purchasers;* or in other words, the *demand price* for each bushel or yard diminishes with every increase in the *amount offered*." (p. 342)

The particular time or period at which or during which any one price may be appropriate to a particular demand and supply setting or may derive from it is presented on page 342 as follows: "The unit of time may be chosen according to the circumstances of each particular problem: it may be a day, a month, a year, or even a generation. . . ." Note, however, (p. 341) that here "we are investigating the equilibrium of normal demand and normal supply in their most general form. . . ." But still (p. 342) the notion has to be not one of schedule or curve, but only of a point in a particular demand and supply setting, enduring, it may be, for decades and leading to a price resultant of equal duration: "In such a market there is a demand price for each *amount* of the commodity, that is, a price at which each particular amount of the commodity can find purchasers in a day or week or year."

There must be, then, many different demands, but if so, no one of them can be *the* demand unless, and until after, the price has been arrived at; and it must be a particular-time price; and there must be a new schedule for every changing situation—each one made up of its particular series of demand prices.

Similarly Marshall at times discusses the supply price. It is obvious that in a supplies schedule there must be reported the various unit-price terms on which the various holders will sell their respective holdings, else nothing can be determinate as to the price outcome. It will be one thing if the goods are to be had at whatever they will bring—reservation prices all at zero—and another thing as the reservation prices are severally modified —all of which is implicit in the notion of a supplies schedule or curve. But commonly Marshall is discussing the problem on the assumption, not of the prices that condition selling, but of those that condition producing. Thus, the supplies curve is implicitly resolved into a costs-of-production curve—not a sellers' but a getting-ready-to-sell curve. And even so, this notion of *the* supply price does not point to the fact that all of the different producers are in face of the same cost-goods markets, but indicates instead some *the-one-price* that all must get—perhaps to come out even—if in the aggregate they are to produce any one particular volume of product. They may, it is true, according as is the particular demand situation, all get less than this or all get more—and some of them therefore differentially more than enough to cover their several costs of production. But *the* supply price for any one volume of product is that price that will call out that particular volume—with, obviously, varying costs for the different individual producers. So far, then, we have arrived at only one point on the curve at which the various volumes of product will be called forth. The supply price turns out, therefore, to imply a curve of the various cost prices—different for various volumes of product—with nothing therefore indicated as to that particular point on the curve at which the demand curve and this supply-cost curve will intersect. The supply price, therefore, if it is to make sense must be after all a schedule—and a cost-of-production schedule at that.

"The demand schedule for gas remains the same as it would be if gas were a freely-produced commodity; it specifies the price per thousand feet at which consumers in the town *will among them* use any given number of feet. But the supply schedule must represent the normal expenses of production of each several amount supplied . . ." (pp. 478-79)

". . . the supply price of a commodity is the price at which it will be delivered . . . in the market which we have in view. On the character of that market will depend how many trading expenses have to be reckoned to make up the supply price. For instance, the supply price of wood in the neighborhood of Canadian forests often consists almost exclusively of the price of the labour of lumber men but . . . to a small retail buyer in an English country town is more than half made up of the charges of the railways and middlemen . . . The possible combinations are numberless . . ." (p. 340) And on page 390, *the* supply price for any one volume of a commodity output is presented as "the expense of production of the marginal element of that product; it is the supply price of which we are in search." It is true that this discussion refers to one commodity of a joint product; and notes (p. 390) that, where there are common costs attaching to "plant, technical skill, and business organization . . . there is seldom any rule of nature to determine either the relative importance of these uses, or the proportions in which the total cost should be distributed among them: much depends on the changing features of markets." But the argument for a marginal cost indemnifying the supply price is not affected; nor the implicit assumption that there is a *one* marginal cost for all of the producers. Thus, even if it be assumed that all producers—agricultural or other—have equal marginal costs, though presumably not equal unit or average costs, it must still be true that that particular cost which is *the* cost for any particular volume of product must remain indeterminate, or can be determinate only in the sense that there must be some one market price at which the particular volume of output will be called forth. This supply price has still to be a point on the supplies curve—many different points together making up the curve. And only in a parallel sense and significance can there be any *the* demand.

". . . When a commodity obeys the law of increasing return, an increase in its production beyond [the] equilibrium point may cause *the* supply price to fall much. . . ." (p. 472)

". . . so long as *the* demand price is in excess of *the* supply price, exchanges can be effected at prices which give a surplus of satisfaction to buyer or to seller or to both. . . ." (p. 470)

In the following passage supply price is merely what the constituents command.

". . . we may regard this supply price of business ability in command of capital as composed of three elements . . . *the* supply price of capital . . . of business ability and energy . . . of that organization by which the appropriate business ability and the requisite capital are brought together. . . ." (p. 313)

Supply meaning output or product is a frequent usage with Marshall. ". . . an inexhaustible store . . . from which additional *supplies* could be obtained quickly and certainly at a *nearly uniform cost.* . . ." (p. 418)

". . . *the* demand for any industrial arrangement is not certain to call forth a *supply,* unless it is something more than a mere desire for the arrangement, or a need for it. It must be an efficient demand; that is, it must take effect by offering adequate payment . . . to those who *supply* it. A mere desire . . . or the need . . . is not a demand in the sense in which the term is used when it is said that *supply* naturally and surely follows demand. . . ." (p. 242)

". . . an increase in its *production* . . . may cause *the* supply price to fall much . . . though *the* demand price . . . may be reduced even more. . . .
". . . a bounty sufficient to call forth a greatly increased *supply.* . . ." (p. 472)

". . . A tax upon the stones . . . would tend . . . to diminish the inducements towards investing capital and effort in obtaining additional *supplies.* It would therefore check the supply. . . .
". . . the stock of stones might be in excess. . . ." (p. 420)

". . . as to the length of life of the stones and the rapidity with which new *supplies* could be obtained. . . ." (p. 419)

". . . an increase in the price . . . may have no perceptible effect in increasing the *output* for some considerable time: while a similar increase in the demand . . . might call forth quickly a great increase in *supply.* . . .
". . . the ultimate *output* corresponding to an unconditional demand . . . would be theoretically infinite; and therefore the elasticity of *supply* of a commodity which conforms to the law of Increasing Return . . . is theoretically infinite. . . ." (pp. 456-57)

A few of Marshall's views as to definition in general may be enlightening here.
". . . we must be clear as to what things we are including, and what things we are excluding. It will seldom make very much difference to our argument [about the national dividend] whether we use all the terms broadly, or all the terms narrowly. But it is essential that our usage should be consistent throughout any one argument. . . ." (p. 523)

". . . In physical sciences . . . as soon as a new notion emerges, a new technical term is invented to represent it. But economics cannot venture to follow this example. Its reasonings must be expressed in language that is intelligible to the general public. . .

". . . bold and rigid definitions . . . lull the reader into a false security.
. . ." (pp. 51-52)

". . . the economist must forego the aid of a complete set of technical
terms. He must make the terms in common use serve his purpose in the
expression of precise thought, by the aid of qualifying adjectives or other
indications in the context. If he arbitrarily assigns a rigid exact use to a
word which has several more or less vague uses in the market place, he
confuses business men, and he is in some danger of committing himself
to untenable positions. . . ." (pp. 81-82)

In the main, doubtless, Marshall's use of the terms *demand* and
supply in variant meanings is in a context which indicates the particular
emphasis or shift of meaning. Not always, however, is this the case—
which fact, in turn, must serve as the excuse for the misinterpretations
that presumably may be contained in any list of examples.

Chapter IV

UTILITY, PRICE, AND MEASUREMENT

THE FUNDAMENTAL requisites of price the classical economists found in *utility* on the demand side and in *scarcity* on the supply side. Nothing that an individual does not want, and nothing that he can have without price, will he pay a price for. The terminology for the case was scant, *utility* being often called *use value*.

Scarcity was more than mere *rarity*. It was rarity in point of volume relatively to desires. Mosquitoes are rare in winter, but take on no price, not being in the economic sense of the term *scarce*. Things of utility that are not scarce were not the less things of utility, but were *free goods*. Any *good* limited in volume in this sense of scarcity could achieve a price, the fact of its desiredness taken to be the adequate explanation of a demand for it, if also the desire were supported by purchasing power.

Cost of production, taken to be the usual explanation of scarcity, was not, however, viewed as the sole explanation of limitation on volume. Any other limitation was as effective as cost, and effective in the same way. It was with "freely reproducible goods" that the cost limitation was effective. Cost affected price solely as an influence limiting goods offers. It explained on the supply side the emergence of price—relative costs of production explaining in this sense relative prices.

With the recognition that price offer is dependent on desiredness, as also on the necessity of paying in order to have, the classical analysis of price offers came practically to a close. Mainly, then, the demand side of the problem of prices and of relative prices was taken for granted—perhaps as obvious, or as clear by mere inspection. Implicit, nevertheless, in this classical view were most of the positions that came to be explicit in the more modern utility analysis at its best of careful development.

Money as such has come to be recognized—perhaps indeed always was—as having only a derivative and representative utility; being, as money, only a general intermediate in exchange; useful only for buying things. But as intermediate it carried an option of purchase over the entire field of desired, offered and unfree goods. To buy a thing was, then, to choose. The individual's buying of any one thing was limited to what he wanted of it, as against buying something else—the primal curse upon the dollar being that one can spend it but once. To buy something is not merely to get something, but to go without something—the ranking attractive thing.

And further things are implicit in this classical position. Utility means desiredness, not desire or desirability. Utility connotes merely the purely individual fact of desire; it is not, for competitive and price purposes, a group or collective category.

The point of stopping, once having started with buying any line of good, involves for the individual at any given time the principle of the falling utility of increments of the good:[1] the principle also of final, or marginal, utility.

[1] The declining incremental significance of each particular line of goods involves also—in a derivative and representative sense—the declining incremental significance of dollars in the individual income. Were there only one line of purchase open to him, the falling utility of income dollars would parallel the falling-utility curve of the particular good. It is the shift from one line of purchases of falling incremental significance to another that draws a curve of falling utility for income dollars much less steep than the curve for each particular line of goods.

This means also, by the way, that, with the wide variety in alternatives of purchase, the income-utility curve must be a relatively flat curve—a fact highly significant for many problems in the distribution of tax burdens, especially with income taxes.

The logical implications of a position may, however, easily carry over-far into the imputing of them as views actually held. Error here in this emphasis is doubtless possible. But it suffices for the present that the logic of the classical position does extend thus far, and that Marshall in his demand discussion is therefore not to be interpreted as denying or subtracting from classical doctrine, but, as, instead, by his incorporation of the relative-utility analysis, merely elaborating and developing it. That you limit your buying of a good at a particular point, turns in part, obviously, on the degree or quantum of your marginal desire for it, but equally also on the marginal appeal of that best thing else that you might buy for the same money. Never can this have been a path-breaking discovery.

This utility analysis is not, then, to be taken to be an issue between the modern—say, the Austrian—and the classical schools. The later view gets no further than to provide a basis for what the classical economist contented himself with taking for granted. Explicitly, as we have seen, he regarded desiredness as conditioning price offer. Implicitly he moved thence to the marginal utility of the good directly under consideration, that one unit, or that last unit of it, wanted; and also—implicitly but obviously—to the setting over of this marginal-utility item, in point of its desiredness, against the marginal utility of the ranking alternative line of purchase.

As, moreover, we shall later see, the actual issue between classical and modern was an issue in the field of cost of production. Classical thought resolved the limiting influence on supply into the marginal discomforts imposed by production; the "modern" view, into marginal utilities cancelled, as conditioning production.

The relative claims of these antithetical views to acceptance will come up for later consideration. All that at present concerns us is to make clear that, on the demand side of the price analysis, there is between classical and modern no issue. No classical economist is committed to deny any step in the marginal utility view. Instead, he is in essentials committed to it. Objections with him can rightly get no further than to denying the importance of it, or even to regarding it as merely a great ado over surprisingly little—hair-splitting about things deserving no emphasis and interesting solely to the sort of people interested in this sort of thing—his part to yawn rather than to contest.

It must, however, be admitted that many classical economists are shrill in their repudiation of this modern utility analysis—whereby, perhaps, both the obviousness and the rightness of it should come in question. But so also do many economists outside of the classical tradition repudiate it. It may, then, be safe for present purposes to assert no more than that no classical economist must be, as such, concerned to reject it. The militant challenge directed against it may have turned on the fact of its use, at important points, as a weapon of attack; or on the over-rationalization often attributed

to it—either objection a matter aside from the present purpose. It
is enough that, so far, the classical economist needs find no occasion for challenge.

In any case, Marshall discovers none. Whether as following
classical thought or as adding to it, he does not find himself in
any way outside of the classical tradition in his adoption of the
marginal-utility analysis, or in his derivation of price offer from
the comparison of alternative marginal utilities. Quite clearly—and
as it seems to me with entire justification—he treats these utility
doctrines as supplementary to classical reasoning, rather than as
concession or subtraction or modification—so far, note always, as
the discussion has to do with the derivation of price offer.

Marshall's definite and entire commitment, not merely to the
marginal-utility analysis, but also—and especially—to the derivation of price offers from individual comparisons of alternative and
quantitative marginal utilities, must forthwith become clear beyond
the possibility of question. With him price offers have their origin
in ratio relations. They are steps toward arriving at further ratio
relations, the exchange relations of money-goods units against other
goods units. Never are values or prices quantities, but ratios—ratios
the terms of which are, as is the nature of ratios, inevitably quantities. Dollars are, no doubt, items of quantity in the sense of definite
amounts of gold. But price means so-much-gold against so-much-
other-thing—never the marginal price offer reporting or deriving
from the separate marginal utility of any one good.

Marshall takes the position (pp. 20-21) that "he [a man] most
often reckons up the advantages and disadvantages of any particular
action before he enters on it." For, practically always, we are under
the necessity of choice, of taking sides. To work is to forego rest or
leisure; and to work at one thing is commonly to forego working
at some other thing. This principle of substitution is widely applicable. Almost always there are debits to set over against credits.
He continues (p. 21): "There will not in general have been any
formal reckoning up of two sides of a balance-sheet: but men
going home from their day's work, or in their social meetings,
will have said to one another, 'It did not answer to do this, it

would have been better to do that,' and so on." In another connection (p. 118) he says that "there is an urgent need for the
free use of money, . . . for that alone can be applied easily in an
unlimited variety of purchases [the option aspect of an intermediate
of exchange]. And in a money-economy, good management is
shown by so adjusting the margins of suspense [expense] on each
line of expenditure that the marginal utility of a shilling's worth
of goods on each line shall be the same"—nothing displacing something else of a higher marginal increment of service. It is like the
case of the primitive housewife—

. . . [who] finding that she has a limited number of hanks of yarn
. . . considers all the domestic wants for clothing and tries to distribute
the yarn between them . . . to contribute as much as possible to the family
well being. She will think she has failed if . . . she has reason to regret
that she did not apply more to making, say, socks, and less to vests. That
would mean that she had miscalculated . . . had gone too far in the case
of vests, and not far enough in that of socks . . . the utility of yarn
turned into socks was greater than that of yarn turned into vests . . .
a general principle, which may be expressed thus:—

If a person has a thing which he can put to several uses, he will distribute it . . . in such a way that it has the same marginal utility in all.
For if it had a greater marginal utility in one use than another, he would
gain by taking away some of it from the second use and applying it to
the first.

. . . .

. . . And this result each one will attain by constantly watching to see
whether there is anything on which he is spending so much that he would
gain by taking a little away from that line of expenditure and putting it
on some other line. (pp. 117-18)

According to Marshall (p. 100) this may occur when, for example, there is "a cheapening of the supply of a rival commodity, or
. . . the invention of a new one."

Further emphasis on the element of individual comparison of
alternative quantitative marginal utilities is provided by the statement (p. 124) that "the price which a person pays for a thing can
never exceed . . . that which he would be willing to pay rather than
go without it. . . ." As also:

. . . a stronger incentive will be required to induce a person to pay a given price for anything if he is poor than if he is rich. . . . A rich man in doubt whether to spend a shilling on a single cigar, is weighing against one another smaller pleasures than a poor man, who is doubting whether to spend a shilling on a supply [volume or stock] of tobacco that will last him for a month. The clerk with £100 a-year will walk to business in a much heavier rain than the clerk with £300 a-year; for the cost of a ride by tram or omnibus measures a greater benefit to the poorer man than to the richer. If the poorer man spends the money, he will suffer more from the want of it afterwards than the richer would. . . . (p. 19)

. . . the clerk who is in doubt whether to ride to town, or to walk and have some little extra indulgence at his lunch, is weighing against one another the (marginal) utilities of two different modes of spending his money. . . . (pp. 118-19)

It is, then, clear that Marshall holds the price offer of any individual for a good to be derived not from one marginal utility alone, but from a comparison, a *subjective valuation* of alternative marginal utilities; and the decision to stop buying to be similarly derived. Emphasis is directed solely to margins, because, as it is commonly assumed, the decision to buy, or to cease buying, is a decision with reference to goods in a series. In principle, nevertheless, it is unimportant whether the buying be of one or of many goods; if only one good is taken, that good is marginal for all purposes of the analysis. The ultimate principle (p. 93) is merely: "There is an endless variety of wants, but there is a limit to each separate want. . . . The *total utility* of a thing to any one (that is, the total pleasure or other benefit it yields him) increases with every increase in his stock of it, but not as fast as his stock increases." Poverty means therefore, other things being equal, high marginal utilities all along the line, both in the getting and in the foregoing. An income, then, as it gets larger is expended at lower margins of utility. In this sense it is possible to speak of the diminishing utility of units of money income. But, accurately, not the money but the thing it purchases has the utility; the intermediate having, as such, no utility in its own right, but only utility attaching to it in this purely derivative and representative sense. And so Marshall argues (p. 96) that "the richer a man becomes the less is the marginal utility of money to him; every increase in his resources increases the price which he is willing to pay for any given benefit." The marginal utilities between which his choice is declared are smaller utilities.[2]

[2] If further proof is desired of Marshall's position that every price offer derives from and reports, not one quantitative marginal utility, but the comparison of alternative marginal utilities, their marginal utility ratio to each other, examples will be found on pages 95, 100, 103, 121, 125, 132, 334, 336, 348, 358, 521, 818, 820.

It is clear also that in substance Marshall interprets *utility* as purely a fact in the individual experience. It is a technical term reporting the quantitative need, want, or desire, of an individual. The object is a *good*. The good, then, objectively viewed, is something that, as desired, affords indifferently pleasure, benefit, gratification, satisfaction, comfort, ease, refreshment, enjoyment, felicity, bliss, delight, amusement, happiness—or anything else that one wants, even the harrowing and the tears of the tragedy or of the funeral. It is, then, not highly important that Marshall occasionally speaks of the desiring of a thing because of its utility—the more accurate view being merely that the desiring of a thing constitutes its utility. Tastes differ: many men, many minds. He says (p. 92): "Utility is taken to be correlative to Desire or Want." And again (p. 17, note) he says that "all incentives to action, in so far as they are conscious desires at all, may without impropriety be spoken of shortly as desires for 'satisfaction' . . ."

Accurately also, *utility* should mean not the mere desirability of a thing but the actual fact of its *desiredness*. But even so, something is lacking; for it is obviously awkward to attribute desiredness to air in view of the usual lack of the consciousness that there is any, and even the occasional lack of knowledge of its existence. It is perhaps enough that in such cases the protest is prompt at deprivation and the consciousness of the lack immediate. At any rate we may safely agree with Marshall in the statement (p. 86): "Human wants and desires are countless in number and very various in kind. . . ."

Rightly, then, there is no place, at least in competitive analysis, for collective or organic formulations of this fact of desiredness. According to Marshall (p. 25), "Economists . . . are concerned with individuals chiefly as members of the social organism . . . the action of the whole is made up of that of its constituent parts; . . . in most economic problems the best starting-point is to be found in the motives that affect the individual. . . ." And again he states (p. 461) that "economic problems are imperfectly presented when they are treated as problems of statical equilibrium, and not of organic growth. For though the statical treatment alone can give us definiteness and precision of thought, and is therefore a necessary introduction to a more philosophic treatment of society as an organism; it is yet only an introduction."

It is, however, fair to say that Marshall's analysis runs almost uniformly in competitive and price terms, as did that of the earlier classical economists, and as was prescribed by Marshall's formulation of the economic problem and his delimitation of the economic field. In his analyses these collective or organic renderings of *utility* count for little or nothing—excepting, however, in his actual working assumption of the possibility of arriving at totals of these individual, and essentially separate and disparate, desirednesses, and thereby of arriving at an average individual utility.

Utility, the fact of individual desiredness, is, to be sure, a quantitative fact

Thus far nothing in the classical account of the relation of *utility* and of its derivative *marginal utility* to price offer, and nothing in Marshall's revision or supplementation of it, offers occasion for serious criticism. In neither are there for present purposes issues important enough, or issues significant enough in their later bearings, to evoke controversy. No criticism, then, will here be urged, or issues raised.

---

with each individual, and capable therefore of comparative uses by the individual. But it is a different quantity with each, inter-individually incapable of being known, as also incapable of being brought into an inter-individual total or report or statement. It is no doubt objective in the sense of attaching to an external object of desire or, more accurately, in the sense of being an externally wanted fact. But it is differently wanted—as many of these objectivities as there are individual wanters—with the aggregating of them into some sort of unity, a vague and unprecise and hypothetical, or even an impossible, thing. Marshall, himself, argues (p. 15): "the pleasures which two persons derive from smoking cannot be directly compared: nor can even those which the same person derives from it at different times."

Nor is it important that not rarely Marshall confuses the notion of utility and value. The following quotations have been selected as cases in point:

". . . being careful of course to get good value in return for his outlay. . . ." (p. 137)

". . . applied to practical problems, the economist . . . must concern himself with the ultimate aims of man, and take account of differences in *real value* between gratifications that are equally powerful incentives to action. . . ." (p. 17)

". . . the more a person spends on anything the less power he retains of purchasing more of it or of other things, and the greater is the *value* of money to him (in technical language every fresh expenditure increases the marginal *value* of money to him). . . ." (p. 132)

". . . a durable good, such as a piano, is the probable source of many pleasures, more or less remote; and its *value* to a purchaser is the aggregate of the usance, or worth to him of all these pleasures. . . ." (p. 123)

Nor even is it serious for any present purpose that Marshall interprets *production* in the competitive process as the achieving of utility rather than of a price outcome. He says (p. 63): "Man cannot create material things . . . when he is said to produce material things, he really only produces utilities; . . . changing the form or arrangement of matter to adapt it better for the satisfaction of wants." Nor again is it of great import that the price outcome is presented as a contribution to the aggregate output of price goods rather than as the individual achieving of price gain. It is quite clear that utility, at any rate, carries with it no connotations of ethical merit, or of wholesoleness, or of contribution to either the individual or general welfare—*desiredness* being the sole test. Marshall says (p. 596): "We must call to mind the fact that the struggle for survival tends to make those methods of organization prevail, which are best fitted to *thrive in* their environment. . . ." (Italics Marshall's) Only, then, when production is interpreted as the bringing about of want-satisfying things or situations to some one other than the actor himself, does the issue become a real one. By any competitive test, attracting

Too much, however, by interpretation and implication may seem to have been read into the classical view. It is doubtless possible fairly to question also whether, as a matter of safe inference, the demand position in classical theory ever advanced so far toward clarity and adequacy as to validate the interpretation here given to it, or to justify the view that Marshall's procedure in regard to it is substantially one of mere extension and elaboration. Such, at all

---

customers by injurious misinformation, or selling bricks with a gold sheen, or robbing the customer *vi et armis,* must rank as productive activities—ethical distinctions either of ends or of methods not to the point.

Some objection is to be made, however—though not of great importance—to the actual development of Marshall's analysis in his presentation of *marginal utility.* It is, to be sure, a derivative from the principle of diminishing utility. Accurately, however, this notion of marginality applies to any individual's holding of goods, one or few or many. Thereby the goods that one has actually purchased contain a *marginal-utility* good as must any stock of any sort of goods. It is therefore difficult to make out whether in the following (p. 93) Marshall appears to be defining marginal utility by offering a particular instance of it, or is instead falling into sheer error: "That part of the thing which he is only just induced to purchase may be called his *marginal purchase,* because he is on the margin of doubt whether it is worth his while to incur the outlay required to obtain it. And the utility of his marginal purchase may be called the *marginal utility* of the thing to him." There is a suggestion here of the identity of marginal utility and marginal purchase price—that second or antithetical view of Marshall's that is shortly to command a deal of our attention. Moreover, at its best and in its typical service, marginal utility is a step in the explanation of price, and not a thing derived from price or explained by it.

Nor obviously does the concept of marginal utility involve the necessity of a time sequence in consumer- or buyer-using. Nor is Marshall to be taken to hold that it does. The method of successive additions, time-wise, one after the other, is merely a device of illustration. No item in a stock needs be taken as coming, or as having come, early or late relative to any other. Take all of them to belong to a stock already in hand, say even by gift: which now is the marginal item? Each has equal potentialities of service with any other. It is impossible to regard any one as entitled, as against any other, to the marginal position. Any one of them may be taken as marginal in the sense that the loss of it would involve that degree of utility dependent on its presence, and as significant, therefore, only according to the strength of the desire frustrate by the loss of it, that weakest desire to be ministered to out of the whole stock. Not all of the items can be marginal at the same time; only one at a time can be taken to be a marginal item; but any one of them may be so taken—no one of them, however, excepting on such terms of regrouping the stock as shall impose the non-marginal position on all the rest.

The point of disappearing or zero utility also is a possible marginal point, as the least utility of a stock. It is, however, only an instance of marginal utility, not a defining case—similarly as in the preceding discussion of the marginal utility of a purchased stock.

One further implication—in no sense controversial—deserves attention here. Marginal utility, as expressing the significance to an individual of the loss of any one item out of his total stock—that utility attaching to the least pressing among

events, appears to be the view of Marshall himself; and this may perhaps suffice for present purposes.

But it is in any case clear that this comparative utility account of price offer must somewhere ahead lead the classical system into serious doctrinal difficulties, or even into sheer disaster. It was, nevertheless, for its immediate purposes, and so far as it went, entirely admirable—needing, and receiving at Marshall's hands, only reinforcement and extension. In its further reaches, however, its course was unsurveyed and its trend unnoted; its security even worse than uncertain. Finally its leading must arrive at an impasse.

For note the actual doctrinal situation. Clearly enough—as indeed merely a matter of objective setting—price is the equating point between price demands and price costs. But the fundamental thesis of classical thought is that back of demand and explaining it are utilities of consumption, and back of supply and explaining it are the discomfort costs, the real costs, of production. Price is then to be accounted for as the equating point between pleasures—or gratifications, or what-not—as over against the total of discomfort—the irksomeness or feeling debits—involved in production, its *real costs*.

But take it as once established that no single offer on the demand side of the price equation can report any utility in quantitative terms,

the wants to be met out of the entire stock—can give no indication of the aggregate utility of the stock. It is not the marginal utility times the number of items. Graphically represented, it is the total area under the falling utility curve, an area of the general nature, not of a parallelogram, but of a trapezoid; or, if the stock were large enough to allow the curve to reach the line of zero utility, of a triangle.

Moreover, the unit by reference to which marginal utility emerges may actually be—or may be conceived to be—a group indivisibly made up of any number of smaller units; precisely as the actual unit of trade—the "dose," so to speak—may be a pound or a sack or a ton or a carload. The total utility of the goods in a stock may then be illuminatingly thought of as the utility of a unit group containing the same number of smaller items.

It may finally be noted that Marshall's discussion of utility and marginal utility *as bearing on price offer* is in substantial harmony with that of the Austrian school of economists, in their most careful and thorough account of their position—or, it may be, in the most sympathetic interpretation of it. Marshall has, however, —most fortunately—avoided in the main the Austrian confusions, perhaps merely linguistic in the larger part, among marginal utility, subjective *Wert*, subjective exchange *Wert*, subjective ratios between subjective *Werts*, objective *Wert*, and finally objective exchange *Wert*; and has—thus far, at any rate—avoided the error of making price offer a direct derivative from marginal utility or a quantitative report of it.

but only a ratio—and at the margin a unit ratio—between alternative marginal utilities; and that the supra-marginal price offers report
no more than ratios in excess of unity; thereupon the entire case
for the quantitative equality of the pleasures of consumption with
the discomforts of production declares its complete and hopeless
insolvency.

Certainly nothing but a ratio relation is present with any item
on the demand side of the situation—a ratio between terms that are
quantitatively comparable to some one individual, and are in any
marginal case in approximate equality. The poor man and the rich
man, as marginal price-offerers, are unalike in the marginal utilities
with which they are severally concerned, and are alike solely in the
ratios between the utilities severally sought and foregone. For the
poor man, the marginal utility of, say, the meat for which he is
bidding, is to the utility, say, of the bread which he must forego, as
one is to one—or as 10 is to 10, and so on—a unit ratio; while for
the rich man, the utility of the meat is to the utility of, say, a cigar,
as one is to one—or 10 to 10—likewise a unit ratio. There is no
other equality between the men. The marginal quantities severally
related by them are entirely disparate—beyond any possible precision in quantitative comparison, and even of the confident assertion
of either more or less.

So much, then, for the demand side of the problem. Price offers
admit of no quantitative explanations other than in the sense of
quantitative equalities between quantities that, excepting as mere
equalities, are determinate and knowable only to the offerer. There
being, then, in the nature of the case no quantity reported on the
demand side, with which any discomfort on the supply side—were
any securely there—could possibly be declared equal, it is not for
the present a pressing matter to determine whether the price costs
on the supply side are in any better case in point of quantitative
standing than the price offers on the demand side. It must be the
task of a later analysis to show that they are not. But it is enough
for the present to note that even could they be so found, this would
avail nothing in support of the classical doctrine under examination.
There being nothing quantitative on the demand side but the dollars

of demand—the process facts to be explained—there can be no quantitative equating against them of whatever quantitative discomfort facts on the supply side might later be disclosed. And that none were finally disclosed would merely declare the classical doctrine to be insolvent, not in one solely, but in two necessary links.

But as has already been noted, the lack of any explicit analysis of price offers in the classical position failed to bring these difficulties into clear definition. In the Marshall analysis, however, they become entirely obvious—wherewith they become supremely menacing to the entire system of doctrine to which Marshall has committed himself as sponsor. His own improvident demonstration that in price offer there is no implication of any quantitative utility for the price offer to report, but, even with the marginal price offer, only an equality ratio between alternative marginal utilities, makes manifest the theoretical impasse. It is a plain abyss—the end of things for the classical system—unless, to be sure, there remains something to be done for the situation, either by retreat or by avoidance.

At this point, however, it becomes obviously imperative to make certain of the view to which Marshall may safely be taken to be committed. Is it true, then, that he holds price to be the equating point between the pleasures, or gratifications, of consumption and the discomforts, or real costs, of production? Such has—by mere assertion—been taken to be the central thesis of the classical system. Practically it has still so to be left—in the manifest impracticability of assembling here the requisite supporting evidence. But Marshall's individual position? This ought not, and must not, be left to go by mere assertion; nor need it be. It is made clear in the following:

. . . it [wealth] includes all those things, external to a man, which . . . are directly capable of a money measure,—a measure that represents on the one side the efforts and sacrifices by which they have been called into existence, and, on the other, the wants which they satisfy. (p. 57)

. . . by the aid of statistics, . . . they [economists] ascertain how much money on the average the members of the particular group, they are watching, are just willing to pay as the price of a certain thing which they desire, or how much must be offered to them to induce them to undergo a certain effort or abstinence that they dislike. The measurement of motive thus obtained is not indeed perfectly accurate . . . (p. 26)

. . . We shall gradually discover a great many different limitations of the doctrine that the price at which a thing can be produced represents its real cost of production, that is, the efforts and sacrifices which have been directly and indirectly devoted to its production. For, in an age of rapid change such as this, the equilibrium of *normal demand and supply* does not thus correspond to any distinct relation of a certain aggregate of pleasures got from the consumption of the commodity and an aggregate of efforts and sacrifices involved in producing it: the correspondence would not be exact, even if normal earnings and interest were exact measures of the efforts and sacrifices for which they are the money payments. . . . It is the average value which economic forces would bring about if the general conditions of life were stationary for a run of time long enough to enable them all to work out their full effect.
. . . existing tendencies may be modified before they have had time to accomplish what appears now to be their full and complete work. The fact that the general conditions of life are not stationary is the source of many of the difficulties that are met with in applying economic doctrines to practical problems. (p. 347)

When considering costs from the point of view of the capitalist employer, we of course measure them in money; . . . His concern with the real costs of their [the employees'] effort and of the training required for it is only indirect. . . . If the purchasing power of money, in terms of effort has remained about constant, and if the rate of remuneration for waiting has remained about constant, then the money measure of costs corresponds to the real costs: . . . (p. 350)

This illustration [of a man building his own house] may serve to keep before us the way in which the efforts and sacrifices which are the real cost of production of a thing, underlie the expenses which are its money cost. But, as has just been remarked, the modern business man commonly takes the payments which he has to make, whether for wages or raw material, as he finds them; without staying to inquire how far they are an accurate measure of the efforts and sacrifices to which they correspond. . . . (p. 352)

. . . the general adoption of semi-mathematical language . . . formally describing these small increments of price as measuring corresponding small increments of pleasure. . . . But he [Jevons] has led many of his readers into a confusion . . . speaking . . . without qualification of the price of a thing as measuring its final utility not only to an individual, which it can do, but also to "a trading body," which it cannot do. . . . (p. 101, note)

. . . Capital needs to be considered in regard *both* to the embodied aggregate of the benefits derivable from its use, *and* to the embodied aggregate of the costs of the efforts and of the saving needed for its production: and it will be shown how these two aggregates tend to balance. . . . (p. 82, note; italics Marshall's)

. . . There is a constant tendency towards a position of normal equilibrium, in which the supply of each of these agents shall stand in such a relation to the demand for its services, as to give to those who have provided the supply a sufficient reward for their efforts and sacrifices. If the economic conditions of the country remained stationary sufficiently long, this tendency would realize itself in such an adjustment of supply to demand, that both machines and human beings would earn generally an amount that corresponded fairly with their cost of rearing and training, conventional necessaries as well as those things which are strictly necessary being reckoned for. . . . (p. 577)

. . . Thus on the whole the *money* cost of any kind of labour to the employer corresponds in the long run fairly well to the *real* cost of producing that labour. (p. 661; italics Marshall's)

Moreover with the disavowal of the quantity-utility reporting function of price offer and of market price, there lapses also the allied appropriateness of either to *measurement*—either of measuring or of getting measured. There is nothing to measure. Ratios are not quantities. Measure has to do with things taken quantitatively, and reports the ratio of two things in respect to their participation in a particular quality. Even if money, as the price quid-pro-quo, a mere quantity of bullion in an exchange relation, were a quantitative thing in the aspect of possessing a quality making it appropriate to the measuring function of something else participating in that quality, it would still be true that a money demand—so much money for so much commodity, a price offer, an *a*-for-*b* thing—could avail nothing for measurement, being not itself a quantity fact, but only a ratio. But more—and much more—of this later.

Nor in fact, as we have already noted and shall later have further to emphasize, is money ever a measure of anything. This interests us at present equally in two aspects—not solely, we repeat, that money as it functions in economic affairs is merely one term in an exchange ratio, but also that it lacks in this function any quality aspect, by reference to which the quantitativeness of another thing can find expression. Wherefore, as a money demand for a good equating against the marginal money cost of production of that good, it can report no quantitative equality of the satisfactions back of the marginal money offer and somehow determining it, with the discomforts taken to be somehow behind the marginal goods offer.

It becomes then still further manifest that Marshall's disavowal of price offer as a utility-quantity fact was a commitment especially disastrous to his ultimate theoretical position. There was, then, nothing for it, but explicitly or tacitly, to steer away from his clearly announced and impregnable ratio interpretation of price offer and of market price. Actually the course chosen by him was to let his ratio analysis stand—to direct no attack against it, but just to leave it—making no effort to carry it over into later theoretical connections, or to follow out its theoretical implications. Instead, he sets up without apology or explanation another, and fundamentally irreconcilable, view. His working doctrine, then, is this second doctrine, antithetical to the other doctrine and contradictory of it.

This second and substitute doctrine declares that the marginal price offer in the demand schedule reports the quantity of marginal utility of the good to the maker of that offer. Implicit in this position is the assertion that each successive offer upward in the demand schedule reports the quantity of the marginal utility of the good to the maker of that offer—the schedule of price offers declining from the highest to the marginal, being, therefore, a schedule of declining marginal utilities.

Moreover, the particular marginal money offer is presented not merely as reporting, but as measuring, the marginal utility to the maker of that offer. Implicit in the position is the assertion that each of the other money offers in the schedule not merely reports, but measures, the marginal utility to other offerers. The money commodity is therefore presented as itself having in the money use the quality of utility in a specific quantitative degree, whereby, in its marginal use, it may serve as the measure of the marginal utility of the good for which it is marginally offered, and whereby the market price becomes the measure of general marginal utility.

Finally, however, the position is pushed much further. Since the marginal money offer in the demand schedule equates against the highest requirement of money for goods among the goods sold from the supply schedule—in a sense, therefore, an equating of money quantities—it gets asserted, but by assumption merely, that the marginal money requirement on the supply side indicates and measures the highest quantity of discomfort, of real cost, on the supply side among the goods sold; whereby it is inferred and asserted, still by assumption, that the marginal utility on the demand side and the marginal real costs on the supply side are quantitatively equal.

On the demand side of this substitute position five distinct assertions are involved: (1) that each price offer is directly derived from the marginal utility of the good to the offerer; (2) and is equal to it; (3) that money is capable of the measure use; (4) that in this case money does actually measure the marginal utility of the good to the maker of the marginal money offer; and (5) that thereby market price measures general marginal utility. For these five assertions argumentative support is offered by Marshall.

On the supply side of the position five distinct assertions are also involved: (1) that each requirement of money in exchange for a good is directly or indirectly derived from the real costs of production of the good at the margin; (2) that this money requirement is equal to the marginal real costs of production; (3) that money is capable of the measure use for real costs; (4) that it actually does measure the real costs of marginal production to the marginal producer of the good; whereby, (5) the market price becomes the measure of general marginal real costs. For these five assertions on the supply side of the case Marshall offers no argumentative support other than that of inference from the argument on the demand side —whether as obvious deductions, or as truths manifest by inspection.

It must be admitted that it does not refute Marshall's substitute position to stress its inconsistency with another view of his, or to assert the entire correctness of the arguments supporting this other view. Any adverse appraisal of this position of confession and avoidance must address itself to the particular arguments by which Marshall arrived at it—and this, if it is in any way possible, entirely irrespective of the reasoning by which the other view was reached—reasoning to which, in Marshall's estimate, no contradictory quality attached: perhaps, after all, there was none. Our immediate task is therefore to examine Marshall's argument for his final position.

The defensibility of the view that marginal price offer and market price do equal and measure both marginal utility on the side of demand, and marginal real cost on the side of supply, must assume the possibility of measurement by price, as a money quantum. With the failure of this assumption the entire position becomes untenable. It must, moreover, be noted that Marshall makes here no attempt to establish the equality of marginal utility with marginal real costs at the equilibrium point of market price. Nothing further than the equating of price offers with goods offers at a market money point is given in the situation as starting point. Marshall will attempt now to show solely the equality of marginal price offer and of market price to the marginal utility of the marginal buyer. But at a later stage of his general discussion he will, without argument, and by sheer assumption, arrive at the position that the marginal goods offer reports and equals the marginal real costs of production, whereby there comes about the equality of marginal utility on the demand side with marginal real costs on the supply side.

It must here again be admitted that with Crusoe an equilibrium of marginal utility with marginal real costs of production must be reached—a quantitative marginal utility in equality with quantitative marginal sacrifices in production—thus paralleling in competitive conditions the equality of marginal price offer with marginal goods offer. And by the very fact of this quantitative equality in the Crusoe situation, the appropriateness of either side to the measurement of the other is established—but only, be it noted, for that one individual who has the experiences both of utility of consumption and of sacrifice of production.

It is, however, this fact that competitive exchanges are exchanges between different individuals, two to each exchange, that introduces a system of exchanges through a money intermediate, and which, it is again to be urged, negatives any equilibrium of pleasures with discomforts, or any inter-individual equality of them; as also it negatives all possibility of measure; and must not the less do all this, even were any inter-individual comparability of feeling experiences safely to be accepted. Without any intermediate of exchange, in barter trading, the case becomes promptly clear. An exchange, marginal on both sides, of A's two plums against B's one peach, indicates no more than that A's desire for a peach is at equality with his desire for two plums, and that B's desire for two plums is at equality with his desire for one peach. It does not in the remotest sense suggest that A wants one peach as much as B wants one, or B two plums as much as A wants two plums, or that A wants one peach as much as B wants two plums. The ratios between A's two wants and B's two wants are the sole things that are equal, with the quantities in the two ratios entirely indeterminate, and impossible of report by either A or B to the other.[3]

Marshall states his position on the equality of marginal price offer and of marginal utility in the following:

. . . it [economics] concerns itself chiefly with those motives which affect, most powerfully and most steadily, man's conduct in the business part of his life. . . .

. . . It concerns itself chiefly with those desires . . . the outward manifestations of which appear as incentives to action in such a form that the force or quantity of the incentives can be estimated and measured with some approach to accuracy . . . the force of a person's motives—*not* the motives themselves—can be approximately measured by the sum of money, which he will just give up in order to secure a desired satisfaction. . . .

. . . the economist does not claim to measure any affection of the mind in itself, or directly; but only indirectly through its effect. . . (pp. 14-15)

Not only, then, Marshall argues, does what one will marginally pay for a thing measure its marginal utility to him, but it discloses

---

[3] The analysis here is doubtless repetitive. But so also is the occasion. The bad necessity for repetition of a similar sort will recur on later pages.

to the observer how great is the individual's marginal desire for it. In the sentence next following (p. 15) Marshall grants that "no one can compare and measure accurately *against one another* even his own mental states at different times: and no one can measure the mental states of another at all except indirectly and conjecturally by their effects. . . ." And still, as Marshall insists, the pains and pleasures of another one may be compared through their indirect effects, the sums of money that this second individual will pay for things. And thus, if a man's limit outlay for two different things is the same, it is inferable that he wants them equally.

So far, it is true, inference may rightly go. But not also as indicating how much he wants either of the two things—excepting solely that he desires them equally. You know nothing absolutely about how large are the potatoes in a bin by knowing them, relatively, as all of the same size. The largest potato in the collection may be a very small potato. And perhaps Marshall means, so far, no more than this, for he continues:

For instance the pleasures which two persons derive from smoking cannot be directly compared: nor can even those which the same person derives from it at different times. But if we find a man in doubt whether to spend a few pence on a cigar, or a cup of tea, or on riding home instead of walking home, then we may follow ordinary usage, and say that he expects from them equal pleasures. (p. 15)

But forthwith—two or three lines further on—Marshall finds something further to assert, a something also most significant for the argument—and a something that he appears to regard as a secure next step in his logic, the necessary derivative from the preceding harmless assertion. He has been comparing through money outlays the desires of one and the same person. Now he will compare the desires of different persons:

If then we wish to compare even physical gratifications, we must do it not directly, but indirectly by the incentives which they afford to action. If the desires to secure either of two pleasures will induce people in similar circumstances each to do just an hour's extra work, or will induce men in the same rank of life and with the same means each to pay a shilling for it; we then may say that those pleasures are equal for our purposes, because the desires for them are equally strong incentives to action for persons under similar conditions. (pp. 15-16)

But note that, as support for these asserted equalities of desires of different individuals, by inference from the equal money outlays to which they will submit, Marshall proceeds forthwith to revert to the consideration of the expenditures of one particular individual (p. 16): "For suppose that the person, whom we saw doubting between several little gratifications for himself, had thought after a while of a poor invalid . . . and had spent some time in making up his mind whether he would choose a physical gratification for himself, or would do a kindly act and rejoice in another's joy. . . ."

But finally—and forthwith also—the discussion appears, though not quite certainly, to shift to inter-individual situations (p. 16): "if he [the economist] finds they [mental states, rather in their manifestations than in themselves] afford evenly balanced incentives to action, he treats them *prima facie* as for his purpose equal."

And thus we have arrived at the gist and substance of this alternative view of Marshall's—pure error, as I regard it. But Marshall does not himself take it to be free of difficulties—these with special reference to the rôle of money as carrying a reporting and measuring function in inter-individual comparisons. He moves then promptly to the consideration of these difficulties, together with presenting the solutions that he holds to be both open and adequate for them —nowhere, however, taking account of the essentially ratio character of price offer and of all exchange relations in the price report of them. He makes no question that

A shilling may measure a greater pleasure . . . at one time than at another even for the same person; because money may be more plentiful with him, or because his sensibility may vary. And persons whose antecedents are similar, and who are outwardly like one another, are often affected in very different ways by similar events. When for instance . . . school children are sent out for a day's holiday . . . it is probable that no two of them derive from it enjoyment exactly the same in kind, or equal in intensity. The same surgical operation causes different amounts of pain to different people. [How be sure about this? Large screams from little children flow.] Of two parents who are, so far as we can tell, equally affectionate, one will suffer much more than the other from the loss of a favourite son. Some who are not very sensitive generally are yet specially susceptible to particular kinds of pleasure and pain; while differences in nature and education make one man's total capacity for pleasure or pain much greater than another's. (p. 18)

Thus with manifest rightness Marshall declares (p. 18) that "it would therefore not be safe to say that any two men with the same income derive equal benefit from its use; or that they would suffer equal pain from the same diminution of it. Although when a tax of £1 is taken from each of two persons having an income of £300 a-year, each will give up . . . what is measured to him by just £1; yet the intensities of the satisfaction given up may not be nearly equal."

But Marshall finds his way out of this difficulty (p. 18), by taking "averages sufficiently broad to cause the personal peculiarities of individuals to counterbalance one another, [whereby] the money which people of equal incomes will give to obtain a benefit or avoid an injury is a good measure of the benefit or injury."

Only—we must ask—the benefit or the injury to whom—to the social organism or the collectivity? Not this; but only the total benefit to the group—a benefit arrived at as a total by taking the one pound as multiplied by the number of individuals in the group that pay it; which, when divided by this number of individuals in the group, gives, not the benefit to any one individual, for this has been outlawed at the outset, but the average individual benefit in the group—not the benefit to the average individual in the group, but the average individual benefit in the group.

Such, at any rate, I take to be the thought. But I am quite uncertain about it. Doubtless, however, the difference on the face of it is not great between the income of an average individual and the average individual income. But there is a difference. Both interpretations must, then, be examined.

There is always danger of fallacy in these mathematics-logic averages. They are often mere blank forms of thought, fitting no objective reality. Take it, however, that this mathematical resultant means not the income of pleasure to the average man but merely the average pleasure income. But first, what is this total income that is numerator over a 1,000 denominator? It is the indeterminate total made up by aggregating 1,000 different unknowns, each of them, to be sure, a quantitative individual experience, susceptible, it is assumed, and perhaps rightly in some loose way—of making up with other individual experiences into a pleasure total of experiences —but each an experience about which, inter-individually, nothing further is here known than that it is quantitative. There results an X that is also quantitative, but only as the total of 1,000 unknown elements. And so the average computed from such an aggregate is merely the 1,000th part of a total and unknown X. We have to do, then, not with any real quantitative aggregate, but only with one in the mathematical sense of an empty die or mould, into which, if there is material quantitatively ascertainable and ascertained, this material may be poured for purposes of making into a total, and may then be carried over into a statement in the form of an average. In the given case, however, we have arrived at totals and averages that are without any actually ascertainable quantitative content.

And this average income attaches to what individual? By assumption to none; we have only the average of individual incomes. We have, therefore, nothing of any use to us. For our problem is one of the influences fixing the terms of the exchanges of goods—each exchange taking place between two individuals. There is no one great exchange of goods in general, or of any particular variety; and no average exchange of either of them, say, of shoes against hats, or of shoes against the money with which to buy hats or this or that other thing, or of hats against bread, or against the money with which to buy bread or some other thing or things. All the buyings in all of these countless exchanges against money, and through money against other goods, are transactions between individual buyers and individual sellers, each buyer with his own individual experience of consumer pleasure, and each seller—taken to be a producer—with his individual experiences of producer discomfort. These different purchases take place, however, on the demand side solely through different individual price-offers-for-goods; and on the supply side through producers, each with his individual goods-offer-against-money.

And we are examining the thesis that each dollar of marginal price offer represents a unit quantum out of the total quantity of marginally arrived at consumers' pleasures; and that each marginal dollar of producer cost represents a unit quantum out of a total quantity of marginally arrived at producers' discomforts. Each consumer price-offer unit, that is to say, reporting at the margin one unit of pleasure out of a homogeneous total of marginal consumers' pleasures; each marginal unit of producer money cost reporting one unit of discomfort out of a homogeneous total of marginal producers' discomforts. The thesis under examination tells us also that the marginal unit of consumer pleasure everywhere is in quantitative equality with the marginal unit of producer discomfort everywhere—as the trend and logic of complete and fluid competition. It is the doctrine of jellified consumer pleasures at the margin, as over against jellified producer real costs at the margin, all arriving at their several individual money correlates in the inter-individual competitive exchange processes of the market.

The criticism is not that this is descriptive of actual things only in an abstract and schematic form—it is offered only as such—but that taken in this sense, it is descriptively unreal and patently incredible, precisely because we are referred to averages of individual consumer pleasures and to averages of individual producer discomforts. Criticism is not, moreover, directed primarily against the descriptive unreality, or against the descriptive mis-account of the way in which consumers' price offers are arrived at—all of them being actually choices between alternative utilities, ratio facts—but against the emptiness of meaning of all these mathematical processes of totals and averages for the purposes of the problem. They make their start with individual unknowns, and with quantities of dubious capacity to be totalled, even could they be individually known. Each is a mere X. And forthwith, in the guise of a mathematical average the total gets distributed into units of unknowns that in this mathematical sense have attributed to them a quantitative equality.

Thereupon this average unknown comes to be attached to an average individual. There is, however, no such individual, but only (a) the mere mathematical average consumption income, or (b) this average consumption conceived as attaching to some one individual out of the entire number in the class—an individual who, with practical certainty, does not exist.

There are, for illustration, four men, two of whom are six feet tall and the other two five feet tall. The average height is $5\frac{1}{2}$ feet. But no service to reality is achieved by asserting that the average man of them is $5\frac{1}{2}$ feet tall. The situation is not improved by the introduction of large numbers, but becomes only less unprecise. These averages are mere mathematical moulds without objective reality.

But suppose, in the case in hand, a report of the pleasure income not of an arithmetic mean but of a median man. This median man there might concretely be, though no one could pick him out to set him to making hats for exchange against shoes, meat, medical advice, cosmetics, or wheat. The intent of the analysis is to arrive at units of gratification which, as marginally set over against units of discomfort cost, are to provide the explanation for the exchange relations of all sorts of goods produced and purchased by men various in position, capacity, tastes and purchasing power. For precisely these exchange relations are the things before us for explanation. Mathematical non-objectivities will not fit into these individualistic activities of the world of many industries and of multiple exchanges of products. The offered explanation, however, diverts us into dealing with unknowns that we could not use, even if we could somehow translate them into knowns. And actually these equalities are equalities of average unknowns—with money units, bullion quantities,[4] offered for the measuring of them. We are merely hypnotized by the mysteries of mathematical concepts and manipulations.

---

[4] It is no part of the argument here to assume that money units must be taken to be bullion units, or that the volume of bullion units of circulating media prescribes on the supply side the values of the other units—or the other way about. The case for the view under criticism is merely intended to be presented here at its strongest. It would seem hopeless to urge the measure function with paper-money or deposit-credit units.

The dollar is set up as the measure. But it measures only in the sense that numerator and denominator of an offer of money for goods, a fraction, can be interpreted back into a ratio between utilities; whereupon we are again at equality ratios between unknowns—and with no individual to whom these ratios can be imputed.

Always, doubtless, measurement is possible with reference to any one quantitative aspect common to any two or more different things, when these different things have specifiable quantities of their common quality. If, however, where the individual quantities are unknowns and therefore where the totals are sums of unknowns, we attempt by division to arrive at an average, the quotient will also be an unknown, a mere blank form or mould of mathematical expression into which, it may be, human experiences might be fitted, were any appropriate to it. An average man? In what respect, and to what quantitative outcome? There can be no average man excepting with respect to some one particular quantitative aspect or character. In weight? Possibly. Or height? Equally well. Or in size of shoe? This also. Or in the number of children in the family? Even this, although this average man may turn out to have 3.47 brothers and sisters. Mathematical children may harmlessly be thus dissected. But a man, an average in some five or fifty aspects? The adverse chances move toward infinity. Kill without fear or conscience the first man you meet, average in this combination of aspects. But average in any one quantitative aspect—weight or height or girth—that is easy, quantities being ascertainable both for himself and for the other members of his group. But in beauty? Or in voice? Or in complexion? One might be average in pleasantness of appearance or in sweetness of voice, but only with reference to some one person to whom these aspects of appeal in different individuals could be quantitative in particulars and in a total. But an average of laughter, or of musical appreciation, or palatability, or of cousinship? Not so easy. How much of it has each member of the class for contribution to the total.[5]

[5] It is not necessary to deny here the possibility of a median for things that in human experience are quantitative. but only vaguely so—things like heat and cold,

And still, why not a man average in point of height, although no one knows how tall are his fellows, or even how tall is he, or how tall he would be if he turned out to be average? This is only a blank form for an average, not an average, but only the assertion that the subject matter is susceptible of being averaged. And so long as we know nothing about how tall the man is who is at the average, we arrive at nothing in saying that a foot rule is his measuring stick. It might measure him. But it does not. Equal

---

for example, that, so far as we can see, are common in general to human experience, and are related to one another in loosely similar fashion. Among the different articles in a room there would probably be a general agreement as to that one with relation to which half the articles were colder and the other half warmer. But there would be no implication that these sensations of heat or cold were equally felt by all the individuals, but only that they were interrelated for the different individuals in approximately the same series. Nor is it implied that mathematical averages are never serviceable, but only that they are serviceable when they are appropriate to the subject matter, and are not misinterpreted or misapplied— as they are prone to be. It may be also that in fields outside of the common run of experience, the best approach to measurement that is practicable is rather ratio-like than quantity-like. Differences of tonal pitch may also have to be experi- mentally handled rather in terms of objective aerial vibrations than of the subjective effects; differences of color or of intensity of light reported in terms of breadth of etherial vibrations; or temperatures through units of expansion with one or another substance—mercury, or air. I am plainly beyond my depth here. It seems to me, however, that in these cases the measure is one of phenomena collateral to the sound or light or heat as items of human experience—casually related, pre- sumably, but not sound or light or heat as psychological items, subjective facts. The roaring of Niagara was actual, as vibratory movements in physics, before there were ears—and susceptible, as such, of pointer readings of some sort, but was not actual as a psychological fact. Because there are no quantitative units for the psychological facts, there can be, as I think, no measuring of them. Not that degree—which is quantitative, a more-or-lessness—is not present, but that no unit for this sort of quality is known. And, in any case, we are discussing measure- ment within the ordinary range of human experience and in the ordinary sense of the term.

" . . . Bodies . . . are primarily spacial and temporal, and both space and time possess what is called 'extensive' magnitude, such as 'number,' 'length,' 'breadth,' 'volume,' 'interval,' etc. Furthermore, the space-filling properties of bodies have a form of magnitude called 'intensive' magnitude, such as 'intensity of light,' 'degree of temperature,' etc. Changes of magnitude, whether extensive or intensive, can be *exactly* described only in mathematical terms." (Ralph Barton Perry, *Present Philosophical Tendencies,* p. 55)

"Measurement must also be distinguished from counting. Counting is a necessary part of measurement but is not itself measurement. Briefly, in counting we assign cardinal numbers to groups of things, in measurement we assign a ratio to represent some property of a thing. The numbers we write down to stand for the results of measurement are always ratios not cardinal numbers. When we say that a thing weighs two pounds we mean that the ratio of its weight to the pound weight is

unknowns are not measured things. Nor do we get nearer to measure by fractioning an unknown total into the average constituent part. How much pleasure does the average man control through his total income of dollars? Taking the dollar to be an appropriate measure thing, it still, so far, measures nothing.

Not yet, however, are we ready to return to the repetitious affirmation that money could not measure, even if there were a measurable something present in measurable form. For we have now—in essentials repetitively—to note not only that nothing is present in measurable form, but also that the thing under consideration could not get into a measurable form—and this irrespective, for the time, of the fact that were it measurable, money could not measure it. For again we have to note that these different things that these different individuals will buy are really different things, and are differently desired by the different men—some of these things, items that will give pleasure; some that will avoid pain;

---

two. When we say a man has two legs we are making a different type of assertion, namely one about a cardinal number. This is seen from the fact that we do not mention a unit, and that we are confined to one definite number. . . .

"The process of measurement as has been mentioned always involves some manipulation of bodies; it is experimental in a sense that counting is not. The process consists in the comparison of two things in respect of some property. One of them is taken as the standard in terms of which the magnitude of the other is expressed. If the standard used and the object to be measured happen to be equal then the comparison is a simple affair, but as they usually are not, it is apt to be somewhat complicated. The most convenient procedure usually is to take a standard that is small relative to the magnitude to be measured or to subdivide the standard, and to find by repeated application in the correct manner to the unknown how many times greater the unknown is.

"The things of the physical world that common sense and science deal with are parts of everybody's experience or have definite relations to experience. This is not the case with mental things. It is only the events in a man's own mind that come within the range of his experience. What happens in minds other than his own, he can only get at in a very roundabout way, utilizing what he knows about his own mind, and a symbolic correlation between mental and physical events. The symbolism is that of bodily expressions and gestures and more particularly of words." (A. D. Ritchie, *Scientific Method,* pp. 121, 127-28, 185)

You may tell me, for example, that so-and-so is "deaf as an adder." But this tells me nothing either about how deaf you hold him to be, or I am to infer him to be. How deaf, then, is an adder? You think very deaf? I don't know—or you either. This exceeding deafness of adders—if you imply it—you may have inferred from their acting as you have noted some deaf men to act. But an adder may be merely trying to fool you—as not rarely is said to be the case with possums, and as looks like it with many excellent bugs.

others that will stop it after once it is started; some that will control the peace of music; others that will open the gates of the Eternal City. They are alike only in the one fact of their desiredness—and not alike even in that—desiredness being also only a blank form for thought, until it is attached to an individual as an experience or activity of his.[6] *Utility* at large is just a word. There is no safety in numbers here, but only vagueness and absurdity.

And now one more repetition: even were all else ripe and right for the measuring process, money could not do the measuring. But more—and wearisomely more—of this later.

"Nevertheless, if we take averages sufficiently broad . . .," Marshall insists (pp. 18-19), "the money which *people of equal incomes* will give to obtain a benefit or avoid an injury is a good measure of the benefit or injury." And so, with that £1 tax levied on each one of "a thousand persons living in Sheffield, and another thousand in Leeds, each with about £100 a-year . . . we may be sure that the loss of pleasure . . . is of about equal importance. . . . " Possibly so, in the aggregate, and in the per-capita average—only how much in each? We have still only a total that is an unknown,

---

[6] And something also about the objective existence, the *out-thereness*, of most abstractions—say, "the hate of hate"; "the love of love"; "the scorn of scorn." We get misled by linguistic uses. There is nowhere *hate* or *love* or *scorn*, any more than *Truth is eternal*; or than, in the old lady's conviction, "music has a soul." These words are verbs in significance, not substantives. There are people who hate, and love, and scorn—hating and loving and scorning men. Not even do we know that there is such a thing as *motion*, but only that things seem to move. Just go out, with telescope, microscope, pointer readers, and balances, and look for the out-there existence of love and hate, piety and faith—and confusion and silliness. Translated into *desiredness*, it becomes a purely individual activity or thought or feeling: attractedness, or inducedness, or temptedness—"all a wonder and a wild delight"—but for that individual only that so sees it or feels it, and therefore as various in degree and kind as men are—about the internal workings of each of whom we other men know nothing, since each of us has to live inside only of his own skin, knowing not much, moreover, about what is inside that.

Not, to be sure, that these individual desirednesses are not, each in its individual bearing, quantitative facts for each desiring individual. They are so; as always any terms in a ratio must be, or be thought of as being. But they are not inter-individually present, as knowable quantities. They are knowable only in the separate-individual sense—and not in any form to enter into totals or to be divided up among individuals, or—still more clearly—to be mathematically manipulated and turned into average units for ascription to some non-existent average human being.

and derivative quantitative equalities that are also unknowns. The total is necessarily one thousand times the per-capita amount. Obviously: but how much is either? And even if we knew, how express either in terms of any unit of quantity, unless merely in some by-and-large sense, and with things in which human experience seems relatively uniform?

But, as we have seen, Marshall is convinced (p. 19) that a working unit, and equalities relative to it, would be still clearer, were all the individuals "adult males engaged in the same trade; and therefore presumably somewhat similar in sensibility and temperament, in taste and education. Nor is the probability much diminished, if we take the family as our unit . . ."—averaging the children, presumably.

And thus while it is clear with Marshall (p. 19) that "a shilling is the measure of less pleasure, or satisfaction of any kind, to a rich man than to a poor one"—in one case a cigar, and in the other a month's stock of tobacco—he continues:

But this source of error also is lessened when we are able to consider the actions and the motives of large groups of people. If we know, for instance, that a bank failure has taken £200,000 from the people of Leeds and £100,000 from those of Sheffield, we may fairly assume that the suffering caused in Leeds has been about twice as great as in Sheffield. . . . By far the greater number of the events with which economics deals affect in about equal proportions all the different classes of society; so that if the money measures of the happiness caused by two events are equal, it is reasonable and in accordance with common usage to regard the amounts of the happiness in the two cases as equivalent. . . . (pp. 19-20)

The ultimate way, then, of getting out of ratios and of unknown equal quantities is to get in still more people, people of all sorts and activities and classes, and then to apply the averaging method—"this source of error also is lessened."

And a hundred-odd pages later, in preparation for his doctrine of the correspondence of money costs with their underlying real costs, Marshall gives a résumé of his argument for the quantitative measurability of the ratio facts of price offer and of market price, as also for their measurement by virtue of the ratio relation of money as the intermediate in exchanges:

Or the real worth of a thing might be discussed with reference not to a single person but to people in general; and thus it would naturally be assumed that a shilling's worth of gratification to one Englishman [and presumably also to all people in trading relations with Englishmen] might be taken as equivalent with a shilling's worth to another, "to start with," and "until cause to the contrary were shown." But everyone would know that this was a reasonable course only on the supposition that the consumers of tea and those of salt belonged to the same classes of people; and included people of every variety of temperament.

. . . a pound's worth of satisfaction to an ordinary poor man is a much greater thing than a pound's worth of satisfaction to an ordinary rich man: and if instead of comparing tea and salt, which are both used largely by all classes, we compared either of them with champagne or pineapples, the correction to be made on this account would be more than important: it would change the whole character of the estimate. . . .

On the whole however it happens that by far the greater number of the events with which economics deals, affect in about equal proportions all the different classes of society; so that if the money measures of the happiness caused by two events are equal, there is not in general any very great difference between the amounts of happiness in the two cases. . . . (pp. 130-31)

The inequalities between the pleasures of champagne drinkers and the discomforts in its production, between the joys of the wearers of pearls and the real costs of pearl-diving, are all absorbed and cancelled in the unproved equalities of general averages.

In turn, then, may now be offered a summary of the objections to this line of procedure.

On the demand side of the price equation, each price offer indicates only an equality relation between alternative marginal utilities, each of which is only individually a quantitative item, but is inter-individually not quantitatively ascertainable. Even more clearly, market price can report no ascertainable quantities of desiredness, being merely the equating point of price-offer relatives with goods-offer relatives.

All the terms in the ratios with which all price-offer schedules have to do, have quantitative implications only in the sense implicit in all ratios, the terms of which have to be quantitative. But marginal price offers indicate ratios of unit value, and the supramarginal price offers ratios of higher than unit value between quantities that are inter-individually not ascertainable.

No measurable quantities, therefore, being presented in any objective market setting—no quantities, that is, that are susceptible of measurement—there is nothing for money to measure. Nor, if there were anything measurable, has money, as exchange medium, any quantitative aspect appropriate to the measurement of it. Value, as non-quantitative, can neither measure nor be measured. And price is merely one instance of value.

The conclusion, then, which Marshall reached and thereupon, for working purposes, abandoned, is the conclusion to which the foregoing critical examination has led. Quantitative utility facts are nowhere reported in price-offer schedules or in the exchange relations termed *prices*, but only ratios, the utility terms in which are always quantitatively indeterminate. Nothing measurable is present, and nothing by which to measure.

No issues of grave theoretical significance turn, however, on the nature of price offer, so far as the purely demand aspects of price determination are concerned. In these strictly demand aspects, the classical economists met no necessity for any clear commitment on whether accurately a price offer resolves into a quantity or into a ratio between quantities. The ultimate ratio logic of their position remained implicit, and, in the purely demand aspect of their analysis, was not required to be more than this. It was only in the supply aspect of the price problem that the logic implicit in their analysis led inevitably to untenable positions that were fundamentally and crucially of controversial quality. And precisely because these classical commitments in the demand analysis were implicit, unexamined, and unconscious, the bearings of them in cost-of-production aspects remain unnoted—their inconsistency with the attempt to present real costs as quantitatively explanatory of money costs overlooked and unrecognized.

Marshall also, in the strictly demand aspects of his analysis, had no clear need of raising the issue between the ratio and the quantity interpretation of price offer. He does, nevertheless, raise the issue— almost, in this aspect, gratuitously. But in the cost-of-production aspect, the issue becomes acute, and, for the fundamentals of value theory, crucial. For it was central in the classical system that quantitative money costs are explained by quantitative real costs, not solely as proportional, but as equa-proportional. And in turn these quantitative real-cost facts on the supply side were to be explained as in marginal equality with utilities on the demand side. Marshall's part-of-the-time denial of the utility quantitativeness of price offer has, then, in preparation for his supply analysis, to give way to a quantity interpretation of price offer—relative prices taken to be proportional with relative, and inter-individual, marginal utilities, so that these could be equated against relative money costs, and therewith, through relative money costs, against relative real costs—which relative real costs must obviously, in turn, be made separately quantitative for use in ratio relations. It is because of this bearing of Marshall's alternative view that price affords, on the demand side of the problem, a quantitative expression and measure of marginal utility, and can therefore serve, on the supply side, as a quantitative expression and measure of real costs, that this wearisome analysis of these utility-price issues has been necessary. For Marshall will make no attempt to prove his discomfort-supply doctrine—taking it, instead, by mere assumption that the principle urged by him in the demand aspect is self-warranting in the supply aspect.

It was the presence of the money intermediate that brought these quantity and measure problems into clear definition. The market equilibrium is clearly one between mere price demands and price offers. It was these price terms that had, therefore, to be resolved into marginal-utility and marginal-discomfort terms. If, however, the situation had presented itself solely in barter terms, the difficulties would have been less obvious, and the offered solution not, on the face of it, an impossible solution. It would have been possible to present the exchange relations or ratios as marginal-utility and marginal-demand *quantities* and discomfort-supply *quantities*, arriving at an equilibrium at the point of quantitative equality. How prove it? That, to be sure, would have been difficult, and in fact impossible. But, in turn, how disprove it? In the lack of anything approximating knowledge of the inter-individual quantities involved, this quantitative view would merely have amounted to the assertion of an equality between unknown quantities—in no sense an impossibility. The exchange adjustment would be in terms of an equality between somewhats. This assertion of an equality between utilities and discomforts would, to be sure, leave the probabilities indefinitely adverse to it, but not a readily demonstrable impossibility. Not that this impossibility could not have been established, but only that the requisite analysis would have been awkward and cumbersome, with much probable confusion or error. The price mechanism carries with it, not merely the advantages of practical definiteness, but also of analytical precision.

We have now to examine the classical view of cost of production as the key to price, and of relative costs of production as the keys to relative prices—in the setting of Marshall's analysis.

Note on Consumers' Surpluses

Not as of strict logical necessity belonging to the present issue or group of issues, but nevertheless as of illustrative significance, is Marshall's discussion of *consumers' surpluses*. He says:

". . . we cannot guess at all accurately how much of anything people would buy at prices very different from those which they are accustomed to pay for it. . . . Our list of demand prices is therefore highly conjectural except in the neighborhood of the customary price; and the best estimates we can form of the whole amount of the utility of anything are liable to large error. But . . . the chief applications of the doctrine of consumers' surplus are concerned with such changes in it as would accompany changes in the price of the commodity in question in the neighbourhood of the customary price. . . .

.   .   .   .

". . . the best plan is perhaps to take that necessary supply for granted, and estimate the total utility only of that part of the commodity which is in excess of this amount. . . ." (p. 133 and note)

We have here certain further steps. The consumers' surpluses now appear as volumes of utility, somehow derivative from the aggregate of price surpluses; and it appears that these utilities are presumably marginal utilities to different people—but possible of being aggregated. Previously Marshall has said:

". . . the task of adding together the total utilities of all commodities, so as to obtain the aggregate of the total utility of all wealth, is beyond the range of any but the most elaborate mathematical formulae . . . even if the task be theoretically feasible, the result would be encumbered by so many hypotheses as to be practically useless." (p. 131, note)

Our difficulty, as Marshall sees the case, is (p. 133) that "we cannot guess at all accurately how much of anything people would buy at prices very different from those which they are accustomed to pay . . ." But there is a more serious difficulty. All these utilities are necessarily individual—as always utility is, because all desires are individual desires. There is no utility at large. Therefore, there is, in the accurate sense, no possibility of aggregating utilities. As well try to arrive at a total of parental affection, or learning, or peace. It is true that parental affection or pride or silliness cannot get bought and sold, as commodities. Market price aggregates are possible only with such things as get traded in. But it is conceivable that price-offer schedules could, by statistical investigation and manipulation, arrive at approximations deserving of serious consideration, with the slopes of the price-offer curves satisfactorily traced. But these would all be price curves, and not utility curves. Any aggregate must be a price aggregate. The various points on the respective curves would be marginal points for the respective volumes of purchases.

Marshall's usual assumption that these price points can report marginal utilities, rather than points of indifference between ranking alternative marginal utilities, is especially misleading for this particular problem. Moreover, as must later become clear, each of these price-offer points can have been fixed only in view of the prices at which the ranking alternative commodities were severally available. That is to say, the price surplus to be computed for the buyer of any particular commodity is conditioned on his option of buying cheaply commodities that are competing to absorb his limited purchasing power.

It must, however, first become clear that in the very terms of the problem these surpluses, no matter what may be the volume of them with any particular product, are for each individual and for individuals in the aggregate, not utility but price surpluses. To assert, for example (p. 133, note), that "the desire for anything is much dependent on the difficulty of getting substitutes for it," confuses price offer with both utility and marginal utility. That for any individual the purchasing power not absorbed by some one commodity is thereby set free for purchasing other commodities, is not in question. So much is implicit in the much-stressed fact that money is only an intermediate commodity. Even thus much, however, Marshall is not always entirely consistent in recognizing. On page 818 he asserts it: "For the price which the various purchasers in a market will pay for a thing, is determined not solely by the final degrees of its utility to them, but by these in conjunction with the amounts of purchasing power severally at their disposal." But, in point of statement, he appears often also to deny it—his identification of price offer with marginal utility a continuing invitation to this error. Thus he says (p. 132) that "every fresh expenditure increases the marginal value [utility] of money to him." But, as an exception, he says, a few lines farther on, that "bread being still the cheapest food which they [labouring families] can get and will take, they consume more, and not less of it." And in discussing an illustrative case of temporary market equilibrium in a later chapter (pp. 334-35) he says: "But we did not allow for any appreciable change in their [buyers of corn] unwillingness to part with money (its marginal utility) ; we assumed that that would be practically the same . . ."

Ultimately, doubtless, one's money surplus gets converted over into a utility surplus, but it is none the less true that it accrues as a money surplus, and that solely in this form can it accrue. And in this form solely are the surpluses of different individuals susceptible of being aggregated or of being approximated. Neither in this nor in other connections is it safe to take utility or marginal utility as interchangeable with price offer; and still less with price.

But the level or point as price basis from which any buyer's surpluses are to be computed is a further difficulty. With any particular purchase the surplus must be, one thinks, computed from the actual price point. But the surpluses attaching to an individual's spending in the aggregate? Marshall says (p. 135 and note) that "we may regard the satisfaction which a person derives from his income as commencing when he has enough to support life, and afterwards as increasing by equal amounts with every equal successive percentage that is added to his income. . . . Of course such estimates are very much at random. . . ." Not inaccurately may it be said that these successive money units control goods of happiness-yielding power—but only in the sense that they report money quantities that the individual can, through his purchases, translate into utility-yielding things.

Say that you buy at 10 dollars six items of a commodity for which your price-offer schedule has been 15, 14, 13, 12, 11 and 10. Your marginal purchase at 10 reports the approximate equality in marginal utility between the good purchased and its ranking alternative purchase. The supramarginal 15 dollar price-offer reports that you hold that first item of the good to signify to you, relatively to the ranking alternative, in the ratio of 15 to 10. Buying it at 10 dollars, you get something for which, because of its marginal utility relative to its ranking alternative, you would have paid 15 dollars—your money surplus in buying it, therefore, 5 dollars—a saved 5 dollars to be used in buying other things controlling marginal utilities. Your surplus in the trade is a money surplus. But because money is merely an intermediate, having no utility of its own, but solely a utility by reflection, these money surpluses have to be got over finally into utility terms. To term the money itself, however, a utility, is to violate the distinction between *utility* and *price*. Moreover, the attempt to translate an inter-individual total of all these individual price surpluses into a total of utility surpluses, assumes price to afford an inter-individual standard of utility—a homogeneous sum of the various individual utilities, with the money unit taken to be an appropriate common denominator of them.

One further aspect of Marshall's analysis of these consumers' surpluses concerns the theoretical issue under examination. How great is any individual's total of surpluses? Marshall, by arriving at an aggregate of the individual's surpluses in any one line of expenditure, arrives at the individual's total of surpluses by adding together these separate-line totals.

How much would one pay for, say, a hat, rather than, say, in the winter, go about hatless? And in turn for shoes? To go without trousers cannot even be thought of—wherefore we shall no longer think of it. And for a coat? For food also—enough, at any rate, to keep one alive to wear the clothing—one would, if he must, pay out pretty much all of his income—excepting for the fact that equally urgently, in solving the problem of keeping alive, one must have shelter also, it being still winter time. In any one of these lines of expenditure, obviously, one would at the outside pay all of his funds that he could divert from his alternatively pressing needs. And if the requirements for these other needs could be cheaply met, the more could be spared for the particular pressing need.

We are again in face of the ratio aspect of all price offers. The limit on any one price offer is the point at which something else has equal appeal for the purchasing power available for buying one of the two. Always in the price-offer schedule for any particular commodity, the several price offers appeal for their explanations to the price situation of the ranking alternative commodities. That is to say: the money-to-goods ratios reported in any particular price-offer schedule—as well also as the goods-for-money offers in any goods-offer schedule—are arrived at only in view of the already existing alternative ratios between the money goods and other goods. The disconcerting fact—fact, nevertheless—that no particular price- or goods-offer schedule exists, excepting within the setting of collateral market prices, demands recognition here. Particular prices—in this manner of explanation—assume other prices—each particular price explained only over against the background of other prices. This is merely one aspect of the principle that all the items in these schedules are arrived at as choices between alternative marginal utilities, and are themselves ultimately ratio facts. To think of a price offer as a simple quantity is error. To think of it as a quantity of marginal utility is profusion of error.

Each particular surplus, therefore, is as a price surplus, interdependent with other price surpluses. Any one surplus reports a differential below the price at which the buyer can buy an equally desired alternative thing.

Say that you have 15 dollars to spend. Paying 10 dollars for A, for which, if you must, you would have paid 15, you have 5 dollars left to spend on, say X—5 dollars more than you would have had, had the actual price of A been at your maximum bid for it. Or, paying 10 dollars for X, when you would at the outside have paid 15, you have 5 dollars the more to extend your purchases of A. The surplus with A depends on your not having to pay 15 dollars for it, but only 10. The surplus with X depends on your getting it for 10 dollars instead of 15. If you had had to pay 10 for A, but 15 for X, your total surplus is 5—and the other way about.

But suppose now that you buy both at 10 each. But you can't; you have only 15 dollars in all to spend. That second surplus is a mirage. It is on only one out of the alternative purchases, that you can have a surplus. The surplus with either one vetoes the surplus with the other.

Substantially this analysis was two or three decades ago directed by Professor Nicholson—and following him, by Hobson—in criticism of the Marshall procedure of aggregating surpluses. Consistently with the Marshall view, a man with only a 1000 income to spend could easily emerge with a 2000 surplus from the spending of it. If, for example, a 1000 gain for you turns on making a New York appointment at 9 A.M. tomorrow, and there is only a dangerously short time in which to catch the train, you might afford—were there nothing else for it—an 800 charge to be got to the station on time. Or, arriving at the station by the usual conveyance and at the usual charge, but missing your train, you might pay 800 for a special; or 800 to be taken by airplane to overtake the train. Or, all things going as usual till you were in New York, you could afford to pay, if you must, 800 to be got across the city on time. But you can afford to make any one of these outlays only on condition that you have not to make any of the others. Your total surplus from the trip cannot exceed the 1000 at stake.

Marshall's reply is as follows (p. 127 note): "Prof. Nicholson says: 'Of what avail is it to say that the utility of an income of (say) £100 a year is worth (say) £1000 a year?' There would be no avail in saying that. But there might be use, when comparing life in Central Africa with life in England, in saying that, though the things which money will buy in Central Africa may on the average be as cheap there as here, yet there are so many things which cannot be bought there at all, that a person with a thousand a year there is not so well off as a person with three or four hundred a year here. If a man pays 1 d. toll on a bridge, which saves him an additional drive that would cost a shilling, we do not say that the penny is worth a shilling, but that the penny together with the advantage offered him by the bridge (the part it plays in his conjuncture) is worth a shilling for that day. Were the bridge swept away on a day on which he needed it, he would be in at least as bad a position as if he had been deprived of eleven pence."

But this reply seems to me not responsive to the issue. The criticism is not against the eleven pence of surplus in any one purchase. If, however, this surplus is taken to be attached to all of this man's trades—eleven pence of surplus per penny of income—it will come about that there is a total surplus of £1100 attaching to a £100 income. Most of the things that one buys *there* are, by assumption, as cheap *there* as here. It is, then, only with reference to, say, half of the income that any *relative* surplus is possible—relative, note, since Marshall has so decreed. One could not, we assume, have any surplus *there* at all in this relative sense. One could not there have bought, say, a radio at any price. If, however, he could have, and would have spent up to £100 for it, but got it at £10, he would have made his £100 income achieve a surplus for him of £90. But neither on the English nor the African basis, could he have achieved more than a £100 surplus out of a £100 income; and practically not that, because some of his alternative purchases would be imperative at some price or other.

That Marshall's reply is inadequate does not here greatly concern us—but only that he is obviously talking—as he should be—of money and not of utility surpluses. The price surplus in any particular trade turns into a utility surplus only at the stage of some later trade or trades. It is commonly worth while to use terms accurately.

Chapter V

COST OF PRODUCTION

COST in the technical economic sense means always cost in the producing of things, as a short term for *cost of production;* not what one has to pay for a thing when he buys it, as is commonly the meaning in popular usage. Cost in this latter sense means no more than the purchase price, and this in turn no more than the price in sale as well as in purchase. In this, a merely superfluous sense, economic usage has no place for the term.

There are, in fact, more than enough different meanings of the term in its actual economic employment. It may mean *money cost* or *real cost.* Your money cost may indicate merely the money debits to which you are subjected in getting a good ready for sale; or, again, the money debits to which your vendor or provider was subjected—his money costs accurately rather than your own, the costs of this seller to you taken to explain, so far, your own production cost.

Moreover, your own efforts and waitings, in the sense of the money debits that attach to the putting forth of your own productive activity or to the time employment of your own property—real-cost facts somehow getting over into a money projection—may require inclusion among money costs; or often also the money return conditioning your displacement of leisure, in its aspect either of rest or of recreation—the money offset against a real cost. Or your cost may have to include the money return that in some alternative gainful enterprise you appraise your time or your property or both to be worth—a displacement or *opportunity cost.* Moreover, note again, the cost directly under consideration may be that of your lender or lessor or employee—the cost to him conceived as lying behind and explaining the cost to you in your own undertaking, cost taken in the *regress* aspect.

Not rarely also money costs are by economists divided into those which are conceived to explain prices, or to cause them, as against costs which are conceived to be explained by prices, or to be caused by them; wages and interest debits taken, for example, to be price-determining, and land-rent debits to be price-determined.

The distinctions between money costs and real costs, and between costs as they are conceived by a particular enterpriser and costs as they appear in the regress view, concur in most aspects with the distinction between costs employer-viewed and costs employee-viewed, and present the same ultimate issues.

With whose and what costs has price-determining cost to do? From what point of view does the cost analysis proceed? Is it more or other than a mere enterpriser process or computation? What costs are they, and whose costs are they, that articulate with the business process and with product prices? Just what in our discussion of costs are we set to study?

The business man is obviously not greatly concerned with real costs—with distinctions between burden costs to some one else and money costs to himself. His affair is with his own money costs—not being interested in any other—precisely as, being a business man, he is interested solely in his monetary outcomes, and not at all in something else that somebody else, for reasons of his own, might incline to approve or to emphasize, such as the stresses or discomforts or the benefits or pleasures accruing to employees or to the public. Similarly the business man, as such, is never—and any other sort of man is rarely—conscious of the distinction between real costs and money costs—and then only as he conceives in some vague way that influences of the general order of real costs may somehow bear to affect his money costs. His business is a business matter, and concerns itself with costs solely in their monetary aspect.

But the economist? What the business man, the bearer of the money costs and the proprietor and seller of the products for money, does or thinks is, to be sure, not final or decisive for the economist. It is true that he is studying things as they occur in the business-man process, in constant mindfulness of it and in strict responsibility to it; but he is not thereby the less concerned with the causes underlying it and so far serving to explain it. For him, therefore, the distinction between money costs and real costs may require attention. In actual practice, however, few economists have been securely conscious of the distinction between costs from the employer point of view and costs from the employee point of view. Rarely, if ever, and never as I think, with the possible exception of Cairnes, has any economist faithfully observed the distinction, when once he has made it. Commonly his discussion will be of *costs*, when clearly enough his meaning is that of money costs solely, typically *expense* costs. Seldom is he actually concerning himself with those real costs that he takes to underlie in some sort, and it may be to explain entirely or in some part, what he is busy in discussing. He will be talking of the employer's labor costs, meaning solely the wage costs. Or he will be talking of capital costs meaning interest outlays, or interest foregoings, or possibly money outlays in the hires of goods. Or along therewith, he may be talking of waiting costs, even though nobody can ever hire *waitings*, but only the things whose present existence may have been conditioned on waiting. This terminological situation must become well nigh intolerable, were it not for the fact that, oblivious of all his earlier distinction-making, the economist is rarely concerned with real costs, and in his talk of real costs has fairly certainly in mind what he originally undertook to designate as money costs. His faith that these money costs, if carefully looked into, would turn out to be explained finally by real costs, and to be equal or proportional with them, explains and, in his view it is to be presumed, justifies the interchangeability of terms as he employs them.

It still holds true, however, that if the distinction is not worth observing, it was not worth making. Commonly, certainly, no attempt is made to observe it. Never is it consistently maintained.

But does not the context commonly suffice to make things clear? Doubtless so, only not always; and then only in the sense that *cost* rarely means *real cost*, but only *expense* or *money cost*. But in view of the fact that in almost every case the enterpriser, computing his costs in the money sense, must include among these costs the price debits attaching to his own labor and possessions—inasmuch as these excuse him from money-hire outlays or deprive him of the hires that he might else collect—*expenses of production* is never better than invitation to confusion. Nor does it avoid the confusion to interpret those foregone incomes as "virtual outlays." Such they may be, but only as a reluctant admission of *opportunity* or *displacement costs*.

But it is enough that these confusions of real with money costs take place and are general—if only it be also promptly said that the harm in it is not especially serious, otherwise than in the underlying and tacit assumption that these real costs are in such sense explanatory and determinant of money costs that the distinction does not need be observed—that a par of exchange between the terms is warranted.

And Marshall? It must for the present and in the main suffice to note—awaiting further discussion—that he makes the distinction, and that he stresses it, not only at large and by implication, but repeatedly and in explicit terms, for ultimate doctrinal purposes; and that in this emphasis he presents the real costs of production as underlying and explaining the money costs; but that nevertheless he is constantly obscuring or overlooking or violating the distinction —and this in the seeming justification that he regards the terms as for most purposes safely interchangeable.[1]

---

[1] But it is still not the less clear that Marshall takes the price problem, as one of relative prices, to be his topic for examination; that he regards it as the central and organizing problem of economic science; and that his approach to it is consistently the demand-and-supply approach. His ultimate appeal, however, on the supply side is to efforts and waitings as the real costs, with expense costs as the money outlays involved in obtaining control of these efforts and waitings. This does not, it is true, in the slightest advance the argument excepting on the assumption—or the demonstration—that the quantum of the efforts and waitings is causal and explanatory of the respective outlays required to control them. In any other interpretation, the costs are no more than what the enterpriser has to pay. And it may in this connection bear repetition that, while the enterpriser does require labor, and pays wages to get it, he does not require *waiting*, but only *capital*, and makes his payments for the control of it—conditioned, it may be, for its existence on the waiting. But whatever outlays he makes, he makes in view of the price serviceability to him of the capital, and not of the waiting.

The enterpriser's outlays take place as conditioning his control of the efforts and the capital. His money outlays are therefore costs to him—not the efforts and the waitings, but only the wages and the capital hires. He may, it is true—and almost inevitably does—subject himself to both efforts and waitings of his own. If so, these also, because they require an indemnity in price, must be counted in

This antithesis of employee cost to employer cost, or of the real costs of production to employers' expense costs of production, receives, however, commonly its full recognition at Marshall's

---

as price resistances. It is in this form that they function as debits in the process of achieving these price results at which he directly aims and to which he looks for his indemnity. Whatever are the efforts and waitings of others—the costs *to them*—the costs *to him* are solely those money hires which the effort-makers and the waiters collect from him. It is to the laborers solely that the efforts can be the costs of the wages. And even so, the efforts are often not the ranking cost. The laborer has no product cost, but only at most a labor or effort cost of his wage. Cost-wise the laborer is not a producer, but only industry-wise—as an item in the mechanical causation of things. His wage is merely a distributive share paid to him out of a price product to the forthcoming of which his labor has, technologically speaking, contributed, but in the price investment for which he has not shared. The employer has bought his productive contribution from him at an employer-price-cost debit against a forecasted price product—an outlay that is in principle precisely like that for the purchase of raw materials or fuel.

And even to the laborer, the determining cost of his wage—the ranking resistance to the performance of the labor for the use of the particular employer—may not have been the stress or irksomeness of the labor, or its attendant foregoing of rest or leisure, but only the resisting lure of an alternative hire.

A repetitive and wearisome elaboration of the obvious? It ought, it is true, to be obvious. But just this it has turned out not to be. The antithesis of the employer to the employee point of view no economist—with the already noted exception of Cairnes—has consistently recognized. In the large, certainly, the antithesis has been more honored in the overlooking than in the observance. For, in the sense of this antithesis, the enterpriser has manifestly no real costs of production, except as possibly attendant on his own efforts and waitings. He has none through his hirings of the efforts or the capital of others. With respect to these, only his wage and other hires of others' labor and capital are costs. And these are in their very terms price costs.

Similarly also with his own efforts and waitings. As costs for him, in such terms as to be set over as debit items against his price products, they have to be reduced to price terms—the *supply prices* for him of his own efforts and waitings; not, that is to say, in terms of their burdensomeness, their real costs, but of the price resistances that these efforts and waitings uphold, whether by title of their burdensomeness, their irksomeness or discomfort, or only of the prospective money gains attaching to their alternative applications. Never does he, and never could he, arrive at any total of his own with his employees' discomforts; or of his own outlays with employee discomforts; or even his own discomforts, as such, with his own outlay costs. The only summing-up of his costs must be in money terms. The only summing-up of employee remunerations must be in money terms. The only summing-up of real costs must be in discomfort terms—a summing-up which is, by the way, a plain impossibility in any other than a loosely conjectural sense. And to sum up employees' costs on the basis of alternative money receipts is a procedure that for real-cost purposes is not only inadmissible, but is, either for the employer or for the employees, concretely impossible.

It is, then, be it repeated, imperative for straight thinking that the antithesis in point of view between employer costs and employee costs—between real and money costs—between efforts and waitings, and wages and interest respectively—be clearly recognized and rigorously maintained. On any other basis, any analysis explanatory of supply, and through supply of price, is a hopeless undertaking.

hands. Always, either explicitly or implicitly, he appeals to employee costs as fundamentally and adequately explaining the employer's expenses; though the precise relation of the employer's efforts, as real costs, to the employer's gains may later present points of doubt. Never is he content with explanations of prices that purport to go no deeper or further back than the prices of the costs, the mere price outlays of the enterpriser. In his regress analysis, however, as we shall later see, his actual point of stopping is commonly just a price point.[2] But more of this later.

Not quite securely, however, is Marshall to be taken to hold that only relative costs are significant for the values of goods, their exchange relations, their relative prices. But this much is thoroughly in the spirit of his analysis, as also in that of the classical economists at large. Exchange values are of the nature of ratios between goods taken quantitatively—ratios the terms in which are quantities, but the ratios themselves mere relations between quantities. Real values, on the other hand, are conceived as quantitative facts, in terms of the human labor pain or discomfort that they respectively incorporate—or, it may be, of the various and different individual pains and discomforts. The various derivative goods, it is assumed, take on relative prices according to their relative *real values*. These ratios between the real values of things are regarded as determining, not only their various exchange relations to the money thing, but likewise, through the money thing, their ratios to one another as reported in their relative prices.

Cost of production in all of these different uses is, by practically all economists, taken to bear on the price of each particular line of products only through affecting the volume of products—or perhaps also through affecting the terms at which the products are held by the respective producers of them. And it is taken as clear that the

---

[2] "The analysis of the expenses of production of a commodity might be carried backward to any length; but it is seldom worth while to go back very far. It is for instance often sufficient to take the supply prices of the different kinds of raw materials used in any manufacture as ultimate facts, without analyzing these supply prices into the several elements of which they are composed; otherwise indeed the analysis would never end. . . ." (p. 339) Nor ever by this method would it arrive at a real cost.

volume of any particular product bears on prices only through its bearing on how low the price must go in order to find buyers for all of it; or perhaps also to decide the producers of it to hold it rather than to sell it—just as a farmer may decide to feed out his hay or grain rather than to take so low a price for it; or to consume his eggs or bacon at home, rather than to submit to the exchange terms that, if he sells, he must accept. Or the producer may hold over in the speculative emphasis, through his expectation of more favorable prices later.

In the main, however, early or late, in the extreme specialization of production under modern conditions, what gets produced gets sold—no matter what the price—within the limits, at any rate, that are credibly to be imposed. Therefore, it may in the large be said that cost bears on price solely by bearing on the volume of output, and thereby on the price at which it must be offered to find an outlet for it all.

This bearing of cost of production through output on price points, therefore, to a process of continuous response of output to the selling prices that are in prospect. If, in view of actual prices, along with the past general run of prices, the prospective prices promise attractive returns to producers, production will respond, with derivative adverse effects on the prices to be had. Unattractive prices in prospect in view of prospective costs, both being inferred in the main from past and current conditions and trends, will restrict output, and will therefore react favorably on future prices.

Prices are therefore in a constant process of tentative and experimental readjustment and modification, with a constant tendency toward conformity with those costs of production appropriate to the existing conditions—always with, however, a process of lag and unprecision in point of its actual working out, precisely because the price-offer situation for each particular commodity is incessantly changing, and because cost conditions are also incessantly changing; and all of this mainly in response to the changing price and cost influences from surrounding industries.

This, in turn, is merely another way of asserting that cost of production is always a forward-looking adjustment. Not that the costs that have been are altogether with the snows of yester-year. If products, earlier provided for, under earlier cost-of-production policies, are now to be marketed, the products—not the earlier costs of them—are now causal for current prices. The activities now being initiated will bear through their results on later prices. It is this forward-looking character of cost-of-production policies, their prospectiveness in point both of debit and credit, and the uncertainties of each, that, for some purposes, has served to recommend the term *cost of reproduction* as more closely descriptive of the manner of causal working. The actual outlays for labor, raw materials, and capital hires may diverge from even the vague and tentative forecasts of them. The selling prices may also be higher or lower than were the estimates that were effective in deciding the inception and the terms of the undertaking. So again the displaced lines of production or of investment will also in one direction or the other have discredited to some extent the earlier forecasts. Only in degree have the later developments in hedging, in forward price-fixed ordering, and in manufacturing to order, shifted the contingencies to other shoulders. It still holds true that, just as the costs later to be incurred may turn out to be mistakenly forecasted, so advance commitments in equipment, in organization, in materials, and in labor may all represent past outlays or fixed charges that the later prices may either fall far short of indemnifying, or may generously reward.

These investment items, therefore, with their disappointing or their flattering returns, will capitalize into low or high present worths—by reference, that is, to their original costs. Purchased or hired, therefore, they must set new levels of costs. And thus, in many industries, and especially in those of long production periods and of high requirements in equipment goods, the prices of products may be wide in either direction from those prices that in prospect were adequate to induce the investment. This divergence of product prices from investment-cost prices may endure long—conformity always in process of coming, but never actually arriving; or arriving to be only temporary.

Prices, then, in the sense that they are determined at all by costs of production, are determined by costs of production in this forward-looking sense, and in the degree and method of its working. And were the process conceived in real rather than in money-cost terms, the essential facts would remain unchanged.

The objective market fact to be investigated is this continuous process of adjustment and readjustment of the money offers for goods to similarly shifting cost situations. Thus far there is practical agreement among economists and business men. All are, in this sense, price economists. Marshall's entire discussion is organized from the point of view of money costs as his central problem. All of his discussions of real costs, of regress costs, of investor costs, and of parent-training costs are directed solely to the explanation of enterpriser costs, separately and relatively.

That these price costs are not self-explaining, and that they are acutely in need of explanation, Marshall consistently assumes and urges. To offer money costs as a final explanation of prices is merely to explain one price by other prices—the prices of products accounted for by the prices of their costs. It was this that, in part, the Austrians stressed in their indictment of classical theory. And as much as this is fairly to be urged: Either the classical view offered no explanation of money costs, or it attempted their explanation by referring them back to discomfort costs—employee real-costs. These discomfort experiences, the efforts and waitings connected with the production of hired or purchased cost goods, were taken as conditioning the presence of these cost goods, whether labor, or capital instruments, or capital funds. This attempt at explanation, the Austrians insisted, achieved no more than to supplement an obviously superficial account by an obviously incorrect account.

The Austrians, in turn, had a cost doctrine of their own. The marginal utilities incorporated in the products constituted, so far, the costs of the products. This Austrian view conceived price not as the equating point between pleasures to consumers and discomforts to producers, but between pleasures achieved and pleasures frustrated—not as demand pleasures marginally equating against supply pains, but as demand pleasures marginally equating against supply pleasure-resistances. Both views were attempts to arrive at the realities underlying price costs; only that the Austrians translated costs, not into realities of marginal discomfort, but into realities of defeated gratification.

On the face of it this Austrian view is easily mistaken for an opportunity-cost doctrine—cost explained through the ranking displacement among alternative price products. But so interpreted, the vice of circuity is forthwith manifest—not, it is true, explanation by direct recourse to opaque items of price outlay, but explanation nevertheless by appeal to opaque price facts—price facts indirectly invoked, price facts one remove more distant, a shifting over to alternative price products. In the Austrian utility view, however, as equally in the classical real-cost view, it was imperative to get out of the price circle by reaching a level of explanation at which price costs were not invoked, but were instead explained. Both lines of explanation purported to move on the level of the real things in human experience, things ultimate in the sense of being at the limits of human knowledge of human beings, feeling facts—in the classical view, things unwillingly undergone; in the Austrian view, things unwillingly relinquished.

The Austrian escape, then, from this price circle was by an attempted recourse, not to discomforts marginally undergone, but to utilities marginally absorbed. In this effort the Austrians invoked the doctrine of *production-related indirect goods*—the analysis having to do, not with consumption goods, but only with production goods, and, at the cost point, with marginal production goods. Cost in the Austrian view was to be discovered at the marginal application of the indirect good—the marginal use reading the cost standing of the good in every supra-marginal application. Iron, for example, is such an indirect, a cost, good with a wide field of industrial uses. High prices as costs could go with it in the making of, say, watch springs or of pen-knives—obtrusively supra-marginal and therefore inelastic uses. In turn, prices less high could be easily borne with tools, machinery and house furnishings; still lower prices for steel rails, locomotives and freight cars.

The price of iron must nevertheless fall to the point at which the entire stock of it can find in industrial uses takers of it, an industrial demand for it. Its marginal use is, say, as structural iron. Then the price in this marginal use is taken to prescribe the cost standing of iron at, say, one cent a pound in all of its supra-marginal uses. This marginal industrial application of iron is thereupon presented as the marginal-utility standing of it, and as prescribing its place as a price cost over the entire industrial field.

And yet it is obvious that this price of one cent per pound does not derive from the marginal utility of iron as an indirect good, any more than the price of apples derives from the marginal utility of apples. The iron commands a price that is derived from, or commensurate with, the marginal demand for it as a price-productive thing. One cent is merely the point to which, not the marginal utility, but the price, must marginally fall in order to find a price market for the entire stock of iron. The fallacy here with the indirect good, iron, is at one with the fallacy with direct goods, by which the price is derived from marginal utility or made commensurate with it. The Austrians get no further ahead than to a marginal price offer. To identify this with marginal utility is sheer error.[3] At the best to be made of it, there is only marginal price productivity. But really the case is still worse; for the enterpriser's choice is actually declared between alternative price productivities—one aspect of the great principle of *substitution*.

It is then clear that equally the "classicals" and the "moderns" regard money costs of production as either circular, or superficial, or both, when offered as ultimate explanations of the prices of products. The later analysis has served in the main as emphasizing this fact. But it is nevertheless true that the Austrian indictment of the classical position as inadequate for circuity or superficiality—so far

[3] It is this confusion in the Austrian cost analysis of marginal utility with marginal price offer that, as reflected back upon the demand analysis, makes difficult any secure interpretation of the Austrian view of the relations between marginal utility and marginal price offer there. Over and again in that analysis the Austrians identify marginal demand with marginal utility—but this commonly in their less cautious and less carefully considered formulations. The better doctrine is not rarely presented with them, as with Marshall—the comparative marginal utility derivation of price offers made entirely clear. But in the majority of cases with both, the idea is in the other emphasis. And with the Austrians, as also with Marshall, later analysis in the cost field follows the bad choice. (Cf. my *Value and Distribution,* especially Ch. XVII)

as the attack was actually thus formulated—was incorrectly formulated. The logical necessity of something further was frankly faced by the classical writers. Ricardo, for example, finding prices proportional with money costs, presented these money costs as proportional in turn with real costs—but without ever finding it convenient to show just how or why.

But true it is that much of the classical cost analysis does run on the level of price costs—as, for that matter, rightly it must, these being the costs that the enterpriser has to concern himself with and use. And true it is also that the recognition of real costs is commonly of the most general and mechanical sort—a formal and ritualistic observance, a Sunday obeisance, or a dignified declaration of something taken as an obvious and undisputed thing rather than the admission of a pressing doctrinal obligation. If it does not explain itself, it ought to; it is left as taken for granted.

Something of this criticism—but in justice not all of it—is perhaps fairly applicable to Marshall's view. His procedure is almost entirely price procedure, and speaks in the main from the point of view, and on the level, of enterpriser cost. But nowhere does he allow it to go unremembered that explanations are to be sought solely at a deeper level. This deeper level he commonly takes to be the real-cost level. Not rarely, however, it is not the real-cost aspect of the cost good that he stresses on the deeper level, but the mere fact that this much of it is present as an objective datum in the situation, of which enterpriser competitions and costs must take account.[4]

But never is Marshall specific in his account of just how these underlying influences work themselves out into money-cost facts. In the main, he does no more than merely to assert the equality-proportionality of money costs with real costs—leaving his earlier argument for the identity of marginal price offer with marginal utility to warrant his identification of the marginal price costs of goods with the real costs that they are taken marginally to impose. And it is fairly to be said that with the earlier position established,

[4] It is solely through this method of approach, on the "basement" level of analysis, that, as I hold, the circuity in the enterpriser-cost explanation of price is to be avoided. This aspect of the discussion, must, however, be a little postponed.

the later could reasonably be left to recommend itself. Only that it is further fairly to be said that, with this earlier analysis discredited, this real-cost position comes to be entirely lacking in support. If it is to be accepted, it must be solely through its self-warranting quality or by mere act of faith. To me it seems plainly contrary-to-fact—in the large, the pleasant employments the best paid, not the worst. And to point in reply to the money costs of parentally-provided training amounts merely to a money-cost change of venue. It can become argumentatively valid only on condition that equal parental outlays are shown to be derived from equal parental real costs—the income dollar of the rich man as grievously acquired as that of the poor man. And if the explanation shifts to differentials in native endowment, the position is not thereby defended, but abandoned. Marshall's extension of the principle of money costs of production to explain the forthcoming of human beings, through the pecuniary investment policies of parents in the rearing and training of offspring, must later come in for detailed examination. But the duty of watchful waiting for whatever arguments Marshall may offer for this real-cost derivation of wage costs should date from the present instant. No mere price-cost regress, it is clear, can serve for this need.

Not rarely, however, and often specifically, Marshall's procedure is that of regress to price costs at earlier steps in the productive process—in the tacit assumption that, pressed far enough, real-cost explanations must be arrived at for the price-cost facts. For example, the price of labor, its wage, is, as we have seen, attributed to the earlier expense costs of nurture and training—alongside, to be sure, of the various wears-and-tears, the anxieties and the burdens, and the attention and loving care, lavished by parents on their offspring—all, as business-wise, and in pecuniary terms, invested in their future. And, as we shall later see, all of these processes are viewed as attaching to periods long enough, and so as attaching to normal-time equilibria, as to leave them difficult of examination for particular times. Or, it may be, the better interpretation of Marshall's position is that, for these interim periods between normal-time adjustments, he does not account for prices as dependent on cost-of-production influences in either real- or money-cost terms, but only on "the general conditions of demand and supply." This issue of interpretation, as well as the query whether demand and supply or the general conditions of them, can be accepted as competent explanations of any item of economic fact, will shortly demand attention.

Whatever may, however, be the right interpretation of Marshall's doctrine of price determination in other than normal conditions, it is clear that with economists in general, as also with the classical economists, the price of any particular article at any particular time depends—in the forward-looking emphasis and subject to the inevitable lags and unprecisions that attend this forward-looking process of price adjustment—on its cost-of-production conditions at that particular time. The price trend is doubtless in the large toward natural or normal prices; these, in turn, being those prices toward which, appropriately to current conditions, prices must be gravitating. But in the usual view these interim prices, equally with normal prices, derive from cost-of-production influences, only that the lags and unprecisions would disappear under normal-value conditions. Always in this view—but under the limitations implicit in the view—prices are governed by cost of production—the marginal cost of production, that is, of the particular time.

It is implicit in this view of the relation of cost of production to price that, as a matter of general principle, no account needs be taken of whether the enterpriser is the owner or the hirer of the equipment goods that he is gain-seekingly employing. His equipment goods, inclusive of land, are as effectively bases of costs when he owns them as when he hires them; his funds, likewise, whether he borrows them, or employs his own in his business undertaking instead of lending them for interest. If, and so far, for example, as in any aspect land rent is a cost, it does not matter whether the property is one under peasant ownership or tenant cultivation. So again, price resistances attach to the enterpriser's efforts as clearly as do real-cost resistances.

But what then, for cost purposes, shall be made of the distinction between fixed or overhead charges and current outlays in production; between supplementary and prime costs; between interest charges and quasi-rents on equipment goods? For obviously for current purposes the worth of equipment goods earlier provided, of organization at earlier investment costs, of training cost-acquired years back, of price-purchased lands, or of raw material inventories, may have at present only a remote connection with these earlier investment costs.

Discussion of this problem has occasioned endless disagreement, not only among cost accountants, but equally, or even more, among economists. The time has not yet arrived for any full discussion of it here. But the difficulties would be far less forbidding, if only always the cost analysis avoided all tests of where the property titles are located. Whatever may be the correct principle for the case, there can hardly be two principles—one for the owner's exploitation, and the other for tenant's or hirer's. In any case, the point of view is not that of employee cost.

Thus, certainly, must cost be presented, when the situation is that of the current hirer or buyer of land or of other equipment goods. If wheat prices are low, then the cost goods may be acquired cheaply. The rents of them are what you have to pay for the control of them. The wage costs of today are the wages of today, not the unknown sums of earlier outlays. You may look to find raw materials cheap of getting, if the products from them are low in price. But doubtless these raw materials may still be high; but if so, it must be that in other lines of production in which they are used the prices have not yet fallen, or that the processes of readjustment between cost goods in general and products in general have not yet worked themselves out. For the prices in different lines of products and the prices of the cost goods in them are closely tied together. No product is independent in its price of other products in point of costs. Nor are the price offers for one product independent of the price offers for others; and all this because of the ratio principle in the price-offer aspect, in the production-cost aspect, and in the selling aspect. These all-round interdependencies of the prices of different goods, and of the costs of different goods, are not so much evidences of any general circuity in the method of approach, as they are of the very functions of cost and of price offer. With respect, no doubt, to the fixation of any particular price through its price costs, the charge of circuity holds. With respect, however, to general prices, the case is not so much one of circuity as of function. In their very nature costs are the way of evening up the prices of goods relatively to one another. They afford the method by which each individual and each line of production goods is guarded from being directed into uses where, for price purposes, better results were open in other directions of production. Looked at in the large, then, costs of production are the method through which individual choices among lines of productive activity and gainful investment are declared—choices made, in view of prices, of the better against the good, and of the best against the better. It still holds true, however, that the ultimate influences do not award to prices the primary place in the causal sequence. Everywhere, moreover, it is ratio relations that are involved. As we shall later further stress, the causal sequence on the supply side of the exchange relations of goods—the sequence, after once the relative desires and the derivative price offers for goods are assumed, begins with the relative stocks of productive agents—not with their prices—individual productive capacities included; thence to the relative volumes of products; thence to the relative prices of products; thence to the relative hires of the agents; and then finally to the capitalization process to explain their relative present worths in price terms. The costs of production find their place as price facts, as the final terms in the causal sequence—as the evening-up influence. It is with things that we set out, and with prices that we end.

To the constant interdependence of prices and costs, and to the constant derivation of product prices from cost prices, most economists—most of the time—appeal. Whether Marshall, however, takes prices to be fixed always by influences of cost, both money and real, or only to be thus fixed in periods and under conditions of normal equilibrium, will be first among our coming problems of interpretation.

Chapter VI

COST OF PRODUCTION (CONTINUED)

TO EXPLAIN the low price of iron by abundant iron resources, or of apples by favorable soil and climate, or of lumber by great forests, or of cheap tropical fruits by plenteous tropical rainfall and temperature, or of dear champagne by scarce champagne lands, or of dear diamonds by limited or niggardly diamond fields, is not to uncover any deeply hidden principle. But not rarely, through the very commonplaceness of it, this simple truth, even with intelligent thinkers, gets obscured—as, for example, when they offer the high rent of champagne lands or the low price of wheat lands as ultimately accounting for the dear champagne or the cheap wheat; or again, the high salaries of prima donnas as accounting for the high prices of opera tickets.

And as preliminary to the discussions ahead, there are further truisms requiring present emphasis. Employers' wage outlays never produce goods. Money is not a factor of commodity production. No more are the discomforts undergone by laborers, or the wages received by them, productive agencies. It is labor that is productive, not the wages received for it, and not the costs of it, either money or real. Nor does the waiting that is assumed to lie behind capital, nor the interest paid for it, nor the rent attaching to any equipment item of it, count causally in the making of the product, but only the capital goods themselves. No one consumes waiting, or makes goods out of it or with it. Not the rents of agricultural lands, but the lands, grow crops. Not urban ground rents, but the urban lots, afford yard-room or the support of buildings.

Doubtless all this is distressingly obvious. And there is yet more like unto it. Rents are not the product of land, but only crops. And it is not the abundance of the good lands to grow crops that explains the high rents of the lands, but only the scarcity of the lands, whereby there arrives the scarcity of products; and the high

123

price of the products; and, at the next remove, the high rents of the lands. It is the lands that are, that make for products; and the lands that are not, that make for rents—a paradoxical way, no doubt, of phrasing the essential truth in the case. It is the high prices of products, deriving from the scarcity of products, deriving, in turn, from the scarcity of lands, that give the high rents of the lands. Admittedly, of course, were there none of the lands, there could be none of the products, no prices for them, and no rents therefrom. But the rents that, so far, report the fact that there are productive lands, afford also, so far, the explanation for the more rather than the less of products; and therefore, so far, the limitation that is on the scarcity of product, and thus on the price of the product—and so on the rent. It is obviously the land that is a productive factor, and not the rent of the land.

And equally clear is it that, not the rent of the land, but the crop from it, is the product of the land. The rent derives from the fact of the scarcity of the product, and the scarcity of the product derives from the scarcity of the land. Nowhere, it is clear, is the rent a causal fact in the process. But precisely so it is with machines and their hires, and with labor and its wages. Wherefore it may seem that to explain the price of anything by either its money or its real costs is to fall into plain nonsense.

Many things, indeed, that in the pecuniary-competitive sense appear to be causal—as, for example, investment outlay, interest, rents, wages, profits—are not in any mechanical or industrial sense causal; but are instead—and often, and in various aspects—the direct antithesis of productive, even in the competitive sense. They are price resistances in production—deductions, debits and not credits. Even where they are not cost outlays, but income receipts, they are no more than the inducement or the stimulation leading up to the application of the causal instruments or efforts—to getting the causal facts to functioning. They are not themselves the causal facts or processes. The rents that as costs the enterpriser pays out for land or machinery are the prices to which he must submit, if he is to have the help of the lands or the machines—hires that report what the land use is worth above free land or land at its margin of employment; or the worth of the machine above no machine or a scrap-pile machine. The rent is a debit against the productive use, an incumbrance, a trammel. Would he could be rid of it—still enjoying its price-productive aid.

The employer pays, say, wages. These condition his achievement in product; are for him hurdles to be passed, debits to bear, intermediate steps—but not means—to product. The employee receives his wages. But this wage is his contractual offset for the labor that he performs—this labor-effort his debit against his wage as credit. Not the wage that he collects, but the work that he does, is the productive fact, the causal thing. Collectively viewed, indeed, all these pecuniary-outlay facts of wage, and rent, and interest costs, vanish from the setting. In this aggregate sense, as Adam Smith observed, it is labor that is the original purchase price of product —product only the return against the effort put forth; a wage, then, in a quite intelligible sense, but in no intelligible sense a causal fact.

Doubtless, however, the quality of the environment may also be causal, in more than the merely conditional sense—the land as much a productive fact as the labor that gets applied to it. This aggregate or collective view regards the product resulting from the land or the labor—not the rent or the wage derivatives—as a total, without reference to any exchange relations inside it of goods with one another. At this point then, there enter the cost aspects of the case, as reporting the relative resistances attaching to the different productive outcomes. How provide against misdirection of productive power, thus working out a right distribution of the fund of effort to be expended in the buying of these things from Nature? The opportunity-cost principle is the guide, as the evening-up process—nowhere any product to be allowed to displace some more important product or leisure, that may carry the ranking resistance. Equally in its competitive and its collective rendering the principle applies.

The important point of present emphasis is that, no matter what may be the type of organization, the fundamental influences in any economic adjustment are the productive resources and capacities, as over against the human desires to be served. All of the competitive process facts have to be articulated with these fundamentally decisive and directive influences—the "basement" level of examination and interpretation. Here also is the remedy for the superficiality of all enterpriser-cost analysis; here the exit from its inevitable circuities.

But here also, through ready and unconscious shifts in the level of analysis, have arrived endless doctrinal confusions and contradictions. For "the great bad is mixing things."

In connection with the relation of money costs to prices, a variety of distinctions has been urged—mainly cross distinctions. Marshall, for example, recognizing the logical inadequacy of the attempt to arrive at a fundamental explanation of prices by recourse to enterprisers' price costs, and convinced that the costs must themselves be explained, directs himself to the regress type of explanation—to the point of view, that is, of employee money cost. For example, the outlay costs of the manufacturer of farm machinery for lumber, steel, fuel and equipment—and for labor as well—are referred for explanation to a step-by-step regress to the respective money costs of the preceding producer-providers. And by the device of isolating price-determining costs at the various stages of the supply process, by taking these costs to be found at the land margins —thereby eliminating complications of rent cost in the sequence of processes—each separate cost stage in the regress finds itself explained by the sum of wages and interest that the respective enterprisers must have advanced in order to compensate the employers next back in the regress for their own particular outlays of wages and interest. In turn also, presumably, these outlays at each backward step are themselves to be explained by real-cost facts of efforts and waitings. Each enterpriser's own labor return is readily referred directly to his own efforts and waitings. At each stage in the regress, therefore, the enterpriser's costs are made up as the sum of all the preceding wage costs, as correlatives of the effort costs, along with the sum of all investment-interest returns as correlatives of the waiting costs. In fact, however, each particular wage outlay is in part traced back to the parental pecuniary burdens of rearing and training the laborer. The enterpriser's outlay should therefore be more than an offset for the discomforts of the laborer. There must then be *for each laborer* a surplus; for included in his hire, as collected by him instead of by his parents, there is an interest constituent on these parental outlays, as also, presumably, on the price offset for the parents' stresses of bringing this child of theirs to birth and for the subsequent cares and anxieties of rearing. These parental pecuniary burdens, in turn, are traced back in point of origin to the discomforts of preceding earning processes, along with the waiting discomforts of saving these earnings; whereby a further surplus income accrues to the later-laboring offspring.

Moreover, as will later appear in other connections, at no stage in this entire regress can either the employer costs of that time, or the employee costs explaining the employer costs, have been commensurate with the appropriate and respective returns on the original investment funds both of parents and of providers of equipment goods—these last, it may be, inclusive of lands. For complications with reference to supplementary costs and quasi-rents require mention here. It is to be recalled that Marshall holds the hires of earlier-produced equipment goods, during their respective reproduction periods, to be, not price-determining, but price-determined—the hires of them temporarily, like those of land permanently, the results and not the causes of the prices of products—as presumably also must be the case with all costs of the supplementary class. It is true that the hiring enterpriser pays them; but inasmuch as they are not price-determining, he cannot find himself in a position to reimburse himself for them from his vendee enterpriser. And thus, at each particular step in the regress series, there is no identity between the employer money-cost and the determining employee price costs one stage back, but instead a further and possibly cumulative divergence—to go along with the previously noted divergences between laborer discomfort costs and laborer income receipts—these last being price determining influences.

Instead, therefore, of this regress method offering a way of escape from the perplexities of the cost-of-production method of accounting for prices, it appears still further to complicate the situation.

In any case, however, it must be clear that so far as this regress method confines itself strictly to the employee money-cost explanation of employer money costs—with nothing pro or con to be made of supplementary cost or with quasi-rent relations to prices—and taking the market facts of wages, interest, equipment rents and land rents as they inscrutably present themselves to the enterprise at each particular step in the regress—nothing to the purpose has in fact been accomplished. This cost-of-production explanation of prices at each point in the regress is itself open to the very charge of circuity that it was invoked to avoid—the regress always from one price-cost analysis to another, and neither the better nor the worse for being more remote. As well have stopped before making the beginning. Only the implicit appeal to real-cost supplementation can save the analysis from logical insolvency. But this method, in turn, appears on examination to lead only into further perplexities, and to recommend strongly the resting of the case for it on pure assumption, or perhaps—if that seems preferable—on the utility-and-price procedure earlier analyzed.

But the validity of this regress analysis is further conditioned on the defensibility of the marginal elimination of rent costs from price determination. For it would seem that if the land rents or the equipment rents, that can as costs be substituted for wage costs, are out of the cost reckoning, wages also will have to go out. But Marshall's position in this regard is here to be taken without argument, as properly belonging to another discussion. Not all problems can be taken up at once. Our examination of this position must similarly be set over for another time. But neither here nor elsewhere is this particular issue of the correspondence of money costs with real costs further examined by Marshall.

Take it that the costs of enterprise A today are valid for the explaining of the product prices of today, but only in the sense that these costs are employee-wise fixed by the different respective costs of B_1, B_2, and B_3, and so on, with their respective costs fixed in turn by different C-group producers—all of different dates of entry into the long regress sequence. If no one of these cost steps in regress is self-warranting as a point of stopping—each one infect by the same defect as in the cost at the A stage—we get nowhere through this regress process, until, at any rate, we arrive at one or both of the terminal points: one at the regress point of the original investment of funds; the other at the forward-looking point of a normal equilibrium. And in either case, we must have in mind all of the different lines of equipment goods and of organization. And equally in both directions we have only fund-investment items to consider and to compare with the pecuniary returns on them. And forthwith upon arrival at these various volumes of investment funds, we have to set out upon new expedi-tions of regress; for these funds must in turn be found to correlate with their earlier real costs of acquisition and of waiting. And thus only by act of faith do we get anywhere; which reliance on faith would have served us equally well at the A stage of our endeavor— this real-cost logic as strong to begin with as ever by the regress method it can come to be.

Marshall himself, however, manifests slight faith in this method of explaining employer money costs through employee money costs:

The analysis of the expenses of production of a commodity might be carried backward to any length; but it is seldom worth while to go back very far. It is for instance often sufficient to take the supply prices of the different kinds of raw materials used in any manufacture as ultimate facts, without analyzing these supply prices into the several elements of which they are composed; otherwise indeed the analysis would never end ... the things that are required for making a commodity ... [we] call ... its *factors of production*. Its expenses of production ... are thus the supply prices of the corresponding quantities of its factors of pro-duction. And the sum of these is the supply price of that amount of the commodity. (p. 339, italics Marshall's)

This means, among other things, that whatever they receive from you, determines what you pay to them.

For later purposes we now note the plural use here—*the supply prices* of any particular product, not its one supply price; the schedule or list or curve notion. Just now, however, we need to note solely that if rightly or safely we may suspend our regress quest at the B stage of it, we might equally well have stopped with the A. Moreover, all along this line, these money costs must have been divergent, either in lack or in excess, from correspondence with the primary investors' money costs—the outlays that were determined by the returns that were taken to be in prospect and that were, as such, held to be adequate inducements by the respective investors. Always, however, excepting, to be sure, in normal equilibrium periods, these forecasts of return must have found themselves discredited, either in excess or defect, by the later outcomes.

But Marshall may perhaps be taken to admit thus much—holding, or it may be urging, that only in periods of normal equilibrium can there be a full correspondence of money costs with prices, or of real costs with money costs—this normal-time period, that is to say, being one in which the forward-looking and the backward-looking sequences of costs arrive at interchangeable sums of real and of money costs, with relative prices proportional with both. He says (p. 497): "In a rigidly stationary state in which supply could be perfectly adjusted to demand in every particular, the normal expenses of production, the marginal expenses, and the average expenses (rent being counted in) would be one and the same thing, for long periods and for short." And again (p. 810): "In a stationary state the income earned by every appliance of production being truly anticipated beforehand, would represent the normal measure of the efforts and sacrifices required to call it into existence."

At present, therefore, only one issue is specifically before us— an issue to which this regress analysis is merely subordinate—*the significance of the money costs of any particular time to the product prices of that time.* Not so much, therefore, the validating of this entire regress method is in question, as the circuity of it. The logic of the analysis at any one stage of the production process is not bettered by the shifting over to an earlier stage. The first step is as secure as any earlier step.

But what then about any one of the steps, early or late in the sequence? What has it to say for the price of the product of that particular time? Whereby we have arrived at the specific problem of interpretation to which the close of the preceding chapter pointed: *What is the relation of the costs of production of any particular time to the prices of that time?* Are the prices of that time derived from the costs of production of that time? Or is it, instead, truth that the hires of the factors of production of that time are derived from the product prices of that time? Have we to do with price-determining or with price-determined costs? Are the prices of products during these interim periods commensurate solely with the prime costs of the time and determined by them? All supplementary cost goods, we infer, command only quasi-rent incomes, which are, for the period, like land rents—derivatives of prices and not causes of them. But the enterpriser who hires these factors of production that were earlier cost-acquired has to pay now a hire for the use of them—a hire that may be generous or scant as tested by the original investor costs; but a hire that, to control the factor good, he can afford to pay, in preference, say, to his alternative costs in labor hires; and a hire that his competitors—if not his lessor—will compel him to pay. What part, if any, of these current quasi-rent outlays are price-determining? If, in truth, the prices of products are not influenced by the hires of the employed goods, whether generous or scant by investment tests, by what, then, are the prices influenced, and how are they to be explained? By the presence, it may be, of the equipment goods, though not by the hires of them. If these quasi-rent hires are price-determined, along with all land hires, what about wages—and especially what about those wage elements that trace back to cost-acquired earlier training? And does the marginal-isolation analysis apply entirely or in part to these quasi-rent or these supplementary-cost groups of factors, thus declaring their hires to be price-determined instead of price-determining? What about the hires of exceptional or of extraordinary native ability? And what, for that matter, about the hires of any ability, whether better or worse, native or acquired? In view of the inter-substitutionary nature of most or all of these costs and of these costs goods, how go about excluding any without excluding all? And with any or with all of them excluded; but with the distributive shares accruing to them still exhausting the price-product to be distributed, and nevertheless with only some part or none of these shares participating in the making of the prices—what instead does the making of them? Marshall says:

The net aggregate of all the commodities produced is itself the true source from which flow the demand prices for all these commodities, and therefore for the agents of production used in making them . . . this national dividend is at once the aggregate net product of, and the sole source of payment for, all the agents of production within the country: it is divided up into earnings of labour; interest of capital; and lastly the producer's surplus, or rent, of land and of other differential advantages for production. It constitutes the whole of them, and the whole of it is distributed among them; and the larger it is, the larger, other things being equal, will be the share of each of them. (p. 536)

And if recourse to *the general conditions of demand and supply* is here an adequate explanation, why ever make the effort to go further with any price investigation? In fact, is ever demand-and-supply a competent explanation of anything; or better, for purposes of explanation, than a pompous pronouncement of lay ignorance—"sound and fury signifying nothing"—or at the best, a mere signboard pointing to the directions of setting forth in the quest for explanations?[1]

Precisely what, then, in Marshall's view, are we to take to be the derivation of prices during these interim periods between

[1] Something, however, quite other, I make no question, than the smug finality of our wise men in industry and finance in their fathoming of difficult issues through pontifical declarations of the obvious or the meaningless, is Marshall's thought in his recurrent retreat for ultimate explanations to *the general conditions of demand and supply*. His appeal, I take it, is to the "basement" level of analysis—not to the hires that are the money costs of things in production, but to the presence of the things themselves, the stocks of them, the going resources, human and environmental, available, absolutely and relatively, for the processes of production. If any criticism is to be offered, it must rightly be to his apparent confusion of two different levels of analysis, to his lack of clear differentiation between them; and to his occasional attempt to replace one cost analysis by another, when in essentials his argument abandons entirely the cost level of analysis for the more significant level—a level, however, that enterprisers' costs of production do not touch. This, for example, he repeatedly does in excluding from price determination the rents of land—and temporarily also the hires of machinery—on the ground that the stocks exist without dependence for their existence on the hires allotted to them. And this argument suffices with him even for cases where the hires are more than adequate to the maintenance of the stocks—these hires being still quasi-rents; an argument carrying some especially disquieting implications with reference to the retention even of wages as price-determining costs. But more of this later.

periods of normal equilibrium? Do the prices derive from costs of production as a whole, or from some part of them, or entirely apart from any of them? And from which ones, if from any—and by what title? Are some of these distributed hires price-determined and others of them price-determining? Or have we, instead, to do with distributive shares all of which are price-determined; and with the determinant prices themselves left unaccounted for; or accounted for only by the general conditions of demand and supply?[2]

[2] I have long been unable to arrive at any secure interpretation of Marshall's position in this regard. But I now seem secure in the conviction that demand and supply, along with the general conditions of them, make up his entire account of prices for these interim periods. Perhaps, however, his reliance for price fixation is solely on prime costs, in which, presumably, the necessary labor returns of the enterpriser are included. Certain of the following quotations taken alone, might, nevertheless, seem to indicate that always the prices of products turn for their fixation on enterpriser money costs, as actually the enterpriser has to compute them, but with land rents excluded. The hires of earlier-produced and cost-acquired goods, as of the time when they are being hired, may seem to function as determinant costs for that time—under the limitations, of course, of lag and unprecision appropriate to the forward-looking cost process. Such also I take to have been consistently the view of the classical writers. And, moreover, such is the present position of economists at large. Marshall's view, however, I take to be that all these instrument hires, and even many labor hires, are price-determined, excepting in normal-value periods.

The following quotations are presented in support of this interpretation:

"This illustration [the case of a man who builds a house for himself on land, and of materials, which nature supplies gratis] may serve to keep before us the way in which the efforts and sacrifices which are the real cost of production of a thing, underlie the expenses *which are its money cost*. But, as has just been remarked, the modern business man commonly takes the payments which he has to make, whether for wages or raw material, as he finds them; without staying to inquire how far they are an accurate measure of the efforts and sacrifices to which they correspond. . . ." (p. 352)

". . . there is a demand price for each amount of the commodity, that is, a price at which each particular amount of the commodity can find purchasers in a day or week or year. . . ." (p. 342)

". . . We shall gradually discover a great many different limitations of the doctrine that the price at which a thing can be produced represents its real cost of production, that is, the efforts and sacrifices which have been directly and indirectly devoted to its production. For, in an age of rapid change such as this, the equilibrium of *normal demand and supply* does not thus correspond to any distinct relation of a certain aggregate of pleasures got from the consumption of the commodity and an aggregate of efforts and sacrifices involved in producing it: the correspondence would not be exact, even if *normal* earnings and interest were exact measures of the efforts and sacrifices for which they are the money payments. . . .

". . . The unexpected may happen; and the existing tendencies may be

It will later be made clear that Marshall's distinction between
land and capital rests finally on the assertion that land is fixed in
volume, while capital stocks are flexible—a distinction of degree,
therefore, as Marshall himself holds. Fixity is not a distinction of
origins, or of the derivation of land from natural bounty, or of
the absence of real costs in its origin. For fertility, as susceptible
of creation or of destruction, and therefore of exhaustion or of
renewal, is by Marshall assimilated to capital. Even, then, were land

---

modified before they have had time to accomplish what appears now to be their
full and complete work. . . ." (p. 347)

"When considering costs from the point of view of the capitalist employer, we
of course measure them in money; because his direct concern with the efforts
needed for the work of his employees lies in the money payments he must make.
. . . But when considering costs from the social point of view, when inquiring
whether the cost of attaining a given result is *increasing or diminishing with
changing economic conditions,* then we are concerned with the real costs of efforts
of various qualities, and with the real cost of waiting. If the purchasing power of
money, in terms of effort has remained about constant, and if the rate of remuneration for waiting has remained about constant, *then the money measure of costs
corresponds to the real costs: . . .* " (p. 350)

"When . . . the amount produced (in a unit of time) is such that the demand
price is greater than the supply price, then sellers receive more than is sufficient
to make it worth their while to bring goods to market to that amount; and there
is at work an active force tending to increase the amount brought forward for
sale . . . when the amount produced is such that the demand price is less than
the supply price [note now the one demand and the one supply price], sellers receive less than is sufficient to make it worth their while to bring goods to market on
that scale . . ." (p. 345)

". . . a cloth manufacturer would need to calculate the expenses of producing
all the different things required for making cloth with reference to the amounts of
each of them that would be wanted; and on the supposition *in the first instance*
that the conditions of supply *would be normal.* But . . . he must give to this
term a wider or narrower range, according as he was looking more or less far
ahead." (p. 364)

". . . this national dividend is at once the aggregate net product of, and the
sole source of payment for, all the agents of production. . . .

"It is distributed among them, speaking generally, in proportion to the need
which people have for their several services . . . the *marginal* need . . . each
agent is likely to increase the faster, the larger the share which it gets . . . if
there is no violent change . . . the supply of each agent will be closely *governed
by its cost of production.* . . ." (pp. 536-37)

". . . periods of time [short-period normal] long enough to enable producers to
adapt their production to changes in demand, in so far as that can be done with
the existing provision of specialized skill, specialized capital, and industrial
organization; but not long enough to enable them to make any important changes
in the supplies of these factors of production. . . ." (pp. 497-98)

brought into being through effort costs or money costs, but were nevertheless, when once existing, unmodifiable in quantity through further human agencies, land would still meet the test on the basis of which it is distinguished from capital. Only in its spatial aspects, its geometrical extension, and by virtue of it, is land fixed in volume. It is not, however, taken to be fixed in the sense that flood or earthquake or subsidence may not change it, but only that it does not respond in volume to the efforts or investment policies of men. As bearing, then, on prices, this distinction is worked out to assert that only such factor hires are price-determining as, during the period under consideration, are modifiable in volume through the economic policies of human beings. It is through this aspect, that the "basement" facts in the situation get their connection with competitive costs. And it is, in this aspect, an analysis in the regress and employee-cost emphasis. The enterpriser pays rent, to be sure. But at no time through the lure of the rent, can anyone, anywhere back in the regress series, have been induced to create land or to contribute to its maintenance in volume.

"Only in a stationary state would average expenses be equal to marginal and to normal expenses." (p. 810, marginal caption)

". . . Let us watch the operations of a 'speculative builder.' . . . He estimates the cost of various sites adapted for each class of building: and he reckons in the price that he would have to pay for any site as a part of his capital expenditure, just as he does the expense to which he would be put for laying foundations in it, and so on. He brings this estimate of cost into relation with his estimate of the price he is likely to get for any given building, together with its site. If he can find no case in which the demand price exceeds his outlays. . . ." (pp. 357-58)— even rent being here a part of his price-determining cost.

"When different producers have different advantages for producing a thing, its price must be sufficient to cover the expenses of production of those producers who have no special and exceptional facilities; for if not they will withhold or diminish their production, and the scarcity of the amount supplied, relatively to the demand[s], will raise the price. . . ." (p. 499)

". . . As the demand for residential and business accommodation in a district increases, it becomes worth while to pay a higher and higher price for land, . . .
". . . a woollen manufacturer finding his expenses of production increased, may move . . . into the country; . . . For . . . the saving in the cost of land that he will make by moving into the country . . . will more than counterbalance its disadvantages. In a discussion as to whether it was worth while to do so, the rental value of the site of his factory would be reckoned *among the expenses of production of his cloth;* and rightly." (pp. 449-50) Here again, even rent is included in the price-determining influences.

This interpretation of Marshall's ultimate basis of distinction between land and capital may be questioned—and rightly enough, until the case in proof has been presented. The present purpose, however, is merely to make clear the setting of Marshall's quasi-rent concept, and of the bearing attributed to it on the determination of price. It is this fixity of land stocks, their unresponsiveness in volume to the hires competitively allotted to them, that in Marshall's thought denies to land rents any price-determining function. It follows, then, that any factor of production, for such time as it is in point of volume independent of the hires attaching to it, must also uphold price-determined and not price-determining hires.

Doubtless it is the land, and not the hire of it, that causes product and thereby affects prices. No matter whether, or to whom, the hires accrue, the land is still present. Its effect on prices is not through its rent, but only through its availability, rent or no rent, for the processes of production.

We have, then, come upon a perfect example of the "basement" analysis. The line of reasoning by which land rent falls out of price determination carries equipment rents along with it, during the period that the stocks of equipment goods are in volume independent of their costs. Not that these cost-acquired equipment goods lack causal significance for the volume of products, and therefore for the prices of the products—as is also true for lands. Thus much the argument admits and stresses. But the *rents* have not in either case this causal bearing. Nor, indeed, causally speaking, can any hire of anything ever have it. It is solely the *things themselves* that have significant bearing on prices—still causally speaking. But, as the Marshall argument holds, if and when and so far and so long—but only so far and so long—as the hires condition the stocks, the hire of the factor can be a price-determining cost. And then not the hire, but the instrument, is ultimately the causal thing. Nevertheless, with the volume of the factor itself as solely influencing the price, but with the hire of it effective, so far as equipment goods are concerned, to react on the volume of the factor, the hire must have, in a roundabout and intermediate sense, some sort of determining influence—of the stimulus sort—on the price; although it still holds true that the hire is not a factor of production, and is not in any mechanical-industrial sense the cause of anything.

But even so it is with the wages that divert a laborer from one line of production to another. This diverting wage, by affecting the volume of laborers in the first industry, must thereby affect the volume of its product. It is in this sense a cause of the change in prices. But the wage does not thereby become a cost of production in the industry in which the laborer no longer works. It does, however, affect the wages of the laborers who remain. But no wages, either there or here, produce anything. And even taking whatever wages are actually paid to be in some wise causal in the case, these cannot be the wages to those that go, but only to those that stay. And precisely similar must be the case with land and its hires— only that, Marshall says, the aggregate volume of labor is conditioned on the wages paid to it. But still the volume is not conditioned on the full amount of the wages actually received, but only on a wage adequate for subsistence, or perhaps for the standard of living—assuming, of course, that the standard fixes the wages rather than the wages the standard. As regards any particular occupation as against competing occupations, this explanation of the stock of available labor through the wages offered for it does clearly hold. But it applies not at all securely for wage-earners or for population in the aggregate. Of this, the falling birth rates of recent decades in the entire western world should stand as proof. And in this alternative-opening emphasis, the argument applies equally to land and to land rents—as in the competition of crops. And still clearer must it be that the fixity in volume that is urged to hold with quasi-rent goods during their reproduction periods is a fixity, not in any particular line of production, but in the aggregate stock of equipment goods. Only implicitly, but still directly, the significance of opportunity costs is here in issue.

Such, then, appears to be the ultimate principle in Marshall's view denying to the rents of cost-derived goods any causal share in price determination. This argument is a necessary corollary of the principle on which Marshall excludes land rent from price-determining costs. This, then, is the doctrinal issue immediately ahead of us.

First, however, must be made clear Marshall's own account of the relation of cost-acquired equipment goods to prices—a position that, in the interpretation here arrived at, has appeared to be in various aspects untenable—a position that is, moreover, inconsistent with the classical account of the determination of price—inconsistent also with the significance attached by business men to cost of production—and a position setting prices adrift from the influences that by economists at large are held to account for them. It denies that most of the hires paid by enterprisers function as price-determining influences. And further, in view of the substitutionary possibilities, especially at the margins of production, between quasi-rent goods and labor Marshall's position leads logically to the denial that wages are price-determining costs—the distinction between prime and supplementary costs being here a cross distinction and a distinction turning essentially on the distribution of proprietorships. Moreover also, because many of the productive capacities of individuals are cost-acquired through earlier training outlays, Marshall's view leads inevitably to the denial of the price-determining rôle to some part or all of the wage expenses of production. And taking it as clear that the things that are not yet in existence cannot uphold price-determining costs, and bearing in mind also that neither the hires of the existing equipment goods that were earlier cost-produced nor the hires of land are price-determining, the prices of products come to be entirely without explanation in terms of cost—even irrespective of wages, and perhaps especially of the wages of exceptional or extraordinary native abilities. And having further in mind that whether the hires attaching to goods earlier cost-acquired are either unduly low or unduly high, as tested by the returns earlier looked for by investors, these hires are equally denied any price-determining rôle; it must follow that no hires of any goods can ever be cost-determining—excepting, to be sure, at those particular and improbable and unrecognizable instants when these hires are crossing the line dividing the too little from the too much—whereby also the principle of the ultimate finality, not of the hires of goods, but of the stocks of them, is implicitly denied; and whereby further the emphasis on the fixity of stocks becomes irrelevant.[3]

[3] A full discussion at this time of the relation of these quasi-rents to prices would involve the examination of certain further aspects of analysis better considered in connection with the relation of land rents to prices, and in further connection with the crucial issue of the distinction between land and capital.

Chapter VII

PRICE-DETERMINING AND PRICE-DETERMINED COSTS: CAPITAL

COLLECTIVELY viewed, all incomes derive directly from labor or from possessions. Competitively viewed, they are so derived either directly or indirectly, the primary distributions in the gain process not always clearly distinguishable from the later distributions by gift, inheritance, parasitism and crime; as witness printing of blue-sky securities, counterfeiting, salting of mines, gainful spread of misinformation, hunting of ivory and catching of slaves. All industry is business, but not all business is industry.

Marshall's *efforts* and *waitings*—occasionally also *sacrifices*—are presented as the *real costs* attaching to the productive uses of labor and capital, for the control of which the *money costs,* the *expenses,* are incurred—the sums of these money outlays being, for each different individual producer, the unit supply prices of each of his different respective volume of output—the sums that some one else receives from you being the sums that you pay out to him. *Capital* in this aspect is merely possessions—legally, *property*—industrially employed. Waiting is implicit in the fact that the possessions are being industrially employed. The correlative hires in the case are, for labor, wages, and for capital, either interest or rent.

Mainly, in these discussions of costs, Marshall's point of view is distinctly industrial—the production of price goods. But waiting refers, nevertheless, either to all investment funds or to the goods in which they have been incorporated. We recall that land is declared by Marshall to be no longer a free good, and that for all enterpriser purposes there is no distinction between capital and land. Rightly, therefore, this fact of *waiting* must attach to land as well as to any other auxiliary good—any indirect or production good. All lessors or lenders wait. Organization and publicity are equally capital, though not quite so clearly so in the technological emphasis.

We have, then, to examine the distinction according to which the hires of stocks of things not dependent for their maintenance on new investment, or on reinvestment, of fund capital, *free capital* —lands, that is to say, in their spatial aspect—are presented both in the short and in the long run as price-determined hires; while the hires of things dependent for their maintenance on investment in up-keep or replacement, are presented as in the short run price-determined—quasi-rent goods—and as in the long run price-determining. Those goods that, through their hires, are taken to be price-determining in the long run are called capital, as over against those goods the hires of which are invariably price-determined— *lands*.

We have then to consider in this aspect a distinction relevant solely to the processes of industry. With the larger general problem of the distinction between land and capital we are not at present concerned. *This purely technological distinction* is important because it is a doctrinal necessity, if the classical position is to be defended that things exchange against one another proportionally with the wage and the discomfort costs embodied in them. This distinction was for Marshall a doctrinal legacy. The classical system stands or falls with it.[1]

In no other aspect, clearly, is there significance for systematic purposes in the land-and-capital issue. Nor for present purposes is precisely this the issue, but only whether, for purposes of price causation, land, as a variety of capital that is fixed in volume, is distinguishable from those instruments of production that do not manifest this fixity—cost-produced items of capital. For we recall Marshall's repeated statement that from the point of view of the

[1] But, as we have seen earlier, the distinction was for classical purposes a distinction of origins. And, as we shall shortly see, Marshall promptly abandons it as such. It is plain, however, that he does not regard this as a tacit abandonment of the fundamental classical principle and thesis, the proportionality of prices with real costs—with price as the equating point of pleasures in consumption with pains in production. Later, therefore, we must examine the question whether escape is possible through the marginal isolation of price-determining costs, with land rents thereby presented as both in the long and the short run price-determined.

142   THE ECONOMICS OF ALFRED MARSHALL

individual enterpriser, land is only one variety of capital.[2] Origins
are in this aspect irrelevant. The enterpriser has now to pay for it,
if he is to have it. Not as a present, but only as an earlier fact, may
lands be called costless. This earlier costlessness is therefore not to
any present purpose as a present-cost fact.

The clearer, then, becomes the present issue. This long run
antithesis of equipment hires to land hires—the equipment hires
price-determining, and the land hires price-determined—is a functional distinction. As such, all distinctions of degree are inappropriate. The distinction between cause and result is not a distinction of
degree. No shading-off, by degrees of time, from price-determined
to price-determining is permissable to distinguish cause-relations
from result-relations—on the hither side of a point of time, a
cause; on the farther side, a result. And similarly, if one part of
the hire of each one of the various productive goods is a cause
of price and the other part an effect of price, the outcome must
be mere doctrinal and practical confusion. If either enterpriser or
economist needs the distinction, neither can actually apply it.

Irrespective, however, of any of these attempted distinctions of
degree, is there any tenable distinction of function, whereby equip-
ment-capital hires are in the short time results of price and in the
long run causes, the while that, both in the short and the long
run, land-capital hires are price-determined? What, for the purposes of this distinction of function, are the objective traits or
characteristics by which equipment capital is to be distinguished
from land capital? By what objective tests draw the line, and how
justify the distinction? By assumption it is for the enterpriser both
meaningless and impossible. But on what lines of objective differentiation shall the economist, for his purposes of a functional distinction between cause and effect, draw and apply it? What, objectively,
is land capital, and what is equipment capital? How tell them apart?

Not precisely, then, for present purposes, are we concerned with
the large and general distinction between land and capital, but only
with the distinction between land capital and equipment capital
—not, therefore, accurately with any distinction in the regress em-

[2] See *Principles*, pp. 400, 535-42, 544.

phasis of origin, whether of a sometime derivation through natural bounty, or through human effort, but only with distinctions of present or future derivation and of functioning—with what are now the origins, and what are now the directive influences, and what are now, in view of the present situation and influences, the modifications in prospect.[3]

[3] It is nevertheless important in aspects collateral to the present issue, as also in other aspects, to make clear what, in Marshall's thought, is distinctive of capital, the trait or traits common to all the different varieties of capital—that large competitive classification of which land is merely one subdivision and quasi-rent goods another.

There are rightly and necessarily offered in Marshall's discussion a number of different kinds of capital: natural, artificial, fixed, circulating, material, immaterial, fund (free or fluid), instrumental, productive or serviceable; and there might also have been offered—but were not—parasitic, predatory and criminal—but all of these as predicates attaching to particular varieties within the major classification, *capital*.

The trait of industrial application which is necessarily in mind when capital is associated with labor as a subject of outlay costs in industrially productive undertakings, receives, on the whole, less emphasis with Marshall than *free capital*, capital funds, a capital fact quite separate from the productive process, and not rarely clearly distinguished in Marshall's discussions. It is the primary form of capital on the pecuniary level of modern business and business-industry. It is the subject matter of the loan relation and of the interest phenomenon. Through investment, it takes on the widest variety of incorporations, as directed into merchandisers' stocks, organization, advertising, credit extensions, dwellings, land, furniture, patents, franchises, formulas, trade-marks, public and industrial bonds, elections, legislative favors, protective tariffs, saloons, dives, gambling and counterfeiting equipment, slave brigs, locomotives, freight and passenger cars, touring cars and trucks, ditches, wells, tile drains, grading, plowing and fertilizing—and finally, no doubt, into the factory lands, buildings, equipment and raw materials of industrial processes.

All of these are in Marshall's account capital items. Materiality is not essential; nor is the materiality of the product or of the return; nor social serviceability; nor wisdom nor wholesomeness nor ethical merit, either in the processes or the results. The bringing about even of desiredness, excepting for the operator himself, is not a requisite, so long as he gets the gain that he was seeking, the thing desired by him. The hire attaching to practically any one of these capital items—excepting land—when employed cost-wise in any gain-seeking process, no matter whether socially productive or not, and no matter even whether industrial or not, is a price-determining cost. Occasionally, it is true, but not commonly, Marshall concurs in the typically classical view that *capital consists of the stored-products of labor set aside for purposes of further production, or of all wealth other than land so set aside*. He opens Book IV on "The Agents of Production—Land, Labour, Capital and Organization" as follows (p. 138):

"The agents of production are commonly classed as Land, Labour and Capital. By Land is meant the material and the forces which Nature gives freely for man's aid, in land and water, in air and light and heat. . . . By Capital is meant all stored-up provision for the production of material goods, and for the attainment

Precisely what, then, is *capital,* in the sense to include both land and equipment goods, and thus to set the background for the distinction between the two sorts of capital?

On the whole, it would appear to include all individually held items of the environment that render *income.* It includes, therefore, indefinitely more than those goods that are means or intermediates in the industrial process, and more even than goods employed as intermediates to individual gain (see p. 78).

Marshall makes, it should be noted, a distinction from the "social" point of view between land capital and equipment capital—a distinction, however, that turns on a test that Marshall urges also from the competitive point of view—the modifiability of stocks. In the main, however, he deals with the distinction as competitively viewed, precisely because it is with competitive processes and ad-

---

of those benefits which are commonly reckoned as part of income. It is the main stock of wealth regarded as an agent of production rather than as a direct source of gratification.

"Capital consists in a great part of *knowledge* and *organization:* and of this some part is private property and other part is not. . . ."

This view he seems to accept, though he has earlier in his discussion of *wealth* (pp. 56-57) appeared to hold that wealth is confined to things "external to him [man] . . . it excludes all his own personal qualities and faculties, even those which enable him to earn his living; because they are Internal." Later, however, he expresses vigorous dissent from Boehm-Bawerk's rigorously technological and industrial view of capital:

". . . Nor does he [Boehm-Bawerk] seem to have succeeded in finding a definition that is clear and consistent. He says that 'Social Capital is a group of products destined to serve towards further production; or briefly a group of intermediate products.' He formally excludes (Book I, Ch. VI) 'dwelling houses and other kinds of buildings such as serve immediately for any purpose of enjoyment or education or culture.' To be consistent, he must exclude hotels, tramways, passenger ships and trains, etc.; and perhaps even plant for supplying the electric light for private dwellings; but that would seem to deprive the notion of capital of all practical interest. There seems no good ground for excluding the public theatre while including the tramcar, which would not justify the inclusion of mills engaged in making home-spun and the exclusion of those engaged in making lace. . . ." (p. 790, note)

It is worthy of note in passing that Boehm-Bawerk, despite his stress on capital as an intermediate good in the productive process, still finds it possible to deny that land is capital—a position more nearly in line with classical authority than that of Marshall himself. From Boehm-Bawerk's position in this regard Marshall offers no word of dissent. His own position, nevertheless, involves no distinction between land and capital, but only between land capital and equipment capital. For it must be held in mind that with him land is merely that particular sort of private capital the hire of which is always price-determined.

justments that he is primarily concerned. What indeed *social* means with him, whether a collective or merely an aggregate view, must be left for a later examination. From the competitive point of view, certainly, capital includes much more than (p. 138) "all stored-up provision for the production of material [external] goods, and for the attainment of those benefits which are commonly reckoned as part of income . . . the main stock of wealth regarded as an agent of production rather than *as a direct source of gratification.*" This formulation does, it is true, run in the acquisitive tenor; but it excludes durable direct goods—those goods commanding a long series of future incomes, say, dwellings and touring cars— and excludes also goods that at some future time will afford a single experience of valuable service—for example, ice stored up in winter for summer consumption, or cider aging to vinegar, or wine taking on new flavors.

The distinction of Marshall's ultimate adoption appears, nevertheless, to attach the capital character to all those individual possessions the incomes of which are felt to be in significant degree conditioned on the passing of time—properties like lands, dwellings, horses, machinery—whether used directly by their possessors, or in the hands of others on lease or bailment; and irrespective of the nature or number of the future valuable returns.

The principle appears, therefore, to be that of dependence on time prospectiveness—capital as present base of future return, individual wealth viewed in its time dimension, affording such incomes as lend themselves to the process of computation of present worths, incomes that get capitalized into present-price terms. In this interpretation, *capital* may be tentatively described as *those price-bearing, durative, individual possessions the prospective price incomes from which are sufficiently remote in time to involve the capitalization process in arriving at a present price worth.*[4]

---

[4] It may be that, as addicted to this particular view of capital, I too readily impute it to Marshall. For immediate purposes, nevertheless, the issue is solely that of the validity of Marshall's distinction between land capital and equipment capital. Inevitably, therefore, our quest for the fundamental characteristics of private capital in the large has carried us somewhat afield. But earlier or later, and especially in its bearing on interest theory, this larger problem has to be adventured. Certain considerations advise the attempt here.

We have seen that Marshall includes in capital all current money holdings directed to the control of later valuable benefits: money in hand; money loaned; investments in patents, franchises, trademarks and vogue; items of income-promising wealth that may not, by the owner, be employed in any industrial process, and that may have no industrial significance to the hirers of them, but that do, nevertheless, afford valuable incomes in time—like dwellings and touring cars. Moreover, Marshall's especial emphasis on funds, free purchasing power, as capital bases for direct owner exploitation or for lending, carries with it the capital quality of all those durable things that are made to incorporate these investment funds. So he says (pp. 585-86) "there is no substantial difference between the loan of the purchase price of a horse and the loan of a horse." The same reasoning imposes, obviously, the inclusion of land as *competitive* capital—a view which Marshall clearly advocates as also it imposes the inclusion of land as a supplementary-cost good.

To the owner, obviously, *waiting* is always implicit in the mere fact of lending—as, for that matter, in the mere fact of his own acquisitive use. That Marshall attaches no weight to whether the good is used by the owner directly or is lent, is clear from the following (p. 586): ". . . all producers, whether working with borrowed capital or not, reckon interest on the capital used by them as among the expenses which they require to have returned to them . . . as a condition of their continuing business." In point, then, neither of cost nor of capital standing is the distribution of proprietorships a relevant fact.

Externality is, however, implicit in the nature of *wealth,* and thereby of capital as a subhead of wealth. Wealth "excludes all his own personal qualities and faculties, even those which enable him to earn his living; because they are Internal." (p. 57) Marshall appears also to emphasize *materiality.* But *material* means with him nothing more than *external*—a passably awkward way of indicating patents, national bonds, deposit credits, and the like:

> *Material goods* . . . include . . . mortgages and other bonds; . . . shares . . . all kinds of monopolies, patent-rights, copyrights; also rights of way and other rights of usage. . . .

A man's *non-material* goods fall into two classes. One consists of his own qualities and faculties for action and for enjoyment; . . . All these lie within himself and are called *internal*. The second class are called *external* because they consist of relations beneficial to him with other people . . . the chief instances . . . now-a-days . . . the good will and business connection of traders and professional men. (pp. 54-55)

.   .   .   .

In the second class [of wealth] are those immaterial goods which belong to him, are external to him, and serve directly as the means of enabling him to acquire material goods . . . it includes his business and professional connections, the organization of his business, and—where such things exist—his property in slaves, in labour dues, etc. (pp. 56-57)

. . . it seems best sometimes to reckon Organization apart as a distinct agent of production. . . .

In a sense there are only two agents of production, nature and man. . . . (p. 139)

It should now be manifest that no distinctions of origin are, in Marshall's view, relevant to this competitive formulation of the capital concept. Nor, as will later appear, do origins ever afford from the social point of view the line of distinction urged by Marshall between land capital and equipment capital. But whatever may be the right interpretation of Marshall's position in this latter regard, it must, to repeat, be entirely clear that origins are without significance for his concept of competitive capital. This position may be replete with difficulty for the classical doctrine—as also for Marshall's own doctrine—that prices tend to be, and in normal times come to be, proportional with real costs in the regress emphasis. Sufficient unto its own time must be this question. But it is certain that in Marshall's view competitive capital includes land capital as one of its subheads. The rents of land, like the rents of equipment goods, are incomes on durative possessions, and in the most inclusive sense of the term are therefore *interest*. Rents assume the interest form of statement whenever they come to be computed as percentage incomes on the price bases. This also is Marshall's view.

It is, moreover, clear, as has earlier been noted, that the distinction between land capital and equipment capital is a distinction of function with reference to the determination of the prices of products. Issues of origin are not issues of function. And even did ever lines of origin parallel lines of function, origins cannot by themselves support the distinction. Admit, then, that the distinction of origins must once have been actual. Admit also both the ascertainability and the relevancy of it to certain problems of that time—costs among them. Admit the existence of present knowledge adequate to making possible the present application of the distinction, for whatever significance it may have now. But even so, this original costlessness can not have lasted over into the present as bearing on the cost processes of the present. The admitted historical validity of the distinction, and even its significance *then* for cost purposes *then,* can establish nothing significant for the cost problems of the present—or securely for any other problem of the present. Would, for example, anything of importance be contributed to any present problem of cost, were a different setting of past fact to be proved—that, say, the existing stock of land goes back somehow for its origins to human devisings or strivings? What then? The present situation would be then no other than it now is.

To urge that a thing carries with it no cost now because it did not earlier impose a cost; or carries with it no cost now because it may at some later time impose a greater cost, or no cost at all— that it must be a cost twice in order to be a cost once—is merely to repudiate the reality and the significance of cost now. Certainly a "basement" explanation of exchange relations could make room for no distinctions of this sort.

There was then no land cost, either money or real? But obviously not, the land being taken to be both a natural and a non-scarce bounty. But what follows for things now? The freedom of the land then from either real or money costs helps nothing now; it is now scarce; it is in neither sense free. Its gift aspect does not hold now. Apply and see. There is scarcity *now;* of this the hires and the derivative prices are the proof. Facts of origin belong now with the snows of yester-year. Admit them; but it can be only as of the past tense. Their significance now is nil—being not now facts in the present tense. We are not talking of *man* over the ages, but only of men in a present situation and in a present process. For, after all, land is not now for any enterpriser a free good in any sense. And in so far as now it is actually non-producible, it is now neither free nor unfree in even the real-cost sense—any more than it is sentimental or pagan or vocal.

But with all of this Marshall is in essential agreement—with reference, at least, to what competitive capital includes as present fact in relation to present enterpriser policies of productive and gainful activity. He repudiates origins as the basis of setting land capital over against equipment capital. But he does on other grounds preserve the distinction.

It is, of course, obvious that this wide inclusion of *capital* imputed to Marshall does not deny that industrial goods are also capital. But often, nevertheless, the inclusion of the instrumental goods appears to exclude these others. In the following (p. 670), the thought is plainly industrially instrumental in emphasis: "If labour and capital increase at equal rates; and if, taking one thing with another, the law of production is that of constant return, there will be no change in the reward to be divided between a dose of capital and labour; . . . there need not therefore be any change in wages or interest." On the next page (p. 671), however, he says: "The influx of foreign capital, . . . becomes less in proportion to the population; wages are no longer paid largely with commodities borrowed from the old world. . . ." But in general "the chief demand for capital arises from its productiveness." The instrument aspect commonly absorbs attention also when the discussion is of capital and labor as bases of real costs. So he says (p. 670): "If however capital increases much faster than labour, the rate of interest is likely to fall; and then the rate of wages will probably rise at the expense of the share of a given quantum of capital."

We have no need for present purposes to examine the asserted relation of a fall in instrument rents to a fall in interest rates, but only to point out the danger in using this instrument concept of capital interchangeably with the funds concept. As Marshall himself says (p. 523) "we must be clear as to what things we are including, and what things we are excluding. It will seldom make very much difference to our argument [about the national dividend] whether we use all of the terms broadly, or all the terms narrowly. But it is essential that our usage should be consistent throughout any one argument. . . ." And yet on this same page the term *capital* is used once in the sense of *funds* and five times in the sense of *capital goods,* exclusive of land; sometimes in the sense of valued capital goods, the only sense in which a rate is possible; and sometimes as mere implementation, a sense in which only *rents* are possible. In the following (pp. 523, 524) the thought is that of capital goods employed in the technologically productive sense: "The labour and capital of the country, acting on its natural resources [non-capital items], produce annually a certain *net* aggregate of commodities, material and immaterial. . . ." and in the next paragraph "all production is followed by the consumption for which it was designed. . . ." It is this factor concept of capital, not the funds or the trade-capital concept, that articulates with the labor theory of value and with real costs; and this concept articulates only by implication—and then indirectly—with interest as a rate on money loans.

But what was the origin of the funds, the interest rates on which are expense-costs in production—even, one thinks, in the normal-value situation? What considerations of the mingled investment of capital funds and of care and effort determined the volume of labor and the particular lines of preparation; and thus (p. 577) brought about in the long run "such an adjustment of supply to demand, that both machines and human beings would earn generally an amount that corresponded fairly with their cost of rearing and training. . . ."? Borrowed funds—possibly from commercial banks—may, it is true, go into capital goods, but also into wages or land hires or land prices; or into advertising or merchandising; or into wars or war bonds; or even into interest or dividend payments; or into face powders, party gowns and fraternity pins; or into the endowment of theological seminaries; or into the maintenance of maiden aunts—with neither labor in the beginning or any contribution to the national dividend at the end.

Giving due weight, however, to Marshall's warning (p. 71, note) against "allowing ourselves to become the servants of words, avoiding the hard work that is required for discovering unity of substance underlying variety of form," it is still true that Marshall often appears to concur in the usual view (p. 138): "By capital is meant all stored-up provision for the production of material [external] goods, and for the attainment of those benefits *which are commonly reckoned as part of income.* It is the main stock of wealth regarded as an agent of production rather than as a direct source of gratification."

But, nevertheless, Marshall will later, and at length, stress as capital-investment outlays the expenses of parents in the rearing and training of offspring, along with the individual's own investment in the acquisition of skill. Two lines of burden will be presented as entering into the cost of production—real or money or mixed—of labor as one of the factors of production. The returns, however, will be regarded, not as interest, but as wages— and seemingly as the necessary indemnity to the offspring for the discomforts of the current putting forth of effort—two costs against a single money return—a return that is adequate for only one of them—with the confusion of wages with interest that inevitably attends the interpretation of parenthood in terms of pecuniary enterprise.

Marshall is not, however, fairly open to criticism as having arrived at circulating and fixed and trade and instrumental and social capitals as merely particular varieties of some inclusive what-is-it. Actually, as I hold, he does far more and better than this. He points definitely to unity in all this variety. As connotations of *capital* he recognizes *income, price-productivity in time, perspectiveness* or *futurity, provision, present-worthing* in price terms, the attendant *interest* phenomenon, individual *investment* and *acquisition,* and finally cites Adam Smith's definition of capital (p. 78) as *"that part of his stock from which he expects to derive an income"* —with only *stock* and *income* left hanging—a formulation to which Marshall accords his definite approval—urging, however, therewith, the recognition of two points of view, the individual and the social; and finally adopting the social; but (p. 78) "making the terms Capital and Income correlative from the social, as we did from the individual point of view."

Inasmuch, however, as the motivations that emerge in price offers, in volumes of products for sale, and in reservation prices, are all individual, the returns also all individual, and the purposes and the results those of private gain, it should, it seems, follow that for all competitive relations and processes the capital concept should run in the individual-competitive tenor—not that (p. 78) of counting "as . . . capital from the social point of view all things *other than land,* which yield income that is generally reckoned as such in common discourse. . . ." Marshall repudiates, (p. 789) even from the social point of view, the "tendency to confine capital . . . to auxiliary or instrumental capital . . . in order to keep clear the contrast between production and consumption . . . there appears no good reason why a thing should not be regarded in a twofold capacity."

Nor does he finally commit himself to the traditional view that capital consists of the stored-up products of labor—or of all wealth other than land—set aside for purposes of further production. Both land and capital must, nevertheless, in his view, be productive— but with this term *productive* not allocated exclusively either to the social or to the private-acquisitive connotation. In the main, indeed, this distinction makes no appeal to Marshall. And still he speaks (p. 138) of capital as meaning in common classification "all stored-up provision for the production of material [external] goods, and for the attainment of those benefits which are commonly reckoned as part of income. It is the main stock of wealth regarded as an agent of production rather than as a direct source of gratification"—elsewhere, however, we have seen, criticising Boehm-Bawerk for this same view.

Note on Marshall's Use of Definition

What, then, is *capital,* so that finally we may know, among other things, what is *land capital,* when functionally distinguished from other varieties of capital, and especially from equipment capital? What is the basis of the distinction? Land appears to comprise all those factor goods that are not equipment capital—land, those factor things that in the mechanical processes of producing saleable goods command hires that always are price-determined; equipment capital, those factor things the hires of which are sometimes price-determining.

The immediate interest, however, is not to debate this distinction between land capital and equipment capital further, nor even the definition of *capital* in the large, but only to stress the function of *definition* and especially the place in scientific discussion that Marshall accords to it, both in principle and in practice.

I feel not at all secure in the view of *capital* that I have attributed to Marshall. I think it, to be sure, the correct definition. But I am not sure that I have correctly reported the rent and quasi-rent issue as Marshall holds it. I have interpreted him as merely attempting to draw a functional distinction relative to the determination of prices. Citations enough could, however, be made from the *Principles* to support the view that land is a something that is entirely outside of that wide range of possessions that Marshall classifies as capital. I get confidently no further in this task of interpretation than that the distinction is to be drawn between those industrial factors of production the hires of which are always price-determined, as over against those that are sometimes price-determining. In my interpretation this distinction is not rightly reported as one between land and capital, but only between *land capital* and *equipment capital*. But I am aware that this was not the classical line of distinction, and that few students of Marshall would concur in my interpretation.

Such as it is, however, I make it. But my fundamental difficulty at this point is that I am unable securely to find out what, in Marshall's meaning, is this *capital* of which I understand *land* and *equipment* to be mere subclassifications. There can be no right objection to this presenting of many different varieties of this one thing—each with its particular designation of subhead—if only the thing to be subdivided is made clear. And this is to specify the characteristics, the differentia of inclusion and exclusion, that delimit this major classification. Only then can we know by what additional aspect of differentiation there arrives the particular subclassification—so that one of them may be Trade Capital, or Free Capital, or Fixed, or Circulating, or Land, or Equipment, and so on. By what title do these sub-groups hold their place in the major group? This is not merely to define *trade* or *free* or *fixed* or *material* or *internal* or *acquisitive* or *consumptive;* it is also to define *capital.* For many things are *free* or *fixed* or *internal* that are not also free capital or material capital or consumptive capital.

Nor it is enough to take *capital* to be what most people mean by *capital.* What then do they mean by it? It is, say, anything that returns *income.* But if also *income* is then to be defined only in terms of what is commonly meant by *income,* or of what is in the market place meant by it—well, then, what is meant? If it can be certain that all traders and all other people mean the same thing, it should be easy for Marshall to tell us what—in his view—is that one thing that they mean. Why leave us to find this out—to surmise what he thinks they think? But if the position is merely that they must and do think something, and that all think the same something—only that Marshall does not himself assume to say just what this something is—he has told us nothing about what he thinks by telling us that he thinks what they think. His definition is a counterfeit definition, if he does not know. But if he means that he does know, his purported definition amounts merely to the assurance that he could define if he would, but will not—that it is easier to let us do it; only that we must do it by arriving at our own interpretation of that one something that they all think, it being taken as given that they all think the same something.

Nor will it do to take the whole matter as obvious anyway—to assume the lucidity and the finality of popular usage—without the need, therefore, of inquiring what is meant or implied. Even for the economists themselves it has not always been easy to find out precisely their own meaning. In fact, Marshall has himself gone far in pointing out this or that misunderstanding or self-contradiction or blunder among them. And when occasionally he has permitted himself to take a definite position, he has—as I think—illustrated the common case—this last, however, as only one further item of evidence that there is no plain agreement anywhere, no obviousness in the situation, no safety in taking capital as self-defining, or as something going without saying in its own right, or to be relegated for definition to the easy and plain interpretation of what people in general or the people of the market place say or think or mean.

The issue is then not at all whether Marshall, in that to which he has committed himself, is right or wrong. In the main, in my own view, he has been right. But in the main—in the affirmative, rather than in the critical or negative, emphasis—he has not committed himself. But the student of Marshall is entitled to know—and not merely, as best he can, to infer—what Marshall means by the technical terms that he employs; and is entitled to expect that Marshall will abide consistently by the terms that he has defined in the meanings that he has ascribed to them. He has, in fact, stressed (p. 71, note) the warning against "the dangers that arise from . . . avoiding the hard work that is required for discovering unity of substance underlying variety of form." (See also pp. 129, 786.) But it is precisely this unity of substance that, with regard to *capital,* Marshall fails to report.

It is, no doubt, true, in view of the nature of the facts with which economics has to deal, the business and pecuniary aspects of commercial and industrial processes—its task the reduction of these to generalization and system—that there is a clear advantage in taking over—so far as it can be made systematically serviceable—the terminology in which business and industry have been generalizing their own activities, and in ascribing to these terms the meanings which can, both by limitation and extension, be made to carry the load of economic analysis and generalization. All of our human living is saturated with generalization—each particular fact recognized both as different from other facts in some aspects and alike in others. There are, for example, these likenesses and differences between *one* and *two*. All grouping is generalization. Language has to do with little else—all common nouns definitive of things; every verb denoting a grouping of activities; every preposition and every case-form a generalization of relations.

But the farmer's generalizations, adequate for his purposes, distinguishing fauna into stock and vermin, and flora into crops and weeds, may not fit the needs of the zoologist or botanist. The classifications of the engineer or the industrialist may be well, or even fundamental, for his purposes, and within the horizon of his interests and problems. What the merchandiser's language indicates that he thinks, may be excellent indicia of clear thinking—for his purposes. Much or little of lay terminology may fit the specialist's requirements, accordingly as, for his problems, it meets the test of "discovering unity of substance underlying variety of form." Something, no doubt, of the formulations of business men, and still more of business analysis—but most of all the methods and organization of business activities—what they think rather than what they say about it, and what they do rather than what descriptively they think about what they do—may be instructive, and occasionally directive, for the economist's thinking in the generalization of the phenomena bearing on the exchange relations of goods. But such is the economist's problem, as against the accountant's concern with divisible gains, and the business man's concern with his individual gains.

Wherever, then, *sheep* and *rats* and *snakes* are serviceable terms in biological science—wherever, that is, there is no good reason to the contrary—these terms may well be used. But still it may be unwise to adopt *fruit* and *vegetable*. Not always, surely, for the purposes of science, are these aspects of similarity and difference rightly reported by popular terms. *Biliousness* and *rheumatism* will not do for straight thinking with diagnosis and remedy.

In the main, then, the following (pp. 51-52) must command acceptance: "In common use almost every word has many shades of meaning, and therefore needs to be interpreted by the context . . . even the most formal writers on economic science are compelled to follow this course; for otherwise they would not have enough words at their disposal. . . ."

And still, the issue is not whether a word may not rightly bear many different meanings, but only whether a technical term must not select one of them. Nor is there question that this technical term may have sub-divisions of meaning, sub-groups within the major grouping; nor that often the context may make clear to what sub-group meaning the discussion is relevant; but only that the basis of the major grouping must be entirely clear and that the sub-groups must be not less clearly defined. If not, there appears to be no occasion for groupings of any sort.

There would, however, be little occasion for protest if Marshall went no further. But both in avowed principle and in actual practice he does go significantly further. Habitual carelessness in terms would be an awkward thing to charge, had not he himself announced it as a policy consciously and purposefully adopted—a policy, not merely defended, but recommended to economists as wisely to be accepted and followed. He is frankly impatient of any other. Courteously, as always, but quite frankly he makes clear his disrelish for the niceties and trivialities of all efforts at the precise definition of technical terms. Meanwhile he leaves *capital* undefined, the while outlining the difficulties connected with some of the sub-groupings of it. But in what purpose?

"... In physical sciences ... whenever it is seen that a group of things have a certain set of qualities in common, and will often be spoken of together, they are formed into a class with a special name; and as soon as a new notion emerges, a new technical term is invented to represent it. But economics cannot venture to follow this example. Its reasonings must be expressed in language that is intelligible to the general public. . . ." (p. 51)

Developing economic analysis ought, we infer, to abide by the terminology of Adam Smith. But Marshall has himself made over the meanings of many classical terms, diverging notably from the classical meaning of *capital*. So with *productive*. So with *profits on stocks*. He has substituted *utility* for *use value,* and has abounded in *utility* and *marginal utility*. Perhaps it would be unfair to urge that his position would require that modern economics should abide by the terminology of mercantilist or physiocratic thinking. It is the issue of new wine in old or in new bottles. In the interest of popular intelligibility as the chief test of terms, Marshall would shift the meanings of terms to the end of retaining the terms.

"Jevons . . . from a purely mathematical point of view, was justified in classing all commodities in the hands of consumers as capital. . . . A true sense of proportion requires us not to burden our work with the incessant enumeration of details of secondary importance, of which no account is taken in customary discourse, and which cannot even be described without offending against popular conventions." (pp. 77-78)

But it is still clear enough that his position does not preclude his telling, once he has adopted this term *capital,* precisely what he means by it—when, as he thinks (p. 51) the reasonings of economics are "expressed in language that is intelligible to the general public; it must . . . endeavor to conform itself to the familiar terms of everyday life. . . ." Only that, as we have seen, this leaves us to find out what these terms, that are "intelligible to the general public," mean to this general public— this not so ready a thing as to find out from Marshall directly what Marshall himself means by them. Does the general public agree as to the meaning? And, if so, to *what* does it agree?

And why not tell just this? But along with this lack of sufficient terms at the disposal of the economists by which they are compelled to use one word in many shades of meaning, Marshall adds: (p. 52) "But unfortunately they do not always avow that they are taking this freedom; sometimes perhaps they are scarcely even aware of the fact themselves. The bold and rigid definitions, with which their expositions of the science begin, lull the reader into a false security." But the possibility, or even the probability, of poor definitions does not argue that there be none, good or bad, but only that bad ones are bad. Moreover, both the basis and the place of definition seem here to be seriously misconceived.

These "bold and rigid definitions" with which these expositions of science *begin* may be defended for the purposes of authoritative and preceptorial exposition—but only so. They reverse the processes of right thinking. Even the beginner in a science would better get definitions only after he is in possession of something to be defined. Definition can organize for him only what he has occasion to organize. No definition therefore is rightly arbitrary. The meaning of any term must depend on the objective material which it must generalize and organize—the relations of similarity and of difference that the facts disclose in view of the problem in hand. A definition is not the point of setting out, but a compact summary of the conclusions reached. As formulated in the first emphasis, it can rightly never be more than a summary of propositions proved or to be proved—a group of theses. To assert that any question is merely one of definition, an arbitrary matter, is to assert that any view of the facts will fit them in their relations to one another. Any issue that is mere matter of definition is no issue at all—the field of inquiry an empty field.

". . . The use of technical terms at starting adds nothing to knowledge: but it puts familiar knowledge in a firm compact shape, ready to serve as the basis for further study." (p. 130)

But to do full justice to Marshall's view of definition, some further report is necessitated. For when the uses of the market place do not suit him, he evinces no extreme solicitude for conformity. And thus, finding the refinements of marginal-utility appropriate to the purposes of his later doctrinal requirements—but converting them, as I hold, to indefensible use—he says (p. 129): "For in this [the consumers' surplus analysis], as in other cases, the apparent simplicity of popular phrases veils a real complexity, and it is the duty of science to bring out that latent complexity; to face it; and to reduce it as far as possible: so that in later stages we may handle firmly difficulties that could not be grasped with a good grip by the vague thought and language of ordinary life."

The immediate purpose, however, we repeat, is not to debate the distinction between land capital and equipment capital, but only to stress the function of definition. Along, then, with other issues, definitions are declarative on issues of relevancy and irrelevancy—in view of the problem in hand. Among the endless possibilities of distinctions which ones are in point? Once again, therefore, it is to be urged that your definitions report conclusions to which, in view of your problem, your analysis of the materials and processes under examination has led you. They are your creed as deduced from your factual observation, from your thought experience and your intellectual experimentation. They are not declared in thunder from Mount Sinai, or imposed by papal encyclical, or by the resolutions of any Synod, or by any authority or any assumption anywhere. Nor are they agreed bases of procedure, like the axioms of the mathematicians—what must follow from this or that assumption. Thinking arrives at definitions. Definitions formulate thought issues. They stand or fall by the test of fitting and organizing the material and processes under examination.

What, then, for example, must *capital* mean if, by this test of fitting facts and processes of the present competitive-pecuniary society, it shall be appropriate to its task—shall formulate a generalization that organizes and clarifies the phenomena? To prove it to misreport the facts, or to confuse or mislead in their interpretation, is to discredit and repudiate it. By this test it stands or falls. Your conclusions are, therefore, in issue at whatever points your definition is in issue—its adequacy in reporting the processes and relations that are the subject matter of your study. Definitions are ways of formulating issues. That you have arrived at "bold and rigid definitions . . . a scanty vocabulary of fastened senses," means nothing worse than that you have arrived at definite conclusions—a specific position that you are willing to present unambiguously—offering plain issues; avoiding weasel words and uncommitting phrases; making clear the similarities and differences on which your thought proceeds. To be specific in definition, actually to *define,* is merely to come out into the open—making yourself accountable for something in particular. That the analyses summarized in the definition are difficult proves the necessity for them rather than providing the excuse for avoiding them. You are wrong? It may be. But such is the way of progress. Now go at it anew. That something has been arrived at—and definitely presented for discussion—affords the hope that there may be later something of the sort again.

My own experience, for example, in the studying of Marshall is not that his avoidance of bold, rigid, precise and unambiguous definitions has made easy my task of finding out precisely what he has meant to say, or has guarded me from perplexity and confusion in trying to interpret him. My chief difficulties have instead been in precisely the other emphasis— in the effort not to ascribe to him positions that he does not hold, that he has not intended, and would not defend—that presumably instead he would promptly repudiate. Secure interpretation I have taken to be my first task and my primary obligation. If in some respects I am still unclear—as I am—or am in error—as is practically certain—in no case is it through my fault of not trying. But interpretation should, I hold, have been my least difficult task—the doctrine itself, and not whether it is held, the sole topic of substantive importance. This book, I am aware, does not so read. Nor has it been so written.

But nothing in all this goes to say that there are not different kinds of capital—natural, artificial, circulating, fixed, material, fund, instrumental, good-will, socially serviceable, parasitic, predatory, criminal—but only that all of these predicates attaching to the substantive, *capital,* assume and assert their common possession of some one attribute or group of attributes by virtue of which each one of the groups can hold its place as a sub-group within a major capital classification. And this presents the necessity—or assumes the achievement—of discovering the attribute or attributes that, as attaching to the major classification, must be taken over by all of these subdivisions—those similarities and differences by virtue of which there can be either one major group or any sub-groups within it, and for the sub-groups their appropriate interpretative words or clauses.

What are with Marshall the marks of this inclusive thing *capital,* for distribution into fund, trade, instrumental, acquisitive, competitive and social, or into this or that other *variety* of *capital?* For it is merely a contented scientific defeatism, a disavowal of obligation, an abdication of function, to renounce thus much of boldness and of rigor. Never can there be any right objection to finding out precisely what you mean and to telling it precisely. If actually there is no one capital aspect common to all these different varieties of capital, it must follow that there can be no different varieties—no substantive to be modified and no interpretative clauses to modify it. And, moreover, if not yet do you know what you mean by that one thing for which the inclusive term stands, you can not know what sub-groups there are of it, or even that there are any. Or if still you believe that there must be such a one inclusive thing, not yet, however, knowing its attributes, but nevertheless, hoping that later you, or some one else, may discover them—then promptly say just that; you take no position; and therefore can offer no present issue—there being nothing either to subdivide or to discuss. But some day you, or that other, may arrive at a view bold and rigid enough to permit of formulation and of examination—if only meanwhile you have not successfully discredited and blocked the attempt.

The nearest approach in the *Principles* to a definition of capital—but a statement neither intended nor specifically adapted as a definition—I take to be the following on page 78 that "almost every use of the term capital, which is known to history, has corresponded more or less closely to a parallel use of the term Income: in almost every use, capital has been that part of a man's stock from which he expects to derive an income."

Setting this alongside of Marshall's other specific commitments, I take the interpretation earlier given of Marshall's position to be justified. So much as this, in any event, is clear: he disapproves of all internal capitals; he attributes capital standing to dwellings, touring cars and household furniture; to the pigs and chickens serving solely for household needs; to money and credits, franchises, patent rights and monopolies; to land fertility, either natural or investment-wise created; to all improvements on, or incorporated in, the land; to land itself, at least as competitively viewed; and, as I infer, to gambling and saloon equipment, slave brigs, and counterfeiting apparatus.

But he neglects to indicate his principle of inclusion or, possibly more accurately, his principle of distinction between land capital and equipment capital, as subdivisions of his major classification. He does not, that is to say, *define*—does not commit himself with reference to the trait or traits that, with some approach to precision, he must have in mind as essential to the notion of capital at large, and of the land subdivision of it. But he has them in mind? He should have, if he holds that people in general or the folk of the market place have them.

But could not all this be inferred from the positions taken by him on specific issues? Possibly so, only that—to me for example—his different specific positions seems to lead directly to a generalization that, as I suspect, he would promptly repudiate. Therefore I don't know what he takes to be ultimate in the notion of capital. I think he intends in general to recognize land capital. I am sure that he does it at times, for the purposes of those times. But I am still uncertain of his general position. If he does include land in capital he is making distinctions within his major classification—for example, between land capital and equipment capital—that, so far as I can make out, are contradictory to the principles on which the major classification must proceed.

Is it a classification consistent with the classical notion of capital? I judge not. But I greatly doubt that he would admit as much. Is it a classification correlative with *income?* It ought to be, as I hold, and in the sense that I interpret income, and as I judge—but am not sure—that Marshall interprets it; but not, I am confident, in the sense that the man in the street interprets it. And why am I left to surmise what the man in the street thinks about it in order to make out what Marshall presumably thinks about it? If Marshall both knows and ratifies, why not tell what it is that he knows and ratifies? Is it utility income that he has in mind by *income?* I so infer. And so inferring, I take Marshall to be in error. But thus, once again, I am at a loss as to his principle of generalization. What has fixity of stocks of spatial extension to do with any principle of inclusion or exclusion? I can't see. But if he can—what does he see? What, if anything, has natural bounty to do with it? And if it has something, why include fertility in capital and exclude spatial extension? Does he, in fact, make any distinction turning on spatial extension? And if so, why should he—by the test of whatever his ultimate principle may be? Is his distinction one of function in the industrial process? I think not—not, that is, under what I surmise to be his principle. But I am certain that the classical view made the distinction; made it between land and capital, and not between land capital and equipment capital; made it a distinction of origins; made it an industrial-factor distinction; and made it a functional distinction—one of result as against cause. And I am convinced that most followers of Marshall interpret him as abiding by the classical, land-capital distinction in the classical sense and significance of it; and that they themselves make it in the same sense and significance. Has, with Marshall, the division of outlay costs, at the margin of land use, into cause and result functions, any relevancy to this issue of classification? He repeatedly so asserts or implies. But, if such is his position, I take it to be error—error by what I hold to be the ultimate principle recognized by him, and that logically he has committed himself to recognize.

If any of these distinctions are functional, are they held also to be distinctions of degree? It is plain to me that they cannot be both; but I note Marshall's repeated statements to the other effect. Taking *competitive capital* and *social capital* to be sub-groups within the major capital classification, what, in point of principle, can be the differentia, in view of the make-up of the major and inclusive group? How, in the social-functional aspect, is land capital distinguishable from equipment capital—unless, indeed, an entirely new basis of grouping and sub-grouping be intended?

How do real costs come to be relevant, not to competitive classifications in general—for this they may be—but to this particular one? Why is it that (p. 82 note) "Capital needs to be considered in regard *both* to the embodied aggregate of the benefits derivable from its use, *and* to the embodied aggregate of the costs of the efforts and of the saving needed for its production . . . it will be shown how these two aggregates tend to balance"? Aside from the impossibility and the irrelevancy of attempting to aggregate *benefits,* I take the entire doctrine as announced to be error. But is this an unfealty—I take it to be such—to Marshall's ultimate principle in the capital classification? Or does it argue for some principle of classification that remains still hidden? And what is that principle?

This protest against Marshall's principle and practice with regard to definition is therefore two-fold in emphasis: a) that in practice he avoids definite and clean-cut commitments; and b) that not only does he defend this practice, but that he disparages efforts in the other direction. Precision in terms makes no great appeal to him. If, in the light of the topic under consideration, the run of the discussion and of the context, you do not understand him, you might easily have been worse off, if he had told you more. Definitions are misleading when they are wrong, and, he infers, not much better when they are right. In particular discussions, it is true, he does not deprecate controversy—if it is not too much trouble:

"When we speak of the national dividend . . . as divided into the shares of land, labour and capital, we must be clear as to what things we are including, and what things we are excluding. It will seldom make very much difference to our argument whether we use all the terms broadly, or all the terms narrowly. But it is essential that our usage should be consistent throughout any one argument. . . ." (p. 523)

Manifestly, however, it does very much matter whether in the distributive problem *capital,* is to mean merely equipment goods, a factor concept, or is to include funds, circulating capital, advertising outlays, patents, franchises and monopolies. The analysis, significant on the first assumption, is worthless on the other. Mainly in these problems, capital means for Marshall that very industrial notion that he has repeatedly discredited.

He deprecates, then (p. 52), the *false security* into which "bold and rigid definitions . . . lull the reader."

". . . If he [the economist] arbitrarily assigns a rigid exact use to a word which has several more or less vague uses in the market place, he confuses business men, and he is in some danger of committing himself to untenable positions. . . ." (pp. 81-82)

But none the less urgently does he occasionally require the acceptance of these terms for certain discussions:

". . . economics . . . must therefore endeavour to conform itself to the familiar terms of everyday life, and so far as possible must use them as they are commonly used." (p. 51)

". . . The real difficulty of our task . . . being the result of the need under which economics, alone among sciences, lies of making shift with a few terms in common use to express a great number of subtle distinctions." (p. 50)

". . . most of the chief distinctions marked by economic terms are differences not of kind but of degree. . . . We shall meet with many instances of the evil that may be done by attempting to draw broad, hard and fast lines of division, and to formulate definite propositions with regard to differences between things which nature has not separated by any such lines." (p. 52)

". . . as to the exact places in which some at least of the lines of definition should be drawn . . . questions at issue must in general be solved by judgments as to the practical convenience . . . there must remain a margin of debatable ground. But there is no such margin in the analysis itself: if two people differ with regard to that, they cannot both he right. . . ." (p. 53)

". . . For in this, as in other cases, the apparent simplicity of popular phrases veils a real complexity . . . it is the duty of science to bring out that latent complexity; to face it; and to reduce it as far as possible: so that in later stages we may handle firmly difficulties that could not be grasped with a good grip by the vague thought and language of ordinary life." (p. 129)

From these passages we return to what appears to be Marshall's summing-up of his position, in the following, quoted, it seems, with complete approval, from Bagehot:

"' . . . as in Political Economy we have more difficult things to speak of than in ordinary conversation, we must take more care, give more warning of any change; and at times write out "the interpretation clause." . . . I know that this is difficult and delicate work; and all that I have to say in defence of it is that in practice it is safer than the competing plan of inflexible definitions. Any one who tries to express various meanings on complex things with a scanty vocabulary of fastened senses, will find . . . that after all he does not come out right, for he is half the time falling back into the senses which fit the case in hand best . . . almost always different from his "hard and fast" sense. In such discussions we should learn to vary our definitions as we want, just as we say "let x, y, z, mean" now this, and now that, in different problems; and this, though they do not always avow it, is really the practice of the clearest and most effective writers.' . . ." And Marshall notes, with similar approval, that "Cairnes also . . . combats 'the assumption that the attribute on which a definition turns ought to be one which does not admit of degrees'; and argues that 'to admit of degrees is the character of all natural facts.' " (p. 52, note)

And I continue to urge the ideal of *no two terms for one thing and no two things for one term*. And I am still denying that any distinctions of subject matter for purposes of the functional antithesis of cause with result can ever defensibly be made a matter of degree—for example, specifically, the attempt to distinguish by degree of duration, price-determining from price-determined hires of factors of production.

Inevitably in later pages this problem of the principle and logic of definition will require some further attention. For the present, however, I am content to shift the issue to the test of practical applications. In earlier pages some examination was made of Marshall's confusions of *utility* with *value;* of *marginal utility* with *price offer;* his occasional notion of *real* value as an exchange relation satisfactory to the trader (p. 137); and of *real* value as connotive of *real* costs. (p. 632), or of merit (p. 205)—not all of these matters of serious import. In earlier pages also, there were noted his shifting meanings of *demand,* and especially of *supply*—matters of far more importance. Shortly we shall have also occasion to stress the perplexities attending his recognition, for purposes of definition, of only two uses of *cost,* money (or expense) and real; with clear definitions of both, but the entire absence of definition of just *cost*—his third and ordinary use of *cost*—an omission that will later take on no small significance. But in this same discussion Marshall says of Mill (p. 339, note): "Mill and some other economists have followed the practice of ordinary life [as Marshall commonly advises] in using the term Cost of production in two senses, sometimes to signify the difficulty of producing a thing, and sometimes to express the outlay of money that has to be incurred in order to induce people to overcome this difficulty and produce it. But by passing from one use of the term to the other without giving explicit warning, they have led to many misunderstandings and much barren controversy. . . ."

Immediately and specifically in point, however, is Marshall's employment of the term *capital*. The notion is, as we have seen, one of wide inclusion. Equipment capital, the capital to which his quasi-rent hires are appropriate, is clearly one of the subdivisions. To land capital he imputes a coordinate standing.

Chapter VIII

THE TESTS OF LAND CAPITAL

THE IMPORTANCE attached in classical thought to the labor-free origin of land—a bounty of nature or a gift of Providence—has already been noted. Mainly the classical analysis concerned itself with agricultural production or with production easily assimilated to the agricultural type. So Marshall argues (p. 805) that "in problems in which the tendency to increasing return is in effective force, there is no clearly defined marginal product." If the exchange ratios of products were to be explained by their relative incorporation of human effort, or of wages paid for human effort, capital had to be regarded as stored-up labor or stored-up wages. Interest was accounted for as indirect wages. Prices were then declared to be proportional with the direct and the indirect labor or wages applied in the production of commodities.

It need not matter for present purposes how, in classical thought, employer wage outlays were made out to be proportional with employee effort costs. Nor need at present the relation of the employer's interest outlays to the waiting costs of the lending or operating capitalist be examined. But in view of the different wheat returns—or of the different wheat-price returns—afforded, per unit of expense or of real costs, by different lands, all free in origin, it would seem to be untrue that the exchange relation of one bushel of wheat with another, or of wheat with other commodities, could be proportional with the respective real or money costs. This difficulty was met in classical thought by recourse to the margin of cultivation of land. Marginal wheat production was assumed to take place on the margin of land cultivation. No rent being paid for any use of the land that, as marginal, was worth nothing, prices came to be presented as fixed by the labor and capital charges on marginal land, or, equally well, by these charges at the intensive margin of cultivation. Rent emerged, therefore, as the result of the prices that wage and interest costs had fixed. The hires of the land factor of production, as the one factor labor-free in origin, were held to have no part in the costs of production of the price-determining units of product—those units, namely, that were produced at the price-determining margin of cultivation. And it is to be noted that this view conceived capital in the factor sense of instrumental goods.

Thus was the labor theory of value supported. This theory imposed, obviously, the distinction between land and capital, or between the land-capital factor and the other factors of production. It invoked a functional distinction between their hires. And by the necessities of its logic, the systematic bearing of this distinction, it invoked obviously the labor-free origin of land as the fact differentiating the land factor in production from the cost-acquired factors. And thus it follows that to abandon origins as the distinguishing aspect of land is, in essentials, to repudiate the central and characteristic position of classical theory.

Marshall, however, as the professed advocate of the real-cost account of prices, could quite certainly not agree that this doctrinal position must stand or fall with the acceptance of the distinction of origins and with the maintenance of it. Marshall rests the distinction instead on another test, which distinction he presents as similarly functional. To me, neither the distinction as drawn in classical thought, nor that as Marshall draws it, can serve as a functional distinction, and thereby as a justification for the antithesis between cause and result. But whatever may be the truth in this regard, it still appears to be true that only this distinction of origins can afford even a semblance of defense for the labor account of prices.

In any case, Marshall does abandon this distinction of origins. The fertility aspects of land he ranks with capital. There may not, after all, be much of this original fertility left. But little or much, that amount suffices for the refutation of the classical doctrine. It was much in the time of the classical writers. Pretty certainly it is much still; only that, affirmatively or negatively, neither inspection nor historical learning is competent to tell just how much, or even to make any secure approximation to telling. And even were any one ever to want to find out, it is quite incredible that any one should ever succeed.

Marshall recognizes this impossibility. The distinction, to be sure, is still valid in the general. If only we knew enough, and cared to, we might not only draw it, but make the application of it to particulars. We simply do not know enough. The situation parallels that with the Visible and the Invisible Church. This invisible Band of the Saved is a non-communicant membership, unconscious of its beatitude. As such, however, it lacks nothing in actuality, but only, for all of us mortals, in discernibility—its sole lack of actuality, the lack of actuality in application.

No matter, then, how great for the classical system of doctrine may have been the need for this distinction of origins—a need which, it must be admitted, Marshall does not recognize—he finds the making of it not only factually impossible but theoretically indefensible. Whatever may have been in particular cases the origins of fertility, always it functions similarly with the cost-achieved improvements in or on the land. Like them fertility is liable to wear and to wear-out. It requires upkeep on terms of the absorption of free capital. Also it can be bought; as commonly also if anyone needs land, it is only by money outlay for it that he can get it. You have to put your own capital funds into it. It may have been free once. It is no longer free, if it is worth the having. Cost-acquired things can be substituted for it, can be put into it or taken out of it. In the main, for that matter, this possibility of substitution applies to all aspects of land, even the positional.

But we have to note again that while the cost-free origin of land, its existence as a gift of nature or a bounty of Providence, was a pivotal assumption in classical theory, it was not thereby the sole necessary assumption. To get doctrinally ahead with it in its systematic significance, the marginal isolation of price-determining costs was a necessary supplement. This marginal-isolation method Marshall employs systematically in both his cost and his distributive analyses, but not as solely applicable to land. It is therefore not the trait presented by him as differentiating land from the other factors of production. And note again that *capital* in all these discussions is capital conceived mechanically and industrially, a factor in typically factory processes.

But first Marshall's position on this origins test must be placed entirely beyond question:

... the greater part of the soil in old countries owes much of its character to human action; all that lies just below the surface has in it a large element of capital, the produce of man's past labour ... the "inherent" and "indestructible" properties of the soil, have been largely modified; partly impoverished and partly enriched by the work of many generations of men. (p. 147)

But the question how far the fertility of any soil is due to the original properties given to it by nature, and how far to the changes in it made by man, cannot be fully discussed without taking account of the kind of produce raised from it. ... At one end of the scale are forest trees; ... the grass on some rich river bottoms ... much of the richest farm land in England ... would give to unaided nature almost as great a return as is got from it now. Next comes land which, though not quite so rich, is still kept in permanent pasture; and after this comes arable land on which man does not trust to nature's sowing, but prepares for each crop a seed bed. ... Lastly ... are the choicer kinds of fruits, flowers and vegetables, and of animals, particularly those which are used for improving their own breeds ... many of the choicest products could not hold their own at all without his [man's] care.
Thus various then are the parts which man plays in aiding nature. ... (p. 148)

Chemically the soil must have the inorganic elements that the plant wants in a form palatable to it; and in some cases man can make a great change with but little labour. For he can then turn a barren into a very fertile soil by adding a small quantity of just those things that are needed; ... and he is now calling in the aid of bacteria to help him in this work.
... He can by sufficient labour make almost any land bear large crops. ... He can even permanently alter the nature of the soil by draining it, or by mixing with it other soil. ... (p. 146)

But further, the order of fertility of different soils is liable to be changed by changes in the methods of cultivation and in the relative value of different crops . . . some of them [clay soils] have a higher value, and are really more fertile, than much of the land that used to be carefully cultivated while they were left in a state of nature. (p. 161)

And, further, fertility is also a question of population, markets, roads, available stocks of machinery and fertilizers, and the prices of them:

We cannot then call one piece of land more fertile than another . . . till we know whether the demand for produce is such as to make intensive cultivation profitable with the resources at their disposal. . . . The term fertility has no meaning except with reference to the special circumstances of a particular time and place. (pp. 160-61)

. . . .

. . . But in fact every farmer is aided by the presence of neighbours whether agriculturists or townspeople . . . they gradually supply him with good roads, and other means of communication: they give him a market in which he can buy . . . what he wants, . . . and all the various requisites for his farm work: they surround him with knowledge: . . . All his produce is worth more. . . .
. . . an increase of population tends to develop the organization of trade and industry; and therefore the law of diminishing return does not apply to the total capital and labour . . . as sharply as to that on a single farm. . . . (pp. 165-66)

Always, in fact, as with *productivity* in general and with individual *skill, fertility* in a competitive society is a price fact within a general price setting:

. . . a mere increase in the demand for produce may invert the order in which two adjacent pieces of land rank as regards fertility. . . . (p. 157; see also pp. 160-61 above)

As there is no absolute standard for fertility, so there is none of good cultivation. The best cultivation in the richest parts of the Channel Islands, for instance, involves a lavish expenditure of capital and labour on each acre: for they are near good markets. . . . If left to nature the land would not be very fertile, for though it has many virtues, it has two weak links (being deficient in phosphoric acid and potash). . . . (p. 163)
. . . the growth of population and wealth will make the poorer soils gain on the richer. . . . (p. 162)

This surplus depends on, firstly, the richness of the land, and secondly, the relative values of those things which he [the cultivator] . . . needs to buy. The richness or fertility of the land, we have seen, . . . varies with the nature of the crops raised, and with the methods and intensity of cultivation. . . . Further, the prices at which the various requisites of the farm can be bought, and its various products sold, depend on the industrial environment. . . . (p. 631)

In fact, fertility is commonly a supplementary-cost good. Its hires fall into the quasi-rent classification; and therefore, in its appropriate time, a fertility hire is a price-determining cost:

. . . But in short periods, . . . no such direct influence on supply price is exercised by the necessity that such improvements should in the long run yield net incomes sufficient to give normal profits on their cost. And therefore when we are dealing with such periods, these incomes may be regarded as quasi-rents which depend on the price of the produce. (p. 426)

. . . In any inquiry then as to the causes that will determine the prices of corn during a short period, that fertility which the soil derives from slowly made improvements has to be taken for granted as it then is, almost in the same way as if it had been made by nature. Thus, the income derived from these permanent improvements gives a surplus above the *prime* or *special* costs needed for raising extra produce. . . . (p. 425)

. . . at any given time he [the farmer] takes for granted all that richness of the soil which results from permanent improvements; and the income (or quasi-rent) derived . . . together with that due to the original qualities of the soil, constitutes his producer's surplus or rent. . . . (p. 630)

And, in fact, the entire distinction is a matter of degree anyway, but still taken to be functionally significant:

. . . Pure rent in the strict sense of the term is scarcely ever met with . . . there is an element of true rent in the composite product that is commonly called wages, an element of true earnings in what is commonly called rent and so on. . . . (p. 421)

Of course there is no hard and sharp line of division between "long" and "short" periods. Nature has drawn no such lines in the economic conditions of actual life; and in dealing with practical problems they are not wanted . . . (p. 378) — [excepting that, at some point a kaleideoscopic reversal of the function of these hires, from a price-determined to a price-determining bearing on products needs to be made].

. . . All appliances of production, whether machinery, or factories *with the land on which they are built,* or farms, are alike in yielding large surpluses over the prime costs of particular acts of production to a man who owns and works them: also in yielding him normally no special surplus in the long run . . . (no special surplus, as contrasted with his general worker's and waiter's surplus). But . . . from a social point of view land yields a permanent surplus, while perishable things made by man do not. . . . The difference . . . is however mainly one of degree: and a great part of the interest of the study of the rent of land arises from the illustrations which it affords of a great principle that permeates every part of economics. (p. 832)

. . . as regards short periods . . . producers have to adjust their supply to the demand as best they can with the appliances already at their disposal . . . there is not time materially to increase those appliances if the supply of them is deficient . . . if the supply is excessive, some of them must remain imperfectly employed. . . . The income is a surplus of total receipts over prime cost; (that is, it has something of the nature of a rent . . .). . . . (pp. 376-77)

In truth, even labor hires contain these quasi-rent elements—functional differences in wage outlays relative to price-determination:

That part of a man's income which he owes to the possession of extraordinary natural abilities is a free boon to him; and from an abstract point of view bears some resemblance to the rent of other free gifts of nature, such as the inherent properties of land. . . . (p. 664; see also p. 623)

But, as we shall later recurrently see, it is characteristic of Marshall's discussions in this connection that, having abandoned in one place a particular basis of distinction, he elsewhere either specifically or by implication sets it up:

. . . separate reasonings are required for those parts of its [land's] value which are, and those which are not, due to efforts of man invested in the land for the purposes of production; . . . the results of these reasonings must be combined in dealing with any particular case of that income which commonly goes by the name "rent," but not all of which is rent in the narrower sense of the term. The manner in which the reasonings are to be combined depends on the nature of the problem. . . . (p. 422)[1]

[1] ". . . Senior seemed almost on the point of perceiving that the key of the difficulty was held by the element of time [that is, long versus short periods]: but here as elsewhere he contented himself with suggestions; he did not work them out.

Nor does the applicability of the marginal-isolation device distinguish land capital from other capital:

... land is but a particular form of capital from the point of view of the individual producer. The question whether a farmer has carried his cultivation of a particular piece of land as far as he profitably can; and whether he should try to force more from it, or to take in another piece of land; is of the same kind as the question whether he should buy a new plough, or try to get a little more work out of his present stock of ploughs, using

He says (*Political Economy*, p. 129), 'for all useful purposes the distinction of profits from rent ceases as soon as the capital from which a given revenue arises has become, whether by gift or by inheritance, the property of a person to whose abstinence and exertions it did not owe its creation.' " (p. 432, note)

Senior, however, said a good bit more than this—all of it relevant to the issue. (See *ibid.*, pp. 112-14 passim, and p. 128) After noting that in the form of freight, warehousing, dock charges, coal and iron values in the mine, and timber values on the stump, practically all items of wealth contain elements that in point of origin are gifts of nature, he finds further difficulties with especial reference to land:

"We may be asked, then, whether the improvements which form the greater part of the value of the soil of every well-cultivated district are all, and forever, to be termed capital; whether the payments received from his tenants by the present owner of a Lincolnshire estate, reclaimed by the Romans from the sea, are to be termed not rent, but profit on the capital which was expended fifteen centuries ago. The answer is, that for all useful purposes the distinction of profit from rent ceases as soon as the capital, from which a given revenue arises, has become . . . the property of a person to whose abstinence and exertions it did not owe its creation. The revenue arising from a dock, or a wharf, or a canal, is profit in the hands of the *original constructor* [investor?]. It is the reward of *his* abstinence in having employed capital for the purposes of production instead of those of enjoyment. But in the hands of his heir it has all the attributes of rent. It is to him the gift of fortune, not the result of a sacrifice. It may be said, indeed, that such a revenue is the reward for the owner's abstinence in not selling the dock or the canal and spending its price in enjoyment. But the same remark applies to every species of transferable property. Every estate may be sold, and the purchase money wasted. If the last basis of classification were adopted, the greater part of what every Political Economist has termed rent must be called profit." (*Ibid.*, p. 129)

But it is obviously unclear whether, had Senior arrived at any new and specific conclusions as to the solution of the question that was perplexing him, it would have been by merging all these properties into the land classification with derivative incomes of rent, or all into capital, with derivative incomes of interest. He got, in truth, not much further than Marshall reports as characteristic of him. He dropped the whole line of thought, making no modification in his allegiance to the general Ricardian view of rent and interest in relation to price. His *Political Economy* was left in such final form as to report Senior as a consistently classical economist, alternating between the labor and the wage theories of value, without any very distinct choice between them, but, on the whole, proceeding in the real rather than in the money cost emphasis. But since the Eighth Edition of Marshall's *Principles of Economics* was published, full information as to the later develop-them sometimes when the soil is not in a very favourable condition, and feeding his horses a little more lavishly. He weighs the net product of a little more land against the other uses to which he could put the capital sum that he would have to expend in order to obtain it; and in like manner he weighs the net product, to be got by working his ploughs under unfavorable circumstances, against that got by increasing his stock of ploughs, and thus working under more favorable conditions. That part of his produce which he is in doubt whether to raise by extra use of his existing ploughs, or by introducing a new plough, may be said to be derived from a marginal use of the plough. It pays nothing *net* . . . toward the net income earned by the plough.

So again a manufacturer or trader, owning both land and buildings, regards the two as bearing similar relations to his business . . . at last he will doubt whether the overcrowding of his workshops or his store-

---

ment of Senior's thought on this issue has become accessible in the volume of Senior's writings entitled *Industrial Efficiency and Social Economy,* edited by S. Leon Levy, New York, 1928. (Vol. I)

"When applied to material objects the word capital includes all instruments used for the production of wealth, from the London docks down to the pillow and bones of the lace-maker; . . . the timber of the shipbuilder and the rough diamonds of the jeweller; . . . the money which a man of business keeps in his own custody or in that of his banker for the purpose of carrying on his trade. If instead of . . . money wages he pays them partly in kind, it includes any store of provisions or clothes which he keeps for that purpose . . . the book debts owing to him from his customers. . . . All these are things enabling an income to be earned. . . . So is a landed estate let to a tenant. . . . Suppose him now to inhabit one of his own houses instead of letting it; it would sound absurd to say that the house, on his inhabiting it, ceased to form part of his capital. . . . However . . . the furniture in a man's house is not considered part of his capital, though it saves him the expense of hiring furniture . . . [but] is capital to a broker who has bought it to make a profit on its resale. (*Ibid.,* pp. 159-60) Land cannot be conveniently excluded from the term capital. (*Ibid.,* p. 170) The same ship may be used alternately as a merchant vessel and a gentleman's yacht. While used in the former mode it is capital; while used in the latter it is not. . . . I include under capital land and all, other brute and inanimate agents which are capable of appropriation." (*Ibid.,* p. 178)

But obviously Senior's main difficulty with the question is in his assumption that the distinction between land and capital is one of origins—a distinction that finally comes to appeal to him as entirely impossible of application, and as useless for any analytical purpose of the economist. That also, though not quite so clearly, appears to be Marshall's final position. And it will, I think, become increasingly clear that Marshall's ultimate defense of the distinction is that of fixedness of stock; even though he is quite definite in his reproof of Professor Fetter for so interpreting him. But we shall see. Moreover, Marshall's distinction is merely a distinction between land capital and equipment capital. In any event, Senior's final renunciation of the test of origins fails of being precisely in point. We need not now concern ourselves with his test of use, this being a line of distinction that Marshall does not stress—and appears not to hold. And clearly enough, Senior is not thoroughly content with it; but, after all, accepts it.

rooms is not so great a source of trouble, that it would answer his purpose to obtain more space. And when he comes to decide whether to obtain that space by taking in an extra piece of land or by building his factory a floor higher, he weighs the net income to be derived from further investments in the one against that to be derived from the other. That part of his production which he just forces out of his existing appliances . . . does not contribute to the net income which those appliances yield him. This argument says nothing as to whether the appliances were made by man, or part of a stock given by nature; it applies to rents and quasi-rents alike. (pp. 430-31)

It is true that in the paragraph next following Marshall goes on to indicate a distinction based on the fixity of land stocks—their unresponsiveness in volume to investment policies—an unresponsiveness that is spatial merely. This line of distinction will shortly claim our attention. But at present the purpose is merely to make clear that the analytical method of marginal isolation is clearly admitted by Marshall not to be a basis of distinction between land capital and equipment goods or improvements on land. There is a wide field for the application of the principle of substitution; land in this aspect is like all the other factors:

. . . the various agents of production . . . are often rivals for employment; any one that is more efficient that another in proportion to its cost tending to be substituted for it, . . . And on the other hand they all constitute the field of employment for each other. . . . (p. 665)

By erecting this floor, instead of spreading the building over more ground, a saving in the cost of land is effected, which just compensates for the extra expense and inconvenience of the plan. . . .

. . . Let him find that the difference between the two plans . . . shows an advantage . . . in favour of the larger area; . . . He might have reached this result by calculating the increased value of the business that could be done with the same outlay in other respects on the larger site as compared with the smaller, or again by building on less expensive ground instead of in a less favourable situation. But, by whatever route he makes his calculation, its character is similar to that by which he decides whether it is worth his while to buy business plant of any kind: and he regards the net income . . . which he expects to get from either investment as standing in the same general relation to his business. . . . (pp. 448-49)

. . . the sum of the prices which he pays for those factors which he uses is, as a rule, less than the sum of the prices which he would have to pay for any other set of factors which could be substituted for them: for, whenever it appears that this is not the case, he will, as a rule, set to work to substitute the less expensive arrangement or process.

·   ·   ·   ·   ·   ·   ·   ·   ·   ·

Thus there are some kinds of field work for which horse-power is clearly more suitable than steam-power, and *vice versa*. . . .

Similarly, if there are two methods of obtaining the same result, one by skilled and the other by unskilled labour, that one will be adopted which is the more efficient in proportion to its cost. . . .

Again, there will be a rivalry between hand-power and machine-power. . . .

. . . He [every business man] endeavours to employ each agent up to that margin at which its net product would no longer exceed the price he would have to pay for it.[2] . . . (pp. 404-6)

It is moreover clear—as occasionally it is to Marshall clear—that items of product that are supra-marginally produced on land do not thereby differ in cost from the marginal item. Rent comes to be paid because of the lower non-rent costs attaching to the supra-marginal production. The costs are merely differently made up: lower labor, machine, and fertilizer charges, and correspondingly higher rent charges. Were these rent costs excluded, the tenant would so far be absorbing the rental revenues attaching to the supra-marginal productive powers of the land—his payment of rent imposed by this fact. So Marshall says (p. 543) that "there is nothing to make the relations between capital in general and labour in general differ widely from those between any other two

---

[2] The distinction between land and capital is in its clearest definition and at its minimum of complication presented with urban lands, where promptly all wage, fertilizer, machine and rent outlays for crop purposes cease from troubling. In this geographical or superficies aspect, to be sure, urban land is a fixed fact. But the accessibility of it, its positional advantage for price purposes, is not thus fixed. And on the land itself there are devices that substitute themselves for surface room. To declare these capital, despite the evident fact that they substitute for land, to rule them out by definition, is merely to paralyze or veto the discussion. In any case, there is no more difficulty in buying or renting all the urban land you want, despite its fixity in aggregate volume, than in hiring all the men you want, despite the fact that with men in the aggregate there are only as many as there are. Moreover, most of the high-rent urban lands are lands on which the priced positional advantages either take the place of merchandisers' advertising costs or are themselves these advertising costs. Shop rents are typical merchandising expenses. And not merely are there substitutes available for the positional advantages that put you nearer to customers—instead of your going to them you may get them to come to you—but also alternative openings for gain-getting are commonly presented by urban land.

agents of production, in the general scheme of distribution already explained"—*capital in general* meaning here, obviously, not free capital but equipment goods.

Marshall asserts, indeed, the equality in the costs of supra-marginal and marginal products:

In a rigidly stationary state in which supply could be perfectly adjusted to demand in every particular, the normal expenses of production, the marginal expenses, and the average expenses (rent being counted in) would be one and the same thing, for long periods and for short. . . . (p. 497)

The aggregate expenses of production might then [in a stationary state] be found either by multiplying these marginal expenses by the number of units of the commodity; or by adding together all the actual expenses of production of its several parts, and adding in all the rents earned by differential advantages for production. The aggregate expenses of production being determined by either of these routes, the average expenses could be deduced by dividing out by the amount of the commodity. . . . (p. 810)

. . . That part of the produce which goes as rent is of course thrown on the market, and acts on prices, in just the same way as any other part. . . . (p. 427)

In connection with his famous meteoric stones *equally hard and imperishable,* Marshall says:

. . . the price of the services rendered by the stones . . . the aggregate surplus or rent . . . could have been reckoned as the differential excess of the aggregate value of the net services of the stones over that which would have been reached if all their uses had been as unproductive as their marginal uses. And exactly the same would be true if the stones were in the hands of different producers, impelled by competition with one another to work each stone up to the margin at which its further use ceased to be profitable. (p. 423)

But the negative position is taken in the following—as is, indeed, implicit in the marginal-isolation analysis, and in the inferred determination of the prices of the supra-marginal items of product by the cost of the marginal items:

When different producers have different advantages for producing a thing its price must be sufficient to cover the expenses of production of those producers who have no special and exceptional facilities; . . . When the market is in equilibrium, and the thing is being sold at a price which covers these expenses, there remains a surplus beyond their expenses for those who have the assistance of any exceptional advantages . . . if the owner of a free gift of nature lends it out to another, he can generally get for its use a money income equivalent to this surplus. (p. 499)

This equivalent money income the tenant, of course, pays as part of his aggregate cost of his aggregate product. And note that now the gift-in-origin aspect of land comes back in as a doctrinally distinguishing fact.

. . . that part of the income derived from the land which the landlord obtains, is governed, for all periods of moderate length, mainly by the market for the produce, with but little reference to the cost of providing the various agents employed in raising it; and it therefore is of the nature of a rent. . . .
. . . the line of division between the tenant's and the landlord's share coincides with the deepest and the most important line of cleavage in economic theory.[3] . . . (p. 636)

Distributive Aspects of Marginal Isolation

Marshall's use of the marginal-isolation device as key to the distributive problem involves the same analysis as that applied to the rent-cost problem. Moreover, the present is our best opportunity for an examination of Marshall's distribution doctrine in the large.

[3] John Stuart Mill, it will be recalled, in most of his analyses, accepted in full assurance the Ricardian distinction between land and capital, interpreting rent, therefore, as a result of the price that wage and interest costs have caused. But, strangely enough, he argued in support of this view—not in refutation of it—that costs of production are neither the greater nor the less on supra-marginal than on marginal land, but are instead, so far as land is concerned, equal; the better lands neither dearer nor cheaper at their higher rents than the poorer lands at their lower rents; the more rent paid, the more land service, and the correspondingly larger price product:
"It is true that all tenant farmers and many other classes of producers, pay rent. But . . . whoever cultivates land, paying a rent for it, gets in return for his rent an instrument of superior power to other instruments of the same kind for which no rent is paid. The superiority of the instrument is in exact proportion to the rent paid for it. . . . The real expenses of production are those incurred on the worst land. . . . Whoever does pay rent gets back its full value in extra advantages, and the rent which he pays does not place him in a worse position than, but only in the same position as, his fellow producer who pays no rent, but whose instrument is one of inferior efficiency." (*Principles of Political Economy*, Book II, Chap. xvi, Sec. 6)
It hardly needs be suggested that the logic of this argument abandons the determination of price at the land margin, either extensive or intensive, asserting instead equal costs of production on all lands and for all units of product.

In the main it continues to be a mechanical-factor analysis, though not rarely it is offered as explanation of the rate of interest on free capital, in entire neglect of the fact that free capital goes indifferently into outlays for land or its rent, into organization, advertising, wage rolls, taxes, royalties, and the like, as well as into machinery, raw materials and fuel. A *dose of capital* means sometimes the application of one or another item of equipment goods, and sometimes a dose of expense, applied quite possibly as a composite of several factor elements. Always, therefore, in the production analysis under discussion, capital must be taken in the mechanical-factor sense of equipment goods. Excepting possibly for the interest problem, *capital as funds* is an irrelevant concept.

Marshall's method of isolating the price effectiveness of any particular factor is to inquire what, at the marginal application of it, a further unit of it would add in price product; or, again, what a unit taken away would subtract. In the analysis excluding rent from price determination, however, the non-land factors are applied, not separately, but as a group, with the price product taken as their joint and aggregate achievement, the purpose being to show that the aggregate hires of them are price-determining for their joint product. Land is isolated, as the one factor taken to have been already acquired—a method equally justifiable, Marshall agrees, as applied to machine margins, for proving the exclusion of machine hires from price-determination; and as well for excluding some or all of the hires of labor.

In the distributive analysis, on the contrary, all the different factors are taken to have equal standing in point of their joint and cooperative contribution to the bringing forth of product, and their several derivative remunerations. The productive contribution of a unit of any one of them, and the derivative hire of this unit, is arrived at by the adding or by the subtracting of a unit, in order to arrive at its independent significance as a unit at the margin of production. It is, then, a factor-dosing method; and it is successively applied to the different cooperating factors to indicate the specific effectiveness of each in its contribution to the joint

price result. All of the supra-marginal items in any stock of interchangeable units must be getting the same hires as the marginal
item, since they have severally price significances interchangeable
with it. So Marshall says (p. 410) that "the withdrawal of (say)
iron from any of its necessary uses would have just the same influence on its value as its withdrawal from its marginal uses. . . . "

It is therefore obvious that this dosing method in the group-unit
sense, as it was used in the earlier rent-cost analysis, or as it is employed when a unit of free capital is incorporated in a composite
unit of mechanical-factor things, can be of no avail for any purposes
of distributing among the constituent factors of the composite
factor-group the value product jointly achieved by them. The case
is where it started, as far as the inter-factor distribution is concerned.

No small part, nevertheless, of Marshall's distributive analysis
appears to run in terms of the unit productivity of a marginal dose
of *free capital*—a fact possibly to be attributed to the ease of error
attending the use of a term of many and ambiguous meanings:

. . . the services of waiting . . . pushed constantly further . . . will prevent
it [capital] from obtaining employment at as high a rate of interest as
before. . . . But this growth of capital will increase the national dividend;
open out new and rich fields for the employment of labour in other
directions; and will thus more than compensate for the partial displacement of the services of labour by those of waiting. (p. 542)

But obviously not fund capital, and not waiting, but capital
goods do these excellent things. *Waiting,* indeed, is not a factor
of production at all. Nor is free capital. Nor does ever a factor of
production achieve a rent through the process here described—a
process that has, no doubt, significance for the problem of the rate
of interest on funds. Marshall is to be understood as assuming that
the funds have been directed into getting more indirect goods
created, or perhaps into land ameliorations. He says:

The ordinary bargain between labour and capital [between employee
and employer] is that the wage-receiver gets command over commodities
[gets wages that carry these commands] in a form ready for immediate
consumption. . . .
. . . there is nothing to make the relations between capital in general

180   THE ECONOMICS OF ALFRED MARSHALL

[free capital?] and labour in general differ widely from those between any other two *agents of production* [free capital is not this], in the general scheme of distribution already explained. . . . (p. 543)

Thus an increase of material capital causes it to push its way into new uses; and though in so doing it may occasionally diminish the field of employment for manual labour in a few trades, yet on the whole it will very much increase the demand for manual labour and all other agents of production . . . it will have forced down the rate of interest, therefore the joint product of a dose of capital and labour will now be divided more in favor of labour than before. (p. 665)

But the increase of *material capital* that forces down the rate of interest is not safely to be taken as the same sort of capital as that which widens the field of employment for manual labor in any trade, or that increases the total output of goods. The outcome here will turn on whether more equipment goods are provided, as also on what kinds. There is such a thing as technological unemployment. In some directions, capital goods are substitutes rather than complements of labor. And for some time—and no one knows for how long—output may outrun the standard of living. Marshall says:

. . . For when it is said that machinery is substituted for labour, this means that one class of labour combined with much waiting is substituted for another combined with less waiting: and for this reason alone [but it does not follow necessarily], it would be impossible to substitute capital for labour in general. . . .

. . . the chief benefit . . . is not by opening out to it [labour] new employments, but by increasing the joint product of land, labour and capital (or of land, labour and waiting), and by reducing the share of that product which any given amount of capital (or of waiting) can claim as its reward. (p. 666)

The ambiguity here in the term *capital* is patent. And so in the following:

. . . A handful of colonists . . . in vast tracts of rich land . . . anxious to reap . . . its future fruits; . . . as they cannot do this directly, they do it indirectly, by selling . . . promises to pay much larger quantities of the goods that their own soil will produce in a future generation. . . . Englishmen and others, who have accumulated the means of present enjoyment, hasten to barter them . . . a vast stream of capital flows to the

new country, and its arrival there raises the rate of wages very high. The
new capital filters but slowly towards the outlying districts: it is so scarce
there, and there are so many persons eager to have it, that it often commands for a long time two per cent a month. . . . For the settlers . . .
are eager to become independent undertakers, . . . so wage-earners have
to be attracted by high wages, which are paid in a great measure out of
the commodities borrowed from the old world on mortgages. . . . (p.
669)

Any consistent meaning for the word *capital* makes this account
preposterous. The *means of present enjoyment* are loan funds, *free
capital*. These funds may flow. But what follows after is not so
clear. The borrowers may use their borrowed funds for the purchase
of anything from anywhere, or, more probably, for hiring labor at
home, or for buying lands and cattle from their neighbors or
terminals or water fronts in town. What filters, and gets loaned
at two percent, and pays wages, is not commodities borrowed from
the old world, but free capital, funds for control. And again:

. . . in almost every business there is a constant increase in the amount of
capital required to make a fair start; but there is a much more rapid
increase in the amount of capital which is owned by people who do not
want to use it themselves, and are so eager to lend it out that they will
accept a constantly lower and lower rate of interest for it. Much of this
capital passes into the hands of bankers who promptly lend it to anyone
of whose business ability and honesty they are convinced. . . . (p. 308)

. . . The ordinary workman . . . having saved a little of his own . . . may
start one of those small shops . . . stock it chiefly on credit, and let his
wife attend to it by day. . . . In these or in other ways he may increase his
capital till he can start a small workshop, or factory. Once having made
a good beginning he will find the banks eager to give him generous
credit. . . . (p. 309)

. . . Thus, in spite of vicissitudes, the able business man generally finds
that in the long run the capital at his command grows in proportion to his
ability. (p. 311)

But the main difficulty with this factor-distributive analysis is
that the capital dose is practically certain to be a dose of money
outlay applied as a composite of factors. If the productive undertaking as an aggregate—the entire complex—were rightly
proportioned at the outset, such must be the added dose, else the

addition of some one unit of any particular factor-good as a capital dose must put the complex out of right proportions. Thus Marshall is justified in saying:

> . . . There are forces constantly at work tending so to readjust the distribution of resources between their different uses, that any maladjustment will be arrested before it has gone far: and the argument does not profess to apply to exceptional cases of violent maladjustment. . . . When the adjustment is such as to give the best results, a slight change in the proportions in which they are applied diminishes the efficiency of that adjustment by a quantity which is very small relatively to that change. . . . (p. 409, note)

But the logic of the argument is not affected by the size of the effects. The productivity of any one factor added to another, say to land, when the land has been having practically no complementation, is not rightly to be taken as including the entire result of the combination. It is to abandon, therefore, the entire theoretical approach to urge (p. 409, note) that with the adjustment such as to give the best results, "a slight change in the proportions . . . diminishes the efficiency of that adjustment by a quantity which is very small relatively to that change . . . and it may therefore be neglected . . ."—just as, in an issue of morals, the smallness of a baby is not a fact of justification or even of mitigation.

For when the adjustment is such as to give the best results, the addition of one unit of any particular factor will modify, unfavorably to the factor that alone is increased, the distributive outcome, apportioning to it a smaller return than belongs to the best adjustment—so far, that is, as among many different enterprisers there can be any one best adjustment. The case is one of an uneconomic dose—small, it is true, and carrying with it, therefore, correspondingly small penalties. And similarly also, if, when the adjustment has come to be the right one for the particular enterpriser, a subtraction of a unit of one particular factor is assumed; a price efficiency that is unduly high gets reported for that particular item, and therefore for all the other items of the stock. The other cooperating factors in the entire productive complex have become relatively numerous to a disadvantageous degree—divergent from their best proportioning—and therefore suffer in returns. Substitutions of factors will promptly set in.

The situation here illustratively assumed is, it is true, one of a *violent maladjustment*. Most of the productive powers of the land —most of its potential responsiveness—have been going to waste, as unutilized powers, and are still going to waste. The case is one of a supplementary-cost good that, as tested by the prices of products, is being starved of its due complement of other factors. Until right proportions are reached, the dosing method by subtraction attributes to the subtracted factor a productive efficiency notably divergent from that which correct proportions would permit for it. And even when the right proportions are reached, this subtraction method, *ipso facto* imposing, so far, a badly proportioned complex, involves error that is merely a smaller error quantitatively. It exaggerates still the share of the product to be attributed to the relatively deficient factor. It is still a supra-marginal responsiveness in the land that is being solicited. The specific productivity of the factor—its marginal contribution to the joint product—must be determined, if ever it can be determined at all, only under conditions of right adjustment. And for this purpose, neither the addition nor the subtraction method is adequate. The addition method attributes too little to the variable factor and the subtraction method too much. Any step toward right proportions over-states, and any step beyond understates, the significance of the particular factor when under right proportions.

Is there then any escape from this unprecision—any accuracy possible—either in principle or through the mechanism of the price market, by which to declare the specific and independent price effectiveness of the various productive factors in any joint and cooperative employment? The objective facts are only price outcomes. And these are merely the market prices of the respective price efficiencies. The difficulty is precisely parallel to that of interpreting the price of a direct good as declarative of its marginal utility. Utility to whom? Or the productive efficiency to whom? There are different enterprisers. The marginal price offer reports not the factor's prospective contribution to the price product, but only what at his margin the particular bidder can afford to pay for it rather than go without it. It is a case of addition to a complex still wrongly constituted. The logical defect is that of the subtraction method. Even when the market price is precisely commensurate with the marginal price offer, and therefore divergent from all other bids of all other competing enterprisers, the successful bidder gets merely a factor unit in complement to his other factors—mainly those of earlier commitment. He is fitting prime to supplementary costs. The price increment is due in part to his possessions already in hand. He would be unable himself to attribute any separate and specific effectiveness to this particular unit complement. It is a case of productivity through togetherness, and of a productivity that motivated the togetherness.

If, for example, from a pair of gloves for which you paid two dollars, and that, were you to lose it, you would replace at two dollars, you now lose one glove, you could at the outside pay two dollars for the return of this one glove. By this test either of the gloves is worth two dollars. But the pair does not thereby become a four-dollar pair. If a horse and wagon can earn ten dollars a day for you, but the wagon alone nothing, they do not together come to be worth to you twenty dollars per day. Even two wagons with one horse may be worth to you only the ten dollars. The rent or the price of a thing is merely the market price of its serviceability rather than the accurate equivalent of it. There is no separate price-productivity to which there can be any possibility of any precise equivalent—even were market price appropriate to the reporting of it.

If, then, the marginal bidder could make no accurate allocation of these specific productivenesses in price, it must be clear that the price process, resting on indefinitely numerous price offers and goods offers, cannot do it. And it is here worth recalling that all these offers are themselves ratio facts between quantities rather than themselves quantities.[4]

[4] The attack directed by J. A. Hobson in his *The Economics of Distribution* against the entire doctrinal validity of this dosing analysis falls somewhat short, it seems to me, of finality. Nor is it clear whether his argument against Marshall's use of the marginal-isolation device has mainly to do with Marshall's

But the decisive objection to this marginal-isolation analysis is still to be presented—an objection that Marshall has himself in other connections admirably expressed. The fundamental principle stresses *substitution* in its bearing on the relative distributive shares of factors—each factor dependent for its openings on the complementary relation of some of the factors, as well as on the substitutionary relation of others—with all of the factors affecting the distributive shares of one another:

. . . There are comparatively few things the demand for which is not greatly affected by the demand for other things to the usefulness of

---

neglect to follow out his distinction between prime and supplementary costs; or with his interpretation of the dose as, in the main, a factor-item rather than as a free-capital unit in the composite-factor emphasis; or with his use of marginal isolation for the purpose of distinguishing price-determining from price-determined costs and equipment capital from land capital; or for the purposes of an adequate and ultimate account of the distributive process. The marginal-isolation method has, in fact, all of these bearings; and in most of them Hobson's argument appears to me to be irrefutable:

"If I rent a piece of land in Piccadilly, in which all houses are three or four stories, the rent I shall pay will take into consideration the capacity of the ground for building a three- or four-story house. If I choose to put a one-story house upon the ground, the rent I pay will be the same as if I had more fully utilized the site. If I afterward add stories, it will seem that I pay no rent for this extra accommodation, but in reality I have been paying it all the time." (*Ibid.*, p. 142, note)

"If a tenant hires a piece of land and puts five doses of capital upon it when he ought to have put six, he pays a rent based upon the supposition that he will make a full economic use of the land, i.e., that he will put six doses on it. If, discovering his error, he afterward adds the sixth dose, he only appears to pay no rent out of its produce, because he has all the while been paying a rent based upon the supposition that he was working his land with six doses." (*Ibid.*, p. 141)

Hobson argues also that when an operator finds it worth while to add a fifth loom to the four that he has been using, it cannot be true that in the new situation the fifth loom is earning less than is any one of the four alongside of it. The four that were earlier together were not earlier earning differently from each other. Together they must have been earning less than now the five together are earning, else the addition would not have been made. It is possible, however, that the five are earning less per machine than the four were earning earlier. It may be that now lower power of response from land or from plant are being solicited—a more intensive utilization adopted.—If so, lower returns per machine are to be expected. For example, there may come a crowding of the available space. Unless for some such reason there is no need that the unit returns fall. And in any case there can be no difference of earning power among the new five.

"The 'dosing' illustration is vitiated by a more fundamental flaw. . . . We may suppose that he [the operator] is in full knowledge of the facts and has a full exercise of choice; as a consequence, he estimates that it just pays him to work five looms instead of four." Why say that the fifth loom pays him less or produces less than earlier any loom out of the four of that time paid him? If there is a fall, it is a fall that attaches equally to the five looms now operated. But why any

which they contribute; and it may even be said that the demand for the
majority of articles of commerce is not direct but is derived from the
demand for those commodities to the making of which they contribute,
as materials or as implements. And again this demand, because it is so
derived, is largely dependent on the supply of other things which will
work with them in making those commodities. And again the supply of
anything available for use in making any commodity is apt to be greatly
influenced by the demand for that thing derived from its uses in making
other commodities: and so on. . . . (p. 403)

. . . Capital in general and labour in general co-operate in the production of the national dividend, and draw from it their earnings in the

---

fall? "The fifth loom after it is added is found to be just as productive as any of
the other four looms. The answer is plain. The fifth loom only just pays because it
addition has injured his work with the other four looms." (*Ibid.*, pp. 142-143)
His own effectiveness, that is to say, is being more intensively applied at a dimin
ishing return for it—a falling incremental return, but an increasing total.

So it is. But nothing in this attack disturbs the dosing principle, but only the
mistaken inference that unequal productivities attach, or that there are unequa
unit costs for the different items of output in each particular situation. Taking the
dosing principle at what it rightly means, there is a significant meaning in it. Le
it be assumed that to the four looms 500 in product was to be ascribed, 125 fo
each loom; but that, under the intenser utilization of some attendant factor, only
600 is obtainable from the five looms, 120 per loom. It certainly is not true tha
in this second situation the four looms of the earlier use are to be now credite
with a return of 125 each, and the fifth loom with a return of only 100. All are
now producing at a rate of 120 each. Hobson is clearly right so far. But a new
distributive situation is presented. The productivity of the fifth loom is achieve
only on terms of the other four having to count at only 120 each. The differentia
for the group of five, all producing equally, is only 100 over the group of four, al
producing equally. Only 100 can, then be paid for a fifth loom. And if it is to be
had at that hire, the hire of all the rest will be at 100. The other factors—presum
ably mainly the land—are advantaging notably. But the dosing analysis stands fo
all that ever it was rightly good for.

Marshall's reply, if taken to be directed to defending this marginal-isolation
method of distinguishing land capital from equipment capital, resumes a position
earlier specifically abandoned—not, however, thereby, necessarily abandoning the
view that land rents are always price-determined as against the temporarily price
determined incomes of quasi-rent goods. This reply is, then, best here examined
(a) as defending the view that costs are higher for the marginal than for the supra
marginal items of product—a view not consistently adhered to by Marshall himself
and (b) as defending the marginal-productivity theory of distribution—the as
sumption that specific and independent productive efficiencies are disclosed in
marginal uses.

Hobson argues, Marshall says (p. 409, note) "that if the marginal application
of any agent of production be curtailed, that will so disorganize production tha
every other agent will be working to less effect than before; and that therefore the
total resulting loss will include not only the true marginal product of that agent
but also a part of the products due to the other agents: but . . . (1) There are
forces constantly at work tending so to readjust the distribution of resource

...easure of their respective (marginal) efficiencies. Their mutual de-
...endence is of the closest; capital without labour is dead; the labourer
...ithout the aid of his own or someone else's capital would not long be
...ive. Where labour is energetic, capital reaps a high reward, and grows
...pace. . . . The co-operation of capital and labour is as essential as that
...f the spinner of yarn and the weaver of cloth. . . . The prosperity of each
... bound up with the strength and activity of the other; though each may
...ain temporarily, if not permanently, a somewhat larger share of the
...ational dividend at the expense of the other. (p. 544)

. . the efficiencies (total and marginal) of the several factors of produc-
...on, their contributions direct and indirect to the aggregate net product,
...r national dividend; and the shares of that dividend which accrue to
...em severally are correlated by a number of mutual interactions so
...omplicated, that it is impossible to comprehend the whole in a single
...atement. . . . (p. 545)

. . an increase in the proportionate share, or rate of remuneration, of any
...gent is likely to bring into play forces, that will reduce that share, and
...eave a larger proportionate share of the dividend to be shared among
...thers. . . .

...etween their different uses, that any maladjustment will be arrested before it has
...one far: and the argument does not profess to apply to exceptional cases of violent
...aladjustment (2) When the adjustment is such as to give the best results, a
...ight change in the proportions in which they are applied diminishes the efficiency
...f that adjustment by a quantity which is very small relatively to that change. . . ."
But this reply seems not to meet the issue, but merely to shift it, and thereby
...o get it over onto even less tenable ground—ground that has, however, already
...een sufficiently inspected. The proportioning of factors is either adapted to the
...est results, or it is not. If it is, the dose will not be an isolated-factor dose, but a
...ree-capital dose. This advances us not at all for the purposes of an isolated-factor
...roductivity: the factors have not been isolated. If it is not the best, the case is
...orse still—the price productivity greater than the factor can command as hire, if
...ll of the stock is to find takers. And in fact Marshall elsewhere (pp. 153-54)
...rges the view that here he repudiates: "The dose is always a combined dose of
...abour and capital, whether it is applied by a peasant owner working unaided on
...is own land, or at the charges of a capitalist farmer. . . ."
It must, however, in fairness be said that Hobson's insistence that, with a best
...roportion of factors already achieved, there can rightly never be applied a unit
...actor dose, but only a free-capital dose, was only later clearly formulated. (See
...he September 1904 number of the *Journal of Political Economy;* "Marginal
...Jnits in the Theory of Distribution.") In this later discussion, however, he adopts
... dosing analysis of his own, though on another issue from that with Marshall,
...nd commits himself to the view that when with four machines—or four laborers—
...here is a product of 500, but with five machines or laborers a product of only 100
...nore, "the competition of employers driving down profits, will raise the wages to
... 20 . . . if we assume . . . [that] the competition of employers is as full and free
...s that of the labourers." More patience with the dosing analysis, at its best of use
...nd implication, might in this connection have served him better.

An increase in the supply of any agent will benefit most other agents but not necessarily all.

. . . the larger the supply of any agent . . . the lower will be the demand price with which it will have to be contented . . . in so far as competition equalizes the price which it gets in all uses, this price will be its price for all uses. The extra production resulting from the increase in that agent of production will go to swell the national dividend, and other agents of production will benefit thereby: but that agent itself will have to submit to a lower rate of pay. (p. 537 and marginal caption)

. . . The increase in the supply of this one agent increases the demand for many others by a little, and for some others by much; but for some it lessens the demand. (p. 538)

. . . The amount of produce raised, and therefore the position of the margin of cultivation . . . are both governed by the general conditions of demand and supply . . . cost of production, eagerness of demand, margin of production, and price of the produce mutually govern one another and no circular reasoning is involved in speaking of any one as in part governed by the others. . . . (p. 427)

The principle in the case—accepted in full, it seems, by Marshall —may be illustrated as follows: say that there are employed four factors of production, any one of which alone could achieve but 2 of product; any two of which together could achieve 5; any three together, 9; and all four together, 14; but that two of any one of them, along with only one each of the other three, would achieve but 17. The best adjustment is plainly one of each of the four or two of each of the four—any deviations from these proportions being, so far, a maladjustment.

The productivity, falling to 9 with the subtraction of any one of the four, would by this subtraction method attribute to each a productivity of 5; but the aggregate productivity is not 20 but 14. If, however, the addition method is chosen—the adding of a second unit of any one of the four—the productivity of any unit of them all will be reported as, say, but 3. The subtraction method attributes to each too much, and the addition method, too little. We seem, then, to be back again at much the same impasse that we faced with the dose of free capital—no specific unit-contribution to product arrived at. We are nevertheless thus far forward: a right composite

lose under the free-capital method must be one that abides by the
earlier proportions—that were the best.

Marshall's solution appeals sometimes to the addition and sometimes to the subtraction method—with a seeming entire indifference
etween them, on the assumption, presumably, that they are
nterchangeable in results.

Specific imputation by addition:

. . . Every agent of production, land, machinery, skilled labour, un-
killed labour, etc., tends to be applied in production as far as it profitably
an be . . . employers . . . by using a little more of any one agent . . .
stimate the net product . . . that will be got by a little more outlay in
his direction, or a little more outlay in that; and if they can gain by
hifting a little of their outlay from one direction to another, they will do
. (p. 521)

. . the earnings of a machine can sometimes be estimated by the addition
the output of a factory which it might effect in certain cases without
volving any incidental extra expense.
. . . If the investors of capital push it into every occupation in which it
eems likely to gain a high reward; and if, after this has been done and
quilibrium has been found, it still pays and only just pays to employ
is machinery [note the interchangeability of free capital and machinery]
e can infer from this fact that the yearly rate of interest is 4 per cent.
. . (p. 519).

Specific imputation by subtraction:

Some things are necessary to them [the hat-making trade]; they must
ave not only some food, clothing, and house room, but also some cir-
lating capital, such as raw material, and some fixed capital, such as
ols and perhaps a little machinery. And though competition prevents
nything more than the ordinary trade profit being got by the use of this
ecessary capital; yet the loss of it would be so injurious that those in
e trade would have been willing to pay 50 per cent on it, if they could
ot have got the use of it on easier terms. There may be other machinery
hich the trade would have refused to dispense with if the rate of interest
ad been 20 per cent per annum, but not if it had been higher . . . finally
e rate being 4 per cent. they use more still . . . the utility of . . .
achinery [the price productiveness of it] which it is only just worth
eir while to employ, is measured by 4 per cent. (p. 520)

. . the loss of that man's work would be likely to cause a diminution in
e net output of that factory, the value of which was about equal to his

wages . . . his wages are about equal to that net product: (of course th
net product of an individual cannot be separated mechanically from th
of others who are working together with him). (p. 538)

Imputation by marginal efficiency, without clear choice betwee
addition and subtraction:

. . . Wages tend to equal the net product of labour; its margin
productivity rules the demand-price for it; and, on the other side, wag
tend to retain a close though indirect and intricate relation with the co
of rearing, training and sustaining the energy of efficient labour. Th
various elements of the problem mutually determine (in the sense
governing) one another. . . . (p. 532; see also pp. 520, 521, and 522

The purpose in this examination of Marshall's distributiv
analysis has been, in the main, to test the validity of the margina
isolation device, through an application of it not directly concernin
the distinction between land capital and equipment capital. Th
doctrinal issues are separate issues. But the underlying analysis
essentially the same for both. Economists, however, there hav
been—and not a few—that repudiate the distinction between lan
capital and equipment capital, holding fast, nevertheless, to th
marginal-productivity theory of distribution.

Therefore Marshall's advocacy of this particular theory of di
tribution does not directly greatly concern us. It is not peculia
to him or to the classical school of economic thinking. It is n
essential even to the classical view of the distributive bearing of th
minimum of subsistence or of the standard of living on wage

Were it, however, strictly a part of our present task, somethin
further would remain to be said. Conceiving production from th
point of view of society or the nation as a whole, this margina
productivity theory of distribution conceives production in th
collective rather than in the competitive and individual sense. Th
processes of production are regarded industrially, and the facto
of production are viewed in their factory or mechanical aspe
Capital, for example, is taken to be equipment goods or fun
invested, or to be invested, in equipment goods. It should inde
in strict logic have no concern with *free capital* funds. Funds neith
saw nor hew. Nor can they be either woven or spun or shaved
cut. Most of the confusions of terms and of analysis with rega

to capital turn on this purely non-mechanical quality of capital funds.

As competitively viewed, this mechanical and industrial account of capital is entirely inadequate. It overlooks as fields of gainful investment, merchandising, advertising, franchises, monopolistic restrictions of output that collectively viewed are negatively productive, parasitism, predation and crime. It forgets, for example, that murder is now financially organized, at surprisingly good investment returns. Business-wise viewed, these traditional factors of production in the industrial interpretation sum up into a travesty of the facts. The four-fold classification is bad enough, even by the test of the industrial point of view; but from a business point of view it is inadequate and naïve to the point of folly.

And thus there are in this aspect definite objections to be directed against the classical system of doctrine, as also against Marshall's particular rendering of it.

Spatial Fixity or Geographical Extension as a Test

Marshall's distributive analysis has made it clear that land rent, whether of fertility or of position, accrues by title of productive contribution, in precise parallel with other price hires. Only the determination of price at the margin of cultivation, with the attendant necessity of isolating at this margin a group of price-determining costs, and of excluding land rents from this group —the non-land costs carrying exclusively the price-determining function—has been here put in question. Not the productivity theory of distribution, but only the marginal-productivity theory, has been made the point of controversy. Issue has, to be sure, been taken upon the specific, separate and independent productivity of any factor of production jointly employed with others. But the price-productivity theory of the distribution of the price shares remains intact. It has not, indeed, been made the subject of attack. Only the attempt at the marginal isolation of price-determining costs has been subjected to criticism. Only the functional identity of the various factor costs has been emphasized, along with the manifest substitutions of the factors for one another within the near-marginal areas.

It is through Marshall's admission of the rivalry of these different cost goods, their usual complementary relation to one another, and especially their occasional substitutionary relation, that his marginal-isolation argument becomes clearly untenable. Moreover, his occasional admission that the supra-marginal and the marginal costs are quantitatively equal, but only differently constituted, amounts by itself to an abandonment of this isolation procedure.

But it remains nevertheless possible for him to urge that not the rent costs solely, but all of the factor costs equally, are price-determined costs. This position, however, abandons the distinction between prime and supplementary costs with reference to price determination, as also, for such time as it applies, the entire cost-of-production method of accounting for prices. For prices emerge, during the appropriate periods—whatever the appropriate period may be taken to be—as not determined by cost of production at all, but only by the general conditions of demand and supply. But, as has earlier been noted, if this be taken as an appeal to the "basement" analysis, the objection is prompt that there is no especial appropriateness of this level of analysis to any particular time or to any particular set of conditions. To accept it as adequate here, is to make always superfluous any recourse to the cost-of-production method. Similarly also it is with the demand-and-supply explanation, in any ordinary meaning attaching to the phrase—a meaning in which, by the way, the assertion of the phrase *demand and supply* is almost meaningless and is entirely without significance.

But still it holds true that Marshall's position denying to the hires of either land capital or equipment capital any price-determining function during these intermediate periods, is not yet refuted. It merely stands as true, (1) that if all of these distinctions are merely matters of degree anyway, everything goes forthwith afloat; (2) that wages, in part or entirely, must go along with the hires of land capital and of equipment capital:

That part of a man's income which he owes to the possession of extra-ordinary natural abilities is a free boon to him [origins again]; and from an abstract point of view bears some resemblance to the rent of other free gifts of nature, such as the inherent properties of land. (p. 664)

Only prime costs in the sense of material costs are therefore left —and even these not securely—for the interim price determination. Only a part of each actual price gets accounted for in cost terms, which is not greatly better than going entirely unaccounted for.

Taking it, then, as clear that Marshall does not attempt to set up the distinction of origins between land capital and equipment capital—no matter how often he may in various connections actually appeal to it—and taking it as also clear that he has both implicitly and explicitly abandoned the distinction of marginal isolation as peculiar to land capital, it remains to examine a third distinction, that of the fixity of land stocks, in their aspect of spatial or geometrical extension.

On the face of it, the distinction would appear to be the same as that between position and fertility rents. But it is not in Marshall's thought precisely this, as is evident from his distributive analysis. In some aspects it suggests a return to the distinction of origins. But it is not that. The supposed manner of origin may, no doubt, infer the fixity of stocks; but, even so, it is merely an item of fact explanatory of the fixity, not the ultimate fact of it. Nor, indeed, are the stocks actually fixed. Wind, river, tide, quake, uplift and subsidence, all disturb the fixity, in any relevant meaning of the term. Even man also may measurably modify it by promoting denudation and erosion.

These annotations, however, are not to the point of the distinction. It is one of responsiveness to the purposed policies of investment—economically motivated responsiveness. It is the unresponsiveness of land capital in this aspect, that is the fact of emphasis. Fertility is responsive; the policies of the individual quest for gain may diminish or cancel fertility, or may reinstate it. But not so with geographical or spatial extension. The changes that ensue—and changes do ensue—do not turn on economically motivated policies, or only inappreciably so.

And thus we come again into view of what with Marshall is the fundamental principle. Only those hires that condition the stocks of factors are for Marshall price-determining hires. Any productive agent that would be here, no matter what the hire, or whether there were any, is an agent the hire of which is irrelevant to price change.

In point of emphasis this is essentially a "basement" view. Relative prices get modified only through changes in the relative stocks of productive factors. Land stocks do not get modified. Traced back to the influences affecting their relative stocks, we come upon policies of investment controlling the newly and continually maturing volume of investment funds. Investors direct these funds into one or another line of provision for production according to the relative prospects of return. The only modifications possible are those with equipment goods. Land capital absorbs no new investment funds, because no new creations of land are possible, in this spatial aspect. There are shiftings of ownership, but these merely redistribute funds. Therefore, the argument runs, price changes through cost influences arrive solely through modifications in the non-land stocks of factors. Investment flows by and around these boulder facts fixed midway of the stream. They do not get modified because, being spatial, they cannot—in response, that is, to investment policies. They are unresponsive. Always, therefore, as Marshall insists, the hires of land lack all bearing on prices, because they lack all bearing on the stocks of land.

But only temporarily is there this unresponsiveness with the stocks of equipment goods or with the stocks of human productive powers. These, then, are of the quasi-rent class, supplementary-cost agents.

Whether or not this argument will turn out to be tenable, it is secure in its purely factual aspects. Later it will be examined in point of its doctrinal merits. The present task, however, is merely to find out what Marshall himself makes of it, factually and doctrinally.

The distinction is ultimately one of responsiveness:

. . . so long as the resources of an individual producer are in the form of general purchasing power, he will push every investment up to the margin at which he no longer expects from it a higher net return than he could get by investing in some other material, or machine, or advertisement, or in the hire of some additional labour . . . the sale replenishes his fluid capital, and that again is invested. . . .

But if he invests in land. . . . The incomes . . . differ from his individual
point of view mainly in the longer life of the land. But in regard to
production in general, a dominant difference between the two lies in the
fact that the supply of land is fixed . . . while the supply of machines
may be increased without limit. . . . (pp. 411-12)

. . . suppose that a meteoric shower of a few thousand large stones harder
than diamonds fell all in one place . . . all picked up at once, and no
amount of search could find any more . . . the owners of them would
have . . . a large producer's surplus . . . it could not be affected by the
cost of obtaining a further supply, because none could be had at any
price. . . .

   .   .   .   .

The total supply of stones is fixed. But of course any particular
manufacturer might obtain almost as many as he liked to pay for . . .
just in the same way as if he were buying machinery, the total stock of
which could be increased indefinitely, so that its price conformed pretty
closely to its cost of production.

   .   .   .   .

. . . Since anyone, who bought stones, would take them from other
producers, his purchase would not materially affect the general relations
of demand for the services of the stones to the supply of those services.
. . . (pp. 415-17)

. . . a manufacturer or trader, owning both land and buildings, regards
the two as bearing similar relations to his business . . . when he comes
to decide whether to obtain that space by taking in an extra piece of
land or by building his factory a floor higher, he weighs the net income
. . . in the one against . . . the other. . . . This argument says nothing as
to whether the appliances were made by man, or part of a stock given by
nature; it applies to rents and quasi-rents alike.

But there is this difference from the point of view of society. If one
person has possession of a farm, there is less land for others to have. His
use of it is not in addition to, but in lieu of the use of a farm by other
people: whereas if he invests in improvements of land or in buildings on
it, he will not appreciably curtail the opportunities of others to invest
capital in like improvements. Thus there is likeness amid unlikeness
between land and appliances made by man [origins now]. There is
unlikeness because land in an old country [different doctrines for different countries] is approximately . . . *a permanent and fixed stock* . . .
on the other hand there is likeness, in that, since some of them cannot
be produced quickly, they are a practically *fixed stock for short periods:*
and for those periods the incomes . . . stand in the same relation to the
value of the products raised by them, as do true rents. (pp. 431-32)

Land is on a different footing from man himself and those agents of production which are made by man; among which are included improvements made by him on the land itself. For while the supplies of all other agents of production respond in various degrees and various ways to the demand for their services, land makes no such response [not origin, but responsiveness]. . . .

It is true that land is but a particular form of capital from the point of view of the individual manufacturer or cultivator. . . .

. . . land (in an old country) does not share the reflex influences . . . which a high rate of earnings exerts on the supply of other agents of production . . . on their contributions to the national dividend, and . . . on the real cost [what now is real cost?] at which their services are purchased by other agents of production. The building an additional floor on one factory or putting an extra plough on one farm, does not generally take a floor from another factory or a plough from another farm . . . the stock of land (in an old country) at any time is the stock for *all* time. . . . He [a manufacturer or cultivator] adds a little more land to his business; but the nation adds no land to its business, the change does not in itself increase the national income. (pp. 534-36)

It is by this test of responsiveness that origins, as reported for example in fertility, do not matter[5]—and that many royalties, on mines, for example, do enter as price-determining costs:

. . . A royalty is *not* a rent. . . . For, except when mines, quarries, etc., are practically inexhaustible, the excess of their income over their direct outgoings has to be regarded, in part at least, as the price got by the sale of stored-up goods—stored up by nature indeed, but now treated as private property; and therefore the marginal supply price of minerals includes a royalty. . . . (p. 438)

But cannot the individual get more, for his own purposes, of these fixed stocks, just as at any particular time he can get more of quasi-rent goods that are fixed for that time, or of labor that also is fixed for a generation? He can:

. . . of course any particular manufacturer might obtain almost as many [of the meteoric stones] as he liked to pay for. . . . (p. 416)

He can not:

. . . Even the individual farmer may not always be able to get an additional ten or fifty acres adjoining his own farm, just when he wants them, save at a prohibitive price. And in that respect land differs from *most* other agents of production even from the individual point of view.

[5] See Marshall, p. 534.

This difference may indeed be regarded as of little account in regard to the individual farmer. But from the social point of view . . . it is vital. . . . (p. 169, note)

We must later look into this word social. It is true that land holdings are checker-boarded. Not rarely, therefore, a piece of land adjoining farm A is so important to the make-up of farm B as a working farm unit, so necessary to its best proportions or to its "best adjustment"—that it can be detached from farm B for incorporation with farm A, in making A into a more symmetrical unit—better proportioned in point of its various land factors— only at a price that will be necessarily stiff, and may even be prohibitive. That is to say, the tract bears a high *togetherness-productivity* to both farms. Often, therefore, the only practicable strategy for the owner of A is to bargain for farm B in its entirety, perhaps to fraction it out in sales on its other fronts, among the neighboring farmers similarly famished for land in their particular urgencies. Often, that is to say, the free capital dose has land as one of its constituents. In such cases, the only practicable dosing unit is a large unit. The principle is not rarely equally well illus-trated with expensive equipment. In the wheat-growing districts of middle Canada, for example, one must jump his farm to double its size if he is to jump from one combination harvester to two. Not the land but the machine is the *limiting factor*. Similar problems are often encountered with male breeding stock, printing presses, power units, and with high-salaried executive ability. Certainly, the principle is not distinctive of land capital.

Investment Motivations as Test

But Marshall is not loyal to spatial extension as the ultimate distinguishing characteristic of land capital. For land in this aspect becomes in some cases capital in the ordinary sense. And oddly enough this is especially apt to happen with the *public-value* aspects of land.[6]

[6] ". . . This (annual) value of the land is commonly called its 'original value' of its 'inherent value'; but much of that value is the result of the action of men, though not of its individual holders. For instance, barren heath land may suddenly acquire a high value from the growth of an industrial population near it; though

Land capital becomes, then, ordinary capital when an investment is made in land with the appropriate motivations—a new test that may have indefinitely broad applications.

It is obvious that the greater part of situation value is "public value." . . . Sometimes the settlement of a whole town, or even district is planned on business principles, and carried out as an investment at the expense and risk of a single person or company. . . .

When, for instance, Mr. Salt and Mr. Pullman determined to take their factories into the country and to found Saltaire and Pullman City, they foresaw that the land, which they could purchase at its value for agricultural purposes, would obtain the special situation value which town property derives from the immediate neighbourhood of a dense population. And similar considerations have influenced those, who, having fixed upon a site adapted by nature to become a favorite watering-place, have bought the land and spent large sums in developing its resources: they have been willing to wait long for any net income from their investment in the hope that ultimately their land would derive a high situation value. . . .

In all such cases the yearly income derived from the land (or at all events that part of it which is in excess of the agricultural rent) is for many purposes to be regarded as profits rather than rent [as was the fertility situation anyway; but what part, and in what cases?]. . . . For in such cases great risks have to be run; and in all undertakings in which there are risks of great losses, there must be also hopes of great gains . . . sufficient to cause those who are on the margin of doubt whether to venture or not, to regard the probable net amount of their gains . . . as compensating . . . that the gains resulting from such ventures are not much more than sufficient . . . is shown by the fact that they are not as yet very common. They are however likely to be more frequent. . . . A large railway company, for instance, can found a Crewe or a New Swindon . . . without running any great risk.

Somewhat similar instances are those of a group of landowners who combine to make a railway . . . which will greatly raise the value of their land. In such cases *part of* the increase of their incomes as landowners ought to be regarded as profits on capital which they have invested . . . though the capital has gone towards making a railway instead of being applied directly to their own property.

Other cases of like nature are main drainage schemes, and other plans

---

its owners have left it untouched as it was made by nature. It is, therefore, perhaps more correct to call this part of the annual value of the land its *'public value'*; while that part which can be traced to the work and outlay of its individual holders may be called its *'private value'*. . . ." (p. 433)

for improving the general condition of agricultural or town property, in so far as they are carried out by the landowners at their own expense, whether by private agreement or by the levying of special rates on themselves. . . .

Thus that improvement of the environment . . . is . . . due to the deliberate investment of capital by the owners of the land for the purpose of raising its value; and therefore a portion of the consequent increase of income may be regarded as profits when we are considering long periods. But . . . any increase in the net income derived from the free gifts of nature which was not brought about by, and did not supply the direct motive to, any special outlay on the part of the landowners, is to be regarded as rent for all purposes [a return to the abandoned test of origins].

Cases somewhat analogous to these arise when the owner of a score or more of acres in the neighbourhood of a growing town "develops" them for building. . . . This collective value, thus created by him, is of the nature of public value . . . that share of it which results from his forethought, constructive faculty and outlay, is to be regarded as the reward of business enterprise. . . .

These exceptional cases must be reckoned with. . . . (pp. 442-45)

Instead, however, of being exceptional these cases suffice in principle to declare all land in a country like the United States to be in part, and in most cases mainly, ordinary capital. The upshot of this particular position is that when individuals invest in land with the purpose of gainfully creating or intercepting *public values,* or mainly with this purpose, land becomes thereby, even its spatial aspects, its quality of geometrical extension, mere ordinary capital —but only in an indeterminate share.

Moreover, the distinguishing characteristic is not the taking of exceptional risks—for whatever that might matter—for these risks are not great in most cases and are approaching constantly nearer to the point of disappearance. The test is in the particular motivations that direct these attempts to secure individual gains through operations in the public-value aspects of land. Real-estate promotions in the wholesale purchase and retail selling of city lands, the smaller speculative ventures in town lots, and most of the farmer settlement of this continent, have moved practically all of the high value lands over into ordinary capital standing. But it is not entirely clear whether they are to stay there, or are, tract by tract, to revert to whatever they earlier were in point of property status.

Fertility Rents Versus Spatial-Extension Rents

If, then, Marshall's line of distinction has been here correctly interpreted as one of investment motivations—a question of praise-worthy intentions, or even of achieved service to the general welfare, gains sought through meritorious speculative ventures—we have thus come into the presence of a distinction of function descriptive of factual price processes—relations of cause and effect —turning on tests of right purposes in achieving beneficent out-comes—ethical distinctions made controlling for scientific classifica-land belong, not in the land-capital category, but go along instead with the quasi-rent classification of productive factors, we arrive tions, a line of distinction not rare among economists.

Recalling now that the fertility and the mineral resources of at the necessity of testing the distinguishability of the fertility of land from its purely extension aspects—and all of this, not as a descriptive or historical or origin task, but as a matter of distinction in principle, an issue of theory.

Transportation controls accessibility, and creates it; though obviously it does not create spatial extension or the geometrical aspects of land—it does not create geography. In one sense of the term also, it does not create position. If, however, it did, or if in any relevant sense it could, there would be no such thing as fixity of land stocks, or as the unresponsiveness of them to gain-seeking activities or to investment policies. And it seems clear enough that in the sense that is relevant to economic problems and issues, transportation does create the positional accessibility of land. Such, in fact, has been Marshall's justification for the gains from speculative ventures in the opening-up of lands. The increments are earned.

Some economists have argued, and especially the single-taxers, that all land values are position values; for, no matter what the fertility of land, its availability accrues only as conditioned on its position—on not being in the moon, for example. But, on the other hand, the ready accessibility of Sahara attaches no value to its lands. There must be at least two legs to this sort of stool—a togetherness of position with land quality—much as, with Webster, neither liberty nor union could be better than a trumpery thing, but glorious together, as one and inseparable.

But take two pieces of land interchangeable in soil qualities and in crop returns to units of expense. Marshall says (pp. 422-23) that "in some cases it is convenient to estimate the rent of a particular agent by comparing its yield to that of an inferior (perhaps a marginal) agent, when similarly worked with appropriate appliances." This is well for lands similarly situated, say in England. It is relatively easy there to reduce all of the rent differentials between lands of equal freight charges to differentials of fertility. But take now two plots of agricultural land, say fruit or wheat land, of equal responsiveness in point of crop outcomes to equal units of expense. But the rent of the one of these tracts that is in California must be mainly fertility rent, as viewed from the California margin of cultivation. The rentless margin of land in England must be found at a much lower grade of land. Relatively to the California land, practically all of the rents of English lands are position rents, spatial rents; while relatively to English lands practically all of them are fertility rents.[7]

But on the Atlantic seaboard in America still another line must be drawn between fertility and position rents. The fact is, then, that with agricultural lands there is no tenable line of separation between rents of spatial extension and rents of fertility. In one setting of transportation facilities, the rents that the Marshall analysis would declare to be price-determining must become in another setting price-determined. A change of freight rates in any one country would similarly draw differently the line of division.

The reply will doubtless be prompt that all these differences

[7] In this connection Marshall says (p. 442, note): "If we suppose that two farms, which sell in the same market, return severally to equal applications of capital and labour [a free-capital dose expended for capital and labor] amounts of produce, the first of which exceeds the second by the extra cost of carrying its produce to market, then the rent of the two farms will be the same. (The capital and labour applied to the two farms are here supposed to be reduced to the same money measure. . . .)"

Marshall has repeatedly pointed out to be matters of degree. But thereupon forthwith it must again be urged that distinctions between cause and effect can never be drawn as matters of degree. Take, for example, the rents on a Massachusetts tract of land. Part of this rent must be price-determined permanently, as spatial rent. Another part of it, as fertility rent, is only temporarily price-determined. But how much of this, and how much of that? There is comfort solely in the fact that, if no one can ever tell, no one can ever want to. And thus it need not matter that in England, according to Marshall's view, one line of division has to be drawn, another in New York, and still others in Illinois, Iowa, and California. As a matter of degree the distinction is logically indefensible; for enterpriser purposes it is non-existent; and for any purpose it is impracticable.

And still the distinction is presented by Marshall as one of degree—even, it may be, with those lands that, for public-utility needs, have been speculatively purchased or speculatively developed:

This series of hypotheses [relative to the meteoric stones] stretches continuously from the one extreme in which the income derived from the stones is a rent in the strictest sense of the term, to the other extreme in which it is to be classed rather with interest on free or floating capital. ... (p. 418)

... between those incomes yielded by agents of production which are to be regarded as rents or quasi-rents and those which ... may be regarded as interest (or *profits*) on current investments. ... The difference is fundamental, but it is only one of degree. ...

Again, pure elements are seldom isolated ... either in the physical or moral world. Pure rent in the strict sense of the term is scarcely ever met with. ... (p. 421)

But in still other connections, Marshall is unfaithful to this distinction of *responsiveness*. We have seen that for short periods he urges no distinction between land-capital hires and quasi-rents. Both are price-determined costs. But if, further, the distinction fails in the long-time equilibrium of the normal-value time, it must fail everywhere:

. . . it is only by accident that an average price will be a normal price; that is, the price which any one set of conditions tends to produce. In a stationary state alone . . . the term normal always means the same thing: there, but only there, "average price" and "normal price" are convertible terms. (p. 372)

In a rigidly stationary state . . . the normal expenses of production, the marginal expenses, and the average expenses (rent being counted in) would be one and the same thing, for long periods and for short. . . . (p. 497)

. . . In a stationary state the income earned by every appliance of production being truly anticipated beforehand, would represent the normal measure of the efforts and sacrifices required to call it into existence. The aggregate expenses of production might then be found either by multiplying these marginal expenses by the number of units of the commodity; or by adding together all the actual expenses of production of its several parts, and adding in all the rents earned by differential advantages for production. The aggregate expenses of production being determined by either of these routes, the average expenses could be deduced by dividing out by the amount of the commodity; and the result would be the normal supply price, whether for long periods or for short. (p. 810)

But the view ultimately adopted by Marshall reformulates the distinction of spatial extension into something that closely approaches fertility, and that thus departs from the principle of the fixity of stocks—of unresponsiveness to gain-motivated human efforts. Indeed, the "speculator distinction" just examined has shown how subtractions from the volume of land capital may be brought about through the transfer of these spatial items to the general-capital category. It is true also that speculative activities with lands may, and not rarely do, shift outlying city additions back into farm lands—a precise reversal of the earlier speculative process. In an occasional "boom" town, houses erected in these outlying areas are brought back into town on trucks. Marshall's basis of distinction now becomes one of the kind of incomes that are derived from these *agricultural* lands that are spatially fixed in volume. But these newly emphasized incomes turn out to be, in ultimate analysis, fertility incomes; and as such are susceptible of wear-out, renewal, or increase.

Having, then, noted (p. 421) that "interest on free capital and quasi-rent on an old investment of capital shade into one another gradually," as indeed being questions of length of time they must, only that this change from cause to effect cannot be thus gradual —and having pointed out (p. 421) that "even the rent of land being not a thing by itself, but the leading species of a large genus," Marshall goes on to say that the case with the economist is similar to that with the chemist "who seeks for the true properties of each element. . . . " He says:

. . . economists . . . have learnt that there is an element of true rent in the composite product that is commonly called wages, an element of true earnings in what is commonly called rent and so on. . . .

They recognize that nearly all land in actual use contains an element of capital; that separate reasonings are required for those parts of its value which are, and those which are not, due to the efforts of man invested in the land for the purposes of production [origins reinstated]; . . .The manner in which the reasonings are to be combined depends on the nature of the problem. . . . (pp. 421-22)

Marshall continues:

Professor Fetter seems to ignore this lesson [from the chemists] in an article on "The Passing of the concept of rent" in the *Quarterly Journal of Economics,* May 1901, p. 419; where he argues that "if only those things which owe nothing to labour are classed as land, and if it is then shown that there is no material thing in settled countries of which this can be said, it follows that everything must be classed as capital." Again he appears to have missed the true import of the doctrines which he assails, when he argues (*ib.* pp. 423-9) against "Extension as the fundamental attribute of land, and the basis of rent." The fact is that its extension (or rather the aggregate of "its space relations") is the chief, though not the only property of land, which causes the income derived from it (in an old country) to contain a large element of true rent: and that the element of true rent, which exists in the income derived from land, or the "rent of land" in the popular use of the term, is in practice so much more important than any others that it has given a special character to the historical development of the Theory of Rent (see above, p. 147). If meteoric stones of absolute hardness, in high demand and incapable of increase, had played a more important part in the economic history of the world than land, then the elements of true rent which attracted the chief attention of students, would have been associated with the property of hardness; and this would have given a special tone and character to the development of the Theory of Rent. But neither exten-

sion nor hardness is a fundamental attribute of all things which yield a
true rent. . . . (p. 422, note)

This fundamental attribute is, as Marshall holds it, *unresponsiveness* to investment policies. Excepting, then, for Marshall's
insistence on distinctions of degree in causal relations, the reply
to Fetter's criticism was adequate, if only this criticism had not
in essentials turned precisely on the practical and logical impossibility of this very distinction of degree. For the principle in the
case, as Marshall has presented it, has been one of spatial relations
as relevant only in this aspect of unresponsiveness. If, then, degree,
as applicable to functional relations in the cause-and-effect
emphasis had been excluded from the analysis, Marshall's position,
in this aspect of it, would have been entirely tenable—though
clearly unserviceable for any purpose of the classical system of
doctrine. For the purposes of this test of responsiveness, hardness
would equally well have met the need.

But the issue takes on an entirely new aspect with Marshall's
attempt—by his reference to page 147—to shift the significance
of this spatial extension to certain particular aspects of the
serviceability of land, that are, no doubt, connected with its spatial
extension:

. . . Those free gifts of nature which Ricardo classed as the "inherent"
and "indestructible" properties of the soil, have been largely modified;
partly impoverished and partly enriched by the work of many generations
of men.

But it is different with that which is above the surface. Every acre
has given to it by nature an annual income of heat and light, of air and
moisture; and over these man has but little control . . . an annuity fixed
by nature for each plot of land. Ownership . . . gives possession of this
annuity: and . . . the space required for the life and action of vegetables
and animals; the value . . . much affected by its geographical position.
(p. 147)

Not, then, the spatial extension is the primary fact, but instead
the annuities of heat and light and wind and rain over which
spatial extension gives control. But the bearing of either space or
geographical position on the rents, and the derivative values
attaching to the ownership of land, are mostly a matter of the

development of transportation, in view of the different changes that derive from it. There is, then, no fixity or unresponsiveness in the sense of the principle involved. Lands that are thus changed from the inaccessible to the workingly available are for every purpose of the present issue added to the stock—not added, it is true, in geographical or surveying sense, but nevertheless both created and added in the sense of economic serviceability.

But the point of particular emphasis for the immediate issue is that these annuities of the general weather quality are themselves not essentially spatial. They are fertility facts. They signify nothing excepting as interdependent with the character and condition of the soil—too many legs here for any one stool. Precisely as with position, these annuities are useless, if the under-soil land carries with it no capacities of fertility response. These capacities can by men be given to the land or by men taken away, accordingly as are the pecuniary policies and methods of cultivation.

And further, these annuities may be devastatingly over-generous —as in Sahara the ruinous sun, and in other districts the calamitous winds, or in still others the floods and tornadoes. They may end in fertility, or put an end to it. And finally, whether they give it, or take from it, or destroy it, the transportation fact is there, to incorporate new lands into the flexibility of the stock, or to enhance their intensive significance, or to limit them, or at the extreme— as with the moon—to exclude them.

Moreover, Marshall is shortly to develop the view that the decisive fundamental fact in any price problem is never the rents of the lands, with the price-determining activity of some of them and with the price-determined passivity of others of them—the hires of some of them causes, and of others of them results of prices; and even the hire of each one split into different functions —but only the available stock of land with which to produce, and the relative stocks of different lands for different directions of production. It is in fact not a question of hires at all, however they may be related to costs of production; for it is not ultimately a question of costs of production at all. Marshall is to abandon, that is to say, the cost level of explanation, and betake himself to what we have called the "basement" analysis. This level of analysis, excellent for its purpose, but needing nevertheless to be articulated with the enterpriser process, since this, in the present working of the competitive order, is the actual process, is to the immediate purpose in only one aspect: it leaves no place for any functional differences among the different factors of production in their bearing on prices. By the test of this level of approach, these distinctions as to price determination are discredited. Something there is to say, no doubt, as to the directions in which to seek for explanations of past changes in this underlying situation and of probable future changes. But nothing in this connection offers comfort to any division of influences into active as against passive—price causes and price effects. Still less in point can be any parallel division of any particular factor item. Marshall himself says (p. 630) that "at any given time he [the cultivator] takes for granted all that richness of the soil which results from permanent improvement. . . ."

A further discussion of this "basement" type of analysis must await a somewhat lengthy examination of opportunity costs in general, and of certain particular aspects of this rent-cost doctrine.

Note on Definition, Continued

What, then, turns out for Marshall to be the accurately distinguishing aspect or quality differentiating land capital from equipment capital in production, so that land rent can be in the long last the sole price-determined cost?

The distinction is not one of any peculiar applicability of the law of diminishing return to land capital; for this applies equally to factory buildings and to plows. It is not by the peculiar appropriateness of land to the analytical device of marginal isolation; for this applies also to equipment goods, plows, for example. It is not by freedom in origin from either effort or expense costs; for fertility is of this character—a quasi-rent good, and thus a capital good, not only in the private sense, as also is land, but equally in the social sense. Not even the price-determined hire of land is peculiar to it—excepting in normal-equilibrium periods; for at all other times the hires of equipment goods, and some or all of the hires of labor, are also price-determined.

It is spatial extension? Not this; because meteoric stones, were they hard enough to be durable enough, would meet the test. Accurately, moreover, it is not the fact of spatial extension that ever is relevant, but only that fixity of stocks that attaches inevitably to spatial extension. Is it the unresponsiveness of land to investment policies that affords the crucial aspect of that fixity in volume that is derivative from spatial extension? But spatial facts, like building locations, may be shifted over into ordinary capital, despite their fixity in volume, if only appropriate investment motivations have directed the investment of free capital in them.

Nor in fact is mere spatial extension decisive of lack of responsiveness. Other things, the meteoric stones, for example, may exhibit this essential fact of unresponsiveness and after all, it is the air and rain and sun and wind (in which the meteoric stones are not especially participant) as attributes of surface extension that make up the ultimate differentia of land from other capital. But these, in turn, not rarely by excess come to be debits rather than credits with relation to land use to its controlling owner. Moreover, their effects are mainly significant in their fertility bearings, and fertility is not to be differentiated from ordinary capital.

And all these spatial-extension income things are, in their income aspect, their price significance and their value standing, dependent on transportation; and this in turn is a capital thing that permits or prohibits —and essentially for income purposes creates or destroys—that accessibility that upholds the position, that defines the spatial extension, that controls the annuities, that gives the fertility, that supplies the income, that takes on the values, and that, all together, in one way or another, refutes the actuality of the fixity of stocks, and thus their unresponsiveness to human devisings in gain-seeking activities.

The truth is that both implicitly and explicitly—as Marshall has admitted in one connection or another—neither origins, nor marginal isolation, nor spatial fixity, nor unresponsiveness, can defensibly be urged as the peculiar aspect or characteristic by which the land-capital category is to be distinguished. But in other and different connections he returns to stress now one and now another of these different qualities or aspects, as the abiding character of differentiation. Often he appeals for the significance of his classification to the social aspects of the situation. But *social* turns out to refer solely to *fixity*. Often again he returns to labor-free origins; still more often to the marginal isolation of rent costs; and again, not less often, to spatial extension in some one or other of the different phases to which, in this general connection, emphasis has been directed.

So far, then, as can be inferred, Marshall does not regard any one of these offered aspects of differentiation as separately and independently necessary or final; and does not urge any one of them as separately and independently defensible. The distinguishability of land is, then, not urged as resting on any one of these various characteristics commonly associated with land, but rather on the sum of them, each one of them usually, but not uniformly and indispensably, present.

Does definition lend itself to this method? Precisely what is it to *define?* Possibly enough the marketplace may have fixed on some line or lines of distinction that may be analytically correct and ultimate. Only on what line or lines of distinction? Marshall, it is true, goes nowhere further than to imply the finality of the marketplace in the technical use of terms. Obviously, however, the market-place would only hesitatingly admit one's home, or even the building part of it, to be capital; but would make no question that a property occupied by a rent-paying tenant is capital. Marshall finds reasons for not concurring in these uses with respect to dwellings occupied by their owners. The market-place makes also no distinction between investments in land, of no matter what sort, and investments in buildings, so long as money returns are derived from them. Not rarely again, there is a business man who regards his residence or its furnishings, his summer place, his car or his carriage, as also the parties and receptions of his wife, as in large share items of business policy. Or he takes money out of his business, or securities out of his safety box, to provide himself a home, thereby excusing himself from the further paying of rent, and also achieving some additional social or financial certification. Or he may sell or mortgage his residence for the funds to extend his business operations. Nor, to think thus far, need he be an economist, or even an especially intelligent tradesman. And not all business men are manufacturers or merchandisers. There are also bankers, and farmers, and repair-station men. Occasionally, it is charged, there are advertisers among the doctors, the lawyers and the professors. There is no reason to suppose that a farmer is so little an economist as to regard only the chickens and eggs that he sells as income, or as a business item only that corner of the hog or steer that he takes to market, or only the land on which he grows cash crops as belonging to his trade capital; or even none of his land as in his trade capital. And if he did, it would not matter; or even if, for trade-capital purposes, he could find no distinction between his barn-yard and his barn. If in the choice of scientific terms the chief purpose is to avoid confusions in the thinking of merchandisers, bankers and farmers, there is something to say on both sides of the precept-ideal that never shall there be two terms for one class or two classes for one term. There are "dangers that arise from . . . avoiding the hard work that is required for discovering unity of substance underlying variety of form." This task of generalization need not, however, fall to the farmer or merchant. Nor need whatever generalizations he arrives at, be definitive for the economist.

It is obvious that any analysis, that either during pre-normal or normal periods will exclude rents from price-determining costs, must likewise exclude interest, unless it is possible to establish a distinction between liquid capital and equipment. But with interest excluded, so also must be wages. For capital is taken to be merely stored-up labor or stored-up wage investment, and interest merely indirect wages—plus, no doubt, a time charge. If, then, interest is not a price-determining cost, wages can not be.

The distinction between land and capital ran originally on the non-labor derivation of land. Capital, it was said, derives directly or indirectly entirely from labor. Land remains over without assignable derivation and without the need of any. Geographically and spatially considered, it is here now, without explanation through past or present human effort. Only so much as this is involved in calling it a *gift of nature* or by making any sort of appeal to its origin, that it has not been provided by human effort. So much is safely to be asserted of anything called land, but in the sole sense, be it noted, that whatever part of it has been due to labor—whether it be now known and recognized as such—is by that fact declared to be not land but capital. It is by definition that land is of non-labor derivation. Our problem, in one formulation of it, is therefore whether this is a defensible basis of distinction. How test the validity of a definition?

Land, then, is a gift of nature solely in the sense—and doubtless an intelligible sense—that through whatsoever effort, edict, or mystery it sometime and somehow had its origin, it was not through human labor. But through other labor? Possibly so; or possibly not. But does it matter, if only it were not through human labor? Only does it any the more matter whether it was or was not through human labor, rather than divine labor, or animal or insect labor or some other labor? Here it is, in any case. Why all this present solicitude as to what quality of past effort it was, or of what or of whom, in point of emotion or temper or even of consciousness? Is present economic analysis to turn on the degree or direction of the economists' sympathetic participation in these far-off, forgotten, or never-known, things of long ago—whether there were any efforts, and if so, whose, and of what sort, or of what temper? Or of what particular order of life or of intelligence, or whether there was the more of beatitude or of woe in whatever creative process there may have been? Is cosmic philosophy or cosmic speculation the necessary starting point for economics—all the issues both of the knowable and the unknowable brought to book through an endless genetic or historical regress?

Across the background, then, of our complete ignorance of origins, the phrase a *gift of nature* hazards only this one insecure and gratuitous affirmation—that however else the land may have come about, it was not through human effort. The rest is silence. It is, however, implicitly taken for granted in the classical tradition that whatever men have actually achieved in either increase of human capacity or of possessions must have been unwillingly and sufferingly achieved. Capital must have been conditioned on discomfort, both in the getting and in the keeping. And even so must it have been of the men's own bodies and minds—or at least of the individual and racial increase in vigor and intelligence. Not only are human beings born in grief and stress both for mother and child, but they get reared through the care, anxiety, sacrifice and expense of the parents; suffer from the measles and the pip; eat their bread in the sweat of their brows; looking forward, the most of them, to dire penances against their sins; a bad mess altogether—whereby not only do all commodities but all human beings occur on real-cost terms—which is good so far, at least, as concerns the labor theory of value—but also, it must be, in terms of real costs running far in excess of the gratifications that attach—a view which, in turn, would seem to be ill for the labor theory of value—there being pretty much everywhere a balance of discomforts over gratifications, even after due allowance is made for all these bounties of nature.

For, as has already been indicated, and as is by authority well attested in general, laborers themselves arrive on cost-of-production terms, both real and money. And thereafter whatever work they undertake is on terms of the further current stresses and burdens attaching to their efforts. And if, moreover, they should grievously achieve any income that they can spare for savings, the griefs of abstinence forthwith set in and pile up. This slight consolation however there has been, that without other griefs than those that attached to their coming to exist, they did—that is, some of them did, in an earlier time—come into the possession of a world wherein to live, a world labor-free in point of origin—though with themselves already damned into the grim necessity of living there. But even from this there was no advantage accruing to the later comers. The earlier comers they found to have already gathered in all that there was of any worthwhile quality—even down to the level of good-for-nothingness, the margin of cultivation. And thus it is that Marshall says:

". . . Capital needs to be considered in regard *both* to the embodied aggregate of the benefits derivable from its use, *and* to the embodied aggregate of the costs of the efforts and of the saving needed for its production: and it will be shown how these two aggregates tend to balance. . . ." (p. 82, note)

". . . There is a constant tendency towards a position of normal equilibrium, in which the supply of each of these agents shall stand in such a relation to the demand for its services, as to give to those who have provided the supply a sufficient reward for their efforts and sacrifices. If the economic conditions of the country remained stationary sufficiently long, this tendency would realize itself in such an adjustment of supply to demand, that both machines and human beings would earn generally an amount that corresponded fairly with their cost of rearing and training, conventional necessities . . . being reckoned for. . . ." (p. 577).

How, if at all, then, as subgroups of *wealth,* are *land capital* and other *capital* to be distinguished—for purposes, be it remembered, of the anti-thesis of price-determining to price-determined costs of production? Shall it be, for example, by some one or by some several differentia regarding—

(1) the character of the incomes
(2) the form in which they accrue
(3) the derivation of the sources (origins)
(4) the relative durability of the sources
(5) the spatial fixity of the sources (unmodifiability or inelasticity)
(6) the marginal exclusion of rent from the determination of price
(7) further or substitute differentia—e.g.
    a) movability of the sources
    b) the social or political status or function of the owners
    c) the divergent trends of interest rates and rent sums.

Say that on one or more of the foregoing lines, separately or together, the distinction is urged. May, then, its tenability be refuted by proving separately and in turn the indefensibility of each of these offered lines? But perhaps if, in any particular case, one distinction does not apply, another will. And if no one of them separately will, perhaps several of them together may.

Suppose it then to be proved that out of the five different aspects in which a thing commonly differs from another thing, there is no one aspect with reference to which it always differs—no one of all these aspects a separately essential condition. What thereby is accomplished? As a matter of procedure, how go about refuting the tenability of any classification? If success is possible, what constitutes success? In point of method, precisely what is the issue? Can some group of proposed differentia, no one of which is separately defensible, together suffice? May it not be true that through the possession at any one time of, say, three or four of those five different aspects, the title to a separate classification is established—correctness of definition possible through large effects, a general smudge of usual qualities—by just looking at the things usually called capital?

Implicit, however, in practically all definitions, is a group of requisites —e.g., a time dimension, externality, price-statement, private gain. Of these several differentia, no one need, it is true, be taken as separately sufficing; each may require with it all of the others; each separately essential, but not independently sufficient. But may it not be true that even if no one of them alone will suffice, several of them together, though not all at once, may suffice? Is it true that each of them separately conditions the adequacy of the sum of them—just as it takes all of the legs of a stool together, and no some near-all, to constitute a stool? May not several of these five attributes—with perhaps some further excellent attributes in addition—eke out the requirement, getting along without the one, or atoning by substitutes for its lack? What degree of the "boldness and rigor of fastened senses" does definition inelastically impose? Are compromises possible? What is it to define anyway? How define *definition*? Must the limits come full circle—much as a pasture may as well not be fenced at all as only four-fifths or nine-tenths fenced? The jump that is not full across the ditch, not better than a half-way jump, or none at all—and possible worse?

Caucasians are, for example, commonly tall; commonly intelligent; commonly quarrelsome; commonly acquisitive; commonly white. If then a particular individual discloses, say, three or four of these five attributes —no one of which always holds for Caucasians—may not thereby his title be made sufficiently clear? It certainly may, if it be true that the one ultimate issue is that of racial stock or of origin—taking it there is such a thing—of which these different aspects of quality are merely separate items of evidence. But stock or origin is still the one differentiating fact. Items of evidence may support the substantive fact; they cannot replace it.

Suppose that I designate an acquaintance of mine as a man, of the name, John Smith, resident in the United States, in State A, County B, in City C, on Street D, in Block E, at Number F. Here are various concentric differentia. There are millions of individuals meeting each of the widest of the specifications; and there are people enough of the name John Smith, even in Cleveland, Ohio; and D Street is well built up; and even so of Block E; and several individuals are resident at number F. But the right individual John Smith has to meet each and all of the specifications. Three or four out of the whole will not pick out the right John Smith. There will hardly be two John Smiths meeting all of the specifications. The individual lacking in one of them will not be the right John Smith. The case will not go off on majorities.

And precisely so with definitions. Whatever requirements there are, must be met. Substitutes for essentials will not suffice. Majorities will not suffice. If too few are met, too much will be included. It is for definition to fix the essentials, and to limit them. Which is to say that it is for definition to define.

We have then to make out through what aspect or aspects an item of wealth that would otherwise be capital becomes *land;* which is the same thing as to make out by the lack of what aspects it fails to become land.

Whatever differentia are alleged, must stand the test of differentia. If, then, it is the relation of land hires to prices which is presented as the differentiating fact, let this be submitted to prompt and thorough inspection; or origins—things due to natural bounty; or indestructibility; or uncreatability; or fertility; or spatial limitation; or the peculiar annuities of sun and rain and air; or the exclusive appropriateness of the marginal-isolation analysis; or the peculiar indefensibility of private ownership in items of the environment; or some combination of these; and so on. But what one, or what ones? And if it be no one of these taken separately, or no group of these, but something else, then what particular thing else? But if no one of these items is separately essential, then not all of them together can be; and still less any inside grouping of them. We ask merely to know what specifically is the test, or what are the tests. And the reply can not rightly be, just other things in general, things vaguely identified, or entirely unidentified, or the contingent togetherness of several specific things, each taken to be separately unessential.

This much of rigidity, at any rate, there must be in definition; that it *define*. A definition is, moreover, as we have earlier seen, not a point of setting out, but a point of arrival, a compact summary of the conclusions to which a preceding analysis has led—conclusions reached as fixing the meaning appropriate to a term as a tool for the intellectual handling of the material under examination in view of the problem-aspects of it under consideration. Call, then, indifferently as you will any particular eminence or hill, Shasta or Tom or Methusaleh. You make thereby no assertions about it but of particularization. But you have not the same freedom about calling a particular thing a hawk or a handsaw, else you may make a mess not only of the dictionary but of some necessary work. The old lady who was quite content about her knowledge of astronomy, excepting that she could not make out how ever the names of the stars were discovered, was lacking in appreciation of the difference between common and proper nouns. Definition, for purposes of thinking, means knowing specifically and precisely what you are talking about.

I do not know, then, what Marshall holds to be the distinctive quality of land capital, as setting it off from equipment capital, and attaching to the hire of it an enduring irrelevance to price determination—its functional relation one of result rather than of cause. I interpret him to hold that no one particular quality or aspect or character is, or needs to be, the abiding test of a scientific category in the social field, but only a fairly high degree of participation in a group of phases no one of which is in its own right and separately a crucial and essential thing. The notion of concentric circles of inclusion and exclusion in the process of subclassification presents the point in issue. Marshall seems to me not to accept it. That I insist in it, sums up my position of thorough-going dissent.

Chapter IX

OPPORTUNITY COSTS: VARIOUS LAND COSTS

THE SECOND glass of water at any particular time is less desired than the first; with increasing consumption, appetite moves toward satiety.

Something analogous, if not identical, holds with indirect goods. A second wheelbarrow with one man, or a second wagon with one horse, affords at best a small increment of advantage. No one tract of land is hungry for indefinitely increased doses of fertilizer or for repeated plowings or hoeings. There arrives a point at which more outlay for labor or more equipment expense gets things out of proportion by the test of net gains. If the undertaking is being enlarged, the time will come when more outlay for land must go along with more labor or fertilizer or machine expense, or with all of them.

The law of the falling utility of direct goods is doubtless a fact in human nature. The law of diminishing return with indirect goods is a fact of industry. The former finds its basis in a biological or psychological limitation on zest or capacity; the second, in a technological limitation on the absorptive capacity of one indirect good for other indirect goods, its valency in industrial combinations: valencies of human desires for successive doses of any one direct good in the first case; valencies of indirect goods for one another in the second case. The law of falling utility refers therefore, in the main or entirely, to the spending of incomes; the law of diminishing return, a law applying in the main to the acquiring of them, a law bearing primarily on the combination of productive factors. Both laws, however, appeal to the same broad and underlying principle. But the law of right proportions deals with the combination of indirect goods; the law of falling utility, commonly with the satiability of desire for any one direct good.

215

There are nevertheless many illustrations of interdependence among direct goods. Potatoes and bread call for pepper and salt, or butter; razors, for shaving soap and brushes. A silk hat is a hazardous purchase, in view of the all-round pressures of dressing up to it—the principle of right proportions. All around the circle we have to line up with each point on the circumference of it, in the effort to achieve not merely right-tasting, but "tasty" combinations.

But not merely are there these supplementary relations—these relations of interdependence and of mutual requirement—to be noted among different goods, both direct and indirect, but also there are aspects of substitution that require no less attention. Bread substitutes for potatoes; eggs for meat; milk or cheese or fish, for eggs or meat; sugar for bread or potatoes—but all of these only within the elastic limit of tolerance prescribed by the balanced ration. Probably also there are some nutritive possibilities of functional substitution among fats, carbohydrates and proteids.

In any case, there are important non-dietary illustrations of the possibilities of substitution. To the end of keeping up appearances, a car will go a long way toward atoning for economies in clothing, housing, neighborhood, servants, entertainment and summer cottages.

With indirect goods the substitutions of factors of production or of gain are familiar; and they are practically without limit, if only they fall within the near-marginal area of application. For these substitutionary relations almost inevitably present themselves —as with foods—at distances never very remote from the margins. Moreover, harvesting or factory machinery must have labor to go along with it, and motor power, and lubricating oils. In most climates feed will not entirely do away with sheds.

Both with direct and indirect goods, these methods of supplementation and of substitution must be adopted in view always of their relative price costs. When potatoes are dear and bread cheap, the competent housewife stresses bread in the household dietary; provides more eggs in the spring and less meat; buys at the seaside much fish and little meat; and with the changing seasons modifies constantly the relative consumption of different vegetables and especially of different fruits.

The farmer follows parallel policies with his different stock-feeds in view of their relative prices. Similarly, fuel oil is displacing fuel coal. So office, hotel, and loft buildings are going higher and at increasing costs per story, in substitution for larger outlays in ground space. The low wage level of some countries discourages invention and any extended use of auxiliaries in production— poverty thus perpetuating itself as does also opulence. Where the need of labor-saving devices is at the maximum, the use of them is at the minimum—a competitive paradox which the collective planning of the Soviets is trying to transcend. There are, in fact, no right distributions of business funds or of expenditures in the combinations of factors, excepting as against the background of the relative prices in the particular field. Outlays in the quest for gain, like outlays for direct goods, take place through comparisons of the prospective efficiencies of the different goods at their respective prices. Always the principle is that of economizing gain efficiency or utility. Always, with the buying of both consumers and producers, the principle of distribution is at one with the principles both of substitution and of supplementation. Always the process is one of choice between competing openings, a comparison of alternative marginal efficiencies for the purposes in hand. The price efficiency of indirect goods is, by their very nature, their sole utility. The principle is the same for price offers with both classes of goods, deriving always from a comparison of marginal utilities —with direct goods, utilities in consumption; with indirect goods, utilities of gain efficiency.

Never are there, then, any direct or indirect serviceabilities to be reported impersonally and in the large. In a society of private property under private initiative for private gain, every account of policies and choices in spending or in investing needs to be consistently individualized. There are no utilities or efficencies at large. All producing and consuming is individual. All price offers and all goods offers, whether for direct or for indirect goods, are individual. And all of these offers report not utility or gain taken absolutely, but only relatively.

The wide application of this principle of comparison is merely another extension of the principle of substitution. It holds not less with indirect than with direct goods. It is constantly illustrated at the point of marginality between the uses of different factors of production. In making a crop, more fertilizer will, as we have seen, atone for cheap lands, or for a limited investment in farm machinery, or for economies in the hiring of labor. And with the utilization of land capital and equipment capital, this law of substitution is at the very heart of diminishing returns and of the marginal exhaustion of factors and of the broader law of right proportions, in view of the relative prices of the factors. It is thereby the ultimate principle of the productivity theory of distribution, and of whatever residual of truth there is in the marginal-productivity theory with its attempted marginal isolation of the various factor efficiencies.

With both direct and indirect goods, therefore, the law of substitution and the law of proportions sum up into the law of the maximizing of efficiency: never an expenditure that sacrifices the greater marginal utility to the less; never a production cost incurred where better price results promise to be achieved through substituted factors or through a different combination of factors. This principle of relativity, of comparative advantage, is everywhere present. The consideration ordinarily decisive against the doing of any one thing is the greater advantage, inclusive of the smaller loss, from doing something else—that broad generalization formulated in the objective world as the line of least resistance, and in the subjective world as the line of least sacrifice—with both resistance and sacrifice taken, of course, as inclusive of the stronger pull or inducement.

In one aspect, therefore, economics sums up into a detailed account of *choice* in the multitude of its settings in the price field. And as a fact implicit in choice, *substitution* is also everywhere. Never therefore anywhere does *choice* or *substitution* afford an adequate explanation of anything until there is pointed out the precise occasion and working of the choice and the substitution. The great law of choice or of substitution explains any particular thing in almost the same sense as does the *Cosmos* or the *Nature of Things*—true presumably, though not, as such, very significant; but requiring often to be made explicit in emphasis or application —as, for example, in opportunity cost—even itself, in turn, prone by its wide extension to hide rather than to disclose definite and explicit explanations. Pushed, indeed, to its utmost elasticity of meaning, all cost has to be opportunity cost—alternatives as resistances.

Had Crusoe only one direction of desire, e.g., for food, and for food of only one particular kind, say bananas, but with these available in plenty for the taking, he would extend his consumption near to the zero limit of utility. For ease of illustration take it to be accurately a zero marginal utility. With all of his needs for food centered on bananas, the point of satiation would arrive late. But were there a second desirable food available, say, breadfruit, on similarly costless terms, but measurably different in flavor, and still in some degree a substitution line of consumption, bananas would be less consumed than before, with the point of zero utility arriving earlier, and at a lower total of banana utility. Inclusive, however, of the bread-fruit utility, the aggregate utility would be greater than with the bananas alone. The principle of the maximizing of utility would apply, but only in the somewhat unusual sense that Crusoe would be economizing, so to speak, as does a lad at a bountiful table, his stock of zest and capacity, so that no desire should arrive at satisfaction on terms of the cancellation of some stronger desire awaiting its equally ready satisfaction. *Hold over some appetite and some room for dessert.* Nothing here implies, however, that by a change in conditions the marginal utility of a good may rise or fall, remaining nevertheless all the while at zero—two zeros of divergent magnitudes. The truth is that, subjectively viewed, the bananas become, through the presence of the breadfruit, a different commodity. The consumption of the substitute commodity lowers the desiredness of bananas. The point of satiation, of zero utility, arrives therefore earlier with either commodity; fewer units of it desired than would be desired were it the sole available commodity.

With only the bananas for food, but with effort costs conditioning the output, there would be a smaller total of output at a higher marginal utility. With both the bananas and the breadfruit, and with costs for both equal per unit of utility produced, the output of bananas would be reduced not only by its cost resistance, but also by the competition of the breadfruit. By itself, the influence of the cost on the marginal utility of bananas would be to raise it; and the influence of the breadfruit by itself to lower it. The influence of each of the two on the other, when both are produced together, is to restrict the output of the other, but to increase the joint total, with a diminished marginal utility for each. By itself, the influence of cost on the two products, when produced together, is to limit the volume of their joint output, and thus to raise the marginal utility of both. It should all the while be held in mind that this is Crusoe discussion, where utility and marginal utility are safely to be invoked consistently with accurate analysis.

A similar line of analysis will be appropriate to a widening field of desires and a widening field of productive opportunities. The effort applied to production will be greater, the intensity of the marginal effort higher, and the marginal utility of products higher, as the volume of each output is restricted by the cost limitation. There is, then, a three-fold explanation for the higher intensity of effort in the temperate than in the tropical zones, and for the higher per-capital wealth and income. Needs in the temperate zone are more intense, even irrespective of their wider variety. Effort is therefore distributed more widely, and thus more thinly, despite the increase of it in the total. But per unit of effort, the concrete product in each line of production is lower in terms of objective results than in the tropics; for if it were not the higher there, it would not get produced at all, in view of the greater burdensomeness of effort there—needs small; effort difficult; product generous.

It is thus clear that with Crusoe, in an environment of more pressing needs his production will be greater, at a higher margin of real cost, and thereby at higher marginal utilities of products —unless, to be sure, the environment is appreciably less responsive to productive effort. So much, indeed, would be true, even had the lines of need and of productive opportunity remained unchanged. In fact, however, the needs are not only more numerous but more pressing. Thereby both effort and output will be the greater. The stress of living grows as new needs are maturing along with new ways of serving them, if only the response to effort be neither over-niggardly nor over-generous. Just here is the significance of Veblen's pithy comment: "You know, necessity isn't the mother of invention." No? "Invention is the mother of necessity." Yes, but—"You see, if we don't know how to do these things, we can't do them, can we?"[1]

It must then be clear that the more things Crusoe had to do, the less he could do each of them. In the main, not the effort costs of any one thing are the explanation for the limited output of it, but the absorption of productive energies in the producing of alternative things. Usually, indeed, it is these alternative things that account for the high real costs of production, the high tension and weariness of effort all along the margins of production. Crusoe's real costs as, by assumption, at balance against the utilities produced at the various margins, may admirably serve as the common denominator of the marginal significance of his various products, or the other way about; but the unit amount of these marginal costs is to be explained only in view of the aggregate pressure of his various desires, and of the competition of his various products for the energies to produce them—these interproduct absorptions of the limitedly elastic total of productive efficiency. The query is, then, a reasonable one how the introduction of breadfruit could ever have carried a barbarous island people

---

[1] No reference; it was in a chat before the fire.

Greatest, perhaps, among the problems in the art of living is *what is all this worth?*—especially in view of the working of competitive consumption. I have elsewhere quoted my sometime friend, then death-stricken: "Why was everything I ever wanted to do either extravagant or immoral or indigestible?"

back to savagery. Needs were so narrow in variety and substitution-ary qualities of breadfruit so wide, in view of the character of the needs, as to illustrate the worthlessness of Paradise. The discussion here has so far assumed near-marginal areas of substitution between commodities of a general separateness of service—commodities responsive in the main to different directions of desire.

If now under these conditions Crusoe were able, through a new method of cultivation or a newly invented tool, to expand greatly his output of one food product, say wheat, the marginal utility of wheat would especially fall. More energy would be set free for the production of alternative goods, food and other, at some decrease therefore of their marginal utilities; decreasing the total utility of each several line of products, but increasing the aggregate utility of the different products. Marginal utilities would still be equal all along the frontiers of commodity production, but the fall in the marginal utility of wheat would be relatively marked.

And similarly, assuming more generous resources of land, with the relations of land products to other products. But the relative inelasticity in the consumption of agricultural products would mean that these products would not greatly increase in output; that in the main the economy of energy would report itself in the expanded outputs of other things; and that suspension of production on land would arrive especially early—the fall in the aggregate utility of those products especially marked, the unit real- and displacement-costs and unit utility low. For a competitive situation, these basal conditions would mean a relative fall in the prices of agricultural products.[2]

---

[2] The immediate purpose here has been to bring into clear relief the fact that whatever may be the bearing of rents on competitive prices, the bearing of stocks of land is not open to question. Relative outputs of goods and relative marginal utilities are modified, and therefore relative prices. Reported in terms of the enterpriser process, land scarcities translate into high outlay costs in rents. Such in the main is the meaning of the "basement" approach. In whatever sense any costs are price-determining, rent outlays, as also indicative of underlying scarcities, are also price-determining. In one emphasis, doubtless, it is possible to regard all hires as, on the enterpriser level, price-determining; in another, to regard all hires as price-determined. The enterpriser must pay hire in order to control the factors, and thus to command their products, and thus to command their prices; but it is these prices that he is to get that reflect back to impose the hires of the factors. High land makes high pork; and high pork makes high land. But, in either emphasis,

Our specific illustrations have, however, so far taken Crusoe to be the sole productive fact in the achieving of his total of product. His first-quality lands have been ample; each one of his two food products, bananas and breadfruit, being taken to absorb units of energy and to impose units of real cost, according to the principle of returning equal amounts of marginal utility—neither of the two being permitted to displace in its production more marginal utility than it affords, or to impose more real cost than it is worth.

These assumptions have now to be modified. Assume that Crusoe is dependent for his food on the growing of two crops, wheat and potatoes—products in some degree substitutionary, but mainly of independent desirability—on a meager area of land that is of first-quality response to the labor applied to it. Land scarcity as well as effort costs come now to be limiting factors. Rule out for the moment any reserves of poorer-quality land as well as all complications of equipment capital.

Crusoe must now make some apportionment of his land resources as well as of his labor. Both will be allocated to wheat and potatoes on such a basis that no unit of either will be permitted to displace more utility of the other or of non-land products than it affords, or to impose more effort than it is worth.

---

all hires go together. It is not possible to divide any group into facts of cause and facts of result. As bearing on prices all these hires trace back to scarcities. At any given time, land is no more limited in volume, or particular lands for particular products more limited in volume, than are men or machines or mules. Any inter- priser can have all of any one for which he wants to pay. But what of the past or the future, or the whence, or the whither? We are talking about the present. It is not necessary for a thing to impose a cost twice in order to impose it once. Nor does it matter to what it is now, whether later it will be more or less, or was earlier more or less—even if any one could securely know.

And even where the distinction from the employer point of view between prime and supplementary costs is in point—the distinction between commitments earlier made and now irrevocable, and those with which the forward-looking analysis still holds, where choice is still open—there is no tenable distinction possible along cause and result lines. The hires of these goods of earlier provision may be more or less than remunerative to the investor; but such as they are, such are the costs —costs that in the given situation are price-determining in the sense that any other cost ever is. Whatever the owner can rent out the goods for, is what the hirer of them has to pay. There are competitors in the given industry, and commonly there are other lines of production offering hires for the goods. Marshall gets so many things under the law of substitution that he forgets this particular one of oppor- tunity costs.

Unit increments of utility-product from the land will be achieved at a rising cost in effort—the law of diminishing return—and at an increasing real cost per unit of labor applied—the law of fatigue as well as of keener desire for recreation. The utility of produce falling, and the resistance to product rising, a point of equilibrium is not distant. Assign it, say, at five o'clock in the afternoon. It would have arrived earlier, had there been only one crop known to Crusoe, or possible of growing. With a wider choice of crops, it would come later. But each crop will suffer the more in volume as the number of alternative crops or other products is the greater. The law of substitution is in this aspect a law of resisting alternative utilities.

This is the principle of opportunity cost. Say that you have been given a dollar, and that you are at choice between buying with it a book and a pocket knife. You take the book; what has it cost you? Nothing, the dollar having come as a gift? That is now an item of history. The actual resistance against buying the book is the lure of the pocket knife.

But what if you must go to work to get the dollar? Assume that a box of candy, as your third choice in spending, is enough to indemnify you for working. The cost of the book is, then, still the pocket knife. Always it is the ranking resistance that registers the cost. Book and knife were the ranking pair of alternative goods. The candy was the third horse in the race, with leisure the fourth. There were doubtless a series of further alternatives grading down from the candy, and if both the book and the knife were out of the reckoning, the candy would find its ranking resistance in that indefinite article next in the declining series. The resistance to the purchase of the book is not all of the different alternatives at once, because not all together could be had in place of the book. It is the ranking one among the different alternatives that is the cost, because the book that overcomes that resistance can still the more readily overcome that of any other. Cost is resistance. The thing that is in issue against the book, the thing between which and the book the problem of choice arises, is the thing that actually the buying of the book displaces. Were not the book purchased, the knife would be. The leisure would not be the foregone thing, because by assumption the knife and the candy outrank it.

The principle may perhaps become clearer, if Crusoe be taken to have a plot of second-grade land that he is finding it worth while to cultivate. There can then be no question of the resistance of effort in cultivating the first-grade tract. His sole problem is how to divide it between wheat and potatoes. The resistance to allotting any part to either is the pull of the other, not the displaced leisure.

How go about persuading a farmer not to plant a particular field to corn? The family labor is there anyway. To abandon the farm is not in contemplation. You have to show him something better than corn to do with the land; that, say, wheat would give a better return—the corn return less than the displaced return. To look for the cost resistance in the real costs of effort could avail only if the corn were the sole practicable crop—the issue coming then to be whether this one crop were worth while as against not working this particular tract of land, so far, then, a partial abandoning of the farm. But this is to abandon all consideration of *land* costs.

And still, is there not at the intensive margin an effort resistance? Doubtless there are real cost aspects in the effort applied. But the question of what in some non-farm direction to do with the labor is another question. Labor-wise there could be such an effort cost, or an alternative-product cost—the alternative, say, of teaching school or soliciting life insurance. But we are discussing the issue of land costs, the resistances attaching to the *land* use. We are trying to determine when and how far there is a *land* cost, what resistances attach to *it*—and this, for the moment, as a question of mere produce, and not of price product.

The cost attaching to the labor applied to the land—not its wage cost, note—may be a real cost fact, or may not, depending on whether the ranking alternative is one of an alternative product or of avoided effort and displaced leisure. But the land has neither pains of producing nor joys in being idle. The sole resistance attributable to it has to be sought in its alternative uses.

Moreover, while the effort is a real cost item of debit attaching to production at the marginal use of indirect goods, all along the line of the various products, it is in its very terms a charge that is common to all of these various products; and thus, as an element common to all of them, it cancels out—the equation neither the better nor the worse for its inclusion or its exclusion as a real cost fact, set over against returns in utility. For we are not now concerned with wages and money costs. If, however, we were, with dollar costs set over against dollar products, there would be a clear case for inclusion as against exclusion—but this an issue for later consideration.

And it is further to be noted that the actual choice in this isolated economy, as far as land uses are concerned, is between the use of a particular area of land for one crop as against another. It is a particular land unit that goes or stays—one crop to be had from it as a whole, as against another crop from it as a whole, or against doing nothing with it as a whole. The marginal line is a division between an area for another use, not a margin of so much wheat and so much corn to be had from a particular area—not a succotash cropping. It is a take-it-or-leave-it decision, a unit shift if any shift there is.

At Crusoe's margins of production, real costs are in equilibrium with marginal utilities, and this equally whether the needs are intense or weak; whether the marginal returns are high or low; and whether the real costs are great or small. In any particular Crusoe situation, any real cost, as equating at the margin against any product at the margin, offers a practicable common denominator of subjective worths, marginal utilities. But equally, any one of these subjective worths is available as denominator, since at the margins all real costs and all worths are equal. The efforts may carry with them high or low real costs, and the respective offsetting utilities may be great or small. But the ratios of effort costs to the derivative utilities are in every case equality ratios, no matter what may be the feeling quantities that are the terms in the ratios. In a given environment Crusoe may desire keenly; may work hard; may work with high intelligence and power; or the reverse of all this may be true. A different Crusoe, whether in the same or in another environment, would differ in each of these subjective aspects and in objective conditions. As the outcome, however, of his desires and of his particular adaptations to different lines of production within the particular situation, his different products would have *relative* worths entirely peculiar to him. But per unit the relative worths of the different products to Crusoe would be proportional both with their marginal utilities and with their marginal costs. But that for each of two men there are marginal equalities of utilities to real costs, gives no support to the notion that inter-individually either the utilities or the real costs are quantitatively equal. One of these two Crusoes may have, *relatively to the other* per unit of product, low real costs and high utilities; the other high costs and low utilities. And thus in an exchange system between individuals, no warrant exists for the notion that goods exchange proportionally either with their marginal utilities or their marginal pain costs. The chances are infinitely great to the contrary—so far, indeed, as comparability of pains and pleasures is possible between individuals. Similarities of ratios assert nothing quantitatively as to the terms in the ratios—the ratios merely relations between quantities. Individual measures by real costs are intelligible as ratios explaining individual appraisals of products. Inter-individual measures are pure folly. The case for the real-cost determination or measure of exchange relations through recourse to averages has been already sufficiently discussed.

Because in economic analysis in general, both early and late, confusing shifts between competitive and collective costs have been chronic—as for example, with Wieser's attempt in *Natural Value* to derive from collective cost safe guidance for competitive-cost analysing and with Marshall's use of *social cost* to deny to rents whatever bearing he attributes to other hires on prices—a further and somewhat detailed and wearisome examination of collective cost and of its articulations with competitive cost, especially with reference to rents, must now be undertaken. It will be made evident that collective cost and Crusoe cost are close to indistinguishable, both being appropriate to a unitary economy; and that the affiliations of collective cost with the "basement" level of analysis are always intimate. Necessary, however, to this "base-ment" view as an adequate explanation of exchange relations, is the opportunity-cost supplementation; and necessary to its articulation with the enterpriser-cost process, is the transition from relative scarcities on the "basement" level to relative price hires on the enterpriser level—a perplexing task at the best as is always true of changes in point of view.

The ordinary man is offended by the old phrase that rent does not enter into the price of oats [for it clearly does come out]; when he sees that an increase in the demand for land for other uses, manifests itself in a rise of the rental value of all land in the neighbourhood; leaves less land free for growing oats; consequently makes it worth while to force larger crops of oats out of the remaining oat-land, and thus raises the marginal expenses of oats and their price. . . . (p. 436, note)

But Marshall will insist that it is not the higher rent on oat land, but the diminished stock of land available for the production of oats that diminishes the output of oats; increases the price of oats; and then, and solely thereby, raises the rent on the oat land. Rent is therefore a result of the price and not a price-determining cost-cause.

. . . A rise in rent does serve as a medium through which the growing scarcity of land available for hops and other produce obtrudes itself on his notice; and it is not worth while to try to force him to go behind these symptoms of the change in conditions to the truly operative causes. It is therefore inexpedient to say that the rent of land does not enter into their price: But it is worse than inexpedient to say that the rent of the land does enter into their price: that is false. (pp. 436-37, note)

But obviously the case is not precisely thus hopeless—the truth outlawed by inexpediency, and solely the error to be frankly adjudged. The difficulty is that costs of production are a mere enterpriser category—the way he has to look at things for the purposes of making them manageable for his purposes of gain. The costs are the debits that he must recognize, as attaching for him to the things through the control and intermediary of which he is to achieve his credits of price return. Doubtless it is the shortage of land that imposes on him the high rent outlays to control it; but equally it is the shortage of the land—so little of it anyway, or so much of it absorbed by other crops—that imposes the shortage of products, and makes these products high of cost for him when he gets them ready to market. True enough that if he could get the land for nothing, and could still sell the products for much, that would be far better. His rent would then be a surplus for him; only that, with the land scarce for growing the crop and the prices high, he somehow can't have the land so cheaply. But so also, if he could get the Pattis for little or nothing, and sell the tickets high—or the wool cheap and sell the cloth high—that likewise would be an excellently good thing. The fact is that, as Marshall has pointed out in another connection and for another purpose, the enterpriser is a middle-man between the sellers of the uses of price-productive agents and the price-buyers of the products. It is on him that these scarcities of agents focus, by reporting themselves to him in the guise of their high hires or purchase prices—his high costs. It is for him, in the interests of his own gains, to work out his adjust- ments to the conditions that are the ultimate and the truly operative causes. These are the scarcities of means, the agents, and the scarcity of ends, the products—all in face of the human desires that are seeking satisfaction. But these are the underlying influences— causes to be appealed to on the "basement" level of analysis. Or, changing a little the figure, the enterpriser process moves on the surface of waters that have depths which the enterpriser only vaguely recognizes, and with which his level of cost analysis is not at all concerned. On this enterpriser level of cost analysis, there is little choice whether one proclaims the price costs as fixing the prices of the products, or the prices of the products as fixing the prices of the cost goods. By the test of appeal to the underlying causes, neither cost prices nor product prices rank relatively to each other as either cause or effect. Both are effects of the under- lying causes. Tested, however, by the causal sequence valid for the "basement" level of analysis, the product prices rank one step earlier than the cost prices. To repeat: abstracting from the demand side of the underlying situation—the desires and the derivative price demands—the causal sequence, shortly and not quite ade- quately formulated to take account of all the relatives involved in it, runs from the relative scarcity of factors, to the relative scarcity of products, thence to the relative prices of the products, the relative hires of the factors, and finally to the relative prices of such of the factors as can get capitalized. Marshall says:

> Jevons asks . . . "If land which has been yielding £2 per acre rent, as pasture, be ploughed up and used for raising wheat, must not the £2 per acre be debited against the expense of production of wheat?" The answer is in the negative. For there is no connection between this particular sum of £2 and the expenses of production of that wheat which only just pays its way. . . . (p. 437, note)

True it is that this particular sum of £2 is connected with wheat prices not as a £2 item of wheat costs, but as a resistance that had to be overcome in expanding the area of wheat land; so far thereby expanding the output of wheat; thereby, so far, an influence to raise the aggregate land-rent costs which the enterpriser process of providing wheat for the market must face. Grass lands, grass, grass prices, and grass rents, as costs for enterpriser purposes, have all been affected in the reverse emphasis. This transfer of land from grass to wheat uses has not, it is true, moved these £2 over into enterpriser wheat costs; but it has affected the location of the wheat margin of production, the volume of wheat, the cost of production of it at the land margin, the rent of wheat land, the cost of all the supra-marginal product, and the prices of all of the products, those marginally produced and the others. Marshall's appeal to the land-margin cost of production as the place of price fixation or determination or governing is a fallacy. The land costs of the product on any given piece of land are all equal.[4] They would be unequal, it is true, but for the rent. There is, then, no occasion for dissent from the following formulation by Marshall:

> . . . And if for the purposes of any particular argument we take together the whole expenses of the production on that land, and divide these among the whole of the commodity produced; then the rent which we ought to count in is not that which the land would pay if used for producing the first commodity, but that which it does pay when used for producing the second. (p. 437, note)

[4] Marshall, p. 497.

But keep in mind the issue: is land rent a price-determining or a price-determined cost? The reply must be that the distinction between price-determining and price-determined is untenable, the issue a false issue. In any sense that any costs are price-determining, all are. And in any sense that any are price-determined, all are. And all attempts to arrive at an explanation of prices by the method of marginal isolation are equally fallacious. But presumably this was in purpose a recourse to the "basement" level. At this level, no cost is price-determining or price-determined; and the argument from the marginal isolation of rent hires has been already shown to be, and admitted to be, untenable. Thus Marshall's present defense for excluding rent from price-determining cost, the while retaining the other expenses, amounts to the repudiation of all these items.

It would probably seem absurd to say that a concert manager should count as within his costs of providing musical entertainments, not the salaries that he actually has to pay, but only such part of these as his singers could command were each employed in his best alternative line of occupation, for example, as a sales-manager or ticket-seller or wardrobe-custodian or cook—not what he does pay them, but what he would have to pay if he had to pay less. It would be similarly unsatisfactory to count, in building costs, not what the bricklayers collect as bricklayer wages, but only what they would collect had each to work as hod-carrier or mortar-mixer or, perhaps, as a section hand on a railroad; or, again, to count in the determinants of passenger charges on an ocean liner only what the boat would command as a cattle ship or tramp steamer.

It is indeed perplexing to be assured on high economic authority —Jevons, Patton, Macfarlane, Johnson, Hobson and von Wieser— that it is only the rent-earning power of land in its best alternative use that is to be computed as cost in the actual employment. And still it is clear that the lower limit to which the rent could fall in one employment, would be the rent waiting as possible in an alternative employment.

Something then is called for in the direction of harmonizing this antithesis of plausibilities and near-absurdities. And this is to be

achieved through holding fast to three clear lines of distinction:
(1) between cost as employer-viewed and cost as employee-viewed;
(2) between cost as collectively viewed and cost as competitively
viewed; (3) between competitive cost as outlay and competitive
cost as displaced price-product.

Were it somehow to the purpose to inquire of the employer, not
as to his cost in the hiring of his employees, but of the employees
as to their costs in working for the employer, the different reports
might vary widely. To the employer, to be sure, the cost of getting
his singing done is what he has to pay as salaries to his singers for
doing the singing. But what is the cost to an employee in doing this
singing? A singer, pain-cost inclined, might report, against putting
forth of the effort attending the rendering of the services for which
he received his pay, his debit of head-aches and weariness and
boredom; another singer, his earlier time or his outlays of training,
or the sum of the two; still another, what a different impressario
would pay him, or what another line of occupation would return,
or the hire necessary to off-set the joys or the peace of leisure—
or to offset both together.

These costs of the labor to the laborer himself, the resistance
terms on which he obtains his labor to sell, are manifestly hard to
come by—so hard indeed, that the business world is fortunate
in not having to estimate them. Sunk costs are everywhere to be
detected. These, however, are of the nature of earlier commitments
—supplementary costs, it may be, from the point of view *of the
employee*. But for the purposes of his present situation, the cost
inquiry would lead him to that necessary remuneration on which
he conditions the rendering of his service. Only, his services to
whom? To the industry as some sort of personified entity? Or to the
particular employer to whom this laborer's services are now being
rendered? Take it as true that his affection for this particular employer is bounded by the disposition to work for him at what
another employer would pay—and not at less. In such case, the
employee's present cost in laboring for his actual employer is presumably the displaced hire from another employer. If, however, the
cost issue were formulated by the employer as what least hire would

suffice to retain this singing laborer at his singing, then the cost quantum would have reference merely to what the laborer would get, were he getting less than he is now getting; his ranking resistance reporting itself in the money terms of a displaced hire or the ranking resistance might equally well be one in the discomfort emphasis—what least salary would indemnify the head-aches and heartaches of his job; or finally at a money statement of his most alluring counter attraction in the field of leisure.

But say that the maximum resistance stated in terms of money were the hire that he could have in a *different field* of activity—as, to be sure, might be the case; although it probably would not be. This alternative hire would concern the employer not at all, unless and until something like a parity should be reached between the actual and the alternative hires. Up to that point, or down to it, the employee's costs do not concern the employer. Later they might, it is true; but then only as they should bear on what does concern the employer—the amount that now, or possibly later, he must pay.

Nor more nor otherwise need the employer who has to pay a rental charge for a machine concern himself with this issue of costs from the point of view of the owner of the machine. I rent you my plow, or draft horse, or slave. After allowance has been made for my debits of wear-out or maintenance or depreciation, my income is precisely what I get as hire. But the cost to me of this hire—this hire the whole of which is cost to you—and which to me, after the debits are allowed for, is all income to me? What *now* does my income cost *me?* Obviously what now I could make my property pay me, either by using it directly in my own operations, whether in the same field of production as yours or in some other, or lending it out to some one else for whatever use he might make of it in this same or in another field. And among my various opportunities, the ranking one will report my cost. But there is no assurance—there is in fact slight probability—that my plow or draft-horse or slave will finally drift into any line of occupation very dissimilar from that in which you are to use it.

And my meadow? You have it from me for growing corn; and pay me for it $100 rent. It would be worth $90 for raising wheat.

Is then, the land-cost to you $100 or is it $90—the $100 that you have to pay for corn purposes, or the $90 that you would have to pay if, say, the corn-borer had made wheat the sole thing or the best thing then to be done with the land? What after all has the $90 to do with the case so long as the corn suit is plainly the best suit to lead? Would it greatly concern you were the rust to cancel in your neighborhood the wheat-growing alternative?

Or suppose now that the singer employed at a high salary, could do nothing else but wash dishes—and poorly at that. This situation —not an improbable one—would not lighten the burden of the impressario's salary list.

All these alternative rent or salary openings signify nothing in the actual situation. But they may, if conditions change enough, come to have significance. If now it interests you or me to know that, if and when the corn industry falls on bad price times, with rents on corn lands falling, my meadow will remain in corn production only for as long as the corn rent on it holds at not less than $90, we have full liberty to employ this knowledge in whatever direction we may please. But under present conditions you will still pay me $100 for the land, or some competitor of yours will get it. In fact, I have been having it in mind, whenever you talk to me about a lower rent, to enter into sale negotiations with a neighboring farmer interested in increasing his acreage of corn. You must not think I can do business with you only. Moreover, I have been thinking of going into corn growing myself. This $90 wheat talk does not appeal to me. It does not sound quite real.

Something not very different from this $90 wheat talk would have reality enough, if only the society were a different sort of society; were collective rather than competitive in the organization of its productive activities; and collective in the traditionally simple sort. The place and time are of a community March meeting, at which, among other issues of collective policy, there is to be discussed the disposition to be made for the year of this tract of meadow land. The executive committee reports its recommendation that the land be planted to corn. You and I oppose—presumably with an argument to offer. I urge that it be put up to competitive bidding. But had this not been our first meeting, I must have known better. There are no rents in a collective society. And competitive bidding is not within the specifications. It is not a profit society.

The sole argument against the report is, then, to be made by you. And your sole basis must be that the community would better use the land for some other crop than corn, or perhaps for some other use than crop land. You stand for wheat. It is then for you to show that the wheat return promises better than the corn—not better, however, in terms of price; the society is not producing corn at money costs for sale on money terms. The issue must be solely one of wheat utility against corn utility. The main cost category in a collective society—and its sole cost category with its store of implemental possessions—is this of opportunity cost, but opportunity in quite other than in the competitive sense; how does the prospective achievement with corn compare with the prospective achievement with wheat? The problem is not one of displaced rent or displaced price but of displaced returns—things regarded solely *as goods* for community consumption.

Suppose now that we have some community marsh land—prodigious for purposes of hay, but good for nothing else; and still our most important community asset. We get, then, hay from it in generous volumes but at no cost; at no cost, that is, as far as concerns the land—no land-cost. Land-wise there are no debits against the hay; no arguments in favor of something else, there being nothing else to raise, and therefore nothing else for which to argue. Only in point of harvesting and carrying equipment can there be implement debits, with these in terms solely of what they could else be used to produce—what other uses the hay use would displace.

And similarly in the main with the labor necessary for the hay harvest; what is there else that needs doing? Something, doubtless, there might remain to say, in the labor aspect, about the special debits of discomfort or danger connected with the marsh mud and mire and mosquitoes. But fertilizer? The marsh attends to its own fertility through tidal backsets and winter floods. And plowing? The less the better, even could it be done. Land-wise the swamp is a great bounty of nature; the hay from it saddled with no land cost. But we may stop to note that were the society competitive, any operator in hay must submit to a stiff land rent for control of this land; else some competitor would get it.

And this collective community of ours has, for its Sunday services and its recurrent merry-makings, a singer of downright prima-donna quality. We are most thankful for her. Perhaps even we should be most thankful that she can do nothing else. Thus we have no alternative-product cost. Moreover she likes to sing. And so no labor cost attaches to her services; further great rejoicings, and sincere offerings of thanks. Our music costs us nothing.

But to return for a little to our analysis of competitive costs. It must now again be recognized that even though you pay me $100 for the use of the meadow, at thus much of manifest cost, it yet may cost you more than that for growing corn. If, for example, you could make the meadow earn you, say $110 in corn—a renter's surplus of $10 to go along with whatever labor and equipment returns you get—and yet could make it pay you $105 in wheat, with a $5 renter's surplus, the ranking resistance to corn is not the $100 of rent that you pay, but the $105 of wheat return from the land that you forego; $5 of your renter's surplus of $10 is necessary to hold you in corn production as against your alternative of wheat. It therefore functions as a cost for corn. Your own labor return also, as similarly your property return, divides into necessary and unnecessary parts. The necessary portions rank as costs, resistances that the corn return must be expected to overbear. The same principle holds also for your hired labor if considered separately. In practice, to be sure, all these different surpluses get merged into net gains of operation. Functionally, however, they are not the less there, and are as separately attributable as comports with the distributive process and analysis.

But on the downward scale from the $100 of rent outlay, there are other doctrines of cost to be considered—and abandoned. As price-determining costs, the classical doctrine made no account of the fact that the poorest of tilled land must carry some rent earning power in the tillage use, to justify this use as against, say, pasture or forestry. But still the isolation of the intensive margin was open, whereby the classical doctrine found it possible to adhere to the view that all land rents are price-determined. With production carried to this intensive-margin limit, a product—it was argued—could be isolated, the price of which was barely adequate to cover the wage and interest outlays requisite to its forthcoming. This is in fact precisely what the intensive margin means. It is a margin at which only prime costs get consideration. There being no valuable land use attaching to this marginal product, no rent is paid for the use. The price-determining rent is thus declared to be zero on what we shall term, somewhat ambiguously, this 5-rent land. This rent of $5 is paid solely because of the supra-marginal bushels.

But in market-gardening and tobacco culture, even the poorest land in use commands a fairly high rent. What about this 50-rent land? Since the $50 of rent is a charge attaching to the use of even the poorest land in the production, say, of garden truck, must there not be here a rent that is to be recognized as price-determining? The reply of classical theory is still in the negative. For turn again to the intensive margin. There has to be a last unit of garden-truck produce that is barely worth while to come by, in view of the wage and interest costs attached to the getting of it. And these wage and interest costs, being marginal costs, are taken thereby to be the price-determining costs; the rent a surplus derivative from the price, determined at the wage-and-interest-cost margin where no rent charges are present.

The alternative product rent of $90 is that one of the series of rent quantities that still demands further attention. We stop in passing, however, to note that these neo-classical views that present some part of the actual rent charges as price-determining and other parts as price-determined must, each in its peculiar fashion, put in hazard the distinction between land capital and other capital—so far, at least, as this distinction is made to turn on the peculiar position of rent as a price-determined cost. The $90-rent view, for example, reports only $10 of the rent as a price-determined surplus. The $50-rent view, in turn, reports only the excess of the actual rent payment above $50 as a price-determined share, with the $50 itself as price-determining.

And now we should be prepared for some further account of the Marshall-Jevons issue. Marshall attacks the $90 rent-cost position of Jevons; and carries his argument without serious difficulty. Thereby, however, he takes the Ricardian zero-rent position as secure against attack. And it is the purpose of this discussion to attack. It must, however, be all the while firmly held in mind that the issue as at present drawn is not in the slightest concerned with real costs. Marshall's entire analysis in this connection treats only of money costs, the point of controversy being solely whether rent costs have any peculiar title as against other costs to be regarded as price-determined—whereby the distinction between land capital and equipment capital may find itself justified. Real costs do not appear even in the background of the discussion. It is, however, no doubt true that this rent-cost position of Marshall, once made secure, will greatly advance the view that real costs are proportional to prices in the long-time norm.

It is indeed clear that in any pre-normal period of price adjustment the proportionality of prices to money costs—the costs results of the prices, and not the prices of the costs—is presented by Marshall as attaching to the new prices that are brought about by the shifting of either equipment goods or lands, and logically also of labor, into some alternative industry. The issue becomes now one not of proportionality but of cause. The ultimate causation is now held to be not with the modification of the hires but only with the available volume of the factor, that modifies in turn the volume of the product—the "basement" level of analysis. Obviously, the hire that is now paid in the alternative industry is not an item of additional cost in the industry in which the item is not paid. It is true merely that the higher rents in the alternative industry have accounted for the greater absorption of the factor in that industry and for the diminished volume of the factor in the first industry. But the cause of the higher price of the product here, Marshall urges, is the diminished volume of the factor and the consequent reduction in the volume of product, and not the greater hire of the factor per area—this new hire deriving from the new price that in turn derives from the diminished volume of the factor:

The argument ... applies, so far as *short periods* are concerned, to the earning power of farm buildings and to other quasi-rents. When existing farm-buildings, or other appliances which could be used in producing one commodity are diverted to producing another ... then *for the time* the supply of the first will be less, and its price higher. ... Thus, when appliances are capable of being used in more than one branch of agriculture, the marginal cost in each branch will be affected by the extent to which these appliances are called off for work in other branches ... in the first branch ... the value of its product will rise. ... The increased earning power of the appliances ... will appear to be the cause of this increase in value; for it will cause a relative scarcity of the appliances in that branch of production, and therefore raise marginal costs. And from this statement it appears superficially to be a simple transition to the statement that the increased earning power of the appliances enter into those costs which govern value. But the transition is illegitimate. There will be no direct or numerical relation between the increase in the price of the first commodity and the income that the appliances can earn when they have been transferred to the second. ... (pp. 437-38)

But with a stock of, say, lands diminished for any particular line of production by the absorption of lands in alternative lines of production, it is not the less true that total land rent in the first industry gets decreased; that the marginal bushels must bear higher labor and capital outlays; and that the supra-marginal bushels must face the higher rent outlays that are imposed for the use of the supra-marginal land efficiencies that are being substituted for wage or interest-bearing labor or equipment efficiencies. Per unit of product, production with supra-marginal efficiencies combines the factors differently from production with marginal efficiencies, the larger rent outlay permitting smaller outlays in other directions. Marshall makes no question that with the new combination of factors following this shift of land out of a particular line of production, and the change in the price of the product, the higher rent is there per area and per unit of product. He denies simply that this higher rent is the ultimate cause of the higher prices. He urges instead that the cause is the more marked land scarcity in this particular line of production. Both the higher rents and the higher prices—or, better, both the higher prices and the higher rents—are results of this increased scarcity. And of the correctness of this as matter of ultimate causation there can be no doubt. But this is a level of analysis underlying that enterpriser-cost analysis to which —excepting when real costs are appealed to—the classical economics is systematically committed. Ultimate causes the enterpriser-cost analysis never discloses. These belong to a different level, a level not contradictory of the enterpriser-cost analysis but supplementary to it and explanatory of it. But as here and as in general Marshall presents this underlying analysis, it is a level essentially repudiating the enterpriser level. Only as viewing the scarcity as reporting itself for enterpriser purposes in the rent are the two lines of analysis to be connected.

Any cost analysis consistently loyal to the enterpriser process and point of view must proceed on the cost level of enterpriser price resistances to enterpriser price products. For whatever price costs of production are or are not worth, they clearly get us no further forward with explanations than to account for each particular price in terms of other prices. But precisely so it is for all price offers and for all goods offers. Real costs also, for whatever they are worth, serve merely as footing for price costs. Each individual functions inside a price situation. Crusoes are mere expositional abstractions. If, indeed, we knew anywhere of an actual Crusoe, we should know of somebody who had actually nothing to do with our case—a mere outsider of our process. The wages that the enterpriser pays are labor prices. His raw-material costs are the prices of his raw materials. His interest outlays and his rent hires are price outlays. His returns are price returns. Whether, either individually or in the aggregate, these cost prices determine product prices, or the product prices the cost prices, this price circuity on this level of analysis is always with us. There may be explanations underlying some or all of these cost facts, but the enterpriser has to take things as they are. And the things that are, are for him, all price things. No matter how ill such a situation logically is, such is precisely his situation.

Moreover, the cost analysis appropriate to this enterpriser process is the only cost analysis that is open to the economist. The objective process discloses no other computation of costs. The enterpriser is the only person who computes these costs, precisely because to no one else accrue the price returns. His are the debits because his are the credits. His employees? Each of them may have his own costs for the wages that he collects, but none against the prices of the products, because no one of these employees collects these product prices. To supersede the laborer's claim to the product was the meaning of the wage contract. The wages are not the laborer's costs, but only the remuneration for his costs. The wage outlays are the enterpriser's costs; they so far condition for him the price products to accrue to him.

All of this, to be sure, may be to declare this price-cost-of-production analysis of little worth; but for whatever it is worth, whether much or little, it is the only cost of production that we have. Abandon it, then? Possibly so. But if we keep it, we must keep it for what it is, else we have to go without it or be misled by it. Any cost-of-production doctrine that, as undisclosed by the objective facts, is merely superimposed upon them is, not only a myth, but something worse than a myth; it is a menace. We shall better get what we can from what we have. Something there is to get.

Marshall makes no question that agricultural lands that are subject to exhaustion or renewal—wearout and upkeep—are quasi-rent properties. Irrespective of origins, and irrespective of whether the point of view is social or not, these lands—in their fertility aspect—are, he holds, equipment capital as distinguished from land capital. Their hires are in the long run price-determining. Not the exclusive applicability of the marginal-isolation analysis to land capital, but the unresponsiveness of the land volume to human devisings, is the basis of the distinction between land capital and equipment capital.

Consider again, then, that salt marsh of ours; that will grow but one crop, marsh hay; that cannot be wasted of fertility or improved in fertility; but can have no marginal dose of anything—not being cultivatable or workable in any way; and that is by nature fixed in area, as it is in fertility. What, then, about the price bearing of its rents?

Note especially the lack of alternative uses. For with their presence, as is the case with most urban or rural lands, and the fact of displacement of product, the resisting rents or the resisting uses —one aspect of the law of substitution—there is no escape from the recognition of costs. Assume then an entire lack of alternative uses. It is, no doubt, an unusual situation, an extreme assumption, in which all possible concessions are made in favor of the view that sometime and somewhere there may be land the hire of which is price-determined at least in some part—not much of it, but some; so little as hardly to be worth noting, save as the setting for a clean-cut doctrinal issue. Is this marsh-land rent a price-determined enterpriser cost?

We have then a case where there is fixity; original bounty; indestructibility and uncreatability of productive power; lack of all alternative uses; the actuality of marginal isolation; and the entire isolation of land productivity, no other factors entering. What now about the rent as cost?

But clearly enough the land is productive of hay, and of hay that sells; and the more that it produces of hay, the lower sells the hay, and the lower also the price of other sorts of hay. The *land* does then affect prices. It certainly is a price thing, and a price-productive thing, and a thing the products of which affect prices. But do its rents affect prices? They are not things that produce, and they are themselves products. But competing operators will offer rent for the land, and anyone that gets it will get it only on terms of rent outlays. Its hire is like other hires—a hire that in the enterpriser process of production is the correlative of the productive efficiency of an agent the existence of which, but not the rent of which, is effective for product; and that is present in such limited volume that the price of its product is not swamped through the very volume of it. To deny that its rent is a price-determining cost, but to assert for the land itself a price-determining standing, is merely to discredit and abandon all price-cost analysis everywhere. It is to get into the "basement," and then to stay there, even after the time that the hires have ripened into facts appropriate for enterpriser purposes in competitive production. A merely scarce factor is not thereby a price factor; nor is a merely scarce product a price product; nor is the price of the product a cost fact. But the price hire of the factor is a cost fact. It is at just this point in the causal sequence that the enterpriser process comes into possession of its appropriate materials, and acquires a logically defensible standing in the price-cost process, And as initiating at this point, factor costs are not infect of circuity. Here factor costs take their surface, but logical, place as certified and warranted by the underlying verities.

Moreover, this salt marsh is not, as a productive factor, either isolated or isolatable. There are different enterprisers, differently appraising, and differently bidding. Under any other than the most effective among them—presumably the victor in the bidding—the volume of hay harvested from the marsh would be a smaller volume, and the price of the hay therefore higher. In a sense, then, there is in the harvesting process a marginal dose. But it is not an isolated dose of harvest effort or of working cattle, since these come along only with the enterpriser. Even with the enterpriser's labor as the sole supplement to the marsh, there are at this minimum these two factors, factors that are, in the nature of the case, joint and inseparable. The argument against marginal isolation is, therefore, an argument decisive also in favor of the price-modifying significance not only of the land, but—cost-wise—of the rent of the land.[5]

[5] And now, what does *social* mean—with reference to costs, and in support of the distinction between land capital and other capital? Marshall, as usual, does not define his term. We shall, then, have to seek out its meaning as best we may by the method of exclusion.

It does not point to *origins:*
Because society now is not concerned with these origins—the past no more relevant than the future; because, as bearing on the distinction in controversy, Marshall has abandoned origins; because his argument, in this connection, runs entirely on the level of money and not of real costs.

It does not mean *collective:*
Because, if it did, it would include the displaced products as costs; because Marshall outlaws that argument in any competitive application, demonstrating that the determining cost must be either what is paid or zero; and because collectively we are not concerned with prices or price costs.

If it is replied that the case is one of real costs, and that thereby displaced product comes to be ruled out of consideration, it forthwith follows that, so far, *social* is irrelevant. And if it is a price-cost issue, there must be price resistances to the limit, at least, of the alternative rent.

It does not, in the competitive aspect of cost, point to spatial or other *fixity:*
Because there is almost uniformly price resistance through displacement, and there are uniformly rent-price outlays as resistance.

Indifferent Alternative Uses of Lands

The land worth $100 for the growing of hops and only $90 for the growing of oats—land for the hire of which the tenant cultivator must pay a rent of $100, and which as cultivated by the owner must displace for him the collection of a $100-rent, a "virtual expense" of $100, imposes, it is clear, in the growing of hops an expense cost not of $90 but of $100. For a tenant the choice is between paying $100 for the control of the land for hops and not having the land. The $90-use for oats is third in order with him,

---

It cannot, in the collective aspect of cost, point to spatial or any other sort of *fixity*:

Because this involves either irrelevancy, or the denial of displacement costs, the primary social-cost category.

It cannot point to the *"basement" level* of approach:

Because this is an approach that has no price relevancy; or if, later in the sequence, it rightly is used, it introduces the competitive price aspect of the actual price hire, thereby not being *social*.

It does not point to *marginal isolation:*

Because this is to deny a cost standing to the displaced products; and because Marshall himself does not make this isolation distinctive of land capital: and because the zero position is a *competitive* argument turning on the tenability of marginal isolation.

It cannot be the 90-rent cost view of Jevons and others, as seen above. It cannot be the 50-rent view—the rent of, say, the poorest tobacco land; because that scuttles the distinction between land capital and other capital; and because Marshall has discredited this view, holding fast to the marginal-zero. It cannot be the 5-rent view, for precisely similar reasons. It cannot be the zero view, because this abandons displaced product as cost, involving also the fallacies of marginal isolation.

Actually, in Marshall's use, *social* appears to connote *unresponsiveness*—the spatial-fixity aspect of land. But then it is not *social* in any analytical or any collective sense as bearing on the point in controversy; and in any case, excepting that of the salt-marsh type, it goes to pieces, both competitively and collectively, against the opportunity-cost actualities.

I am unable, then, to attach any meaning to the word *social* that justifies the distinction for the support of which the term was invoked. I have no clear notion of what the word means. Unfortunately, however, this decides nothing; the word may be used in some meaning that has entirely escaped me. It is impossible to not-see a thing out of existence. But all that I can, I have done. I can get no defensible meaning out of the term. Marshall, not having himself defined the term, has left it to his reader to grope for a meaning, to surmise it, or to infer it as best he may from its various contexts. So much I have tried to do, not thereby, it is evident, having got very far. No adequate examination is possible of a position that has not been taken. The primary requisite for a discussion is to have something to discuss. A position that cannot be located is an irrefutable position.

and the $90-payment lacks visibility. It has not even a third rank among his possibilities. Nor with the owning culvitator is the growing of oats a thing to be considered. Its third-rank place excludes it from his problem. Nor with him is there any question of the payment of any rent. His ownership means that he does not have to pay rent. Nor commonly is there any question of a rent to be foregone, the practicability of leasing having only a third-rank standing—not one of the terms in his choice between policies. It is a sub-marginal datum. He is occupying and cultivating his farm, commonly without thought of moving off or of disturbing its unit symmetry. Ordinarily his choice in policy is one between alternative crops.

Jevons' error of employing a collectivist-cost category in a competitive analysis led him to fix on the $90-rent as the land cost of, say, hops. Accurately, however, there is no place in this collective analysis for rents, price hires of land, but only for displacement costs in products. But Jevons' argument could rightly go no further than that the land cost in the growing of hops must be not less than $90. His collective approach, nevertheless, led him to fix it, not at a minimum of $90, but at precisely $90. But it was no part of his thought to make the land cost the sum of the $100 and the $90; nor, in fact, does Marshall so interpret him.

Marshall's reply was two-fold: (1) if the land cost of hops were either $90 or $100, it must be $100 in the price-governing sense; (2) it could be neither of the two, but instead by the argument of marginal isolation, must be zero.

Refutation of Jevons' $90-rent view we have seen to have been a matter of no serious difficulty. But Marshall attempted no case for his own zero-cost position, other than to return to his recurrently abandoned device of marginal isolation.

. . . It is therefore inexpedient to say that the rent of land does not enter into their price. But it is worse than inexpedient to say that the rent of the land does enter into their price: that is false.
. . . there is no connection between this particular sum of £2 [Jevons' alternative rent] and the expenses of production of that wheat which only just pays its way . . . that which is produced on the margin of profitable expenditure. . . . (p. 437, note)

But now Marshall undertakes the discussion of a situation where the alternative uses are at an equality of appeal, at the substitutionary margin—a situation that would be presented were the price of hops so far to fall that the return from the land in hops was no greater than that in oats. What then would be the land-cost for hops?

For the owner-cultivator, the choice has now to be made between cropping the land for hops as against either accepting $90 of rent for the land, or using the land himself in the growing of oats—alternatives that by assumption are equal in point of appeal. He must do one or the other. If you order your eggs poached or fried, they will not be both. At less than a $90-return in hops he must himself shift to oats, or turn the land over to a tenant-cultivator who will make the shift into a $90-rent oat use of the land. To the owner-cultivator, then, there can be no cost of hops unless he actually grows hops. If he does grow them, his cost is his ranking alternative, either the growing of oats or the collecting of a $90-rent from a lessee. Presumably, then, the displaced $90-return in oats is his land cost for hops. If the cultivation is by a tenant, his land cost must be the rent that he pays (or, it may be true, something in excess). The problem is not formulated to take account of all of the relations turning on individual peculiarities.

What, for the price problem, does *cost* mean? It points to price resistances. It is that price total below which as return the indemnity is inadequate to justify the product. It is the limit at which what one gets is barely worth while, in view of what one must undertake. In the instant problem, then, the cost to the tenant is the $90 of rent that he has to pay; to the owner-cultivator, it is, by assumption, indifferently the foregone $90 of rent from the tenant, or the foregone $90 from his own crop use of the land in oats. For, as Marshall has said (p. 430), "land is but a particular form of capital from the point of view of the individual producer." Of thus much, indeed, Marshall makes factually no question:

> . . . The farmer can evade . . . a yet further part [of a general tax on hops] by substituting another crop on land which he had proposed to devote to hops. He will have recourse to this second plan in so far as he considers that he would get a better result by growing another crop . . .

than by growing hops . . . the surplus which he could obtain from the land by growing, say, oats upon it would come into his mind when deciding where to set the limit to his production of hops. . . . (p. 436)

But still, as Marshall insists (p. 436, note), "it could not be truly said that the rent which the field could be made to yield by growing other crops, 'entered into' the marginal price of oats."

And why not? Marshall's reply here is not two- but three-fold: (1) if any rent is a price-determining cost for hops, it must be the rent that is paid for the use of the land in growing hops—[the assumption of a cultivating owner abandoned], (2) the rent for oats is obviously not an amount to be added to the hops rent, (3) the price of hops is governed by the cost at the intensive margin in the cultivation of hops.

Here is again to be noted the recurrent return to the recurrently abandoned device of marginal isolation. It must suffice in this aspect of the argument to note the fact, and to recall Marshall's statement (p. 430): "The question whether a farmer has carried his cultivation of a particular piece of land as far as he profitably can . . . is of the same kind as . . . whether he should buy a new plough, or try to get a little more work out of his present stock of ploughs . . ." Marginal isolation, that is to say, applies to plows in the same sense as to land.

In fact, however, the rest of the argument gets mixed in with the marginal-cost analysis:

. . . For there is no connection between this particular sum of £2 [the rent for pasture or oats] and the expenses of production of that wheat [hops] which only just pays its way. What should be said is: "When land capable of being used for producing one commodity is used for producing another, the price of the first is raised by the consequent limitation of its field of production. The price of the second will be the expenses of production . . . on the margin of profitable expenditure. . . ." (p. 437, note)

What takes place, that is to say, is the limiting of the amount of land available for hops. Thus there is imposed a higher marginal cost of production for hops. But this is essentially a shift to the "basement" level of analysis, along with an attempted articulation of it with the marginal-isolation analysis. It goes directly from the limitation of agents to the limitation of products. Rightly, however, on this level of fundamental causes, not the higher marginal cost of production of hops explains the higher price of them, but only the smaller volume of product. The higher price, in turn, justifies higher unit costs of production; and thus justifies higher rents on what land is left; and therewith higher unit costs, both marginal and supra-marginal, for hops.

> The ordinary man is offended by the old phrase that rent does not enter into the price of oats; when he sees that an increase in the demand for land for other uses, manifests itself in a rise of the rental value of all land in the neighbourhood; . . . consequently makes it worth while to force larger crops of oats out of the remaining oat-land, and thus raises the marginal expenses of oats and their price. A rise in rent does serve as a medium through which the growing scarcity of land available for hops and other produce obtrudes itself on his notice. . . . (p. 436, note)

We have, then, here an interesting fusion of the "basement" view of things with the marginal-isolation view; and an illuminating account of connections between this level of analysis and the enter-priser level; but without attempt at a precise articulation of factor stocks, on the one level, with enterpriser cost outlays on the other level. While the reduction in the volume of the land for hops raises the rents of this land, it is still, Marshall insists, the *rent* for the use of the land for hops that gets paid, and not the rent for oats; and manifestly, the oat rents do not get added to the hops rents:

> . . . there would be no simple numerical relation between the surplus, or rent, which the land would yield under oats, and the marginal costs which the price of hops must cover. . . .
> . . . it could not be truly said that the rent which the field could be made to yield by growing other crops, "entered into" the marginal price of oats [hops]. . . . (p. 436 and note)

And still there are perplexing confusions in the analysis. They turn on the shift between point of view of the cultivating owner and that of the cultivating tenant. The tenant's problem of costs in leasing land for the growing of hops has to do with the rent that he must pay to the owner in order to get the land. But the owner-cultivator is never concerned with any rent to pay. As has already been pointed out, his concern is commonly with an alternative crop.

And we have seen that this much Marshall admits. The owner's situation presents, then, one of the simplest applications of opportunity cost. The tenant's arrival at a decision whether to rent the land, and at what payment, is not of the same sort, though problems of opportunity cost may later present themselves with him.

In this opportunity aspect, therefore, the following attempt to assimilate the problem of opportunity cost to the no-rent land cost of the marginal-isolation procedure, is worthy of careful examination:

... when appliances are capable of being used in more than one branch of agriculture, the marginal cost in each branch will be affected by the extent to which these appliances are called off for work in other branches ... the value of its product will rise. .... The increased earning power of the appliances due to the external demand will appear to be the cause of this increase in value: for it will cause a relative scarcity of the appliances in that branch of production, and therefore raise marginal costs. And from this statement it appears superficially to be a simple transition to the statement that the increased earning power of the appliances enter into those costs which govern value. But the transition is illegitimate. There will be no direct or numerical relation between the increase in the price of the first commodity and the income that the appliances can earn when they have been transferred to the second industry and adapted for service in it. (pp. 437-38)

The untenability of relative real costs, marginally isolated, as the ultimate explanation of relative price costs, and thereby of relative prices, should now be wearisomely clear. And with the recognition of opportunity costs, the entire case of real-cost determinations lapses. There are, no doubt, vagabonds of one sort and another with whom the griefs of labor fix a limit on even their predatory activities. Likewise there are the scavenger laborers—hewers of wood and drawers of water—so ill adapted to any alternative occupations as to experience pain-cost margins of effort. But your concert ticket comes so high, not because of the grief associated with the possession of the voice that rings and thrills—mainly, however, "a rare disease of the larynx." You do not pay the painter or the lawyer according to the discomforts of his occupation, or even for those at the afternoon cessation for a game of golf. The brick-layer's wages are collected from you because another employer will pay them if you do not; and never by virtue of your appreciation, or the other employer's, or his own, that brick-laying is a half more uncomfortable job than carpentering.

The high wages in the United States are not due to the exceptional dislike here of work, or to exceptionally uncomfortable conditions of working. Wages are not at the starvation level in India or China because the disinclination to labor in those parts is small, or effort relatively easy under the blistering sun. Most occupations, and most men in them, are well paid, when they are well paid, because of a generally prevailing high level of wages. The productivity theory of remunerations is itself a flat denial of the real cost theory. The pleasant occupations are, in the large, the well-paid occupations. Their products are high-priced products.

Real costs are almost never the sole consideration in the choosing of occupations. Commonly they are only minor aspects in the choice, a choice turning always in the main on total relative advantages, with the returns in price the chief of these. These facts, doubtless, Marshall's wide law of substitution adequately covers; but covers them so unprecisely or so vaguely that Marshall himself fails to discover in it the refutation of real costs as the ultimate determinant of prices, particular or relative.

But to establish this real-cost explanation of relative wages alongside of the doctrine that prices are fixed, or governed, by marginal money costs of production—exclusive of certain other hires—would amount merely to asserting that prices are not in general proportional with both real and money costs. The principle would apply only on the marginal fringes of productive activity—with merely this hair-line area of jurisdiction for the plenary truth—a doctrinal exemplification of the fable of the mountain and the mouse, or, perhaps, of the fly on the axle of the chariot.

Moreover, the real-cost explanation of exchange ratios gets rather worse than better, with a better view of the function of money costs. For the truth is not that the proportionality of money costs with prices is restricted to this hair-line breadth of jurisdiction. From the owner or investor point of view, in the long-time, forward-looking aspect of costs, where the division of costs into prime and supplementary is out of place, supra-marginal and marginal costs are equal, and are different only in their makeup. And from the tenant and hirer point of view, where the supplementary and quasi-rent cost goods all command hires in the price-cost emphasis, there is still less occasion for any differential between marginal and supra-marginal costs.

The truth is that the ordinary view declaring prices to be determined by *marginal* costs and to be proportional solely with them, credits money costs with entirely too little significance. The proportionality of prices with costs—so far as it holds at all, and in the sense that it holds after lags and unprecisions have been allowed for—holds inclusively of all products and of all their price costs.

But nothing of this inclusive sort is to be credited to real costs in their relation to price. Only the marginal proportionality holds—so far as anything holds. The law of increasing fatigue—or something like it, when recreation aspects are included—is a law applicable only to the marginal items of product. For the purely individual analysis—a Crusoe or collectivist view, as distinguished from an inter-individual view—there are, doubtless, aspects of truth in the real-cost approach, but for marginal production solely. And it is inevitable in this real-cost view that recourse be had to production at the land margin of production. Tempted thereby—and as its sole claim to plausibility—the labor-wage analysis adopted the marginal approach, creating the fallacious marginal-isolation device for enterpriser-cost analysis. In this real-cost view, fatigue resistances are increasing with increments of product, the while that utilities are diminishing. The lines of equation are therefore mere lines, and lines that are changing. Products in general that exchange in proportionality with money costs, cannot exchange in proportionality with real costs, excepting so far as marginal items of products are concerned.

The real-cost view, therefore, can never purport to establish the proportionality of prices with costs over an area wider than these hair-line frontiers of productive effort. There is then a disastrous lack of coincidence between the labor-pain and the labor-wage theories of price determination. The proportionality of money costs with prices is as wide as the field of price; of real costs, only as wide as the marginal frontiers of price.

The classical account of prices has thus been declared to fail in other aspects than its appeal to real costs as explanatory of wage costs. For real costs, it is now clear, would not do, even if, for inter-individual purposes, they were relevant. The classical account would not be tenable, even assuming that relative real costs could explain relative wage costs; for these real costs are applicable only to the marginal units of product. It further would not do, because marginal isolation, while an appropriate method with real costs, is entirely inappropriate with money costs.

The real-cost support, therefore, for even the wage-cost share of money costs, does not hold. The wage-cost elimination of other price costs by appeal—whether with land or with other instruments of production—to the device of isolation at the margin, does not hold. The case, therefore, for the explanation of price costs of production by real costs has not even the logical standing of an inquiry as to what would be true, if something were true that is not true.

Chapter X

QUASI-RENTS: EQUIPMENT AND EFFORT

MARSHALL'S occasional references to the *general conditions of demand and supply* as offering explanation of each particular price, and thus of prices in general, can be taken as a mere truism. Given all the various desires for different things, and all the various abilities and instruments for producing them, it must hold that somewhere inside this total situation the explanations of all prices must be sought—and may be found. The determinants are all there, hidden it may be; or if not hidden, still refractory to generalization; or inadequately or incorrectly analyzed and generalized. For Economics is precisely the effort to uncover and to generalize this complicated and perplexing mass of fact and of factual process. Mere reference, however, to these facts and processes, along with the assumption that somewhere therein there are explanations, is not explanation. Tested by what, for us human beings, are the requisites of explanation, the assertion is something less than a mere truism; it is meaningless.

Interpreted, however, to point out that, taking desires and demands, for granted on the one side of the price problem, the explanation for the various prices must further be sought, not in the hires of things as enterpriser costs attaching to them, but solely— for any ultimate view of the problem—in the available stocks of them for each particular productive purpose, this appeal to the general conditions of demand and supply points to a most illuminating method of approaching the price problem—accurately the problem of relative prices. Forthwith, on the supply side of the problem, the movement of thought must be from the relative scarcities of the productive agents, to the relative scarcities of their products, thence to the relative prices of the products; and finally to the relative price-hires of the factors; or, also, through the capitalization process, to the purchase prices of the factors. It is only at the factor-hire stage of the logical movement that process relations are so far disclosed that price costs are available for the enterpriser-cost level of analysis.

This "basement" level of approach has the supreme merit of offering a method of escape from the crass circuity that otherwise infects all the logic of the traditional enterpriser-cost explanation of prices. Always it is wholesome to recognize that not the hires of things, but the things themselves, explain the more or less of products—that only *things* have productive applications. Moreover, this "basement" view of the problem of the relative standing of products invokes the facts that are ultimately controlling for no matter what particular form or order of economic life. It is the basis for the Crusoe, or the collective, or the competitive systematization of economic material. It was, then, in this "basement" emphasis that Ricardo was led to stress the niggardliness of nature as fundamental to the price standing of agricultural products; as also that Malthus was led to stress the good fortune attending the presence of such natural bounties as there are—Ricardo noting what makes prices so high; Malthus noting what prevents them from being higher.

Making, then, no question of the serviceability of this "basement" view, it is still clear that, once its accomplishments are secure, the way has merely become open for the right use of the enterpriser level of process and analysis—an account of the actual gain-seeking activities of industry and business.

The very mass and complexity of these total situation materials and processes unfit them for *explanation* in any intelligible sense of the term. Omitting from consideration the desire and demand aspects of the case; the variety and the interrelations of the utilities of things; the limitations that the multiplicity of desires imposes on the satisfaction of them severally; the relations of desire to price offer and of price offers to one another; and directing attention solely to the means available for the satisfaction of the desires of men, the data become scarcely more manageable. The human being has still to be taken into the account, not as a desiring being, but as a being of productive and gain-achieving capacities; and this in all the aspects relevant to these activities: the various degrees of capacity in the various lines of price achievement; in mental and physical powers; in industriousness; in willingness to labor and in aversion to labor, along with the counter inducements of rest, amusement and play. And there are also productive and gain-serving possessions: the various agents in their varying lines of application; in their substitutionary and complementary aspects relatively to one another—one aspect of the laws of return. And more puzzling still, there are the various advantages of individuals in differential rights and opportunities: advantages of organization, good-will, privilege, patent, franchise and monopoly. And, perhaps most puzzling of all —and almost uniformly overlooked—there are the clashings of private right and private effort with the industrial process; complications of parasitisms, predacity or crime—gainful and cost-wise relevant items of fact in the entire competitive setting. And finally, all of these are to be considered against the background of further property rights, laws, customs, traditions, taboos—institutions at large; and all within the further setting of the "state of the industrial arts," the vast inheritance of industrial science and technique. Offered as explanation for prices, the *general conditions of demand and supply* are not chips and stones, but poisons, in place of bread.

It is seemingly in the second and significant sense that Marshall's recurrent reference to the general conditions of demand and supply is to be understood. But therewith certain of its implications should be noted. It is a recourse to existing conditions solely. Consistently with it, no regress in the time sense is permissible. It makes no appeal to origins, or to preceding periods of investment policy. It makes no call for an account of whence the situation was derived— genetics out of place—or of whither it is tending. Normals also in the sense of long-run views are irrelevant if stressing influences other than those implicit in things as they are. Normals as trends or conceptual outcomes by which the functional bearings of things in the present are to tested and declared, are logically outlawed. The analysis is not concerned with *termini a quo* or *termini ad quem*.

Moreover, all the hires that for the cost-of-production analysis are to be explained by the phrase, and taken over from it, stand in one and the same relation to prices. If any are result, all are. If any are cause, all are. Distinctions between governing and governed are outside the pale. And they are worse than irrelevant; they are are pure misinterpretations. Take all of the hires to be price-determined. It is well, unless the processes of enterpriser production are expediently to be retained for purposes of explaining prices, and if some other process is offered as adequate substitute; or unless the quest for explanations is frankly renounced.

But in the sense of the enterpriser process all of the hires must be included in the enterpriser's costs. Whether he hires a machine that earlier was cost-produced, or land that was not, or a mule that was, or a man that was not; or whether the machine hire is more or less than adequate by the test of its earlier cost, or the land hire by this test entirely excluded; or the machine hire more or less than adequate by the test of what the bailor paid for it, or the land hire more or less than adequate by the test of what the lessor paid for it, are all alike irrelevant questions—from the point of view, note, of this "basement" approach in general conditions of demand and supply, and of its articulation with enterpriser costs.

The curtain rings down—for this purpose—on all these items of knowledge, or of lack of it; on all discussions of origin; and on all historical regresses in either the real- or the money-cost tenor. Nor is there occasion—that is, for the purpose—to ask whence human nature was derived, or why the sun shines, or the seasons change, or the rains fall, or cows give milk, or sheep shear wool, or why the flora and the fauna are what they are. We may be supremely indifferent—for the purpose—as to whether petroleum is of animal or vegetable origin; or as to the forces or selective processes or the propensities or the desires by virtue of which corn grows upwards and potatoes downward; or as to why osage oranges will neither digest nor nourish, while jerusalem artichokes will. The cosmos and its derivation—the nebular hypothesis and Einstein's humps in space that explain why gravity is something else than Newton got us to imagine it to be—are items of historical learning or of speculative outlook beyond our responsibility. For us, as price economists, these things just are, and act and interact. How, being thus, do they grind out prices?

And further, against the background of this "basement" level of things, the analysis does not turn on what may be the individual ownership of things. Whether the cultivating operator is also the owner can impose no significantly different lines of analysis. If the hire that the tenant pays for the use of a machine or for a tract of land is a price-determining cost, the property in the use of the owner must equally impose a similar cost. The distinction between prime and supplementary costs, for whatever it is worth, will have to be re-examined. Whatever sort of cost the hire is to the tenant who pays it, it must be the same sort of cost to the operating owner who foregoes it. And if the wage that the employer pays is a cost, it will not matter whether part or all of the hire is to the laborer a surplus above *his* cost, or is only the scant indemnity for his effort, or how much he could get in another occupation; or whether part of it is due to his expensively or wearisomely acquired training, or attaches instead to his native ability; or whether the laborer's skill is specialized, or is commonplace, or is extraordinary.

All regress methods, that is to say, and all the different aspects of the employee point of view, will be beside the point. The difference between a quasi-rent and a true rent, between a "true-effort" hire and a quasi-rent effort return or hire, will not interest the gain-seeking employer; it will find no report in his computation of costs; it will be as far outside of his interests as it will be beyond his knowledge; and thus, for all purposes of the cost analysis on this level, will be similarly unregarded by the economist.

The fundamental defect in this quasi-rent type of analysis, now further to be examined, is that it belongs to the employee point of view, as is inevitable to the making of room for real costs. It shifts from telling what the enterpriser has to pay, to telling why he has to pay it—possibly because the recipient has to get it; or it tells how much of the hire the recipient does not need to get; or how much of it traces back to bounties of nature at his birth, or to a long series of expenditures by his forbears—or is a mere windfall—a conjuncture income. Presumably, however, the employee himself knows little or less about these things; more probably he doesn't care; and certain is it that his employer cannot know and does not care. For neither of them is there a penny in it. Wherefore, as taking no part in that process of choice which the cost-of-production analysis formulates, it is—so far—of no interest to the economist.

Precisely because the business man in the business process is not concerned with the derivation of the cosmos, neither, so far, is the economist. Granted that the business man cannot know the answers to these questions, or that, knowing all or any one of them, he would not in the slightest modify his cost-of-production computation by which he decides what and how much to do, it follows that the economist also—for the purpose in hand—is also quit of them, one and all. And similarly, for the purpose, he is not interested in forecasts of what will be the normal, or would be the normal, adjustment of any particular prices or of all prices together—though as economic technician in the general welfare or even as human being with a wide assortment of interests and curiosities, idle and other, the problems of the past or the future may greatly allure him. But they do not concern the cost-of-production problem—particular costs, relative costs, particular prices, relative prices, or the price system as it is, or, in the proximate business process, is about to become. Other conditions later will bear on their several price outcomes. Some of them, it may be, the economist, as such, may be able to forecast. And if among them some will be unfavorable, the economists as economic technicians may see something that ought to be done, may want to get that something done, and may move to have it done.[1]

---

[1] As far as I can make out, there are several varieties of institutional economists, all of them, I suppose, under the temptation of recommending their particular views by staking out priorities in this bouquet-dispensing term. There are, I am sure, certain differentiations to be noted among them that this one commendatory term must inevitably somewhat obscure.

(1) There are some of them that urgently insist on a close-up and detailed description of the entire economic field—not merely a near-to-the-ground contact with the underlying facts in all their complexity, a full descriptive account of the situation, but a constant vigilance to keep the account complete in the numerous and interacting details of change and development: all excellent and admirable, I take it, but requiring not only a treatise of 57 volumes, but a fortnightly revision. Nevertheless is this admonition to stick by the facts, never permitting generalization to smell too much of the cloister and the lamp, a wholesome admonition. Always, in large degree, the subdivisions of the economic field require this detailed study, and

The enterpriser faces a general situation in the making of which he has commonly had no part that he himself appreciates, and

are drawn in the recognition of this need. Subordinate generalizations supplementary to those appropriate to the broad-stroke generalizations of any general-system treatment, are in place with the specialized topics.

(2) There are those economists whose interest is in genetics, economic and industrial history, the study of which—as notably with Veblen—concerns itself with the processes of cumulative change, and with the generalization, so far as may be, of these processes—his *Economic Factors in Civilization* being chief of Veblen's marvel courses in his university teaching, excellent exceedingly in its suggestiveness and stimulation and in its vistas and horizons of inspiration and of lure.

But the conviction that these generalizations in the genetic emphasis, these economic laws of the time sequence, may be made applicable to the price-equilibration processes of the cross-section analysis, and in large part may displace them, appears to me to be a disastrous error—an error that, for a period—that in which he considered of Economics as an evolutionary science—seriously infected, as I hold, much of Veblen's high achievement; but of which he later became weary—a fact that his intellectual discipleship has not sufficiently taken into reckoning—not, however, I admit, by their fault. These genetic studies look for laws in other dimensions than those of the price-adjustment process. And are they better worth while? It may be; but this asserts them to be a different sort of thing of their own peculiar quality and jurisdiction. The thing in which one is interested has to be for him the worth-while thing—issues about which there is no disputing; push-pin versus poetry; but each of us with his own opinion of which is which.

(3) We have institutionalists who take problems of description and problems of appraisal to be indistinguishable, or, at all events, inseparable; or who take categories of appreciation as competent bases for generalization of description and of process; the welfare economists—specialists in economic engineering—who find either impossible or unserviceable the distinction between fact and appraisal, description and appreciation. With these economists I do not so easily agree—not by the test of their interests, which are their own affair; or of their competency, which I do not question; but of their assumption of what is science.

(4) And finally there are the economists who make central to their particular variety of institutionalism the test of scientific generalization by its serviceability for forecast—what will later come out of this or that situation—or, in the same emphasis, set the economic problem as one of accounting for the progressive unfolding of economic situations in the past—history in the forecast view; forecasts formulated from the point of view of an earlier time-venue—not the perfect tense of the present or the future tense of it, but the future of the past tense, a reckoning from a point in past time chosen as the then present for forecast exercises.

The issue in this regard is not as to the practical or scientific serviceability of science in the forecast aspect, but only the issue whether this is the sole worth or the sole test of science—astronomy, for example, a science solely by its competency to compute eclipses or to date the cosmic smash-up or to fix the age of the stellar system, or to report how long it will endure. I do not myself especially mind that by this test the class rooms of the sociologists and the historians—and both the class rooms and laboratories of the biologists—are to be deserted.

I do not make out clearly the affiliations of the behaviorist psychology, or of determinism, or of statistics, with institutionalism. But I am informed that there are these affiliations. In the main also, I intend no issues with any of these views. But I am persuaded that institutionalism as a term is too narrow a cover for all of the people in the bed.

commonly no part anyway. And such part as he has, or has had, is attendant mainly on his purely individualistic and gain-seeking activities, his enterpriser part in modification and readjustment. He faces a system of prices declarative of the terms at which he must obtain his cost goods and of the prices at which he may expect to market his products. There are stocks of goods from which to buy, both arrived and on-coming. Some of these are on-coming as the outcome of the enterpriser activities of other enterprisers, under situations and motivations similar to his own. Some of the accrued stocks are remainders from an earlier stage of competitive enter-priser activities. Some of them attach to environmental conditions. And further items in the system of prices are the more distinctly consumer aspects of the market situation; and behind these are the desires of human beings.

Little of all this is he able to explain; and little of it would he as enterpriser be concerned to explain, if he could. As a business man, he needs hail or tornado or drought or fire insurance. Why there is hail or tornado does not concern him. Whence come the suns and the winds and the ocean currents that make the climate, he may never know and will not inquire. Why the world is so big or so small; what set the proportions of sea and land; what decided how much of what land there is, is desert or mountain or marsh or forest or jungle is not his problem. His concern is with what he must pay for what land he wants in his business. Why there are so many men; or why the climate is so cold that they need woolen garments; or why they need woolen garments where the climate is cold; or whether the desires are traditional or imitative or decorative or competitive, can be to his purpose solely as bearing on his outlook for pecuniary margins.

There are presumably ways of accounting genetically for this situation, in some and perhaps in many aspects of it. Other aspects are presumably beyond the possibility of accounting. But even were all of the various explanations all wrong, the enterpriser need be none the worse off thereby. Doubtless many of them are wrong. It does not matter to him. His need is merely to know how to act within the situation as, for him, it unaccountably is.

And were it at all to his purpose, he might reflect that if economic

processes are never explained until the derivations of a present
situation are known, these explanations must always be in large
part wanting. Even the price system of any particular time is to be
explained in the genetic sense only as a modification of an earlier
price system. The regress is endless—excepting at some not distant
point of entire ignorance.

Moreover, Marshall's attempt to escape the circle of explaining
the prices of products by the prices of the costs, through a regress
to an earlier situation of prices, never leads back to a time which
does not pose the very problems of the present—and a time about
which even less is known than about the present. You must pay
to B thus much for the cost goods that he provides for you, because
he in turn had to pay such and such other prices to various C's;
who in turn had to pay such and such other prices to various
D's. All this with Marshall is, no doubt, in the faith that ultimately
—land hires of course excepted—these various costs can all be
reduced into wage costs, and these wage costs in turn accounted
for in terms of real costs. If, however, this recourse to discomfort
costs does not suffice for the present case, it will be regressively
the more satisfactory only because the factual grounds of attack on
it are less clear. But try out the method where you—or some one
else—may know something about its factual setting. You have to
pay some one of your men $5 a day in wages. Why? Perhaps he can
help you toward the knowledge that you have not. But he will
not talk to you—or you to him—about the griefs attaching to his
efforts; or his preference to sleep or play; or about how much his
father and grandfather paid out to achieve his present existence;
or about the gestation worries of his mother or his grandmother, or
their bedside vigils and anxieties. He will tell you what other jobs,
and at what other pay, are open to him—what your competitors are
offering for men, and the conditions of work with them; or about
what employers in other industries are willing and offering to do.
Or he will tell you about what he can make "on his own"—in
leasing that neighboring farm, or in soliciting life insurance, or in
taking over the district school, or in clerking in the store, or in going
on the road peddling, or soliciting orders.

And your further regress will merely lead you into a new setting

of circuities—only that the further back you go, the less glaring—
because of the increasing unprecision—will become the difficulties
with your tests. Your security will be merely that of the thicket or
the darkness.

This present-situation view is essentially, as we have seen, a
cross-section view. It is not genetic or historical. It takes for granted,
it is true, an on-going process—but only as a present fact. As an
on-going process, it derives, doubtless, from somewhere, and is
probably going somewhere; but the whence and the whither of it
are irrelevant, excepting solely as bearing on what the situation
is now, what it is at present doing. All past accountings for it may
be wrong, and all forecasts of its movement impossible—as long as
between the two eternities of unknowns there is a ribbon of light
bright enough and wide enough, as a specious present, for enterprisers to operate in. The enterpriser is a here-and-now person,
neither historian nor prophet. He has a situation to deal with, to
adapt to, to gain from. So far, indeed, as it is plastic to his efforts
—and thus not far—he will set himself to making it nearer to his
heart's desire. But even so, his problem being as it is, and he himself
being as he is, the case is one of present action within a given
situation for his individual gain. The derivation of himself or of
his human nature, or of the habitat, or of human nature at large,
or of the numbers of human beings, or of human institutions, as
over against what these things now are, is no part of his problem.

Admittedly, however, the economist's problem is not precisely
the enterpriser's problem. The enterpriser's particular problem is
that of achieving his individual gain within a situation that is in
part made up of other enterprisers in processes that are in the large
similar to his, and under motivations that are practically identical.
But the economist must see these different activities in the large, as
also the situation in the large; must generalize them; and therefore
must study them in the aggregate, as well as in their inter-individual
adjustments. But still it is for the economist an on-going process,
within a given setting of situation—facts, that he has to study—so
far, at least, as he is occupying himself with the processes and the

mechanics of price-equilibration: the value problem as a system of relative prices, the exchange relations of goods, the relative prices of things.[2]

It is, then, inevitable that the cost-regress analysis should present practically all the problems of the cross-section analysis, along with its own cumulative opportunities for error. And if, as Marshall insists, it is commonly enough to go back only one stage with it,[3] it must be as well not to go back even thus far. For real-cost purposes, the regress procedure has to assume that there is a functional differentiation in outlay costs, some of them price-determined and some of them price-determining, else, by the very purpose of it, it must be promptly discredited, only the non-labor costs at each step being price-determining. And unless the cross-section analysis in the present situation discloses this difference between price-determining and price-determined costs, no particular situation in the past could find room for it. If relative wages now are not explained by relative real costs, never were they so explained. And in whatever sense and emphasis the present population is not explained by the pecuniary costs of production of human beings, or by their real costs of production, inclusive of the maintenance and training costs incurred for pecuniary ends by earlier and later progenitors, in precisely this same degree and emphasis the wages of labor at any earlier stage of the period concerned in the regress procedure cannot have been so explained.

[2] This is, to be sure, not to say that there are no other fields of economic interest or problems, it may be, of far greater appeal to the right and wholesome scientific interest: industrial history; the history of economic thought; institutional genetics; institutional forecasts; or even price trends, present and future. There is, be it repeated, no disputing about the worthiness of interests. *Nor again is there any disputing that they should not get confused.* The study of the process of price-equilibration within a given situation is one problem. But never is the past or future of prices, or the relations of one price system to another, or even of any price items in one system to others in that system, safely to be undertaken for study, until the processes by which a particular system of prices within a given situation is arrived at, have become clear. To account for the degree of change over a period of time in any price system, or for the time changes among price systems, requires an understanding of the equilibration process, not only at the beginning and at the end of the period under examination, but continuously all the way along. Dynamics may be better than statics, in the sense, at any rate, of a further step; but not in the sense of denial or of displacement or of independence.

[3] See Marshall, p. 339.

Logically, as we have seen, no point of stopping in the regress offers any advantage over stopping before the regress began. Analytically this type of analysis offers no advantage over the cross-section method, precisely because the regress involves whatever functional analyses the cross-section method employs. Whatever time in the past is selected, that is then its cross-section present. There is only one analysis for that period and the present. And if regress is called for now, the necessity for it is not to be escaped by pushing the time-venue back by days or years or decades or generations. Historical explanations explain only when they cease to be historical—when they stop; and if the start was logically infect, the stop declares a collapse. The regress method may carry peculiar dangers or difficulties or uncertainties of its own, or it may have the dubious merit of shifting the issue over into times of factual vagueness or ambiguity; but doctrinally it stands on a precise level with the cross-section analysis of the present.

And thus, through another approach, it again becomes necessary to decide whether costs are functionally to be differentiated in their bearing on prices. In principle, enterpriser cost points to the price sum of the forecasted resistances to forecasted price returns. It is an individual computation, a purely competitive phenomenon in business policy. Along with other costs, discomfort costs there doubtless may be; but all costs have equally to arrive at a price expression of their resistance.

Are there, however, distinctions requiring recognition among factors, for purposes of our problem of relative prices? The ordinary employer cost is a regress cost, but of the present time—what a particular enterpriser is paying to another because of what things are now costing this other. Under close examination, how in this employee aspect do these costs look relatively to one another? What does Marshall himself make of his quasi-rents, and what is their bearing on the general movement of his doctrine? Doubtless there is the logical necessity for them, when once the price-determined standing of position rents is asserted. If land rents are price-determined because of the fixity of land stocks—their unresponsiveness to investment policies—the hires of all agents must be similarly price-determined for their respective periods of unresponsiveness.

The first step with Marshall in this analysis is to apply the land-rent principle to machinery and tools. But equally it is admitted to apply to labor and its hires for such period as the stocks of labor are also unresponsive to the hires of labor; and to apply also —and permanently—to such varieties or instances of labor agents as are never price-determining or wage-responsive. And in the degree that the multiplication of human beings is not the outcome of investment policies, or worked out through cost-of-production influences, the hires of labor—wages, salaries, exceptional and extra-ordinary labor incomes—must rank as price-determined incomes. Possibly even, their place in supplementary costs may seem at hazard.[4]

The hires of machinery and tools are quasi-rents—are, that is to say price-determined in the short run, but price-determining in normal-value conditions:

. . . so long as the resources of an individual producer are in the form of general purchasing power, he will push every investment up to the margin at which he no longer expects from it a higher net return that he could get by investing in some other material, or machine, or advertisement, or in the hire of some additional labour. . . .

But if he invests in land, or in a durable building or machine, the return which he gets from his investment may vary widely from his expec-

---

[4] But prime and supplementary costs have rightly no place in this quasi-rent discussion—excepting in the sense that they go a long way toward outlawing it. They belong entirely to the employer point of view. As such, they include whatever money costs are still within the enterpriser's field of choice, as over against his earlier and perhaps now entirely inelastic commitments. As distinctions, therefore, between different times, rather than different lines, of outlay they are quite irrelevant. Prime and supplementary costs have nothing to do with the employee point of view. It is true that wage and raw material outlays are the typical—in the sense of the most usual—instances of prime costs. But outlays for machines, or even for more land, or rights of way, or water royalties, or for emergency requirements in pasture lands or forestry rights, might be items of prime cost. As an employer category, prime costs are not concerned with any of the distinctions with which the present analysis deals—purely employee distinctions—a fact that should conclusively have warned against them. One of the two, this prime-cost distinction, or these employee-cost distinctions, must be abandoned. It would in fact be possible, though admittedly improbable, that all of the enterpriser's prime-cost outlays were in quasi-rent or true-rent directions. Some of them, for labor especially, are almost certain to be.

tation. . . . The incomes . . . differ from his individual point of view
mainly in the longer life of the land . . . the supply of land is fixed. . . .

. . . .

. . . "That which is rightly regarded as interest on 'free' or 'floating'
capital, or on new investments of capital, is more properly treated as a
sort of rent—a *Quasi-rent*—on old investments of capital. . . ." (pp. 411-
412)

Just how soon after it gets produced, a machine turns into a good
price-determined in its hire, is not clear; but presumably when the
hire has come to diverge from the interest return at the time of
production. And it is clear that it does not matter whether the
divergence is upward or downward. The point of emphasis is the
temporary fixity of stocks. It will not, then, matter if the hire
should return to the investment level in crossing the line to the
other side or even, it may be, if it should remain on the line, since
during the reproduction period nothing can be done about it. What,
however, about other *its*? Other instruments are, or may be—
especially if the return on this first one has been high—coming into
readiness. The stock is changing, though this particular item is
fixed. It should be true, then, that items of equipment, interchangeable in other respects, are some of them price-determining and some
not. Moreover, these shifts in a flash of any particular item of
equipment from cause to result, or from result back to cause (all
become causal in the normal value time), are difficult to picture.
At any rate, all of these interchangeable goods, some with interest
and some with rent returns, are plainly substitutionary with price-
determining wages.

The same quasi-rent standing holds for the cost-achieved fertility
of land:

. . . In the long run, then, the net returns to the investment of capital
in the land, taking successful and unsuccessful returns together, do not
afford more than an adequate motive to such investment. If poorer returns
had been expected than those on which people actually based their calculations, fewer improvements would have been made. (p. 426)

Suppose, however, that in the first year these returns ran true
to expectation, in the second year fell below, in the third year ran

true, and in the fourth year ran above. This would, it is true, be the merest nagging, and sticking-in-the-bark, criticism, were the issue something less serious than a series of functional transformations. The logic here is not a quantitative issue. The citation continues:

That is to say:—for periods which are long in comparison with the time needed to make improvements of any kind, and bring them into full operation, the net incomes derived from them are but the price required to be paid for the efforts and sacrifices of those who make them: the expenses of making them thus directly enter into marginal expenses of production, and take a direct part in governing long-period supply price. But in short periods . . . no such direct influence on supply price is exercised by the necessity that such improvements should in the long run yield net incomes sufficient to give normal profits on their cost. And therefore when we are dealing with such periods, these incomes may be regarded as quasi-rents which depend on the price of the produce. (p. 426)

Notice here—but solely for later reference—this *long-period supply price,* in the singular; and, further, *efforts* and *sacrifices,* instead of the more common *efforts* and *waitings.* Not far ahead we shall have to inquire whether *sacrifice* has not some reference to the principle of substitution—the fixing of each productive margin where the enterpriser "no longer expects from it a higher net return that he could get by investing in some other, etc." For it may be that employee costs are getting mixed here with opportunity costs. *Sacrifice* seems nowhere to have been defined; wherefore it will mean to you about what you think the argument should require it to mean.

The functional significance of fertility does not turn on whether it is natural or artificial:

. . . In any inquiry then as to the causes that will determine the prices of corn during a short period, that fertility which the soil derives from slowly made improvements has to be taken for granted as it then is, almost in the same way as if it had been made by nature. . . . But it is not a true surplus, in the same sense that rent proper is. . . . (p. 425)

It is to be noted, then, that quasi-rents are not in the last analysis distinguished by origin in investment costs, but solely by the short-time inelasticity of stocks. It is true merely that stocks are commonly responsive through the investment process.[5]

Real-cost considerations, therefore, have no present relevance. This is all money-cost analysis. It is solely with enterpriser costs that we have to do, but with enterpriser costs in their regress aspect —why they are as they are; what they must be, if they are to indemnify the provider of the cost goods.

[5] The characteristic, therefore, by which human abilities belong to the quasi-rent class is not that they are native, and thereby cost-free, in origin; or even that they are cost-acquired, the results of training outlays; but that temporarily they are not subject to modification in volume through investment—and that in the long run they are so subject. If, then, human abilities are neither in the long or in the short run responsive in volume to investment policies, their hires should be regarded by Marshall as of the true-rent, and not of the quasi-rent, character.

To extraordinary native abilities Marshall ascribes true-rent hires. Investment does not bring them, though, when they are present, it may train them to increased efficiency. There is commonly, therefore, in the actual incomes an admixture of quasi-rents, as also there is presumably some trace of pure-effort wages—these last price-determining always.

The fact is, nevertheless, that Marshall treats the abilities of business enterprisers as of the quasi-rent class. He says that (p. 622) "of the profits of the business man . . . the greater part is quasi-rent." But later, (p. 623) he contends that "the class of business undertakers contains a disproportionately large number of persons with high natural ability; since, in addition to the able men born within its ranks, it includes also a large share of the best natural abilities born in the lower ranks of industry. And thus while profits on capital invested in education is a specially important element in the incomes of professional men taken as a class, the rent of rare natural abilities may be regarded as a specially important element in the incomes of business men, so long as we consider them as individuals." And on page 606 Marshall says: "There is . . . no other kind [than business power] of useful, rare, and therefore highly-paid ability which depends so little on labour and expense applied specially to obtaining it, and so much on 'natural qualities.' And, further, business power is highly non-specialized. . . ."

The explanation that appears to be offered for all this confusion confounded, does not seem to be to the point—it being merely that little of his income is thought of by the business man himself as effort income. Even, however, were what the business man thinks of his own case decisive of the nature of his income, and of all those subdivisions of it for normal-time purposes, it would still be true that to declare any part of his income not effort income, is not to declare it to be therefore quasi-rent income. Marshall says (p. 622) that in business on a large scale, with great investment, and with "violent fluctuations from a considerable negative to a large, positive quantity . . . he [a business undertaker] often thinks very little of his own labour in the matter . . . there is so little difference between the trouble of having his business on his hands only partially active, and that of working it to its full capacity, that as a rule it scarcely occurs to him to set off his own extra labour as a deduction from those gains: they do not present themselves to his mind as to any considerable extent earnings purchased by extra fatigue. . . ."

Why Marshall calls these incomes quasi-rents, as against ordinary labor hires, on the one hand, or true rents on the other hand, is not clear. But it is clear that

And further, the logic of the position applies equally to the existing stocks of raw materials, or, at all events, to those that are not still within the control of investor policies. The fact that any item of producers' goods, or for that matter, of any other sort of good, is either a good presently existing out of the past, or not existing at all, is perhaps a logic too heroic to be fairly applicable to this particular issue. Even if logically there is no present, but only a hair-line between two eternities—you and I not in the room here, but only, just before now, here, and just going to be here—it is still left true that there is a psychological present, the specious present of the psychologist; and this may justify the distinction that is above suggested between the on-coming and the arrived, or between *made* and *making*.

Note also that in Marshall's view this temporary fixity of stocks has to do solely with the total stock of any particular class of factors of production—land, power engines, ordinary machinery, trucks, factory buildings, manufacturer lofts, or any sort of structure. No account is taken of the various and changing distributions of these aggregate stocks among the various industrial uses competing for them, accordingly as prices and other conditions are shifting. One passage, however, in the *Principles* looks specifically in the other direction:

... the argument ... with regard to the special earnings (whether of the nature of rents or quasi-rents) of appliances capable of being used in several branches of production, is applicable to the special earnings of natural abilities, and of skill. When land or machinery capable of being

---

investment in any sort of preparation for later earnings is not taken to be essential to quasi-rent standing; that lack of specialization is no more to the point than the presence of it ought to be; that cost-free origins have no significance for the purpose; and that in Marshall's thought these enterpriser labor incomes do not, in the long run, remain in the price-determined class, but become instead price-determining like ordinary labor and capital hires.

A possible explanation for this view that the incomes from business ability are not in the long run of the true-rent class, but go along instead with ordinary price-determining wages, might seem to be that, in Marshall's thought, business ability, no matter how exceptional, arrives in the long run as a sort of by-product of the general reproductive process—a process that proceeds in the large along investment lines, and thus conforms in general to the principle of the cost-of-production process. If so, however, the same reasoning should cover all extraordinary natural abilities, whether general or specialized, and should attach the quasi-rent standing equally to them. It does not.

used for producing one commodity is used for another, the supply price of the first is raised, though not by an amount dependent on the incomes which those appliances for production would yield in the second use. So when trained skill or natural abilities which could have been applied to produce one commodity, are applied for another, the supply price of the first is raised through the narrowing of its sources of supply. (p. 579)

Precisely so; but therewith all talk of fixity, unless from "the social point of view," goes for naught. It is also to be queried whether the argument from marginal isolation—admitted by Marshall to apply as well to equipment goods as to land—does not outlaw this entire discussion.

It does, however, appear decisive for this entire fixity analysis that, practically always, outlays for equipment goods can be substituted for outlays for labor. Such is the essential meaning of the popular term *labor-saving devices*. If, then, the wage costs are price-determining in the short run, the equipment-good hires should be equally so; and if the equipment-goods costs are not, the wages can not be.

This conclusion is not, however, as devastating as, on its face, it may appear to be. For in fact, as will shortly appear, Marshall holds labor incomes to be in large part quasi-rent items, with their hires price-determined incomes. Only the *true earnings of effort,* which are everywhere a constituent of all labor incomes, are to be understood to be indisputably of the price-determining function. Inasmuch, however, as the substitutionary aspect of all these quasi-rent goods for pure-effort labor—and, as well, of most quasi-rent labor for pure-effort labor—applies in quite unlimited degree, the fundamental difficulty persists. It is, indeed, particularly serious by the fact that these labor-saving devices appear to apply in especial degree to the displacement of the cruder grades of labor.

The perplexities under the head of *financial capital* are also serious, though adequately to be discussed only in connection with interest theory. It is, in fact, not altogether clear what relation to prices interest is reported to have. It is clear that earlier commitments in buildings and equipment are regarded as now commanding quasi-rent hires. Outlays in fixed-charge directions belong to the same class. Overhead divides, one thinks, into prime and quasi-rent costs. But what about holdings in cash, money or deposit credits, bills receivable, and circulating capital in general—quick assets? These, although they are not industrial-factor costs, would appear to be price-determining, as easily within the field of investor choice. But not rarely also, investment goods of the extremely permanent sort, land for example, can be marketed. Mainly, therefore, the view that these items are not bases of price-determining costs, is not tenable in the competitive sense, but only in the aggregate or social sense. Some enterprisers are merchandisers of lands as truly as others of canned goods and pumpkins.

But it may be true that the distinction between long and short-time commitments, being by Marshall recognized to be one of degree, is intended to leave a wide margin of discretion in applying it; or, it may be, is without significance excepting in view of all the circumstances in each particular case of its application. The purpose of the distinction is nevertheless to be clearly held in mind. The line has to be drawn, no matter what be the point of its drawing, so that on the hither side of it any particular item of cost goods shall be price-determining, the while that, just on the further side of it, the hire is price-determined—a lightning transformation from cause to result. Distinctions of degree are tenable in their due place. But if the distinction under examination is one of degree, it is one in which degree is taken to run so far as to amount to kind, and to run therewith into a glaringly antithetical kind—a reversal of function from governing to governed. The distinction, by the way, between what is not *determining* but is *governing* appears to be purely defensive ambiguity—another case, it may be, where some serious effort at clear definition would have made secure interpretation less difficult.

Efforts and Quasi-rents

But how does the principle of Marshall's quasi-rent doctrine, the responsiveness principle, work out in point of its application to the sums received by the makers of effort for those services that they render to the enterpriser—services for the control of which the competitive employer is submitted to outlay costs? All pure-effort earnings are by Marshall taken to be always price-determining hires. Some part, therefore, of every labor income to the employee, and of every wage or salary outlay by the employer, is a price-determining hire:

. . . when the artisan or professional man has once obtained the skill required for his work, a part of his earnings are for the future really a quasi-rent of the capital and labour [funds?] invested in fitting him for his work, in obtaining his start in life, his business connections, and generally his opportunity for turning his faculties to good account; and only the remainder of his income is true earnings of effort. But this remainder is generally a large part of the whole [but sometimes not?]. And here lies the contrast. For when a similar analysis is made of the profits of the business man, the proportions are found to be different: in his case, the greater part is quasi-rent. (p. 622)

Just imagine yourself engaged in making this analysis—with all of the laboratory equipment in experimental psychology that you could ask—even for any particular business man, to say nothing of assembling the material for a large number of business men to the extent necessary to afford the basis for a generalization. Or you might sample. But what answer could any one of all these business men give to any one of your relevant questions. How much of your labor return traces back to your earlier training—and how much of this earlier training was investment-acquired? But there are these parts? Conceptually, no doubt; but not as objectively distinguishable. How much of your earning power derives from native or acquired specialized ability?

But whether or how far any particular artisan or professional income accrues to specialized efficiency does not appear to matter in this cause-and-effect aspect. The ease of transfer to some alternative field is not relevant to the question of what part of the ability was cost-acquired:

. . . the gross earnings of management which a man is getting can only be found after making up a careful account of the true profits of his business, and deducting interest on his capital. The exact state of his affairs is often not known by himself; and it can seldom be guessed at all accurately even by those who are in the same trade with himself. . . .
. . . And though it may sometimes be a more difficult task for a business man than for a skilled labourer, to find out whether he could improve

his prospects by changing his trade, yet the business man has great opportunities for discovering . . . and if he should wish to change his trade, he will generally be able to do so more easily than the skilled workman could.

On the whole then we may conclude that the rarity of the natural abilities and the expensiveness of the special training required for the work affect normal earnings of management in much the same way as they do the normal wages of skilled labour. . . . (pp. 607-8)

. . . a great part of what appears to the borrower as interest, is, from the point of view of the lender, earnings of management of a troublesome business. (p. 588)

Of course, this appeal to the normal earnings of management and to the normal earnings of skilled labor is also a procedure of the purely conceptual sort; for no one has ever witnessed a normal-value situation; nor, if some one had, would he ever have been able to recognize it as such.

But as to the specialization, no criticism is here offered. For, doubtless, the degree of specialization has to do with the distribution of the stocks of any factor among the different industries. But this aspect of things Marshall nowhere takes into account in drawing the line between pure-effort hires and those quasi-rent hires deriving not from native abilities but from cost-acquired training. And rightly, for specialization has nothing to do with the relation of the hires to the investment costs, though it may have something to do with the amount of these hires.

And as has earlier been noted, this recognition of distribution between industries, and of specialization as a limiting influence in this distribution, draws the curtain on all talk of fixity and unresponsiveness of factors, as far as any particular price outcome, or relative price outcomes, can be concerned. Land may be shifted from one crop to another, or from gardening to residence lots, or from pasture to forestry, or from apartments to merchandising— and vice-versa—and so on indefinitely.[6] There is no escape from this difficulty by asserting, as Marshall does (p. 434), that "farming is a single business so far as the main crops are concerned; though the rearing of choice trees (including vines), flowers,

[6] Marshall, pp. 436, 448-49.

vegetables, etc. affords scope for various kinds of specialized business ability. The classical economists were therefore justified in provisionally supposing that all kinds of agricultural produce can be regarded as equivalent to certain quantities of corn; and that all the land will be used for agricultural purposes, with the exception of building sites which are a small and nearly fixed part of the whole."

But shoes and hats are not a single business. Trucks are used in farming, merchandising and hauling sand. Even if we adopt the standpoint of the original investor, the volume of funds directed into any particular line of production goods must turn in the main on the alternative prospects, the lure of substitutes—on opportunity costs—that are here evident, as pretty much everywhere else. Marshall himself says:

... It is ... not unreasonable to assume for the present that the owners of capital in general have been able in the main to adapt its forms to the normal conditions of the time, so as to derive as good a *net* income from their investments in one way as another. (p. 592; see also pp. 450-52)

But this principle of opportunity costs Marshall finds to have more to do with the pure earnings of labor than has the discomfort aspect of this labor:

... the disagreeableness of work seems to have very little effect in raising wages, if it is of such a kind that it can be done by those whose industrial abilities are of a very low order. For the progress of science has kept alive many people who are unfit for any but the lowest grades of work. They compete eagerly for the comparatively small quantity of work for which they are fitted. ...
... the dirtiness of some occupations is a cause of the lowness of the wages earned in them ... this dirtiness adds much to the wages they would have to pay to get the work done by skilled men ... and so they [employers] often adhere to old methods which require only unskilled workers. ... (p. 558)

In total effect, this view is incontestible. The wages are low because there is nothing else open. It is the lack of alternatives that congest the particular occupation. But the explanation is not precisely that the abilities are of a very low order. Low-order ability, like that of the fat woman or four-eared man in the side-show, might get high pay if it were not too plentiful. Excepting with interchangeable jobs, ability has no economic test but money returns. Mainly it is the lack of alternatives that imposes the particular congestion, and that results in wages not even remotely proportional with relative discomforts. If the four-eared boy were especially happy in being able to listen in on two radio stations at a time, his wages would not thereby suffer. The issues are of stocks; and are of discomforts only as affecting stocks. What you can get elsewhere is a cost to you here, with labor equally with capital.

Moreover, many of these perplexities in attempting to subdivide returns on effort, or on investment-acquired individual abilities, into investment returns, true labor incomes, rents and near-rents—but not all of these perplexities and confusions—are due to confusions in points of view. From the point of view of the prima-donna receiving her salary, as from that also of the unskilled laborer, whatever income is received, may be variously reckoned as a surplus, accordingly as (a) it is so much more than nothing; or (b) so much more than the minimum necessary to overcome the disinclination to the particular effort, as such; or (c) so much more than could be had in some similarly burdensome alternative occupation; or (d) so much more than could be had under another employer in the same occupation. But to the employer, no part of whatever he has to pay to hire the labor is a surplus, but only what more he would pay, if he had to, than he does pay.

But inasmuch as the test of quasi-rents is one of responsiveness, why is not any grade of native ability a cost-free thing; and the hire of it a quasi-rent, so far as this hire is in excess of pure-effort earnings? In fact, however, as we are shortly to see in detail, Marshall takes practically all laborers to exist as conditioned and limited by cost-of-production influences. All along the line he holds the cost-of-production explanation for the volume of labor and for the wages of it. Consistently with this view, there is no place for training costs, excepting as a particular variety of the costs of production of particular grades of labor, as over against the reproduction and maintenance costs of the general mass of laborers. For Marshall holds that, with ordinary labor, parents are neither able nor disposed to enter into investments in training. They have, it is to be assumed, more than enough to do to make face against the pressing necessities of birth and maintenance and the current temptations of unthrift. But if, with the better-to-do, these training outlays promise well enough for the future incomes of offspring, then both the resources and the disposition prescribe the making of the pecuniary outlays as investment undertakings. On terms of lower investment returns, the outlays will not be undertaken. Thus, Marshall argues, there are cost-conditioned abilities limited in volume, not only in general, but in different directions and kinds:

. . . the investment of capital in the rearing and early training of the workers of England is limited by the resources of parents in the various grades of society, by their power of forecasting the future, and by their willingness to sacrifice themselves for the sake of their children.

This evil is indeed of comparatively small importance with regard to the higher industrial grades. . . . They exert themselves much to select the best careers for their sons [and daughters?], and the best trainings for those careers; and they are generally willing and able to incur a considerable expense for the purpose. The professional classes especially, while generally eager to save some capital *for* their children, are even more on the alert for opportunities for investing it *in* them. . . .

But in the lower ranks of society the evil is great. . . . (pp. 561-62)

Doubtless, but it does not follow that the reproductive processes are, on the whole, or exclusively anywhere, business policies, or that even where training is afforded, it is in the main in the emphasis of pecuniary investment. This is, however, a topic for later examination in the large. It is important at present to make clear that Marshall does hold a cost-of-production explanation of the processes and outcomes of reproduction with human beings. The underlying principle is that manifest with the raising of mules, slaves, cattle and hogs. And the purpose of the discussion is to establish not only a theory of wages but a basis of the quasi-rent relation of many labor returns to enterpriser costs—an employee account of the reasons why enterpriser costs are as they are; and in what shares these costs divide into price-determining and price-determined parts:

. . . the only persons . . . very likely to invest much in developing the
personal capital of a youth's abilities are his parents. . . . This fact is very
important practically, for its effects are cumulative. But it does not give
rise to a fundamental difference between material and human agents of
production. . . .

. . . on the whole the *money* cost of any kind of labour to the employer
corresponds in the long run fairly well to the *real cost* of producing that
labour. (p. 661)

Just what, in view of the money tenor of most of these investments by parents in the future earning prospects of offspring, is
the significance of this emergence of *real* cost in the discussion is
not readily apparent. But it is to be recalled that always real costs
are taken by Marshall to be the underlying and adequate explanations of money costs. It is, however, clear that neither with the
ill- nor the well-to-do does this particular analysis go off on any
doctrine of the minimum of subsistence or of the standard of living
—the effects of restricted economic incomes on births or deaths,
as directive of population increase. Each is a sufficiently dubious
doctrine in view of the near-truth in the adage that *the fools have
all the luck and the poor men all the children,* or that *it is the
poor that are prolific;* and in view of the especially falling birth
rates of the outstandingly well-to-do countries and of the outstandingly well-to-do classes in most of these countries.[7] But Marshall's
view rests instead, for present purposes, on the assumed disposition
of parents not to bear, or rear, or train children, if the prospects
of these children—not the prospects or situation of the parents—
are unsatisfactory. This view appears to have slight factual basis
in reference to those countries about which trustworthy information
is available.

For Marshall's purposes, the better view would seem to be to hold
all labor incomes to be of the quasi-rent class for whatever the
wage is above an indemnity for the real costs of effort.

[7] ". . . though a temporary improvement will give a good many young people
the opportunity to marry and set up house . . . yet a permanent increase of
prosperity is quite as likely to lower as to raise the birth-rate. But on the other
hand, an increase in wages is almost certain to diminish the death-rate. . . ." (p.
529)

Unusual Abilities

But what about the exceptional native abilities of business men? Marshall finds a relatively small share of pure-effort incomes among business men. But in the main, it appears, their labor returns are still to be regarded, not as pure rents, but merely as quasi-rents, so long as we consider these business men as individuals. Not so, however, with the exceptionally successful professional men:

. . . the class of business undertakers contains a disproportionately large number of persons with high natural ability; since, in addition to the able men born within its ranks it includes also a large share of the best natural abilities born in the lower ranks of industry. And thus while profits on capital invested in education is a specially important element in the incomes of professional men taken as a class, the rent of rare natural abilities may be regarded as a specially important element in the incomes of business men, so long as we consider them as individuals. . . . (p. 623)

But we recall that the distinction between a quasi-rent and a pure rent turns on what will be the relation of the hire to prices under normal-value conditions. Wherefore Marshall goes on to say:

In relation to normal value the earnings even of rare abilities are . . . to be regarded rather as a quasi-rent than as a rent proper.
. . . on the other hand, the greater part of incomes earned by exceptionally successful barristers, and writers, and painters, and singers, and jockeys may be classed as *the rent* of rare natural abilities—so long at least as we regard them as individuals. . . . (p. 623)

It has already been noted (p. 622) that "of the profits of the business man . . . the greater part is quasi-rent," as distinguished from the income of the artisan or the professional man, who, when he has "once obtained the skill required for his work . . . only the remainder of his income is true earnings of effort. But this remainder is generally a large part of the whole." And this is held to be true (p. 623) despite the fact that "when an artisan or professional man has exceptional natural abilities, which are not made by human effort, and are not the result of sacrifices undergone for a future gain, they enable him to obtain a surplus income . . . a surplus which is of the nature of rent." For it has now become clear that there are quasi-rents that do not derive from the fact of an earlier investment of funds capital. There is much human ability that does so derive, but Marshall does not urge that native ability is thus derived; and native ability is a basis of both quasi-rents and true rents. If so, however, what is to be made of the following, in view of the assertion on page 622 that with the profits of business men the greater part is quasi-rent?

. . . Everyone . . . can gain some training for business management, if he has the natural aptitudes for it. There is therefore no other kind of useful rare and therefore highly-paid ability which depends so little on labour and expense applied specially to obtaining it, and so much on "natural qualities." And, further, business power is highly non-special-ized; because in the large majority of trades, technical knowledge and skill become every day less important relatively to the broad and non-specialized faculties of judgment, promptness, resource, carefulness and steadfastness of purpose. (p. 606)

It may be. It probably is. But why then assert (p. 622) that of the incomes of "the artisan or professional man . . . the re-mainder . . . true earnings of effort . . . is generally a large part of the whole" while " . . . of the profits of the business man . . . the greater part is quasi-rent?" The suggestion is strong, though per-haps not intended, that the differentiation is due to the lack of specialized ability with the business man. It can hardly need repeti-tion that, from the point of view of investment cost, the specializa-tion of native ability is no part of the case.

And now what about extraordinary native ability—neither the more nor the less native or costless than mere exceptional ability? There is, to be sure, some admixture of pure-effort income; but incomes to these abilities are mainly pure rents:

. . . those extra incomes which are earned by extraordinary natural abilities. Since they are not the result of the investment of human effort in an agent of production for the purpose of increasing its efficiency, there is a strong *prima facie* cause for regarding them as a producer's surplus, re-sulting from the possession of a differential advantage for production, freely given by nature. This analogy is valid and useful so long as we are merely analysing the component parts of the income earned by an individual [which is precisely what we have all along been doing]. And there is some interest in the inquiry how much of the income of successful men is due to chance, to opportunity, to the conjuncture, how much to the good start they have had in life; how much is profits on the capital invested in their special training, how much is the reward of exceptionally hard work; and how much remains as a producer's surplus or rent resulting from the possession of rare natural gifts. (p. 577)

But Marshall insists (p. 578)—not at all denying the actuality of the pure rent—that "we are not at liberty to treat the exceptionally high earnings of successful men as rent, without making allowance for the low earnings of those who fail." This is not the place for taking issue on this exception; but it still holds true that other grades of ability have similar, and perhaps equal, chance of failure; and that no consideration in this emphasis at all disturbs the advantage of inheriting extraordinary ability. Seemingly, then, *exceptional* natural ability carries, in the main or entirely, rents of the quasi-sort; but *extraordinary* natural ability, a considerable loading of pure rent. All of which may be the fact, though one does not entirely understand why. But still less easy is it to understand by what methods Marshall found these things out.

But the ability that is native has aspects manifestly differentiating it from the capacities that are cost-acquired. Marshall takes native ability to be in the main similar, in its bearing on prices, to machinery, to cost-acquired fertility, and even to natural fertility—to the extent, indeed, that he debits against the individual's net return from ability a risk charge, commensurate with the chance that the individual might not have succeeded; and an additional debit in the nature of a depreciation charge, commensurate with the gradual wearing out of the individual's life and productive energy:

. . . the greater part of incomes earned by exceptionally successful barristers, and writers, and painters, and singers, and jockeys may be classed as the rent of rare natural abilities—so long at least as we regard them as individuals, and are not considering the dependence of the normal supply of labour in their several occupations on the prospect of brilliant success which they hold out to aspiring youth. (pp. 623-24)

A long period of time is however needed in order to get the full operation of all these causes, so that exceptional success may be balanced against exceptional failure. . . . (p. 619)

. . . the miner is as liable to wear-and-tear as machinery is; and a deduction must be made from his earnings also on account of wear-and-tear, when the special return of his skill is being estimated. There is some ground for regarding this special return as a quasi-rent. (p. 576 and note)

These debits appear to apply as obviously to native as to cost-acquired ability. The implication, however, that these risks or wear-outs would discourage the particular grades or types of ability from being born, is presumably not to be drawn.

Meanwhile it becomes again clear that the ultimate test of distinction can not be that of origins, or of derivation from training costs earlier borne; but only the test of responsiveness, either in decrease or increase, to investor policies. Many incomes therefore, whether those from exceptional native ability or those from ability reinforced through costly training, contain some slight elements of pure-effort returns; some pure-rent elements; and, along there-with, residuals of the quasi-rent character—but residuals varying in ratio-shares according to the particular origins of the respective income-returning abilities.

But Marshall takes all but the incomes from extraordinary natural ability to consist mainly, and almost entirely, of pure-effort returns, along with a residual of return of the quasi-rent sort. He quite clearly does not restrict these quasi-rent abilities to those deriving from training costs. These cost-acquired incomes are mingled in varying proportions with native-ability incomes.

Are, however, Marshall's reports of the varying constituents of these different sorts of incomes—his relative allocations of price-determining and price-determined elements—to be taken as founded on any secure bases of fact? Marshall himself would probably not so insist. They appear to be frankly such estimates and approximations as Marshall finds to be reasonably hazarded. How, indeed, could he get further or achieve more? Or how could you, or I? No ways of precise knowing are open. But does knowledge or precision matter here? Would it hurt if nothing in it all were even an approximation to the credible—or even were plain and sheer error?

Practically, it could not matter in the slightest, for the prices under consideration are those of the pre-normal period—else there could be no quasi-rents to talk about.[8] In fact, one way of defining a normal-value situation is that of a time when all quasi-rents have disappeared, when the hires of investment goods have equilibrated against the investment expectations which directed their production —the later responses justifying the earlier responsiveness.

But in this pre-normal time, some or all of the hires of the factors of production are indefinitely divergent from the expectations of the investors who provided the agents. It is thus that they are the results of the prices, and not the causes of them. Costs of production do not, for these pre-normal and interim periods, explain prices. The lines of causation run just the other way about. For purposes of explaining prices, it therefore does not at all matter what these various hires may be, or into what parts they are apportioned. Practically all of them have hires that are mainly of the quasi-rent function anyway, and are—at least for the time—in the price-determined class. Only the pure-effort parts of these labor returns —with certain other prime costs, it is to be assumed—could go, in even their short way, toward a causal account of prices.

[8] I am, I repeat, not confident in this interpretation. Quasi-rents, it is clear, may be distinguished from true rents by this reference to normal conditions; for all quasi-rents have by that time shifted into causal bearing, through costs, on prices. But it does not follow that some quasi-rents may not earlier than this have become causal. The logic of the parallel with true rents should limit the price-determined status of the quasi-rent goods to their respective periods of getting replaced through the investors' direction of funds into the creation of additional items of the goods. Were, however, the returns on investment running disappointingly low, this process of replacement might stretch out to even the normal-period situation. But were any new stocks promptly coming in—and possibly coming in rapidly in view of stimulating returns—some of these equipment goods must remain price-determined, the while that others of equal quality were taking on, or had taken on, the rôle of price-determination.

Moreover, the meaning of *normal* is unclear in this connection. It points, no doubt, to a situation in which investment activities are maintaining an output-schedule of goods equilibrating against the price-offer schedules of buyers or hirers. Possibly, then, any particular line of equipment may reach its own particular normal—or even attain at several different times its normal—during a period that, in the large and general aspect, was merely an interim, or pre-normal period.

But whether or not this interpretation is defensible need not greatly matter so long as it remains clear that, for the period of at least a generation, the hires of both native and acquired, and of both exceptional and extraordinary abilities—and perhaps of all abilities—are excluded from the price-determining function. For the criticism that is here urged as ultimate is that for part of the time—if, indeed, not always—Marshall's analysis leaves prices unaccounted for in cost terms—or, for that matter, in any other terms. I have, however, in earlier pages quoted passages from the *Principles* that indicate the continuous dependence of prices on costs.

Marshall is, then, dividing these quasi-rent or similar incomes into those distributive elements that would—some of them—be price-determining in a normal-value situation, and into others that would not. But no one of them is so now. Whether, then, he divides them rightly or wrongly does not signify for any interim price outcome. For these hires are themselves, in practically their entirety, irrelevant to the determination of actual prices. It is part of the argument that when normal-value conditions shall have arrived these subdivisions will matter—but only then. According, however, to Marshall's view of this normal-value situation certain of the hires that now are price-determined will continue to be price-determined—namely, true rents, portions of the returns on exceptional abilities, and the major part or the entirety of the returns on extraordinary natural abilities. But the hires of cost-acquired goods, that now are price-determined, will then, presumably at some particular instant, have shifted over into the price-determining class. And the true-effort hires that now are price-determining will so remain.

But it must be obvious that the few price-determining hires of these interim periods must commonly, or always, be altogether inadequate to explain the prices of these interim, pre-normal times. Prices, then, in all these times are without any cost explanation, or, in any significant way, any other explanation. In times of depression, clearly, the prices of products may fall far short of indemnifying the total costs of the products; and yet it may remain worth while, even though a new dollar may not replace an old one, to maintain the organization and to retain the clientele. Commonly, however, as Marshall rightly notes, the prices will be high enough to allocate some residual and meager returns to the quasi-rent goods and agents. The *general conditions of demand and supply*—not the prime costs that are obviously inadequate, and not the quasi-rents that are by assumption excluded—are solely invoked to account, so far as any account is offered, for the prices of products in pre-normal periods.

But it is also to be noted that not rarely these quasi-rent goods and agents are getting returns generously in excess of adequacy.

What part, if any, have these returns as costs in making prices? It may be lessees, or tenants, or purchasers, that are the actual enterprisers. But even the more clearly, Marshall would insist, the hires can not explain the prices; it must be the prices that explain the hires.

But whence come, then, these hires into the hands of the owners of the quasi-rent goods? How do these quasi-rent laborers get their pay? From the employer enterpriser, certainly. But why? Because of the prices that are ruling on the products. The hires that the employers must pay are going up—or going down—with the prices of the products; or, it may be, the prices up or down with the hires. Some nexus there is, at any rate, between the prices of the products and the hires paid out by the enterprisers in getting the products produced. Lag and unprecision once allowed for, this connection must be clear and close. Inter-enterpriser competitions make it so. Something further, then, than the general conditions of demand and supply might be offered in explanation of these product prices —namely, these enterpriser costs. In fact, these enterpriser costs might be regarded as the manner in which, for the purposes of the cost-of-production account of prices, these general conditions have to report themselves. Perhaps, even, these costs are themselves items of fact in these general conditions. Circular reasoning? No doubt; but not more so than in that future time of normal conditions; and not more so than belongs always to enterpriser costs of production as explaining the supply side of the price problem. Moreover, it is this or nothing for these interim prices.

And there is a further dour fact to be faced. If it should later turn out that never can any normal price situation or system actually arrive, prices, must, in this Marshall view, always be awaiting their explanation; the labor of the economists terminating inevitably in the discovery that prices can never come into any remote prospect of getting accounted for—the central problem of the science solved only in the sense of being found a mystery.

But taking it also as both clear and unquestioned that ordinary pure-effort hires are always price-determining, but that exceptional-ability hires—in non-normal times—are not so; and that extra-ordinary-ability hires are entirely, or almost entirely, not so, it would seem to follow that if you as enterpriser spend 50 dollars on the hires of ten men for one day, and another 50 dollars on the hire of one very extraordinary man accomplishing per day ten times as much in the same task as each one of the ten ordinary men—two labor ways, cost-wise equal, of getting a particular job done—the first 50 dollars as a composite hire is all price-determining, the while that the other 50 dollars, as a single-man wage, is all price-determined—excepting a few dollars of true-effort wages.

And so again if a machine, labor-saving in its purpose and its actual functioning, were to displace one of these ten men of yours, it would get a price-determined hire in place of the price-determin-ing hire of the man. Nothing so strange, however, would be the fact, were the machine so admirably efficient as to displace that one employee with the 50-dollar extraordinary ability—a man whose abilities, we recall, were of the pure-rent order. And if a pure-effort employee of yours displaced a machine, you would then have to do with a price-determining outlay in place of the earlier price-determined hire. And note that all these extraordinary out-comes would hold for normal times, so far as the extraordinary-ability laborer were concerned.

And after all, do outlays for extraordinary ability ever fall within prime costs? Unquestionably they sometimes must. And still they are in the main of the nature of pure rent. The solution of most of these difficulties appears to be possible only by abandoning this entire quasi-rent position. But then, it seems, land capital must rank with equipment capital in point of bearing on the prices of products.

But interest on free capital appears to be a price-determining cost. If now you invest your funds in near-town lands that excuse you so far from trucking charges, you have, it seems, purchased a property the hires of which are temporarily price-determined, while your trucking charges were not. And if you use your funds in hiring an artisan or a machine, you have a quasi-rent investment. If, however, you hire an artisan of extraordinary natural ability, these hires have the standing not of quasi-rents but of true rents; but if you hire ordinary laborers, then the outlays are price-determining.

And certain further things become also clear: no human abilities that are not cost-acquired ought logically to be assigned to this quasi-rent classification. For the native abilities of human beings are not responsive to the investment policies of any one. Precisely, therefore, as exceptional and extraordinary abilities command, not quasi-rent, but pure-rent hires, so also must ordinary ability, since this is as cost-free as are the higher grades. Thereby ordinary wage outlays, even when they are granted to be prime-cost outlays, become price-determined hires—excepting so far as, by the burdensomeness of labor, pure-effort wages have to be recognized. We arrive, then, at the conclusion that the ultimate outcome of this quasi-rent doctrine is to exclude from the price-causing function by far the larger part of all labor hires; and to do this, not only for all the pre-normal periods with which we are familiar, but as well for those normal-value periods that we have so far never seen, and that may possibly turn out not to be merely hypothetical but also essentially conceptual.

And if the hires of exceptional or extraordinary abilities become pure rents by virtue of their cost-free origin, there must be a clear case for the inclusion of all native abilities, whether exceptional or ordinary.

Marshall is then bound to hold either (1) that only the hires of cost-acquired abilities can ever—even in the long-run time of the normal-value situation—become price-determining, or (2) that in the last analysis all human beings—and therefore all human abilities—are cost-explained in origin. Logically thereby, the bearing and the rearing of offspring must be presented as finding their motivation and their limit in investment policies, in full parallel with the abilities that have been presented as tracing back to parental investment in training costs.

In fact, however, Marshall makes little attempt to support the cost derivation of exceptional and extraordinary native ability. To these abilities incomes of pure rent appear to be attributed. But he does, nevertheless, note that such considerations of resources as limit the forth-coming and maintenance of offspring, and such investment policies as set limits to the training of what offspring there are, are in some respects to be distinguished from ordinary investment:

... whoever may incur the expense of investing capital in developing the abilities of the workman, those abilities will be the property of the workman himself; and thus the virtue of those who have aided him must remain for the greater part its own reward. (p. 565)

Whatever deficiencies the modern methods of business may have, they have at least this virtue, that he who bears the expenses of production of material goods, receives the price that is paid for them. . . . (p. 561)

. . . human agents of production are not bought and sold as machinery and other material agents of production are . . . those who bear the expenses of rearing and educating him [a worker] receive but very little of the price that is paid for his services in later years. (pp. 560-61)

. . . the income expected to be derived . . . is of the nature of profits . . . the rate . . . is often high for two reasons: the people who make the outlay do not themselves reap the greater part of the reward . . . they are frequently in straightened circumstances. . . . (p. 622)

Marshall does not, however, recognize that to hold practically the entire stock of existing laborers to have been cost-produced, is to declare all to be quasi-rent productive agents, and is therefore to deny all of them in pre-normal times the price-determining function. And all of this amounts to wiping the slate clear of almost all prime costs for price-determining purposes. Practically all hires, labor as well as machine, become quasi-rents—unless they are pure rents; though doubtless there remain some pure-effort hires.

This quasi-rent doctrine was a perilous adventure.

Chapter XI

EMPLOYEE AND ENTERPRISER LABOR RETURNS

CERTAIN of Marshall's quasi-rent analyses, with especial reference to labor hires, are still to be examined; though the case with quasi-rents may seem to be ill enough without any cost-of-production account of the forthcoming of human beings as workers, whether as units in the great general stock or in particular stocks.

The quasi-rent doctrine reports all cost-produced instruments of production, during the period required for their production, as receiving hires that for the employee recipients of them, are like true rents, and that therefore are to be excluded from price-determining costs of production. Certain difficulties with this view have already been urged. We have now, however, to examine further difficulties superimposed upon the earlier, through Marshall's advocacy of the cost-of-production derivation of human beings. For the logic of this doctrine is to reduce all labor to a quasi-rent standing, and thereby to declare all labor hires during non-normal periods to be price-determined hires.

The reasons here to be adduced for not accepting this particular view are urged not at all in the purpose of avoiding further difficulties for the quasi-rent analysis, but rather impartially to clear the way of both the equipment and the labor quasi-rent doctrines.

Marshall was, however, almost inevitably committed to both of them through the logical necessities of his general doctrinal standpoint: to the hires of machinery as temporarily price-determined, to go along with true rents as permanently price-determined; and to the cost account of human beings, in order to provide a real-cost explanation of wages. The exclusion of land rents from price-determining costs was also imposed by this labor-cost theory of prices—land being in classical thought the one productive agent not subject to real costs of production in its origin.

For Marshall, however, the fertility aspects of land invalidated the classical reasoning—still, none the less, leaving the conclusions secure. Natural fertility and cost-free fertility are the same thing. But fertility can be worn out or created by men. Two sorts of fertility, cost-free and cost-achieved, are only conceptually distinguishable. Marshall abandons the test of origins, admitting the fertility of land to be capital in the sense that any other equipment good is capital. The ultimate line of distinction Marshall takes to be not that of origins but of responsiveness to human devisings in gain-seeking activities. In many cases the two lines of test concur, and thus are easily confused. But the classical choice of the wrong test left the classical conclusions defensible, on the whole, under the other test. Obviously, therefore, in the Marshall view, only the position or the spatial-extension aspects of land remained as bearers of those permanently price-determined hires that differentiate land from other productive agents.

This insistence on the fixity of land stocks has, however, nothing to say as to the relation of the hires to prices. There is, so far, no reason why these fixed-stock hires should or should not be taken as price-determining. Whether the hires will in the future be less or more, or the rents higher or lower, has in itself no bearing on whether the rents will then be price-determining or price-determined, or on whether now they are the one or the other. On this functional issue, for either the present or the future, these prospects or possibilities are irrelevancies.

It has, in fact, been through quite other doctrinal considerations that the peculiar relation of the spatial rents to prices has been urged. For it has been precisely here that the method of marginal isolation has taken on its chief significance. It is at any rate clear that the inelasticity of land stocks has had much to say to the movements of prices in the past, and will have much to say as to the trend of prices in the future, in view of the various possibilities with regard to population. But Marshall's reasoning directs itself not precisely to the explanations of prices at particular times, but rather to the causes of changes in prices. Land being taken as fixed in stock, all changes in prices must turn on the flexibilities of stocks of other factors of production, these being by assumption the sole possible influences for price change. But fertility, while a cost-free thing, is still a thing that is elastic in stock. By the test of responsiveness, therefore, its relation to prices must be that of capital goods. But this view of the case stood squarely across the path of making prices proportionate to real costs, a proportionality that was the essential thesis of the classical system—as it is also of Marshall's revision of the system.

The sole exit from this difficulty appeared to be by extending widely this classical principle of recourse to the margin of cultivation of land for the fixation of prices. There was also isolation of price-determining costs with equipment goods. By this procedure, the fertility as well as the position of land would have price-determined rents. Thus the hires of the cost-free elements in land would still stand as having no part in the making of prices.

But it has in modern analysis become clear—and is to Marshall clear—that this method of marginal isolation is not less applicable to the cost-produced agents of production than to the natural agents. Not only are there fertility rents, but there are machine rents. With both of these quasi-rent agents, therefore, marginal isolation is as applicable as with land capital; and with both the case is as strong as with land for declaring the rents to be, for their appropriate periods, of the price-determined sort.

In view, however, both of the substitutionary and the complementary relations among factors, this extension of the marginal-isolation principle carries with it its peculiar hazards. It purports, it is true, to avoid in real-cost connections the difficulty of regarding, not only cost-free fertility, but equally cost-achieved fertility as like machinery in point of bearing on prices. The marginal-isolation approach excludes both, for the period appropriate to the quasi-rent position. How this analysis will apply in normal situations, we shall not at present inquire. Temporarily, at any rate, cost-achieved fertility goes along with natural fertility and with machine equipment.

The marginal-isolation principle purports also to justify *unresponsiveness* in place of *origins* as the line of distinction between land capital and equipment capital—thereby in point of function classifying both natural and artificial fertility along with equipment goods. It leaves position rents as the sole hires price-determined in the long run. Machine rents are the typical case of temporarily price-determined standing. Clearly then, this original quasi-rent doctrine and the extensions of it follow unescapably from Marshall's earlier positions: spatial extension, in its aspect of fixity, as the essential characteristic of land capital and true rents; the derivative exclusion of both natural and artificial fertility from land capital—and the inclusion of both in the quasi-rent-bearing equipment capital; the extension of the marginal-isolation device to all of these quasi-rent agents; and thereby the exclusion of the rents of all of them from price determination during their appropriate reproduction periods.

And why not? For if true rents are to be permanently denied the price determining function by virtue of the permanent non-dependence of the stocks of land on the hires of the land—the ultimate meaning of *unresponsiveness*—then also fertility rents, and therewith also machine rents, must be excluded during the period of their unresponsiveness. Thus is the rent-cost position in classical theory defended; the distinction between land capital and other capital maintained; the wage-cost explanation of prices justified; and room provided for the proportionality of prices with real costs—after once due allowance has been made for the real costs attaching to the waiting aspects of capital investment, and thus for the money-outlay costs of interest. On the face of things, then, it might seem that all things have become well for classical theory.

But by equally good title certain other doctrinal steps become inevitable. Why must not also the hires of labor be included among the price-determined costs of production, for the period during which the stocks of labor are similarly unresponsive to the hires of labor? Marshall does, in fact, as we have earlier seen, accept this as an inevitable step for certain of the hires of labor—those of cost-acquired abilities.

But what, in turn, about native abilities and the hires of these? Must these not also be of the quasi-rent class? And does not in fact the logic of the argument go further yet—declaring them rather of the pure-rent class? For it does not appear to be true that the output of native ability can ever come to be responsive to the hires that are expected later to accrue to it. If parents have any choice about it, they presumably produce in any case as capable children as they can. If the wages in prospect are unattractive, the parents may scrimp on training. But this has to do not with native ability but with training costs, another question, and leaves the native abilities neither the more nor the less. The extent to which parents, price-allured, are likely to attempt to breed for native ability does not seem at present impressive or promise to become so later. Even were it within their horizon to try, they would not know how to go about it, or to get any one to tell them. And still clearer is it that in the past they have neither known nor tried. What they may sometime know how to do is irrelevant to the present stocks of labor and to the wages of it. Thus the native-ability hires are true rents, if they are rents of any sort. And if the hires are ever price-determined, they are enduringly so. The principle of responsiveness does not apply.

And thus much Marshall appears also both to admit and to assert—with respect, at least, to abilities of the extraordinary class. For if the hires of these abilities are included in the price-determining class, the entire real-cost determination of price costs becomes an impossible position. By the test of its very purpose, the analysis is self-refuting. With relative real costs accounting for relative price costs, the hires of extraordinary ability must be taken to be price-determined—and this not temporarily, but permanently. They must be true rents and not quasi-rents. Even in normal-time situations, they must be results and not causes of prices.

But the argument applies equally to exceptional abilities. Factually, indeed, the distinction is an impossible one between exceptional and extraordinary abilities—a distinction definite and intelligible only in point of words, or purely conceptual. Those hires of ability that are quasi-rents as distinguished from true rents can attach only to cost-acquired abilities. These also are only conceptually distinguishable. The economist can reason about the distinction, but nowhere can either he or the "market place" apply it, or the market place be concerned with it.

It being, then, clear that the hires of exceptional and extraordinary ability have no real-cost correlates, it is a logical necessity for the labor theory of relative prices to rule them out of price-determining costs, and to rule them out permanently.

Moreover, whatever ability any worker inherits must be native ability. Why then are not all labor hires price-determined costs? From the employee point of view, to be sure—and all of this analysis is from this point of view—there are, or may be, real costs attaching to any item of productive effort. And there are reproduction and maintenance costs that perhaps are to be recognized, as real or money costs, or perhaps as both. But still, there must be alternative methods of explanation—*either* the labor available for hire limited by its pure-effort costs, *or* limited by parental real and money costs; but not by both at once. The classical economists should make their choice here, and abide by it, not now the one and again the other, or the two together; else the employer would commonly become insolvent in the paying of the wage—his sale prices inadequate to cover his wage outlays. Only why should the laborer refuse to work when his wages were high enough to make it worth while, if only his parents had not spent so much on him?

Moreover, neither of these alternative explanations can credibly be adequate. We can securely know not much about it anyway, but we may still suspect that employee surpluses are fairly common. But it must at any rate be clear that once the burdens of bearing and of maintenance have been incurred, these must be the basis of quasi-rents—the hires not in the short run price-determining. Pure earnings of effort—in the emphasis of real-cost limits on effort— must be the sole remaining price-determining hires in the labor field.

But before entering on our examination of the analysis in the regress and employee emphasis by which Marshall presents labor as a productive agent subject in volume to cost-of-production limitations, there are some further points of interest in this quasi-rent doctrine. For now we recall that when the normal-value time arrives, if ever it does arrive, the situation will have changed in certain very important particulars. All of the quasi-rents will have been absorbed into price-determining costs. True rents will remain as price-determined. And there will be some pure rents of labor. All of those hires that are at that time price-determining will find themselves explained by earlier real and money costs, and equated against these costs—mainly those of the original investor of funds in equipment lines. Those hires of labor that are price-determining will have behind them, and explanatory of them, some real costs of the pure-effort type, and other money costs of the parental investment type. And these costs will be somehow combined with the laborer's own true-effort costs of his current labor, in such wise as to offset and explain the actual wages.

But what in these normal-value conditions must be the significance of that marginal-isolation method that has been the chief reliance of Marshall's earlier analysis? True rents will of course remain price-determined. Marginal isolation, that is to say, will still remain as applicable to the spatial extension aspects of land. But for all other hires this method of marginal isolation must seemingly become entirely inappropriate:

In a rigidly stationary state in which supply could be perfectly adjusted to demand in every particular, the normal expenses of production, the marginal expenses, and the average expenses (rent being counted in) would be one and the same thing, for long periods and for short. . . . (p. 497)

In a stationary state then the plain rule would be that cost of production governs value . . . no fundamental difference between the immediate and the later effects of economic causes. . . . (p. 367)

All of the rents of fertility and machine agents become, then, price-determining. Supra-marginal units of product have the same cost as the marginal units, only differently constituted—an analysis that has earlier by Marshall been discredited, not for true rents solely but for all rents.

But with the rents of natural fertility admitted to the price-determining function, the central thesis of the entire classical position lapses. For prices turn out to be disproportionate to real costs. And unless the hires of exceptional and extraordinary abilities are interpreted as true rents—and therefore as always price-determined—a further decisive objection in the same emphasis is to be urged. And no matter what place is made for the hires of all native abilities, high or low, the pure-rent status of them must be recognized, unless, to be sure, the real costs of effort or the costs of rearing—one of the two, but not both—are presented as adequately accounting for the hires that are received by the agents—there being never any occasion to account for these hires from the employer point of view. But there is no warrant for asserting or assuming that the hires of ordinary labor, skilled or unskilled, are proportionate to the real costs of effort or to the costs of rearing. If they were so, it would be merely as an inscrutable item of fact. But they are not so:

. . . the wages even of a working man depend on the start he has had in life almost as much as on the expense which his father has been able to afford for his education. (p. 608)

. . . even in modern England the accident of birth counts for a good deal in the access to posts of command in all kinds of business, to the learned professions and even to skilled manual trades. . . . (p. 649)

. . . the son of a man already established in business starts with very great advantages over others. He has from his youth up special facilities for obtaining the knowledge and developing the faculties that are required in the management of his father's business: he learns quietly and almost unconsciously about men and manners in his father's trade and in those from which that trade buys and to which it sells; he gets to know the relative importance and the real significance of the various problems and anxieties which occupy his father's mind: and he acquires a technical knowledge of the processes and the machinery of the trade. Some of what he learns will be applicable only to his father's trade; but the greater part will be serviceable in any trade that is in any way allied with that; while those general faculties of judgment and resource, of enterprise and caution, of firmness and courtesy, which are trained by association with those who control the larger issues of any one trade, will go a long way towards fitting him for managing almost any other trade . . . if they continue their fathers' work, they [the sons] have also the vantage ground of established trade connections. (pp. 298-99)

These advantages, then, are merely collateral items of fact attaching to general status. They are neither native nor, to either father or son, cost-acquired. Therefore, for all the purposes of the present analysis, they are mere wind-falls—good luck or conjuncture things. Moreover, they appear to be of the class of pure rather than of quasi-rents, neither in the long nor in the short run deriving from investment policies.

If, then, there still can be a normal-value period, and a period that can be recognized as such, or if for doctrinal purposes one can be assumed, these real and quasi-rents and these pure-effort hires, and these mixtures of all of them, must occasion many difficulties that appear to be insuperable. But for all pre-normal periods, there can be no occasion for perplexity—on the assumption, that is, that practically all enterpriser costs are price-determined anyway. Thereby, no problems of cost attach to them; they cease from troubling.

Marshall's distributive explanation of wages as the price hires received by laborers, derives these hires from the price productivity of the efforts. It turns on the assumption of competition among employers, and of the effectiveness of these competitions for the control of the productive services of the laborers.

We need not enter at present into the theoretical precision of this productivity theory of distribution, as affected by the interdependence and the togetherness of the factors in practically all productive processes. It is sufficient for present purposes to point out that the forecasted returns from labor to any employer of it are always conditioned by the stock of labor in general, and especially by the stock left available in his particular field of production, after allowance has been made for the absorptions of other industries. The principle of alternatives is important here, the question for any employer never accurately one of the entire volume of laborers:

But we must not omit to notice those adjustments of the supply of labour to the demand for it, which are effected by movements of adults from one trade to another, *one grade to another,* and one place to another. The movements from one grade to another can seldom be on a very large scale. . . .

But the movements of adult labour from trade to trade and from place to place can in some cases be so large and so rapid as to reduce within a very short compass the period which is required to enable the supply of labour to adjust itself to the demand. . . . (pp. 572-73)

In any case, however, the available stocks of labor are here taken for granted on the supply side of the distributive situation. These stocks, or this stock, Marshall purports to explain as determined by the money costs of production of human beings. There can be no price productivity of labor excepting in view of the stocks of laborers. These stocks, then, are by Marshall accounted for on cost-of-production terms. That it must have been the cost-of-production computations of twenty years ago that account for the various volumes of labor today, or the computations of today that will account for the volumes twenty years hence—the productivity of one decade equating against the supply influences of other decades—does not need to disturb Marshall in this connection. For the present analysis has to do solely with adjustments in the normal-value equilibrium. Until that time the wages are mainly quasi-rent items anyway:

. . . the income derived from the appliances for the production of a commodity exerts a controlling influence in the long run over their own supply and price, and therefore over the supply and the price of the commodity itself; but that within short periods there is not time for the exercise of any considerable influence of this kind . . . this principle needs to be modified when it is applied not to the material agents of production, which are only a means towards an end, and which may be the private property of the capitalist, but to human beings who are ends as well as means of production and who remain their own property.
. . . since labour is slowly produced and slowly worn out, we must take the term "long period" more strictly, and regard it as generally implying a greater duration, when we are considering the relations of normal demand and supply for labour, than when we are considering them for ordinary commodities. . . . (pp. 573-74)

Moreover, this cost-of-production inquiry is an inquiry in the employee and regress emphasis: why the labor stocks are thus or thus—whereby the employer must, in the long run, pay this much or that much for labor, if children, born, and maintained and trained, are to remain available. The output of goods, reacting through cost of production on the hires, will in the long run determine the hires. These hires must, then, in the stabilized conditions of normal-equilibrium times, be equal to the stabilized costs of producing the laborers. Meanwhile, as is to be inferred, the hires must be price-determined, either true rents or quasi-rents —surpluses not to the employer who pays, but to the employee who receives—and thereby price-determined items all. Training costs have been earlier noted to be quasi-rent facts; and now, with the rest of the outlays connected with parenthood, all of the labor hires must be of the quasi-rent character, with the exception, it may be, of the earnings of exceptional and extraordinary abilities, which appear to rank as true-rent hires—unless, indeed, these also have their long-run determinants in parental costs.

The doctrinal significance of this cost-of-production explanation of the available stocks of workers—and so far of their hires—is clear. Behind all employer money costs—when these become price-determining and to the extent that they become price-determining —there must be the explanatory real costs. This is a classical fundamental. Therefore the wages of the workers must be explained either by the current true-effort costs, or by the parental money costs of the past; which parental costs must, in turn, come to be resolved into real costs. But these current true-effort costs Marshall has made a matter of relatively small account. He has not seriously urged them as adequate. And even the most cursory survey of labor incomes supports him here. This account of the parental costs of production of workers he takes to make good this lack. And it is a lack that for classical purposes must be made good. The account will, it is true, run almost exclusively in money-cost terms. But, as commonly elsewhere, the conversion of money costs into real costs is left as self-warranting to make good its own case —as a thing not only possible of doing, but easily to be done— and therefore to be turned over to the capacity and the responsibility of the reader. A self-evident truth needs no proof; and is always the most difficult of truths to be proved.

We may, however, at this point query whether the offered explanation of laborer costs of production runs in terms of the iron law, the law of the subsistence minimum, or that of the standard of living. It comes nearer to being the latter. His general position Marshall sets forth as follows:

But the incomes which are being earned by all agents of production, human as well as material, and those which appear likely to be earned by them in the future, exercise a ceaseless influence on those persons by whose action the future supplies of these agents are determined. There is a constant tendency towards a position of normal equilibrium, in which the supply of each of these agents shall stand in such a relation to the demand for its services, as to give to those who have provided the supply a sufficient reward for their efforts and sacrifices. If the economic conditions of the country remained stationary sufficiently long, this tendency would realize itself in such an adjustment of supply to demand, that both machines and human beings would earn generally an amount that corresponded fairly with their cost of rearing and training, conventional necessaries as well as those things which are strictly necessary being reckoned for. But conventional necessaries might change. . . . As it is, the economic conditions of the country are constantly changing, and the point of adjustment of normal demand and supply in relation to labour is constantly being shifted. (pp. 576-77)

There are, however, Marshall notes, a number of significant aspects in which the growing of offspring differs from those ordinary pecuniary and business processes in which the cost-of-production computation has its place:

. . . human agents of production are not bought and sold as machinery and other material agents of production are. The worker sells his work, but he himself remains his own property: those who bear the expenses of rearing and educating him receive but very little of the price that is paid for his services in later years.

Whatever deficiencies the modern methods of business may have, they have at least this virtue, that he who bears the expenses of production of material goods, receives the price that is paid for them. . . . (pp. 560-61)

. . . whoever may incur the expense of investing capital in developing the abilities of the workman, those abilities will be the property of the workman himself; and thus the virtue of those who have aided him must remain for the greater part its own reward. (p. 565)

The tax-payer may possibly deserve mention here:

We may then conclude that the wisdom of expending public and private funds on education is not to be measured by its direct fruits alone. . . .

All that is spent during many years in opening the means of higher education to the masses would be well paid for if it called out one more Newton or Darwin, or Shakespeare or Beethoven. (p. 216)

But this rearing of offspring Marshall does nevertheless present
as essentially a capital investment, with some intermixture of pure-
effort costs, in the production of human beings—a pecuniary and
business undertaking for pecuniary results:

. . . The market price of everything, *i.e.*, its price for short periods, is
determined mainly by the relations in which the demand for it stands to
the available stocks of it; and in the case of any agent of production,
whether it be a human or a material agent, this demand is "derived" from
the demand for those things which it is used in making. In these relatively short periods fluctuations in wages follow, and do not precede,
fluctuations in the selling prices of the goods produced.
But the incomes which are being earned by all agents of production,
human as well as material, . . . exercise a ceaseless influence. . . . (pp.
576-77)

. . . There are many problems, the period of which is long enough . . .
to justify us in regarding the average prices of those commodities during
the period as "normal," and as equal to their normal expenses of production in a fairly broad use of the term; . . . The average earnings of labour
during this period therefore would not be at all certain to give about a
normal return to those who provided the labour; but they would rather
have to be regarded as determined by the available stock of labour on the
one hand, and the demand for it on the other. . . . (p. 574)

During this period, then, the wages are of the nature of quasi-
rents. But in the long run—that is, in the normal adjustment—
labor, like other agents of production, bears hires conforming to
cost-of-production principles.

It must be admitted that occasionally the growing of children
may be pecuniarily motivated in the usual sense. On some immigrant
farms in the United States, children doubtless may pay from the
investment point of view. In England in the early nineteenth
century they were sometimes desirable claims against the poor
rates; and there are poor people with whom, it is said, children
are important as one method of provision against old-age penury
and public charity. But neither you nor I can have greatly profited
our parents from the investment point of view, or were ever

expected to; nor is there any intention or expectation that our children in turn will profit us. If in most western countries there were no children excepting where the adventure promised to pay the adventurers in it, there would be practically no children. Mainly also the same truth holds for most marriages, in many or most modern countries, on most income levels.

And still it is not a final objection to Marshall's position that the incomes later to be collected will accrue, not to the investors, but to the offspring. Much investment is actually directed to providing estates for wife and children—but rarely in the purpose of expanding their earning powers. With the estates the greater, the earning will the less be needed. The issue is merely, then, whether this line of investor motivation is adequate to cover the facts of reproduction, of maintenance, and of training. As an investment procedure there are certainly quite exceptional aspects of it to be examined. It is distinctly peculiar from the point of view of investment; and therefore calls for an exceptionally sceptical and critical examination. Is it so far away in motivation from the raising of cattle or hogs as to weaken the attempted parallel? Even cats and dogs and canary birds fall not clearly within the field of pecuniary investment for pecuniary returns to anybody. They cost, it is true; but they do not by investment tests pay as well as chickens. They are nearer to the expenditure of income than to the gaining of it. And so of our flower gardens—though not so of vegetable gardens. Just how much has one accomplished toward pecuniary prosperity who has a wife and a half dozen children—plus, it may be, a few dogs?

Certain of these difficulties Marshall recognizes: for example, that most parents, and perhaps especially those who accomplish most in providing offspring for the later labor markets, have no funds to invest, or no wish or forward purpose for the investing of them—the investment motivation far from accounting for the phenomena; that commonly other motivations are the more important, or are decisive; that it is a family matter—support of wife and daughters to be taken into the account—children conditioned on having mothers, and one being never secure of only boy babies;

that the earning powers of the offspring are in large part not dependent on any sort of pecuniary planning or outlay, but derive instead from family connections, social relations, and trade affiliations:

... the birth-rate in every grade of society is determined by many causes, among which deliberate calculations of the future hold but a secondary place. . . . (p. 572)

... But it is very difficult to ascertain the causes that are likely to determine the distant future of the trades which they are selecting for their children; and there are not many who enter on this abstruse inquiry ... the supply of labour in a trade in any one generation tends to conform to its earnings not in that but in the preceding generation. (p. 571)

... But the investment of capital in the rearing and early training of the workers of England is limited by the resources of parents in the various grades of society, by their power of forecasting the future, and by their willingness to sacrifice themselves for the sake of their children. (p. 561)

... in the large majority of cases the son follows the father's calling. In the old-fashioned domestic industries this was almost a universal rule; and, even under modern conditions, the father has often great facilities for introducing his son to his own trade. Employers and their foremen generally give to a lad whose father they already know and trust, a preference over one for whom they would have to incur the entire responsibility. And in many trades a lad, even after he has got entrance to the works, is not very likely to make good progress and obtain a secure footing, unless he is able to work by the side of his father, or some friend of his father's. . . .

And the son of the artisan has further advantages. . . . (p. 563)

... The most valuable of all capital is that invested in human beings; and of that capital the most precious part is the result of the care and influence of the mother. . . .
... in estimating the cost of production of efficient labour, we must often take as our unit the family. At all events we cannot treat the cost of production of efficient men as an isolated problem; it must be taken as part of the broader problem of the cost of production of efficient men together with the women who are fitted to make their homes happy, and to bring up their children vigorous in body and mind, truthful and cleanly, gentle and brave. (p. 564)

All of this appears to be wisely and truly said; most of it is as wholesomely thought as it is beautifully stated; a part of it is economics; some of it merely edifying; and most of it not argumentatively to the purpose. All of it is presumably intended to support the thesis that the production of human beings takes place as pecuniary investment for pecuniary returns, mainly to the offspring. But most of it appears to be effective argument to precisely the contrary conclusion. For it turns out that the father's incomes are expended in rearing daughters not even to earn incomes even for the sons of other parents, but to make the husbands happy and the children trustworthy, cleanly, brave and kind. Much also of this training for future success—inclusive, it may be, of purely pecuniary success—is through the mother's influence—not, it is clear, a money cost, and almost as clearly, not even a real cost; but instead the happy privilege of the loving mother, one of the chief meanings of life to her. Moreover, most of the children—for most people are poor—have little or none of this pecuniary solicitude lavished on them, or even directed toward them. The mother and daughters get a reasonable share of the scant family revenues, without prospect of pecuniary return anywhere. These pecuniary devisings also, while often actual, are entirely secondary matters with reference to birth rates in every grade of society—most people having neither the desire nor the intelligence to undertake this sort of investment, even if they could. And finally, even where the motivations are actual, the success of the son, while largely dependent on the opportunities open to him through his home and father, and the father's or the family's connections, is not in the main pecuniarily devised or cost-achieved.

More and more, also, training for particular occupations is becoming futile. Marshall has already stressed this fact for exceptional business ability. It seems to hold also for artisans; and still more clearly for the lower and unskilled grades of labor. More and more investment in income prospects must be directed to general intelligence; and intelligence in this aspect is probably mainly native. Perhaps also general intelligence is, in the large, better worth while, and better deserving of expense, and more widely recognized, than is pecuniary efficiency. This view seems to be fairly common among the very sort of people and the very grades of society that are well-to-do enough to undertake the outlays. The case comes down then closely to the issue as to whether the reproduction of laborers as one total stock is more than secondarily motivated to pecuniary ends, and is pecuniary in its methods and emphasis. Marshall has some relevant observations for this aspect of the problem:

... independently of the fact that in rearing and educating their children, parents are governed by motives different from those which induce a capitalist undertaker to erect a new machine . . . the circumstances by which the earnings are determined are less capable of being foreseen, and the adjustment of supply to demand is both slower and more imperfect. . . .

Not much less than a generation elapses between the choice by parents of a skilled trade for one of their children, and his reaping the full results of their choice. And meanwhile the character of the trade may have been almost revolutionized by changes, of which some probably threw long shadows before them, but others were such as could not have been foreseen even by the shrewdest persons and those best acquainted with the circumstances of the trade. (p. 571)

. . . That general ability which is easily transferable from one trade to another, is every year rising in importance relatively to that manual skill and technical knowledge which are specialized to one branch of industry. . . . (p. 573)

Marshall has, it seems, left no very strong case for pecuniary investment, as conditioning the output of human beings of highly specialized efficiency. Nor does the cost-of-production account of the forthcoming of workers of the ordinary grade make a more impressive showing. It may meanwhile be well to find out, as far as may be, what sort of expenditure the people that you and I know, do actually make in and for the home—for the wife, the daughters, as also for the sons—and to what ends, social as well as pecuniary. Marshall has sufficiently set forth the situation with the people not, we flatter ourselves, so much like you or me, or like the people that we see and meet and know.

It is probably safe to say that there are sexual urges, and that there are desires for offspring, that have to do with entering marriage. It is clearly safe to say that no one enters marriage in the purpose of opening to himself fields of gainful investment in the rearing of his young. As the affairs of life actually run, the kind of woman that prompts your devotion will not be yours—and enduringly yours—excepting on terms of marriage. And if you want children, as probably she also wants them, you will recognize marriage as the necessary condition, for their sake, for her sake, and for your own. Whether or not this is a fact near to the fundamentals of right living, an ultimate requirement of good conscience as against a mere convention, needs not be debated here. It is quite certainly a convention and a definitely rigorous one. You have to comply; and probably you not merely comply, but approve. The point of special insistence is that you are not entering marriage for the investment opportunities that it may offer to you. These are less than secondary influences.

There are, however, certain other requirements that are clearly conventional in your rearing of children, that not rarely may amount to a veto on the plan, and that often must amount to a veto on it from the point of view of an attractive investment program. These are the socially imposed necessities of competitive consumption; the charges going with seeing and being seen; outlays in the emphasis of keeping up with the Joneses, of living reputably and decoratively—not your own eyes, but the eyes of other people, disordering your budget. Against having a home or children, they are interferences and debits, like expense-loading, or service-dues against the opening of an account, or like admission dues to the lodge. They don't pay, either from your own point of view or that of your children. Nor are they outlays incurred in the expectation of enhancing the future earning powers of the children. Nor even are they incurred for the immediate health, or welfare, or training of them. They are, in short, conventional—efforts for their social standing or your own. They make home and marriage and children cost, and without credits to any future capital account. Presumably they limit the number of marriages and of the children born to the marriages; but they are not outlays in the interest of larger earnings of offspring in the future. If your motive were that of later interest collections on your capital, these expenses must be outlawed under the investment test.

Remember that this is all employee-cost analysis. Marshall's argument is that, just as how much the enterpriser has to pay for raw materials or machinery is prescribed by the money costs of the providers, so what he has to pay in wages is prescribed, in the long run, by the money costs of parents in rearing offspring for the labor market. Nor is this a real-cost regress, excepting so far as the real costs may have imposed a money charge to overbear them, and thus may have contributed to money costs. The argument is, then, that the same processes and computations of money cost as lie behind the existence of machinery and raw materials, lie also behind the existence of human beings for hire. There is, so far, no reference to real costs. But without this reference, the chronic circuity in these money-cost analyses is uncured—the regress ultimately purposeless by logical tests.

These maintenance costs of the laborers were money costs of maintenance—for food and shelter. The training of the offspring was a training that was money-cost provided; their skill a price-tagged skill; the teachers of them, in turn, were money-cost maintained and money-cost trained; the food for them bought from farmers who in their turn had wage outlays to meet, or to hire, and money land-rents to pay. (We do strange things when we put lumber prices into costs and leave land rents out.) A wage-cost explanation of the prices of foods is not a real-cost, but a price-cost, explanation.

Moreover, are human beings any sort of cost-tagged product? The money-costs aspects of the case have already been sufficiently examined. But the real-costs aspects? Recall that the two will not mix; that it is either the one or the other, not both—no sum of the two possible. How did the economists go about it to discover that children are a sorrow and a burden rather than a joy? Or means—as investment items—and not ends? That real costs have been submitted to in the acquisition of later price benefits—to some one else? Who so informed Marshall and his fellowship? Suppose, for a moment, the truth to be the other way about, as in the balance it very probably is: what effect would this have on wages? And if it is pain costs that impose the wages, what would the fact of net pleasures in parenthood do to those costs?

But do financial conditions limit marriages, and births, and maturities? It may be so; but this does not declare these conditions to be costs. So also do railroad accidents and snake bites. And so again do expensive foods; and the social climbing of parents. It is the poor that are prolific.

At any rate, there are only so many human beings—of working age—as many as there are. Admit it. And stop there. The number that there are attaches no money-cost or real-cost tag to any one of them. We do not in fact know why there are not more, or fewer —any more than we know why there is not more land; or why squashes do not grow bigger; or why the nitrogen in the air is not as digestible and as nourishing as it is plentiful; or why grass is neither appetizing nor nourishing for us humans.

But we have not yet done with these conventional costs. Are they investment outlays? And for whose benefit are they incurred? How about the daughters with their music and painting and finishing schools? And the sons—your sons, for example—that, along with the daughters, you cherish and indulge? Did you really think that last gown or cloak, or sport suit or Tuxedo would return later to you or yours in greater earnings; or the clubs and the fraternities and the pins; and the tours and the fishing trips and the tackle for both? You have to do it, though you know that the most of it were better not—even by the test of health or of getting educated. These are conventional necessaries and therefore, hag-riding you, they nearly break your neck. But you must give your young their pleasures, as these pleasures actually offer themselves, along with the taxis and flowers that are fitting. For you love your children.

But, nevertheless, just why do you do it all—or even send them to college? You might look at *The Theory of the Leisure Class,* if you are seriously thinking that these outlays are not mainly— or surely partly—your own certification, or your own defense against ranking as a *piker.* The saving of faces is not exclusively a

Chinese game. And if some economist other than Veblen interprets you as, with most of those outlays, busily investing in the present worth of your offspring's putative salary increments, you will prefer to believe it; but unless you are pretty much a fool, you will not. Why did you get all this money anyway? And somebody may— or may not—urge that all the opera coats and party gowns and receptions of your wife, are the expressions of the love you bear her; or that not quite all are. But probably no one has ever yet discovered them to you as investments in her future earning power, or in that of the children.

The present issue is, however, whether money costs are competent to explain the numbers or the gain-seeking efficiency of workers. Admit that larger outlays by parents for their children do make, not only for better preparation of the offspring for the high-paying posts—which is sometimes true, and often not—but also make for more births and more maturities—which seems to be commonly not the fact—it still appears to be true that native ability has a large, and perhaps the larger, share in pecuniary success; and that the production and the rearing of children are mainly a matter of the sexual urge and of the cost-careless longing for children rather than a gain-motivated process. Practically never is it pecuniary in motivation or successful by the self-seeking pecuniary test. It is even dubious how far it is successful by the test of pecuniary gain to offspring. Pecuniary considerations doubtless have bearing; pecuniary self-seeking motivations have little or none, otherwise than mainly by restriction and limitation rather than by incentive and stimulation. The generalizations of business policy do not apply. Almost as well extend the cost-of-production doctrine to the biological costs of plants in maturing seed, or of the egg in becoming a chicken.

Were, however, the analysis projected on the real-cost level, as it is not, the objection would be pertinent that these parental costs are money costs and not real costs; and that, for real-cost purposes, these parental processes are those of things sought rather than of things shunned.

There is a suggestion in Marshall's argument that by the pecuniary test the parents' investment in children must be expected to justify itself through the future achievement of an item of personal capital, offsetting in price terms, at this later date of dawning income, the sum of the investments earlier made, together with the interest charges thereon. And thus Marshall finds it necessary to capitalize these items of mature humanity, as of the time when they are at the opening period of their income-earning careers. Possibly, however, such is not the purpose of his capitalization analysis in the course of this general discussion. But if such is not the purpose, no other is manifest.

Marshall believes that the workers, both the skilled and the unskilled, can be capitalized into cash items of wealth. For the parents? Presumably not. For themselves? Clearly it is not possible. At any rate for the country? There will, then, have to be an interest basis. Suppose, however, that we first try to outline a man's own capitalization of himself. He certainly has a rate of interest. Take him, say, at age 25 in good health, with his training complete—for himself to get what he can out of himself and it. A fair forecast of his salary is say, $5,000 per year, and his probable life is, say, forty-five years. How much is he now worth to himself? He must fuel and shelter himself—and this better than he would his machine or ox or slave. Take it that he computes $4,000 per year as his maintenance charge. He will then have only $1,000 to debit against the strain and stress of earning his salary. He would certainly be entitled to compute a similar sort of debit against his mule or slave or machine if to get the services out of it he must clean or groom or whip or swear. Perhaps, then, after all one is an item of net liability to himself rather than an asset. In fact, Marshall himself urges (p. 576) that as machinery must have a high per-period hire if it wears out rapidly, so similarly is the miner "as liable to wear-and-tear as machinery is; and a deduction must be made from his earnings also on account of wear-and-tear, when the special return of his skill is being estimated."

It might, of course, work the other way, if he enjoyed his labor. But what about the fun that he gets in spending his income? That is what he got and spends his income for; what in terms of income the fun costs him. But, at any rate, he may enjoy his leisure? That, however, may be an extraneous matter—neither debit nor credit with reference to his getting or spending his income. He might have lived off other income. Or he might, like the tramp, have got more fun out of making all of his hours leisure hours. Which consideration suggests that his $5,000 per year should have been debited with a money price against the leisure foregone through earning the $5,000. And this, in turn, suggests that the entire question of one's money worth to himself may have to turn on whether or not he has a sunny disposition and a good liver. A pessimist would find that the average man, if he knew how to go about his life-value computations, would come out at a minus quantity. What would he take to die? He couldn't get it. Or at what price would he sell himself? His purchaser would get the price, along with him.

But no matter about this; what is he worth to society—to people other than himself, taken in the aggregate? What will they get out of him? First take account of his maintenance—along with what further he actually spends on himself. He will contribute, as an average man, an aggregate of, say, 100,000 bushels of wheat worth a dollar per bushel. But if he takes out of the national dividend $100,000 worth of cloth and shoes, neither you nor I will make anything off him. But the profits of the cloth and shoe producers? He had also his profit from the wheat. How much the poorer were you and I, or either of us, by the deaths of 100,000 of our soldier boys in the great war? Perhaps we should pity them, cut off in their youth. But who needs pity us? All economists are aware that the world—and America—became less crowded. Malthus explained all this. But a particular young man might have saved and given us, the public, a school or church or library. If so, we clearly lost by his death just that much. But not his parents; they would never get a dollar out of him; but might still have to put up more to go along with all their earlier pecuniary sacrifices. Or his children that now will never be born; how much is their loss? Or if he already had children, they would inherit what previously he might have saved. Something in that, for them, but nothing for you or me; and to talk of another's loss by your death or mine does not, as I think, make economic sense.

. . . Many estimates have been made of the addition to the wealth of a country caused by the arrival of an immigrant whose cost of rearing in his early years was defrayed elsewhere, and who is likely to produce more than he consumes in the country of his adoption. . . . (p. 564, note)

Suppose that he does; some one later as representing him is going to consume more than he produces, with interest accumulations to offset whatever socially productive services may or may not have attended the capital meantime.

. . . if we might neglect provisionally the difference between the sexes, we should calculate the value of the immigrant on the lines of the argument. . . . That is, we should "discount" the probable value of all the future services that he would render; add them together, and deduct from them the sum of the "discounted" values of all the wealth and direct services of other persons that he would consume. . . . (p. 564, note)

This would mean that now the aggregate wealth of all of us to all of us is the aggregate present worth of the estates that we shall have together accumulated when we severally die.

. . . Or again we might estimate his value at the money cost of production which his native country had incurred for him. . . .
. . . But it is clear that the above plans put the value of the male immigrants too high and that of the female too low: unless allowance is made for the service which women render as mothers, as wives and as sisters, and the male immigrants are charged with having consumed these services, while the female immigrants are credited with having supplied them. [But what about the husbands' and brothers' services to the feminine half of society?]
. . . We may . . . guess that the total amount spent on bringing up an average child of the lower half of the labouring classes . . . is £100; for the next fifth we may put the sum at £175; for the next fifth at £300; for the next tenth at £500, and the remaining tenth at £1200; or an average of £300. But of course some of the population are very young and have had but little spent on them; others have got nearly to their life's end; and therefore, on these assumptions, the average value of an individual is perhaps £200. (pp. 564-65, note)

Perhaps all that needs be said for this is that it is an excellent illustration of what happens to an analysis when it is lifted from the plane of the competitive price process which we know something about, and carried over into the field of social or collective processes and appraisals. It is gratuitous at best. I think it worse. Unless it seems worth while to ask what a dead man loses by his death, or an unborn person by not being born, the sole talk should be of the parents. And from the pecuniary point of view they were all the while losers, or charity dispensers, or spenders of current income for the current satisfactions that children afford to their foolish parents. To make of the rearing of children an investment program, or a business process, or a gain-seeking quest, or a cost-of-production set of debits to set over against a forecasted pecuniary lure as credit, is thought-wise to travesty human experience—for purposes of doctrinal exigencies in economics. But Marshall further says, with reference to adult training and the apprentice system:

. . . Here again we meet the difficulty that whoever may incur the expense of investing capital in developing the abilities of the workman, those abilities will be the property of the workman himself; and thus the virtue of those who have aided him must remain for the greater part its own reward. (p. 565)

Precisely so. And even were it not, the economist has to explain only those things that his categories are fitted to handle. He does not have to explain whence came the world, or why there are mosquitoes or stars, or what urges lie behind the conception and the rearing of children, so long as the explanations are not in his competitive price process.

Risks in Parenthood

Marshall's account of the relation of risk to the prospective returns from parental investments in training deserves attention at this point. With regard to "those extra incomes which are earned by extraordinary natural abilities" he argues (p. 577) that "there is a strong *prima facie* cause for regarding them as a producer's surplus, resulting from the possession of a differential advantage for production, freely given by nature. This analogy is valid and useful so long as we are merely analysing the component parts of the income earned by an individual."

But whether the ability was or was not freely given by nature Marshall's earlier analysis is declared to be irrelevant. And it is not clear what else we can be doing than analysing the component parts of an income earned by an individual. Presumably, however, the emphasis is on averages. This section of the *Principles* (p. 577) begins: "We may now discuss the question under what head to class those extra incomes which are earned by extraordinary natural abilities." Marshall implies that not all of these incomes are either rents or quasi-rents. Some are returns on training outlays; some are true earnings of effort; and some are "due to chance, to opportunity, to the conjuncture" and some "to the good start . . . in life." But some are true rents:

But when we are considering the whole body of those engaged in any occupation, we are not at liberty to treat the exceptionally high earnings of successful men as rent, without making allowance for the low earnings of those who fail. For the supply of labour *in any occupation* is governed, other things being equal, by the earnings of which it holds out the prospect. The future of those who enter the occupation cannot be predicted with certainty: some, who start with the least promise, turn out to have great latent ability, and, aided perhaps by good luck, they earn large fortunes; while others, who made a brilliant promise at starting, come to nothing. For the chances of success and failure are to be taken together . . . and a youth when selecting an occupation, or his parents when selecting one for him, are very far from leaving out of account the fortunes of successful men. These fortunes are therefore part of the price that is paid in the long run for the supply of labour and ability that seeks the occupation: they enter into the true or "long period" normal supply price of labour in it. (p. 578)

Because this discussion seems to be concerned with the division of labor incomes into pure-effort elements, therefore price-determining elements; into quasi-rent elements, therefore temporarily price-determined elements; and into pure-rent elements, therefore permanently price-determined elements—general objection is, of course, here, as earlier, to be registered. So far, however, as the analysis is intended to refer to training expenditures; so far as it is assumed that these training outlays are actually incurred by parents in the investment emphasis; and so far as the particular occupation is being considered with relation to the openings, prospective or present, in other occupations, with its unattractiveness through hazards regarded merely relatively to those of other occupations—the conclusions are not fairly open to question. But native abilities appear to be included in the discussion.

Marshall is not, one infers, asserting that there are no permanently price-determined elements in these incomes of extraordinary ability. Instead, indeed, he asserts that there are; or merely that in many or most cases, what looks like extraordinary ability is in the main good luck; or that these windfalls of the good luck or conjuncture sort, when taken in the average rather than individually, are not in the long run price-determined hires; but that these incomes of extraordinary natural ability, like those of other native ability, and like those of cost-acquired ability, are not promptly responsive to the current level of hires, and are therefore of the quasi-rent character, irrespective of the degree of hazard attending the training for earning the incomes, or of good luck in the receipt of them, and therefore are temporarily price-determined.

And it is perhaps also to be inferred that in the average these elements of quasi-rent in the hires of labor are not the smaller for the risks, but rather the larger; since the effect of the hazards of failure, along with the fact emphasized on page 622 that "the people who make the outlay do not themselves reap the greater part of the reward arising from it," has been to discourage the investment, and therefore to make fewer the well-trained men in the occupation, and thus to raise the level of compensation to such well-trained men as are in it.[1]

[1] Not only, then, has it been the purpose here to deny that population or skill in general, or population or skill in particular trades, can be accounted for on money-cost-of-production lines; or even, could it be rightly so accounted for would be better than a circuitous or superficial explanation; but also to put in issue the validity of the antithesis presented of supply to demand in this process of wage fixation. For however the stocks of labor may be taken to be accounted for, the wage theory that is presented by Marshall is merely a productivity theory of wage —as are also the iron-law and the standard-of-living theories. Laborers are taken to be paid for, under enterpriser competitions, according to the price-productivities of them in view of their numbers. The significance, therefore, of the changes in numbers—and commonly not a great significance—is precisely in its effect in changing the productivities—productivities that are, in turn, to be worked out through the distributive process and to be interpreted in the light of it.

The truth is that the demand and supply formula, adequate in the main for the simple case of *direct* present goods, is gravely misleading in connection with the prices or hires of indirect goods, that, since they function along with other factors must receive their remunerations as the outcomes of distributive processes. More labor can affect wages only, (1) by affecting the national dividend—which effect

But it is at any rate clear that Marshall commits himself in this discussion to certain significant positions: that there are labor incomes of the permanently price-determining sort that are due to opportunity and to the good luck of a favorable start in life—incomes that are not cost-achieved or cost-explained, but that, perhaps even in the short run, are price-determining costs; that there are other incomes that are due to mere ordinary chance, but that are not thereby excluded from the price-determining function—being necessary to the inducing of entrants to the occupation; as also finally there are incomes of native ability which are similarly free of cost limitations and permanently price-determined.

In fact, even with marked talent or with so-called genius—the great musicians and painters as possible examples—Marshall inclines to regard the great incomes as mostly matters of lucky choice or of favoring opportunity or of fostering parental support, rather than as the clean-cut good fortune of native endowment. Occasionally, no doubt, there are these incomes attaching definitely and in the main to the good fortunes of birth; true rents, therefore, and price-determined permanently; but on the whole, he insists, the run of the facts is the other way:

It may be conceded, however, that if a certain class of people were marked out from their birth as having special gifts for some particular occupation, and for no other, so that they would be sure to seek that

---

in the per-capita sense is commonly very slight; and (2) by affecting the apportionment of this dividend into distributive shares. In the simple case of direct goods, a change in available stocks involves merely a new point of equilibrium with an unchanged demand—a supplies curve that has moved, intersecting with a demands curve that has not moved. With indirect goods the very fact of a change in the stocks brings about a change in the total production and thus a change in the gain-motivated bidding of enterprisers expressed in the demands curve price-offers, and therefore a change in the distributive allotment.

The bids of these enterprisers for the increased stocks of factors that react on the total of products, approximate, to be sure, the price efficiencies of these factors, taken in some sort of average, in view of the changed ratios in which they are now available. The changed ratios change the relative efficiencies. Thus the redrawing of the one curve requires the redrawing of the other. Irrespective of the fact that no one factor of production ever works in isolation, it must remain impossible for any one factor of production to be separately set over against a productivity-demands schedule for that factor, because this very change in stocks involves by itself a new productivity schedule. It is impossible to make productivity a thing separate from stocks, so that stocks on the one side and productivity on the other can get equated. Nor, again, at any time are stocks of labor, either general or in particular, cost-determined.

occupation in any case, then the earnings which such men would get might be left out of account as exceptional, when we were considering the chances of success or failure *for ordinary persons*. But as a matter of fact that is not the case; for a great part of a person's success in any occupation depends on the development of talents and tastes, the strength of which cannot be clearly predicted until he has already committed himself to a choice of occupation. Such predictions are at least as fallible as those which a new settler can make as to the future fertility and advantages of situation of the various plots of land that are offered for his selection. And partly for this reason the extra income derived from rare natural qualities bears a closer analogy to the surplus produce from the holding of a settler who has made an exceptionally lucky selection. . . . (pp. 578-79)

Nevertheless, as we are elsewhere told, (p. 204): "Some people . . . seem to be fitted from birth for an artistic career, and for no other. . . ."

Precisely what as a conclusion Marshall expects to derive from making these cases interchangeable with settlers' land rents, unless it be to put his entire land-rent doctrine out of drawing, is not clear. And it must be obvious that whether these incomes are true rents or quasi-rents—and one or the other in Marshall's doctrinal view they have to be, unless, indeed, they are true-effort hires—distinctions along these lines could not greatly serve or interest any enterpriser; but still they might be there. But only for normal-value times does Marshall take them to interest even the economist.

Marshall thus reports his lack of concern with the rent aspects of these incomes of talent or genius and with their ways of getting themselves distributed into their vocational niches; whereby the hires of them and the cost status of them get left out of the account as exceptional, and therefore of slight bearing when we are "considering the chances of success or failure for ordinary persons." All this advises, however, some especial degree of attention to the serious risk problems connected with ordinary persons. To these aspects of risk Marshall accords slight or no discussion.

But these risks are there. The children may die before either they or their parents have collected any returns on the expenses of either rearing or training. Or invalidism or death may arrive in the early years of the income period. Or the offspring may turn out to be all-round failures in the disposition or the power of earning income. Or, if there has been special training—or if there has not —the offspring may choose badly the field of activity; or the training may turn out to be futile in view of such tastes or capacities as may later develop, or in view of the shifting or disappearing openings for income. With the girls especially there are risks of small earning power, or even of life-long dependency, or of marrying an incumbrance. Perhaps, indeed, no one expects his girls *to pay,* unless, possibly "marrying well" may meet the test.

Recall Marshall's general position that the volume of bread-winners, not only in general but in particular occupations, is determined on the one side by the ordinary principles of cost of production, as over against the prospective earnings on the other side. If the labor incomes are high relative to the parental investment charges of providing bread-winners for the prospective labor market, these parents will respond with more children, or with more expensive training, or with both. Low wage levels, on the other hand, are taken to diminish both births and training—fewer bread-winners and bread-winners of lower earning powers—and to diminish these through discouraging these lines of productive investment.

What bearing, then, have these aspects of pecuniary risk on the number and the training of children with ordinary people— influences restricting or postponing marriages, or the number of children born to the marriage, or the outlays for the training of the children? Deaths among children restrict, doubtless, the total of maturities, and may, so far, affect favorably the wages of those that do not die. But the present issues are other: how far are these risks of death or of other misadventure a pecuniary influence with parents to discourage expenditures on children, by diminishing the number of marriages, or of births to the marriage, or by restricting the per-individual expenditures for rearing and training —so much outlay turned futile by the shipwreck of its purpose? Such, obviously, must be the meaning of similar conditions in the raising of cattle or mules or slaves. Only as limited output reacted to improve the conditions of sale or lease in the market, could the output justify itself in terms of pecuniary enterprise. Where costs of production are the dominant influence on output, they must find a point of equilibration against the price-offer schedules of bidders for purchase or lease.

But there is also the possibility that parents, facing the chances that children may die at an untimely age, might, so far as planning were an influence in the situation, contrive for more children to be born, or might spend more on the health or training of each of what there were—though not this, certainly, from the point of view of pecuniary purposes or investment policy. Just the reverse from this pecuniary point of view should be—and Marshall takes to be—the fact.

It is difficult, it is true, to articulate these risk considerations with any doctrine of quasi-rents for the mass of the earnings of labor in wage-earning society, and, perhaps, especially difficult for societies of a low level of incomes and of living standards. But if there are quasi-rents on the higher income levels, there should be on this, only that they must be quantitatively smaller, though not by necessity at a lower percentage rate on the investment. Certainly, by the investment test, there must be quasi-rents large enough to afford investment surpluses—else there can be no children. For it is obvious that by these investment tests, many of the children must be a sheer loss. Such is the meaning of the risks for those cases where the cards fall out badly. There must, then, be offsetting margins. In fact, also, if the children arrive on this investment basis —themselves, to be sure, the collecting agents for the investment returns—not part of these returns solely, but all of them—whether high or low by investment or by any other tests—must be quasi-rents. For these offspring are, we recall, investment products. All of them, therefore, are items in the total existing stock, and are collecting price-determined hires—so far, that is, as they are not collecting true-effort hires and, it seems also, true-effort hires in addition to the investment indemnities. For the period of a generation at least—for their life periods in fact—each particular hire will have nothing to say as to any newly-provided human beings of wage-contracting age. It is not decisive of the quasi-rent status of this labor that it be not ill paid, but just that it be paid. Quasi-rent agents often collect disappointingly low hires, or again find flattering market conditions. It is *unresponsiveness,* and not the quantum of the return, that is the badge of quasi-rent things. Wherefore, that earlier suggestion that all native abilities, so far as they are not cost-tagged or are not entirely cost-covered, carry quasi-rents, affirmed only the smaller part of the truth. For, note again, it is not freedom from costs of origin, or some cost-free balance in the hire, that attaches the quasi-rent status to some part or the entire hire of an agent, but only the temporary fixity of the stock of it.

And thus it is that by still another route we arrive at the doctrine that all labor hires are—for their respective and appropriate periods —price-determined items of cost—excepting, it is true, for the true-effort portions of them; whereby a trace of real-cost wage doctrine comes into view.

Enterpriser Labor Returns and Costs

It belongs to the logical movement of Marshall's general analysis to make practically no account of the relations of enterpriser effort to cost of production in any pre-normal situation, and to find no occasion in this regard for any close analysis of this problem under normal conditions. These labor returns in pre-normal periods are taken in the main to be price-determined, along with other quasi-rent returns, as also are the returns on investments in equipment goods and in organization. Always, to be sure, there are true-effort hires that at all times exercise the price-determining function; but these seem already to have been sufficiently examined; as also, for most purposes, the returns on both native and acquired enterpriser abilities.

Most of the earnings of enterprisers are, in Marshall's view, quasi-rents on native ability. The enterpriser makes, we recall, small account of effort resistances. His abilities are, in the main, native, and thus, though not in any considerable part cost-acquired, are nevertheless of the quasi-rent quality, although, doubtless, there is some intermixture of pure rents:

... before free capital and labour have been invested in securing the skill required for the work of the artisan or professional man, the income expected to be derived from them is of the nature of profits . . . when the artisan or professional man has once obtained the skill required for his work, a part of his earnings are for the future really a quasi-rent of the capital and labor invested in fitting him for his work, in obtaining his start in life, his business connections, and generally his opportunity for turning his faculties to good account; and only the remainder of his income is true earnings of effort . . . when a similar analysis is made of the profits of the business man . . . the greater part is quasi-rent. (p. 622)

On the whole . . . we may conclude that the rarity of the natural abilities and the expensiveness of the special training required for the work affect normal earnings of management in much the same way as they do the normal wages of skilled labour. . . . (p. 608)

. . . Everyone has the business his own life to conduct; and in this he can gain some training for business management, if he has the natural aptitudes for it. There is therefore no other kind of useful rare and therefore highly-paid ability which depends so little on labour and expense applied specially to obtaining it, and so much on "natural qualities." And, further, business power is highly non-specialized. . . . (p. 606)

Marshall's analysis under the head of enterpriser incomes has, then, mainly to do with the division of these incomes into their different functional elements, *for distributive purposes,* from the point of view of *normal conditions.* The analysis is therefore primarily concerned, not with enterpriser labor returns, but with the aggregate returns of the capitalist enterprise, where the capitalist is at once investor, employer and laborer:

During all this inquiry we have had in view chiefly the ultimate, or long-period or true normal results of economic forces; . . . the way in which the supply of business ability in command of capital tends in the long run to adjust itself to the demand; . . . how it seeks constantly every business and every method of conducting every business in which it can render services that are so highly valued by persons who are able to pay good prices for the satisfaction of their wants, that those services will in the long run earn a high reward. . . . All his [a business undertaker's] prospective gains enter into the profits which draw him towards the undertaking; all the investments of his capital and energies in making the appliances for future production, and in building up the "immaterial" capital of a business connection, have to show themselves to him as likely to be profitable, before he will enter on them: the whole of the profits which he expects from them enter into the reward, which he expects in the long run for his venture. And if he is a man of normal ability (normal that is for that class of work), and is on the margin of doubt whether to make the venture or not, they may be taken as true representatives of the (marginal) normal expenses of production of the services in question. Thus the whole of the normal profits enter into true or long-period supply price. (pp. 618-19)

Accurately, then, it is not the earnings of management but the total gains of the manager that Marshall makes the subject of his analysis; and this, in the main, not from the point of view of the relation of any part of this gain to cost of production, but of the distributive titles into which this gain is divided, and of the influences by which these shares are severally determined, *under normal conditions*. *Profits* is the term covering the entire gains of the capitalist enterpriser:

The causes that govern Earnings of Management have not been studied with any great care till within the last fifty years. The earlier economists ... did not adequately distinguish the component elements of profits, but searched for a simple general law governing the average rate of profits— a law which, from the nature of the case, cannot exist.
... the head of a small business does himself much of the work which in a large business is done by salaried managers and foremen, whose earnings are deducted from the net receipts of the large business before its profits are reckoned, while the earnings of the whole of his labour are reckoned among his profits. ... (p. 609)

This is obviously distributive rather than cost doctrine. It is in this distributive aspect that he is examining how great are the labor, the investment and the risk shares in the aggregate enterpriser income, with especial reference, however, to what on the face of things would look to be pure labor returns. But the ability and skill of the enterpriser have their origins partly in native and partly in acquired qualities. And practically always, effort, as itself a burdensome thing, requires its offset in money returns. Often, and perhaps sometimes mainly, these cost-acquired abilities are due as much to burdensome effort as to investment outlays, but efforts that equally with expenditure were conditioned on the prospect of later pecuniary returns—as, of course, the returns on native powers and the current pure-effort returns cannot have been. Though quantitatively indefinite, then, the returns to current enterpriser effort trace back to investment outlays or burdens, and are therefore in this aspect interest. And inasmuch also as these outlays were made prospectively, and are now fixed commitments, the returns on them are now of the nature of quasi-rents—price-determined in the short run, results of price rather than cause. Doubtless these composite hires contain also returns on native ability, cost-free returns, therefore; but these returns Marshall regards as similarly quasi-rents, by virtue of a fixity that he somehow takes to be temporary, or so in the main—the intermixture of true rents being not large, even in cases of extraordinary natural abilities.

That lines of division—definite, it may be, in principle, but entirely undiscernible in any other sense—are hereby drawn for every enterpriser labor return, between the permanently price-determining elements in the return, pure-effort hires; the temporarily price-determined elements, quasi-rent hires; and the permanently price-determined elements, true rents, does not greatly matter. For with the exception of the pure-effort hires, these distinctions purport to have no functional significance on the hither side of normal-value periods. And even in normal-value periods, only the true-rent elements will need to be distinguished. They will be like the rents of spatial extension. The other elements in the hires will be like those of the natural fertility of land and of cost-acquired equipment. No difficulties, novel in point of degree, will then be introduced for these normal-value conditions. And no difficulties with distinctions between different kinds of risk can attach for any pre-normal time, all these risk returns being equally price-determined anyway.

Further quotations from the *Principles* are here offered, in the purpose mainly of indicating that Marshall's attention is directed to the inter-relations of these various hires, but particularly to the inter-relations of the subdivisions of enterprisers' labor returns, from the point of view solely of normal-value conditions; that for pre-normal conditions he regards most of these incomes as price-determined receipts; that only for purposes of distinctions between pure-effort hires, quasi-rents and true rents, and then not in the cost but only in the distributive aspect, are any of these incomes taken to call for especial attention; that the point of view is still essentially that of the employee, the distributee of income; that no attempt is made, for either normal or pre-normal times to divide enterpriser incomes into shares of necessary and unnecessary cost; that all incomes save those from the spatial extension of land are presentèd for normal times as price-determining; that all surpluses, even those of enterprisers, are surpluses in the employee sense, differential incomes with respect to past costs, and, with whatever surpluses there are, surpluses by this test:

In a sense there are only two agents of production, nature and man. Capital and organization are the result of the work of man aided by nature. . . . If the character and powers of nature and of man be given, the growth of wealth and knowledge and organization follow from them as effect from cause. . . . (p. 139)

. . . we may regard this supply price of business ability in command of capital as composed of three elements. The first is the supply price of capital; the second is the supply price of business ability and energy; and the third is the supply price of that organization by which the appropriate business ability and the requisite capital [Funds? Instruments? And note *the one* supply price.] are brought together. We have called the price of the first of these three elements *interest;* we may call the price of the second by itself, *net earnings of management,* and that of the second and third, taken together, *gross earnings of management.* (p. 313)

. . . For these gains or profits [those derived from the aid of accumulated wealth in the attainment of desirable ends, especially when that wealth takes the form of trade capital] contain many elements, some of which belong to interest for the use of capital in a broad sense of the term; while others constitute *net* interest, or interest properly so called. Some constitute the reward of managing ability and of enterprise, including the bearing of risks; and others again belong not so much to any one of these agents of production as to their combination. (pp. 582-83) [This last means, it may be, *organization.* At all events, the bearing of risks imposes mainly capital hazards.]

. . . all producers, whether working with borrowed capital or not, reckon interest on the capital used by them as among the expenses which they require to have returned to them in the long run in the price of their wares as a condition of their continuing business. . . . (p. 586) [Items that to the owner or the hirer of them may be in the short run either more or less than the rate that is conditioning in the long run.]

... the postponement of gratification involves *in general* a sacrifice on the part of him who postpones, just as additional effort does on the part of him who labours. . . . (p. 587) [Whether *sacrifice* means here the undergoing of waiting or the foregoing of alternative returns, the principle applies equally to the owning of land.]

... But the gross earnings of management which a man is getting can only be found after making up a careful account of the true profits of his business, and deducting interest on his capital. . . . (p. 607)

It is, then, becoming increasingly clear that Marshall's principle, even with the effort income of the enterpriser, is one of fairly rigid adherence to the point of view of employee cost. In accounting for the price of any product, and therefore intermediately for its hire, recourse is had not to the money debits computed by the enterpriser against his forecasted credit of price product. Instead, attention is directed to the burden, whether in expense or effort or waiting, borne by those who, for enterpriser pay, have submitted to the exactions; have experienced the muscle aches; have sacrificed the leisure; have undergone the waitings and the deprivations that attach to lending; and have endured the strains and cares of child-bearing and child-rearing—*real-cost* items all of these—or who have provided the raw materials, the fuel, and the equipment goods; or have met the expenses of food and training for the children under the financial hazards of later pecuniary misfit or failure—items all of *money* cost.

It is the costs behind the enterpriser's outlay costs, the costs of those that he hires or buys from, and not the enterpriser costs themselves; the *why* in terms of origin of these enterpriser costs, and not the sheer fact of the making of them, to which Marshall has recourse for the identifying of those enterpriser costs to which attach the price-determining function. It is only those items of enterpriser hires that have, either directly or indirectly, a cost-in-origin, either money or real, with which, as Marshall holds, the final meaning of costs is to be discovered and the ultimate explanation of relative prices to be sought. Only when actual prices are proportional with these costs-in-orgin as fundamental determinants, are actual price relations explained; and this may turn out to be the meaning of *normal*.

The point of view of the employer . . . does not include the whole gains of the business; for there is another part which attaches to his employees. Indeed, in some cases and for some purposes, nearly the whole income of a business may be regarded as a quasi-rent, that is an income determined for the time by the state of the market for its wares, with but little reference to the cost of preparing for their work the various things and persons engaged in it. In other words it is a *composite quasi-rent* divisible among the different persons in the business by bargaining, supplemented by custom and by notions of fairness. . . . (p. 626)

. . . It is not true that the spinning of yarn in a factory, after allowance has been made for the wear-and-tear of the machinery, is the product of the labour of the operatives. It is the product of their labour, together with that of the employer and subordinate managers, and of the capital employed; and that capital itself is the product of labour and waiting; and therefore the spinning is the product of labour of many kinds, and of waiting. . . . (p. 587)

But obviously, the land on which the material was grown and the land supporting the factory building had part in the production —from both the employer and the industrial point of view—as truly as the machines, and also is as clearly an item of waiting. And it is confusing, especially from the industrial point of view, to call waiting a tool or an implement. As well call lending so. It is part of the thinking that makes *waiting* an existence in its own right, like the Good and Peace and Hate and Love, as objective and existential facts, rather than as words of mere verbal or adjective significance, and as substantives only linguistically. There are individuals who love and hate, or loving and hating individuals, but no Love or Hate. And even were there not merely waiting individuals, but *waiting,* no mechanical applications could be made of it.

On the whole then we may conclude that the rarity of the natural abilities and the expensiveness of the special training required for the work affect *normal earnings* of management in much the same way as they do the *normal wages* of skilled labour. . . . (p. 608)

Notice the *normals;* and also that only two pages back training outlays were reported to be almost entirely absent or inffective with business ability.

There are in Marshall's discussions in this connection a few passages having possible opportunity-cost implications:

. . . the manufacturer who is doing a large business with comparatively little capital of his own will reckon his labour and anxiety almost as nothing, for he knows that he must anyhow work for his living, and he is unwilling to go into service to another: he will therefore work feverishly for a gain that would not count much in the balance with a wealthier rival, who, being able to retire and live in comfort on the interest of his capital, may be doubting whether it is worth while to endure any longer the wear-and-tear of business life. (p. 603)

Thus then each of the many modern methods of business has its own advantages and disadvantages: and its application is extended in every direction until that limit or margin is reached, at which its special advantages for that use no longer exceed its disadvantages . . . these modern methods . . . render possible a much closer correspondence between the earnings of undertaking and management and the services by which those earnings are got than could be generally attained under the primitive system in which capital was scarcely ever applied to production by any save its owners . . . that share of the normal expenses of production of any commodity which is commonly classed as profits, is so controlled on every side by the action of the principle of substitution, that it cannot long diverge from the normal supply price of the capital needed, added to the normal supply price of the ability and energy required for managing the business, and lastly the normal supply price of that organization by which the appropriate business ability and the requisite capital are brought together. (pp. 605-6)

. . . the average rate of profits in a trade cannot rise or fall much without general attention being attracted to the change before long. And though it may sometimes be a more difficult task for a business man than for a skilled labourer, to find out whether he could improve his prospects by changing his trade, yet the business man has great opportunities for discovering whatever can be found out about the present and future of other trades; and if he should wish to change his trade, he will generally be able to do so more easily than the skilled workman could. (pp. 607-8)

. . . as a rule a person will not enter on a risky business, unless, other things being equal, he expects to gain from it more than he would in other trades open to him, after his probable losses had been deducted from his probable gains on a fair actuarial estimate. . . . (p. 613)

These excerpts appear mainly to have reference to normal periods, and to have a distributive rather than cost bearing—why one gets thus much, rather than what part of it one must get in order to justify his productive process as against whatever else most strongly deters. The quotations have to do also with total gains rather than with the separate functional elements in the total. And some of them, obviously, are discussions of the bearing of risk on the necessary total of gain. And still the principle, not merely of substitutional outlays and methods, but also of substitute lines of production may be found in them. The analysis could easily have been carried over into a doctrine of necessary returns as costs, in view of alternative openings. Seemingly, however, Marshall did not have this in view.

Interpreted, however, as opportunity-cost analysis, it would need to take account of the separate alternative openings for gain for the enterpriser's abilities and efforts, and of the alternative uses for the capital goods and funds, and in addition, note, for lands in point both of fertility and of spatial extension, else the proportionality of prices with money costs would fail. Moreover, because the analysis must take on the inter-individual reference, real costs in the quantitative sense could not serve, since they are not proportional with the price hires or incomes. Think of the prima donna and the servant girl, the barrister and the pearl-diver. Nor will averages do, since the inter-individual facts are ratio facts, as the sole bases of comparability—if and so far, that is, as opportunity costs are in the case. Opportunity costs and real costs get on ill together. But they are none the less in the background of the thought in most of the quotations under discussion:

... the alert business man is ever seeking for the most profitable application of his resources, and endeavouring to make use of each several agent of production up to that margin, or limit, at which he would gain by transferring a small part of his expenditure to some other agent ... he is ... the medium through which the principle of substitution so adjusts the employment of each agent that, in its marginal application, its cost is proportionate to the additional net product resulting from its use. We have to apply this general reasoning to the case of the hire of labour. (pp. 514-15)

But why *proportionality* is used here instead of *equality* is not easy to see. And different agents have different productivities to different employers. Each employer has his intensive margin; therefore it is a lower instrument margin with some than with others; whereby some are reaping renters' surpluses.

Chapter XII

NORMALS AND REPRESENTATIVES

IF POTATOES are at four dollars a bushel—as once in central New York a few years ago—it is certain that this price will not endure beyond the next crop, or at the most a second or third crop. If wheat is at twenty-five cents a bushel, it is a good purchase to anyone who can hold it. It must be merely a question of time before it will rise. Thus all of us recognize in a general way the meaning of norms. Production will expand with potatoes, and contract with wheat, until the prices concerned get more nearly into line with other prices. Wages are too high to permit of 25-cent wheat long, as also are fertilizers and machinery. This means that other things are commanding prices, and so are paying wages and are buying supplies, that impose for wheat costs too high to make it worth while to produce a 25-cent product. For the costs in any one line of production are in the main due to the competition of producers in other lines, that not only absorb the cost goods but attach to them prices which the producers of wheat must face as their own costs.

All this is commonplace enough. The principle of substitution holds in selecting the factors and the methods that, at their prices, promise the various producers of the various goods their several best margins. But the principle holds also in the selection of that line of production promising the best returns—no line of production to be allowed to displace more price returns than it achieves. It is the principle underlying the distribution of investment, and of wage outlay, and of enterpriser effort, over the entire field of production. It is the ultimate principle of opportunity cost. Likewise it is the ultimate principle of normality. When potatoes are returning—and, so far, are promising—relatively high margins of gain, in view of the costs that the general situation is imposing in raw materials, interest rates and the various hires of men and things, and as well in the alternative openings for enterpriser effort and earning power, the output of potatoes responds in volume, thereby lowering prices, and therefore abridging the prospective margins of gain.

On the demand side also the same principle holds. One's price offer for any particular thing turns in large part on what other things the money will command. Thus the price-offer and the goods-offer sides of the determination of any price are interdependent with the general situation of prices. On both sides of the problem all prices are linked with all others. The costs to which one will submit are commonly influenced by what the same outlays or the same energies will achieve in other lines of production; as also the costs to which one must submit turn on what the cost goods would achieve in other lines of production.

And thus the price problem for any line of goods must be examined on both sides of it, against the background of a general price situation. The enterpriser-cost process is, in this aspect, a process of the evening up of pecuniary openings and of price levels. In principle it is a general system of opportunity-cost adjustments. And because it is an enterpriser process, where all outlay costs and all displacement costs are price items, it is a process that for explanatory purposes is both superficial and circuitous. But it is, no less, the actual process. Whatever explanations there are appealing to a deeper level of causation, the underlying and determining influences in the case have to be articulated with this enterpriser process, precisely because it is only through this process, and in terms of it, that the ultimate influences can arrive at expression in competitive industrial activities. It is to this enterpriser process solely that pecuniary costs of production are an appropriate computation, as explaining on the supply side of the price problem the particular and relative resistances to the forth-coming of products. It incorporates and reports, for enterpriser purposes, the conditions that the ultimate causes have created. Only through this enterpriser cost process can these influences obtain expression in competitively organized production. On this enterpriser level, and in the supply aspect, particular costs explain particular prices, and relative costs explain relative prices. Price offers are opportunity-cost facts, the getting of one thing only through the displacing of another. Goods offers are opportunity-cost facts, the getting of the money only by the foregoing of the goods. Costs of production also are always opportunity costs in principle; to get the products as against keeping the money, or to get the product on terms of foregoing the producing of another. For costs of production are merely reservation prices pushed back to the stage of getting ready to sell.

It is thus evident that there is thought-wise such a thing as the normal price of any particular good. It is the price harmonious with the general price situation, the price that the processes of readjustment will bring, taking the general price situation for granted as background, and allowing for the time requisite for the processes of readjustment. Whether in point of stock or of the terms of its offering, it is true, as Marshall says (p. 384), that "if the supply of one factor is disturbed, the supply of others is likely to be disturbed also." Take it that general prices are not changing: then any particular price, say of the potatoes or the wheat, must adapt itself, both on the demand side and the production side, to the price situation about it. All that is needed is time enough for the process to complete itself—a process that in both aspects involves the application of the opportunity-cost principle in the redistribution of producing, selling, buying and consuming.

Moreover, there is thought-wise such a thing as a normal general situation of prices, in the sense of a system of prices completely adjusted to one another, not, however, in the sense of objective and concrete achievement, but only in the conceptual sense, a mental fabrication. But in this conceptual sense, prices may be thought of as adjusting to one another within a given situation of desires (styles and fashions included) and of methods and of productive individuals and instruments—a short-time or an intermediate-period normal—within a general setting of influences taken for granted as stable for the particular period, an other-things-remaining-the-same concept.

A further reach of conceptual normality is one for the outcome of still longer-time processes: an adjustment that assumes the working, and the termination of the working, of a wide variety of changes in the general setting of things: in population; in general intelligence and strength; in desires and interest, *e.g.,* fashions; in environmental resources and conditions, *e.g.,* oil; in technical knowledge and methods, *e.g.,* transportation and the need of it; in the progressive exhaustion of mines and forests; as measurably also in fertility; in climatic fluctuations; in the redistributions of property rights; and even in the redistribution of sea and land areas—and finally, note again, in the termination and cessation of all these changes. All this, obviously, is extreme intellectual abstraction, each term of it and the time of each term, an heroic assumption—and all of it running in the conditional or sub-junctive mood, *if* this and that, and *when* this or the other thing— and finally, all other things to remain the same for the period requisite to the later processes of equilibration.

Most of these concepts of normality—they are purely conceptual things in the very nature of their assumptions—run in the forecast emphasis, and involve even in the short-time sort, a passably wide range of assumptions. In purpose, however, forecast is not always conscious. Repeatedly Marshall is talking of this or that item of fact as normal in the present tense. In fact, however, the assumption that any present situation or any item of fact within it is normal must involve assumptions, if not about the past, then certainly about the future. For the meaning of a present normal is that the future is not to modify it in relevant and significant aspects. Otherwise the present thing cannot be in any significant sense normal. If, however, a price could be said to be normal at present through reporting now the effects of forecasted future prices, no price could ever in a speculative market be other than normal.

Mainly then, it is clear, these notions of normality are not merely mental attitudes, but they are attitudes of estimate, of opinion, of probability in the emphasis of expectation. They are outlooks and forecasts. Moreover, they are commonly not merely conceptual attitudes, but they connote specific outcomes, areas of probability, strips of the expected, rather than the setting-up of precise outcomes in prices or in other specific conditions. What, for example, in the short-time sense, is the normal price of potatoes, as the price either that present conditions are making toward, or that the future will mill out as derivative from the present processes and conditions? No present declaration of any particular price is attempted, but only, at the most, that the future will bring one— a price that in any specific case is not at present known, and that is assertible in the present only as a thing to become in the future knowable in the specific sense. No assumption of a normal price in present assertion could go further than one of a ribbon area of a future price range, or, possibly, a price in the not-far-from emphasis.

As the years run, potatoes sell, say, at harvest at from 60 to 80 cents per bushel. Somewhere along about this is about what you may, with fair assurance, expect. Or possibly 70 cents may be reported as a price approximately at the center of oscillation—as about the price that one may look for, or as the average run of the years; it being assumed, of course, that the controlling influences are to continue much as, during the past period of observation, they have been—no new bugs or weevils or blights.

Will potatoes or wheat ever arrive at the conceptual normal price, or stay there, if either should once get there? Doubtless a thought is one sort of fact, an event actual in its own order of actuals. But no normal is ever actual otherwise than as subjectively factual, a mental activity, an event that, while it is conceptually actual, is never actual by the test of fulfillment in the order of things in the world "out there," the world of objective fact. Objectively speaking, then, in the out-thereness sense, as part of the order of the external world, there can be no normal price for potatoes or wheat. For normal prices are only concepts.

Always, therefore, there is danger to clear thinking in accepting a fact in the conceptual order of events as indicative of objective actuality, or as affording a basis of inference as to the quantitative sequences, or the times of them, in the order of events not *in here* but *out there*. That normal-price adjustments can be thought of does not argue for their objective actuality either present or future. For to conceive of a normal price for potatoes argues not so much that potatoes ever will achieve that price, or will be stable there, as that they never will—the necessary assumptions being incredible of realization.

And still less credible is the assumption of the actual arrival of any normal-price system of prices, either early or distant. Nothing in this, however, need disturb the validity of the notion of normality as an item in the order of purely conceptual facts. Will parallel lines ever meet? As thus badly formulated, it is a futile question. Lines that are conceptually parallel can never conceptually meet; nor were there objectively any lines fulfilling the conceptual terms, a matter of definition, could they ever meet. That there are no lines, seeming to us to be parallel, in the objective world that will ever meet, is not to the purpose; this merely asserts that meeting lines parallel in the way that we conceive of them are not objectively actual. It is the concept, the definition, that prescribes the impossibility of the meeting—consistently with the concept. That all the actual lines in a spherical universe must be curved—space having curvature everywhere—says nothing as to what is true of straight lines as we think of them—excepting that objectively there are none. In fact, a line that actually is curved has to assume conceptual straightness as the thing that a curved line is not.

The test of conceptual validity is freedom from contradiction, a thinkable and clearly defined notion, and not the objective actuality of something fulfilling the notion. Neither is objective actuality tested by conceptual validity, nor conceptual validity by objective actuality. An assumption, indifferently true or false objectively, may serve as an axiom in mathematics as the basis on which the derivation of corollaries is to proceed—the implicit becoming explicit. Hidden contradictions in the concept may thus be uncovered, or the objective unactuality of it is indicated. It was once much argued where a ball in a cannon on the deck of a moving ship and pointed in the direction of the course of the ship would drop, were the cannon touched off and the ship to move as swiftly as the ball. Would the ball get out of the cannon? Would not the powder have to blow it out? But this would violate the assumption. Let it then; but the ball could not stay in the breech of the cannon. The conceptual fact ran afoul of the actualities of the objective world. And still, conceptually speaking, a powder that, in deference to experimentors' needs, should suspend for the moment its usual habit or proclivity of expelling cannon balls, is not unthinkable, but only incredible as a phenomenon in the actual universe. In fact, just on the day of this writing, I have been reading in a popular journal that "scientists have found in Alaska the bones of an animal with a head like a camel and a body like a fish"—an idea having conceptual validity enough so that I find myself much doubting its objective fulfillment. These normals I suspect to be also of similar standing. But the concept of a normal, or of normals, may nevertheless be a serviceable tool of thought, if only objective actuality be not too confidingly ascribed to it.

It is, as we have seen, mainly in the forward-looking business process that normals appear to be especially in place. An enterpriser, before going into a business, will probably do a good bit of forecasting, pro and con. Among the various openings that he is seriously considering, what will their several costs be? He will be interested in the outlook for both costs and selling prices in the general average of the periods during which he has it in mind to be producing and selling. And in arriving at these prospective averages, he will get what information he may from the averages of the past. He will also look carefully at existing conditions in order to make out whether and how far each may afford significant evidence of what may be anticipated.

But these averages, past, present or future, are not themselves normals, but only evidence of the particular normal sought. They are particular bases of getting at an opinion as to particular normal prices or conditions. Your estimate of a man is not the same thing as the man himself, and may be wide of the truth. But you have bases of inference for your opinion or estimate. Some of these may be averages of one sort or another. Your opinion of what would be a normal price is similarly founded on evidence, much of it of this average sort.[1]

But the thing about which you have an opinion, the normal price, is a different thing from your opinion about it. And this *it?* It is not something that is expected to arrive or that is believed possible ever of arriving. It is itself conceptual—that unknowable outcome that would become precise and actual if things were such as it is well recognized they are not, and are not going to be, and would not long remain if they were. If only things would stop changing—the flux of them suspended long enough—there would arrive some prices, or a price, that would be both actual and precise

[1] ". . . For suppose that the disuse of meat causes a permanent distaste for it, and that an increased demand for fish continues long enough to enable the forces by which its supply is governed to work out their action fully (of course oscillation from day to day and from year to year would continue: but we may leave them on one side). The source of supply in the sea might perhaps show signs of exhaustion. . . . On the other hand, those might turn out to be right who think that man is responsible for but a very small part of the destruction of fish that is constantly going on; and in that case a boat starting with equally good appliances and an equally efficient crew would be likely to get nearly as good a haul after the increase in the total volume of the fishing trade as before . . . since fishermen require only trained aptitudes . . . their number could be increased in less than a generation to almost any extent. . . . If therefore the waters of the sea showed no signs of depletion of fish, an increased supply could be produced at a lower price . . . and, the term Normal being taken to refer to a long period of time, the normal price of fish would increase with an increase in demand." (pp. 370-71)

The present thought about the normal must, then, be clearly distinguished from the thing of the future that is now being thought about—the present error from the possible later truth. Normals are in the present purely individual outlooks; are therefore as numerous as are the outlookers; are present mental attitudes regarding later objective facts; are not now specific price things; are many of them wrong— with no certitude that, by the test of the later objectively right thing, if it comes, any will ever be right—the only thing certain being that, if things ever stay put long enough, there will be a stable and specific objective price fact, an objectively right *normal,* instead of numerous present errors about it. And certain it should be also that these present attitudes—right or wrong, and mainly or entirely wrong —are the process facts with which any economist can rightly have to do. And if any normality fact is process-wise ever to declare what costs are price-determining and what are not, it must be the present fact, the price fact, the error fact. The only other fact that could ever serve for this functional distinction must be the future fact—the fact that is at present the unknowable fact; the fact that may never be, and that credibly can never actually be; and that if later it should ever become actual, could never by anyone, even the economist, be recognized as such. For no later current situation could ever possibly declare its immunity from later change, either proximate or remote. Normals must then be as conceptual as in the current present they have to be.

—but this only a conceptual precision, in the sense that in the assumed conditions a precise price would arrive, but a price that still is quantitatively unknowable as an item in the present outlook. And when it should arrive, if only it could, the individual holder of the present conceptual forecast would not be able at that time to recognize it as the fulfillment of his conceptual view. His view was not, in fact, a how-much view, but only a view that there would arrive a how-much thing. And so one's conceptual assertion that some sort of individual would be a normal man, or even one's belief that some one person of the present—perhaps, indeed, himself—is normal, is at the most only an opinion about a normal, along with the opinion that the particular individual conforms to it. One cannot know whether one is, or is not, himself a normal man in his particular trade. But one may none the less take oneself to be so; or may take some one or another unparticularized individual among all of those in the trade to be the normal individual. If, for example, through the different lines of evidence examined, an enterpriser could settle on what would be a normal individual in the trade, he might then have an opinion as to what particular individual would fit the requirements.

Or say that he takes himself to be in his particular trade a normal producer in point either of unit costs or of net gains. Perhaps this opinion is arrived at on the basis of his knowledge that his unit costs have been running close to the average of market prices; or possibly on his opinion that his net gains have been running close to what he believes to have been the average net gains in the trade. But does either of these situations mean that in the future he will be normal at future prices? And at what prices? To take himself as a producer that will be normal at that time at the prices of that time is not, as of necessity, to have in mind any particular price for that time, but only that there will be such a price and that he will be a normal producer by the test of it. A present belief in the coming at a specific time of a specific normal price involves no present attitude on what that normal price will specifically be, but only the assertion that there will be one—the present conception lacking, as of the present, all quantitative definiteness. I have, for example, a friend who reports himself as believing the apostles creed. "But what do you take it to mean —'conceived of the Holy Ghost,' etc.?" "I don't know." "You believe, then, in something, but don't know what?" "I believe merely that whatever it means it is the truth." And I have to admit this to be an intelligible and intelligent belief. You do not know what evidence your friend gave in court yesterday, or will give tomorrow; but you are convinced that anything sworn to by him is the truth.

And you may similarly hold that enterpriser X in your trade is the normal or the representative producer, or that he will be so, without knowing what his costs are, or will be, or at what price he will in the future sell his product. Somewhere there is that appointed woman for you, as you desire or dream. Which one? Where? When? These particularizations are not essentials or prerequisites to the concept. There is an old ballad opening somewhat as follows:

Where and how shall I earliest meet her? What are the words she first
    will say?
By what name shall I earliest greet her? I know not now, but 'twill come
    some day.

You may believe in Heaven, without committing yourself to descriptive details of where or how or what: just a most excellent place in which, as you may perhaps hold, every one will be normal; and normal prices will be ruling; and every producer will be normal with relation to the different several prices. And of these normal individuals and these normal prices you will have assurance as adequate as of any on the hither side of the hereafter.

And not much thereby is asserted? Then also there is not much to be put in issue. You are sovereign over your own concepts, so long as you refrain from attaching to them the objective validity of fulfillment. They are dangerous merely as keys or guides to actualities in the external order of events, or as working tests or measures of facts or trends anywhere.

The effort thus far in this chapter has been, for purposes of the discussions to come, to distinguish from each other two different orders of actuality—in the hope of holding them separate. There are, it seems clear, different things that Marshall includes under the one general head of *normal*. At least one of them appears to have no need of any of the foregoing hair-splittings. But much of Marshall's discussion does, as I hold, run on the level to which the foregoing analyses are relevant. Much also of his discussion appears to obscure that one particular position of his deserving a further and most careful—and in large part, a sympathetic—examination.

There are, then, various types of normality to be deduced from Marshall's analysis in its different connections: (1) normality, belonging as a *fact* of *process* to the objective world, either as trend or as accomplishment; (2) a something purely conceptual, an ultimate goal attributed to the facts of process, an ideal, a fabrication of what would be if and when things were what they neither are nor will ever be; (3) the way in which, severally or as an aggregate, the various investors think of the ultimate goal or goals—investors' conceptual processes; (4) the way in which investors are taken actually to arrive at their actual decisions in investment policy—descriptive forecast as a process fact.

Normal must be understood in this fourth sense, if any validity for the objective economic process is to attach to it. Moreover, Marshall's analysis does clearly embrace this fourth interpretation —with this as seemingly the one interpretation out of the four, possible of logical articulation with the movement of his general system of thought. The forecasts, then, having to do in this sense with normals—normals that are to the point for the actual economic process—are not your forecasts or mine or those of any economist. Nor even are they those of any investor or investors, in any conceptual sense of normal, or of any interest in such conceptual senses. Each investor thinks about his own particular problem, in view of what it is and of what he has to decide to do, and therefore to decide not to do. He is thinking of what particular business to go into, or of what policy to follow with the business that he is already in. He may, it is true, be concerned with more than one line of activity to the end of deciding on one of them or on one set of them. But even so, he is not concerned with any entire system of normals, a complete and definitive equilibrated system; or with what at any particular time the situation in any aggregate view will be; or with any early or intermediate equilibration of prices or conditions in general. The terminus-a-quo with him is the particular present situation in those aspects of it that he takes to bear on him, and on the future policy to be adopted by him, without reference to whether it is normal or not, or is ever likely to be, or even ever could be. His concern is with those prospects that are relevant to his program. Neither normals in name nor normals in significance would help him, even were they available. What shall he undertake, and how far shall he go, and for what time? Shall he or shall he not best divide his investment resources? Or, holding them as a unit, how far shall he employ them jointly with his own personal activity? Or how differently combine them with it? You and I, for example, invest dividedly here and there, and, in the aspect of individual earning activities, teach school—with never a thought of normals.

Each enterpriser is seeking the best prospect of aggregate gain open to him, in view of what he can make out with regard to such part of the future as he is at present interested in. Continually new investment funds are maturing, if not with him, then with other investors actual or potential. Continually new forecasts are being made as the situation is changing and unfolding. It is a continuous process of the tentative adjustment and readjustment of investment policies and activities, as conditions are changing, or are in prospect of change.

Normality is, in this view, the general outcome taken by each of the investors to be probable in view of all the evidence available to him, and the way in which it appeals to him as bearing on the particular thing he is considering doing or not doing, for its appropriate period. No joint or aggregate notion of the probable is within the facts. And in no sense of normal other than this can any investor be interested in whether he is himself normal, or the situation is now normal or will ever become normal, or in any sort or direction of ultimate trend or outcome, or in whether things will ever stop changing, or whether by the time he is through with them—his particular terminus-ad-quem—they will have stopped changing. Actually they will not; and of this he is presumably aware.

What, in this emphasis, Marshall must mean by a *true long-term normal* is presumably a time of a completed adjustment of the terminus-ad-quem to the terminus-a-quo, a time when nothing will advise any one at either terminal to any further processes of readjustment. Such time could arrive only if at both terminals conditions would stop changing long enough for all readjustments to become complete—no further advantage promised anywhere by any further change; all relevant conditions, numbers, climate, desires, land areas and land resources—both mineral and agricultural —health, strength, industriousness, and methods, stabilized; that fourth variety of normal which Marshall terms the Stationary State. Any normal short of this is merely a normal of a lesser degree of improbability or impossibility, a less heroic exercise of conceptual ability. For certainly the stabilization of mineral resources is a paradox.

But these investor decisions and policies belong to the process facts in a world of countless changing economic conditions. Normals in any other sense are conceptual items—ways of thinking about the facts, rather than of thinking in them to the end of acting on them. The facts of process make no place for normals in any other emphasis.

One of Marshall's views of *normal* appears to be that of a purely type thing, like *man;* something that no one ever saw or will see; conceptual thinking in an extreme form. But this notion of *type,* as meaning something like *mode,* is not by Marshall distinguished from the merely *ordinary* or *commonplace* or *usual;* or from the *expected* or, perhaps, the *rightly-to-be-expected;* or from the *median;* or from the *mean average.* But as referring to only one quality or character and signifying the mode in that quality or character, *typical* is a term of descriptive and external reference, and is not subject to suspicion for its purely conceptual standing. So again of the *usual* or the *ordinary* or the *commonplace,* the thing that in most cases you find. The conceptual character of *the expected* is clear: it points to the internal fact of your expectation with regard to what may or may not later be. The extreme conceptual quality of a computed average as something assuming no objective representation or fulfillment, especially where several aspects are involved, has been stressed in earlier discussions.

But with distinctions of this sort Marshall does not here concern himself. Nor in general does definition with him permit of them. And in this particular case, doubtless, they are especially difficult of making; wherefore also they are in especial need of being made. In Marshall's thought, it is clear, *normal* covers indifferently the type, the usual, the expected, and the mean average. Whereby the normal comes to be in Marshall's thought an objective reality, a term descriptive of the objective facts—normal *thises* and *thats,* presented as objectively actual in the order of economic events— these conceptual things taking on a causal character as of explanatory significance for factual processes and outcomes. It is a case of several meanings for one term, a shifting of connotations, in such sort that one can never be certain of precisely with what one has to deal. In one case, it may be with merely the usual or the ordinary; in another, with the typical, in the possible objective sense of mode or median, or perhaps of thought-of comingness; or solely with a mathematical quotient. In what one or what several of these different meanings you may, in any particular connection, interpret *normal* may seem to have been left to you to infer from the context. In fact, however, any effort of yours at interpretation in these regards must be futile—precisely because Marshall has not concerned himself with any one of these distinctions; has not, it seems, had them in mind. You would be gratuitously imputing distinctions —discovering things not there. Marshall's use of the term *normal* cancels these perplexing but necessary distinctions, by ignoring them—all to the final outcome that Marshall takes the *normal* —and that you are to take it along with him—as carrying the attribute of actuality in the objective order of economic events, like The Good, The True and The Beautiful, or like Peace and Hope and Love—all of them as objects in the *out-there*.

... the course of action which may be expected *under certain conditions* from the members of an industrial group is the *normal action* of the members of that group relatively to those conditions. (p. 34)

The italics are Marshall's. Note that this view of normal refers solely to the actions of the members within a particular industrial group, and this only under certain conditions. But it does not yet appear, and may not later appear, what a *group* is or what these *certain conditions* shall be taken to be. Perhaps the group will turn out to be whatever industrial classification you may have in mind or may infer to be in Marshall's mind; and pretty certainly the conditions will themselves be presented as merely *normal conditions*. Marshall continues:

This use of the term Normal has been misunderstood; and it may be well to say something as to the *unity in difference* which underlies *various* uses of the term. When we talk of a Good man or a Strong man, we refer to excellence or strength of those particular physical, mental or moral qualities which are *indicated in the context*. A strong judge has seldom the same qualities as a strong rower; a good jockey is not always of exceptional virtue. In the same way *every use* of the term normal implies the predominance of certain *tendencies* which appear *likely to be more or less* steadfast and persistent in their action over those which are *relatively* exceptional and intermittent. ... (p. 34) [Italics supplied]

Perhaps this means the *mode* of many aspects at once: what you see the most of.

But the normal which starts off here by being typical, grades off into becoming the expected-to-be. And forthwith it will have become the usual or ordinary or commonplace. These shifts are obviously easy, and the temptation to them great. For if you have clearly in mind what is the type or mode of a class, you will know what to take to be likely with that member of the class that next comes along. And because what is usual at any particular time is what at the next time you would commonly find, and would expect to find, the meaning of normal in the sense of typical or usual readily shifts over into the expected. And with these starts, or with any one of them, the notion of means is not far in the offing, either as arrived at directly from the notion of type, or from the notion of the usual as the to-be-expected thing. This paragraph from page 34 continues as follows:

Illness is an abnormal condition of man: but a long life passed without any illness is abnormal. During the melting of the snows, the Rhine rises above its normal level: but in a cold dry spring when it is less than usual above that normal level, it may be said to be abnormally low (for that time of year). In all these cases normal results are those which may be *expected* as the outcome of those *tendencies* which the *context suggests;* or, in other words, which are in accordance with those "statements of tendency," those Laws or Norms, which are appropriate to the context.

The shift to emphasis on tendencies and the expected, with some suggestion of means, is clear. But bearing in mind that on the preceding page "a social law" was defined as "a statement that a certain course of action may be expected under certain conditions from the members of a social group," we find that normal results are those actions which may be expected from the members of a group as the outcome of the tendencies which are in accordance with those statements of tendency appropriate to the context.

It may be that this means no more than that normal is what you are to look for in view of the tendencies which you believe to be actual; or, perhaps, just the expected under the conditions, or within the conditions, if they are themselves normal—just as a river may be abnormally high, if it is higher than it commonly is at so dry a time. Similarly Marshall says (p. 35): "The normal price of . . . eggs may be taken to be a penny when nothing is said as to the time of the year: and yet threepence may be the normal price in town during January; and twopence may be an abnormally low price then, caused by 'unseasonable' warmth." This seems to be an expected computed average that is deduced from the usual; or the expected thing deduced from the usual computed average.

But does it matter which it is? It is the event, and not your recognition of it, that must stand as the fact in the external run of things. The expectation is a mental attitude with regard to the external and factual event. And an arithmetic average is a mathematical quotient. It matters in this talk of normals, to be sure, just what we are talking about. By the test of the external order of things there are no normals. Usuals, however, there may have been in the past; and there may be usuals in the present. And there may be a present belief that similarly there will be usuals in the future.

Is this all that Marshall means? Instead, he will make distinctions of function by the test of whether and when an event is normal—as, for example, with the bearing of the hires of quasi-rent goods or of labor of different kinds and grades on prices. Moreover, not yet having been told what a *tendency* is, we are tempted to suspect that that also may be a mere mental fabrication, a conceptual fact, something belonging to the internal order of events. And we note that now *normals* are reported (p. 34) to have something to do with remoteness in time, or perhaps that there are different grades or degrees of normality according to the length of the run, for "normal economic action is that which may be expected in the long run. . . ." And what is the long run? It may have to do with the time requisite for the processes of equilibration in view of the swiftness of working of the particular tendency with which the processes have to do.[2]

---

[2] Below is a list, far from being complete, of *normals* or of normality or of "representativeness" reported in the *Principles*—it being clear that representatives are always normals, though *normals* are not quite certainly to be interpreted as always *representative*. Try to fit the particular use with its precise form—typical, usual, mean, mode, median, etc.

Farmers—   "of normal ability relatively to the task" (p. 631)
               "of normal ability and enterprise for that class of holding" (p. 635)
Earnings—   "representative of the normal earnings of management in his grade" (p. 600)
               "The normal earnings of management are . . . high . . . when, etc." (p. 612)
Ability of
  enterpriser— "business ability up to the normal level of that grade of industry" (p. 600)
               "if he is a man of normal ability (normal that is for that class of work)" (p. 618)
Harvest—   "in a year of normal harvests and normal prices" (p. 635)
Employer—   "of normal ability and normal good fortune" (p. 667)
Profits—   "inequalities in the normal rates of profit in different trades" (p. 612)
               "a worker of normal efficiency; whose additional output repays an employer of normal ability and normal good fortune and normal resources with normal profits, but not more." (p. 667)

In the main, however, Marshall appears to hold the purely conceptual fact of a computed average in several aspects at once to be decisive of normality, both as it is forecasted and as conceivably it may later arrive. These averages, then, are not taken to be merely

	"yields only a normal rate of profits to that class of industry" (p. 615)
Shepherd—	"of normal efficiency . . . to assume him to be thus exceptional would be most inexpedient. He should be representative: that is, of normal efficiency.
	"If he is representative, and his employer is representative, etc." (p. 516)
Tenant farmer—	"it being assumed that that farmer's ability and enterprise are such as are normal for farms of that class. . . .
	. . . .
	"if he is successful . . . to retain something more than mere normal profits" (p. 657)
Management—	Causes that "affect normal earnings of management . . . as they do the normal wages of skilled labour." (p. 608)
Efficiency—	"The eleventh man (supposed to be of *normal* efficiency)" (p. 517, note)
Skilled labor—	"normal wages of" (608)
Worker and conditions—	"if the worker and his conditions of employment are both normal" (p. 517)
Conditions—	"the owners of capital . . . have been able in the main to adapt its forms to the normal conditions of the time" (p. 592)
Expenses of	
	"that share of the normal expenses of production of any commodity" (p. 605. See also p. 805)
Good fortune—	"an employer of normal ability and normal good fortune" (p. 667)
Resources—	"an employer of normal ability . . . and normal resources" (p. 667)
Prosperity—	"The time chosen must be one of normal prosperity" (p. 667)
Wages—	"the normal rate of earnings will still be the same in all trades" p. 512)
Supply of labor—	"the dependence of the normal supply of labour in their several occupations on, etc." (pp. 623-24)
Firms—	many, and many *representative*
Demand—	numerous cases
Supply—	" "
Prices—	" "
Interest rate—	" "

But there is no *normal farm* (pp. 649-50) for "every farm has slight peculiarities of its own. . . ." And whether or not it is significant, functionally or otherwise, *normals* appear to be lacking for the following: merchants, buyers, sellers, borrowers, lenders, factories, railroads, machines, dwellings, town lots, land-lords, parents and individuals. (See *Principles* p. 557.) Why? The objective unreality may be too obvious.

items of evidence in making up a forecast in the present of the particular future normal. Instead, the averages are taken to be the factual items that, in the future time, will make precisely the normal of that time, an objectively actual normal. This normal, when as an objective fact it arrives—that objective fact of the later time about which present forecast is attempted, mainly through the use of averages—may turn out entirely to discredit any particular forecast of it, or even all of the various forecasts of it. The normal of the present forecast is merely a present estimate of what in the later time, the particular normal time under consideration, the normal will then actually be.

But when at its later time this normal arrives at objective actuality, the test of it will be not that of the mode, a thing susceptible descriptively of an external counterpart, but that of the mean, a purely mental fact, a computed thing of which there may not be, and presumably where several aspects are involved, can never be, any objective exemplification.

. . . the normal, or "natural," value of a commodity . . . is that which economic forces tend to bring about in the *long run*. It is the average value which economic forces would bring about if the general conditions of life were stationary. . . . (p. 347)

Thus, when it is said that the price of wool on a certain day was abnormally high though the average price for the year was abnormally low, that the wages of coal-miners were abnormally high in 1872 and abnormally low in 1879, that the (real) wages of labour were abnormally high at the end of the fourteenth century and abnormally low in the middle of the sixteenth; everyone understands that the scope of the term normal is not the same in these various cases. (p. 363)

. . . looking forward a long time he [a cloth manufacturer] must take normal wages at a rate rather higher than the present average.

Again, in estimating the normal supply price of wool, he would take the *average* of several past years. . . . (p. 365)

. . . Thus the whole of the normal profits enter into true or long-period supply price.

The causes which govern the normal levels of wages and the various elements of profits, resemble one another. (p. 619) [This is partly a marginal caption—the purpose of quoting it being merely to indicate that it is normals that are under discussion.]

. . . to find the average profits of a trade we must not divide the aggregate profits made in it by the number of those who are reaping them, nor even by that number added to the number who have failed: but from the aggregate profits of the successful we must subtract the aggregate losses of those who have failed . . . and we must then divide the remainder by the sum of the numbers of those who have succeeded and those who have failed. . . . (p. 621)

. . . a farmer's calculations as to the rent which it is worth his while to undertake to pay, are further hampered by the difficulty of deciding what is a normal harvest and a normal level of prices . . . many years are required to afford a trustworthy *average* of them. . . . (p. 656)

. . . Let us suppose that a person well acquainted with the woollen trade sets himself to inquire what would be the normal supply price of a certain number of millions of yards annually of a particular kind of cloth. . . . (p. 343) [—necessarily a mean, unless it be the median or mode of the entire year, if, indeed, norms for periods are permissible.]

. . . a price at which each particular amount of the commodity can find purchasers in a day or week or year. . . .

The unit of time may be chosen according to the circumstances of each particular problem: it may be a day, a month, a year, or even a generation: but in every case it must be short relatively to the period of the market under discussion. . . . (p. 342)

. . . If . . . a thousand things of a certain kind have been produced and sold weekly at a price of 10*s.*, while the supply price for two thousand weekly would be only 9*s.*, a small rate of increase in normal demand may gradually cause this to become the normal price. . . . (p. 464)

Interpreted, then, in the sense of the process facts and in the emphasis of the expected, irrespective of the evidence on which the various individuals concerned may have arrived at their expectations, normals are in prospect only through the forward-looking policies of investors. In the light of all sorts of data and by the aid of all sorts of analyses, the various investors judge as best they may with regard to the relative prices in those various futures with which they are severally concerned, and with regard also to the derivative hires for funds and for the various materials, equipment goods and agents and make their investments in line with these forecast estimates. With new investment funds continually maturing, with the current situation constantly changing, and with changing influences continually entering into the forecast processes, the total process is one of continual readjustment. Were it, however, a timeless process, a logic purely, the adjustment would always be complete, no matter what or how rapid were the changing conditions. And similarly, with conditions stable long enough to allow for the processes time enough, a perfect adjustment would arrive, stable for the period of stable conditions.

Such is presumably what Marshall means by the true long-time normal, a view that, as intended to abide by the movement of the investor process, may be interpreted to be descriptive rather than conceptual in emphasis. The unrealities attach solely to the assumption of conditions stabilized long enough to afford the process time for its working out into a complete equilibrium. In this aspect Marshall is concerned with the logic of the process, but still with an objectively actual process.

This interpretation of the *normal* of whatever degree or period, combines, it will be noted, the notion of expectation or forecast with the notion of accomplishment. As a present-process fact, normality points to the outlook as estimated by the investors in view of the facts as they see and estimate them—the usual, past experience, averages as they have been and are, along with the various prospects of relevant change and development:

. . . The motive force is the competition of undertakers: each one tries every opening, forecasting probable future events, reducing them to their true relative proportions, and considering what surplus is likely to be afforded by the receipts of any undertaking over the outlay required for it. All his prospective gains enter into the profits which draw him towards the undertaking; all the investments of his capital and energies . . . have to show themselves to him as likely to be profitable, before he will enter on them. . . . (p. 618)

. . . he [a cloth manufacturer] might . . . looking forward over several years so as to allow for immigration . . . take the normal rate of wages at a rather lower rate than that prevailing there at the time. . . . He might argue . . . that parents had already begun to choose other trades for their children. . . . (pp. 364-65)

But *tested by outcomes,* each of these normals, differing in degree according to its kind, will report, if and when it arrives, its particular objective fact of equilibrium—an achievement possibly diverging widely from each and all of the earlier forecasts; registering, perhaps, effects outside of the range of any earlier reasonable expectation; outcomes discrediting all the earlier *usuals* and all the earlier *averages*.

... On the other hand, those might turn out to be right who think that man is responsible for but a very small part of the destruction of fish ... and in that case ... the term Normal being taken to refer to a long period of time, the normal price of fish would decrease with an increase in demand. (p. 371)

Moreover, the assumptions that are implicit in this notion of a true long-time normal need to be made explicit. It is no doubt possible to think of a particular price as being normal relatively to other prices that are not normal, and that are not taken to be normal: an adjustment of one price to whatever are the conditions surrounding it—for example, the normal prices of wheat or of cotton sheetings during a war period of general disturbance, or especial stress in particular directions, or even of a general credit and price inflation. But a true long-time normal for any one price requires and must assume normal prices generally; a system of productive activities and of prices that is normal in the all-round sense. The normal demands curve or the normal supplies curve for any direct good requires not only normal prices for all other direct goods but also for all of the different cost goods for all the different commodities, inclusive of the price costs and the product prices in all alternative openings; and together with all this, normal rates in general, and in particular, of wages, rents and interest.

The truth of this is obvious on the demand side of the case: the price that any individual will pay for any item of any particular good is conditioned on what his money will buy of other goods— his price-offer schedule the outcome, at each point on it, of a comparison of alternative marginal utilities. And similarly on the supply side: the prices of the cost goods derive from the prices at which their products can be sold, as also from the prices at which alternative products are selling. What the producers of carpets must pay for wool, must turn in part on the prices of all the other products into the making of which wool enters. What one must pay for cotton for blankets, must be affected by the absorptions of cotton for sheetings, and for shirtings, for tents and for gun-cotton. Fuel coal goes down with cheaper fuel oil. Long-term normality anywhere pre-supposes normality everywhere. Implicit, therefore, in Marshall's normal supplies schedule for each particular commodity is the assumption that all of the different supplies schedules and all of the different demands schedules have also become normal. All of the processes of adjustment have had time to work themselves out, with no motive or occasion of disturbance remaining—all buyers, all sellers, all producers, all equipment goods whether land or other, taken to be each so acting or so used that no individual could, to his own thinking, advantage himself by any further modification of his method or direction of producing, or buying, or selling— a complete and systematic price equilibration.

Obviously, however, this view that the normal for any one com-modity assumes a systematic normality does not in any sense deny that each several buyer has his particular price-offer schedule and that each several producer or seller has his particular goods-offer schedule. As at all other times, so at any normal time, it is error to talk of *the* demand price or *the* supply price of any good. A market price-offer schedule for any particular good implies the summing-up in one schedule of all the different individual price-offer schedules. The total supplies schedule is similarly a composite of all of the individual goods-offer schedules. And each of these individual schedules, along with the composite schedules for each particular good, assumes a surrounding and conditioning price system. True long-time normals are, therefore, nowhere unless they are every-where.

At all times, normal or other, enterpriser computations of cost are mere forecasts, as is commonly the fact also with selling prices. In true long-time normal conditions as well as in ordinary conditions, the aggregate outputs of the respective lines of products will be the outcomes of countless enterpriser programs of production in view of the situation as it presents itself to each enterpriser. Accord-ingly as results turn out to be gratifying or disappointing, are the next steps to be chosen. When normals should arrive, therefore, no individual enterpriser could know it, even with regard to his own product. The nearest he could come, would be to be satisfied with his own situation, in the sense of finding no occasion to undertake new things.

It belongs, however, to the assumption that at this normal-price level each product is allotting to the investor those returns that, as expected at the time of the investment, conditioned the making of it, and that now condition the maintenance of the rate of it:

... when we are investigating the causes which determine normal value "in the long run," when we are tracing the "ultimate" effects of economic causes; then the income that is derived from capital in these forms enters into the payments by which the expenses of production of the commodity in question have to be covered; and estimates as to the probable amount of that income directly control the action of the producers, who are on the margin of doubt. . . . (p. 500)

Nor can anywhere the returns be more than adequate by this test, else a relative increase in this line of investment is due—the normal-value situation not yet attained. The returns must, therefore, be neither more nor less than the precisely adequate. All of the different effort returns for the different grades of efficiency are also at the respective levels at which the reproduction of human beings will be both absolutely and relatively constant—at those levels, then, that will maintain fixed stocks of native ability, of trained skill, and of extraordinary natural ability, and that will distribute them stably over the entire field of production. The prices of final products, of raw materials and of fuel; interest rates over the entire field of loan relations; the prices of cost-produced goods and the rents of them; the prices and the rents of lands of all sorts; wages over the entire field of effort returns; dwellings and house rents; advertising and sales costs; and so on—must all have arrived at stability absolutely and relatively, along with stable general prices, the values of money, and therewith stable costs and rates of banking credit—else further readjustments are in waiting, a normal-value situation not yet reached, and therefore no single price item in the entire system yet stable.

More, however, than the foregoing appears to be involved in Marshall's thought. Not only must there be normal prices everywhere, but also, as he holds, there must be, as conditions to these normal prices, normal enterprisers—or a normal enterpriser—normal laborers, normal wages, normal efficiencies, normal harvests, normal prosperity, normal good fortune, and so on to limits that are not entirely clear—to the outcome, at any rate, that most of the differentiations that are at the heart of the competitive process must get erased:

The net product to which the normal wages of any group of workers approximate, must be estimated on the assumption that production has been pushed to that limit at which the output can be just marketed with normal profits, but not more: and it must be estimated with reference to a worker of normal efficiency; whose additional output repays an employer of normal ability and normal good fortune and normal resources with normal profits, but not more. (Something must be added to or subtracted from this net product to find the normal wages of a worker whose efficiency is more or less than normal.) The time chosen must be one of normal prosperity . . . if the building trade is exceptionally depressed, or exceptionally prosperous . . . then the occasion is one which does not afford a convenient opportunity for estimating the relations of net product to normal wages of either bricklayers or carpenters. (p. 667)

. . . a farmer's calculations as to the rent which it is worth his while to undertake to pay, are further hampered by the difficulty of deciding what is a normal harvest and a normal level of prices. For good and bad seasons come so much in cycles that many years are required to afford a trustworthy average of them. . . .

The landlord in determining what rent to accept is met by this difficulty and also by another, arising out of variations in the standards of ability among farmers in different parts of the country. The producer's surplus, or English rent, of a farm is that excess which its produce yields over its expenses of cultivation, including normal profits to the farmer: it being assumed [by whom?] that that farmer's ability and enterprise are such as are normal for farms of that class *in that place*. . . . (pp. 656-57) [italics Marshall's].

The landlord will take the best terms he can get, different for different sorts of tenants. He has no more concern than the tenant with normal costs or prices of product. What he gets is a surplus only in the sense that he gets it. But he may look ahead to decide whether to make a short lease or a long one. He is not concerned with tenants some where else; and excepting for his ignorance of tenant farmers, he has no reason to assume that any man is normal even for farms of that class in that place. But the mere process notion of a terminus-a-quo in equilibration with a terminus-ad-quem involves no such heroic assumptions.

And still it is to be noted that normal conditions are themselves so far variable with any particular commodity, and perhaps with commodities in general, that a distinction has to be drawn between average prices and normal prices:

. . . the term Normal being taken to refer to a long period of time, the normal price of fish would decrease with an increase in demand.

Thus we may emphasize the distinction already made between average price and normal price . . . the conditions which are normal to any one set of sales are not likely to be exactly those which are normal to the others: and therefore it is only by accident that an average price will be a normal price; that is, the price which any one set of conditions tends to produce. In a stationary state alone . . . the term normal always means the same thing: there, but only there, "average price" and normal price" are convertible terms. (pp. 371-72)

Seemingly, therefore, the normal employer and the various other normals implicit in the true long-time normal must be changing. This, however, is not an interpretation confidently to be presented. Such is plainly the fact, as will later appear, with *representatives*. In truth, different stages and degrees of normality have clearly to be recognized. There are short-period and long-period normals—the last term of them all being, however, not the true long-time normal, but a still further variety of normal, the Stationary State:

. . . in fact a theoretically perfect long period must give time enough to enable not only the factors of production of the commodity [one commodity, note] to be adjusted to the demand, but also the factors of production of those factors of production to be adjusted and so on; and this, when carried to its logical consequences, will be found to involve the supposition of a stationary state of industry, in which the requirements of a future age can be anticipated an indefinite time beforehand. . . .

Relatively short and long period problems go generally on similar lines. In both use is made of that paramount device, the partial or total isolation for special study of some set of relations. . . . In the relatively short-period problem no great violence is needed for the assumption that the forces not specially under consideration may be taken for the time to be inactive. But violence is required for keeping broad forces in the pound of *Ceteris Paribus* during, say, a whole generation. . . . (p. 379, note)

But of what Marshall terms normal cases there are several. They are questions of degree; and might, it seems, be indefinitely numerous, as convenience should advise, in parallel, for example, with the non-competing groups of Cairnes' discussion:

Of course there is no hard and sharp line of division between "long" and "short" periods. Nature has drawn no such lines in the economic conditions of actual life; and in dealing with practical problems they are not wanted [unless, perhaps, we want to know when quasi-rents and other hires change from the price-determined to the price-determining function]. Just as we contrast civilized with uncivilized races, and establish many general propositions about either group . . . so we contrast long and short periods without attempting any rigid demarcation between them. . . .

Four classes stand out. In each, price is governed by the relations between demand and supply. As regards *market* prices, Supply is taken to mean the stock . . . on hand, or at all events "in sight." As regards *normal* prices, when the term Normal is taken to relate to *short* periods of a few months or a year, Supply means broadly what can be produced for the price in question with the existing stock of plant, personal and impersonal, in the given time. [One price or an average price for the entire period on the supply side of the case; that is, the supply price of that volume· of product in that time.] As regards *normal* prices, when the term Normal is to refer to *long* periods of several years, Supply means what can be produced by plant, which itself can be remuneratively produced [by many and different competing producers, presumably] and applied within the given time; while lastly, there are very gradual or *Secular* movements of normal price. . . . (pp. 378-79)

And finally, we have the Stationary State; which logically may be taken to be a fourth or a fifth variety of these degrees of normals.

Is, then, the trait of that sort of normality under consideration to be taken to attach to all the other facts and influences in any particular normal situation? Not, it is certain, in such sort that the one particular price that is presented as a price normal to the situation needs assume a general setting of normalities of equal rank or kind. The fairer interpretation is presumably that the shorter-time normals are merely partial normals, normals with reference to one particular price, or perhaps some limited group of prices—normal in the sense that, for that one particular commodity or group, an adjustment is reached in view of what the surrounding conditions actually are. This then is a price that may be normal to a situation that is not itself normal—not, therefore, a normal in any general sense, but only a *so far* normal, and, even at that, a normal that will be cancelled with the later and certain modification of the environing situation. These short or mid-term normals refer solely to particular, and not to systematic, prices and conditions. In any other interpretation—that, say, of an all-round but partial normality, grades and degrees by this general and all-round test—the notion promises no great service-ability, and especially little for Marshall's purposes as they are later to become clear.

Certain, however, of the mere mechanics of Marshall's concept of normals have here to be examined. We have earlier noted, with reference to the fixation of ordinary prices, Marshall's shifts in use from the schedule notion of demands and supplies to the purely quantitative view, the notion that reduces both the demand and the supply sides of the price problem to arbitrarily chosen points on the respective curves—a quantity, the volume of the particular good that will be parted with by holders, or that will be purchased, at some one putative price. No method of explanation, it is clear, of any price adjustment can be reached by this approach. The price being somehow once arrived at, the volume of goods that will be produced or sold or purchased may then be explained—the pro-ducing or selling or buying responsive to the price. But this is to conceive of volume of output, and of sales and of purchases, not as causal of price, but as derivative from price—to define your explanations of the price problem in terms of your solution of it, an account of causes in ex-post-facto terms, consequents transformed into antecedents—demand, for example, as explanation for price turning out to mean merely what you buy at the price. It is funda-mental in price analysis that only through demand and supply in the sense of schedules or curves on both sides of the demand-and-supply setting, are prices to be explained.

And still clearer must it be that for purposes of explaining any market adjustment there is nothing to be arrived at through any one supply quantum, or even any one supply quantum at its terms of sale. Nor is the situation bettered through the adding of a demand, in the sense of how much would be purchased at any one price, even though it somehow were that price attached to the particular stock for sale. There are, for example, 100,000 bushels of wheat that would be parted with at one dollar per bushel, and there are purchasing dispositions that will absorb 50,000 bushels of wheat at that price—*the* supply at the price and *the* demand at the same price—but with nothing more to be inferred as to the market adjustment than that the price must be less than one dollar.

It is obvious, then, that the price problem is wrongly formulated and the solution of it rendered impossible, when any one price is found or assumed as an account of supply, *the* supply price; and the case is little better, even when an amount at the price is also declared. We get nowhere with the price of the 100,000 bushels, unless we are also somehow assured that it is just 100,000 bushels that can find buyers at this price of one dollar each—the terms of the problem rigged to fit the one-dollar price, and then proclaimed as the explanation of it. Only with both sides of the price equation reported in the schedule sense must prices emerge. They are merely remote possibilities in the point-on-the-curve sense, and are impossibilities where either demand or supply means no more than quantity solely or than price solely.

In fact, also, the demands schedule is merely a summed-up report of an indefinitely large number of individual price-offer schedules —a composite schedule reporting the different volumes of the particular commodity that purchasers will take on terms of the different prices. Mere quantity statements misinterpret the factual situation and bar the way to any price outcome. Equally hopeless is it, and theoretically even worse, with no more at hand than *the supply* price and *the demand* price. In any sense appropriate to the price problem, there is no such thing as *the supply* price or *the demand* price.

At present, however, we are interested neither in Marshall's analysis explanatory of the process of price fixation, nor in his terminology for the purpose, otherwise than to the end of a better understanding of his procedure with respect to normals and normal prices. For, as we shall see, the same defects, confusions and impossibilities attach to his analysis of normal demand and supply as to the earlier analysis. In point of process facts there is the same analysis for the two.[3]

But may it not reside in the very nature of a normal situation to provide some one particular price which, as the one particular point of adjustment, may serve to justify the notion of *the one* demand price and of *the one* supply price—these assumptions derivative from the very fact of normality? Defensibly, no. And all-round

[3] Under the ordinary price analysis the following instances from the *Principles* may be noted:

Supply as quantity—"the supply of business ability in command of capital" (p. 313) ; "an increased supply could be produced at a lower price" (p. 371) (See also pp. 242, 272, 273, 525, 528, 530, 534)

Demand as quantity—"their number could be increased . . . to meet the demand" (p. 371) ; "how closely the supply of labour responds to the demand for it" (p. 530) (See also pp. 161, 187, 242, 313, 370, 534, 576)

Supply in terms of "a" or "the" supply price—"The first is the supply price of capital; the second is the supply price of business ability and energy; and the third is the supply price of that organization, etc." (p. 313) (See also pp. 142, 144, 317, 338, 340, 345, 470, 521, 806)

Demand in terms of "a" or "the" demand price—"We may revert to the analogy between the supply price and the demand price of a commodity" (p. 338) ; "so long as the demand price is in excess of the supply price exchanges, etc." (p. 470) (See also pp. 313, 336, 345, 501, 806)

Demand price as merely market price—"a rise in its demand-price increases the supply of it." (p. 532) ; "If he [a man considering building] can find no case in which the demand price exceeds his outlay . . . he may remain idle." (p. 358) ; "A rise in the rate of interest offered for capital, *i.e.,* in the demand price for saving, tends to increase the volume of saving." (p. 236) (See also pp. 217, 219, 455, 456, 534, 570)

Under the normal analysis, as in the ordinary price analysis, the following usages may be noted in the *Principles*:

Demand and supply as schedules—"Let us suppose a list of supply prices (or a supply schedule) made on a similar plan to that of our list of demand prices: the supply price of each amount of the commodity in a year, or any other unit of time, being written against that amount" (p. 343) ; "An increase of normal demand for a commodity involves an increase in the price at which each several amount can find purchasers; or, which is the same thing, an increase of the quantity which can find purchasers at any price" (p. 462) ; "If we could trace the lists of demand and supply prices far ahead, etc." (p. 809) ; "the representative firm being always of the same size . . . its normal expenses . . . would be always the same. The demand lists of prices would always be the same, and so would the supply lists; and normal price would never vary." (pp. 367-68) (See also pp. 346, 405, 407, 463, 465, 810)

Supply in terms of "the" supply, or of "a" or "the" supply price—(pp. 317, 330, 375, 378, 440, 470, 500, 573, 574, 577, 605, 607, 806, 809)

Demand in terms of "the" demand, or of "a" or "the" demand price—(pp. 339, 340, 341, 342, 343, 345, 347, 365, 470)

normality without an explanation of how the different price relations in it were arrived at, as long as competitive production at varying price costs and competitive buying at varying price offers were conceived to be going on, must take prices as somewhat mysteriously deriving from the void; else separate demands and supplies schedules for each commodity must belong to the processes by which the various prices in the normal system of prices arrive for summing up into the system of prices.

. . . when we are investigating the causes which determine normal value "in the long run," . . . the income that is derived from capital . . . enters into the payments by which the expenses of production of the commodity in question have to be covered; and estimates as to the probable amount of that income directly control the action *of the producers,* who are on the margin of doubt as to whether to increase the means of production or not. . . . (p. 500)

. . . it appears reasonable to argue that the marginal supply price for each individual producer is the addition to his aggregate expenses of production made by producing his last element. . . . (p. 501)

Not in point of the process, but only of the setting of the conditions within which the process is going on, must a normal situation differ from any ordinary situation. Moreover, Marshall is entirely clear—part of the time—that in normal periods both the normal demand and the normal supply of any one commodity must be understood in the list sense. The process does not become unitary and organic by the mere fact of becoming normal:

When we say that a person's demand for anything increases, we mean that he will buy more of it than he would before at the same price, and that he will buy as much of it as before at a higher price. A general increase in his demand is an increase throughout the whole list of prices at which he is willing to purchase different amounts of it, and not merely that he is willing to buy more of it at the current prices. (p. 97)

. . . It is to the persistence of the influences considered, and the time allowed for them to work out their effects that we refer when contrasting Market and Normal price, and again when contrasting the narrower and the broader use of the term Normal price. (p. 348)

. . . the demand and supply schedules do not in practice remain unchanged for a long time together, but are constantly being changed; and every

change . . . thus gives new positions to the centres about which the amount
and the price tend to oscillate. (pp. 346-47)

. . . on the supposition that the conditions of supply would be normal. . . .
Let us suppose a list of supply prices (or a supply schedule) made on
a similar plan to that of our list of demand prices. . . . (p. 343)

An increase of normal demand for a commodity involves an increase
in the price at which each several amount can find purchasers; or, which
is the same thing, an increase of the quantity which can find purchasers
at any price. . . . Similarly an increase of normal supply means an increase
of the amounts that can be supplied at each several price, and a diminution of the price at which each separate amount can be supplied. . . .
(pp. 462-63)

Representative Firms and Factors

A clue to the *how* and *when* and *what* of the Representative Firm,
as of any other one of the various representatives presented by
Marshall, seems possible only through careful attention to the shifts
of thought from the descriptively objective to the purely conceptual.
The representative firm in its least conjectural interpretation belongs to the true long-time normal period—itself a conceptual fact
at the extreme—that period, note, at which the costs of the representative firm in producing a commodity first become price-determining.

Thus the history of the individual firm cannot be made into the history
of an industry any more than the history of an individual man can be
made into the history of mankind. And yet . . . the aggregate production
for a general market is the outcome of the motives which induce individual producers to expand or contract their production. It is just here
that our device of a representative firm comes to our aid. . . . (p. 459)

These results will be of great importance when we come to discuss the
causes which govern *the supply price* of a commodity. We shall have to
analyze carefully the normal cost of producing a commodity, relatively
to a given aggregate volume of production; and for this purpose we
shall have to study *the expenses of a representative producer* for that
aggregate volume. . . . (p. 317)

The representative firm has replaced the departed economic man.
That firm is representative in the normal period with any particular
commodity, the marginal costs of which are commensurate with
the price of the commodity at that normal time. This commensurate-

ness of costs with market price is seemingly to be taken as the basis or the test by which representativeness exists, and is indicated as also the test by which the costs of the representative firm—its marginal costs—are declared to be price-determining; and this comes about through the fact that in this normal period the investors' earlier forecasts of income have come to be the incomes that are actually accruing:

> In long periods . . . all investments of capital and effort in providing the material plant and the organization of a business . . . have time to be adjusted to the incomes which are expected to be earned by them: and the estimates of those incomes therefore directly govern supply, and are the true long-period normal supply price of the commodities produced. (p. 377)

Not always, therefore, it seems, is the firm representative by definition; since, in these normal periods, at least, the representative firm is one that, at a particular aggregate of product in the industry, carries marginal costs that not only equal the market price, but also determine or govern it. At this period, then, and at this aggregate of product, it is a firm that is—or would be under the conditions— a firm distinctly functional in character.[4]

---

[4] Perhaps, however, this is an incorrect interpretation. For though on page 317 Marshall says that "when we come to discuss the causes which govern the supply price of a commodity . . . we shall have to study *the expenses of a representative producer* for that aggregate volume," and speaks on page 377 also of the investors' estimates of income that govern supply "and that are the true long-period normal supply price," he does not in either of these places assert that it is the marginal cost of the representative firm that governs the price. Elsewhere indeed, he has said the precise contrary; costs neither determine nor govern price:

"The part played by the net product at the margin of production . . . is apt to be misunderstood . . . many able writers have supposed that it represents the marginal use of a thing as *governing* the value of the whole. It is not so; the doctrine says we must *go to the margin to study the action of those forces which govern* the value of the whole; and that is a very different affair. Of course the withdrawal of (say) iron from any of its necessary uses would have just the same influence on its value as its withdrawal from its marginal uses. . . ." (p. 410)

". . . the general relations of demand and supply govern value. But marginal uses do not govern value; because they, together with value, are themselves governed by those general relations." (p. 411)

". . . it [cost of production] does not govern price, but it focusses the causes which do govern price." (p. 428)

If this means merely that, on the supply side of accounting for price, the marginal costs of the enterpriser are not an ultimate explanation, assent is clearly due. The position is also entirely in line with classical thought. If, however, the appeal to

There are, it seems, representative firms in non-normal periods. But we are talking of the representative firm as it is conceived to be functioning in normal periods. The normal period being, however, conceptual, the representative firm of that time must be also

these *general conditions* intends the view that ultimately in the price process discomfort costs on the supply side are marginally equated against marginal pleasures or utilities on the demand side, the position becomes definitely intelligible only by becoming plainly erroneous. The identification of marginal demand with marginal utility, and of marginal cost with marginal discomfort, becomes obviously untenable when once the ratio nature of all the items in either schedule is recognized. Quantitative marginal utilities, as distinguished from relative marginal utilities, are never indicated by price offers or by goods offers. Nor more are quantitative discomforts indicated by marginal money costs.

If, however, Marshall intends no more by this appeal to the general conditions of demand and supply than the declaration that the superficial facts of price or goods offers, and especially of enterprisers' price costs, can attain ultimate explanation only on the level of the general underlying conditions—such is no doubt the truth; but it is so far an obvious truth as to stand for the purposes as not greatly significant. All things may safely be asserted to have explanations of precisely this sort—one and the same explanation for all—excepting that to assert only thus much does not, in any human sense of the term, offer an explanation. Instead, it merely asserts that somewhere there is one, if only it may be found. To serve as explanation for any price, these facts of ultimate appeal have specifically to be articulated with the actual process through which these ultimate causes find their expression.

Moreover, if Marshall intends to deny as a process fact the fixation or determination of price by cost of production, he is repudiating a central thesis of the classical economics. Interpreted in this sense, the general conditions of demand and supply offer, indeed, not a substitute explanation, but no explanation at all. Nor is there any virtue in the term *govern* instead of *determine*. Certainly a safer statement for Marshall would run that, on the supply side, not marginal costs of production but just the costs of different producers account for a volume of product such that the price adjusts at the marginal price offer and at the costs of the marginal producer. It is doubtless clear that price offers and goods offers are schedule facts, with each schedule reporting a series of ratios. It is certain also that each several producer in his productive commitments plans a volume of output not gainfully to be extended in view of the prices to be expected. In this sense, then, he has such a thing as a margin of production. But whether in ultimate analysis increments of product bear on prices by the test of their peculiar incremental costs, or only as affecting the average unit costs of each enterpriser's output is a further matter. It is possible that the presence of these differential marginal costs in the output of any particular enterpriser turns merely on the presence of both prime and supplementary costs, the different datings of different commitments, or on those post-commitment readjustments that are imposed by unstable price conditions. The cost analysis in the completely forward-looking view, as also the analysis appropriate to conditions meeting accurately the expectations of the investment period, may plausibly be presented as leaving no room for different costs for different items in the output of any particular enterpriser. But this is an issue for later examination.

In any case the underlying causes that account for the demands and the supplies schedules for any commodity must account also for the determination of the market price *through these schedules*. In this intermediate, this non-ultimate, sense, it is conceptual. But inasmuch as at no other time is it taken to be functioning in point of costs as a price-affecting influence, it does not greatly matter whether for other periods it is or is not similarly conceptual. Clearly, however, the representative firm of the normal

---

these schedules that determine the price. If there is in this aspect any perceptible difference in meaning between *determine* or *fix* and *govern,* it is a distinction that escapes me. And Marshall has made no attempt to indicate or explain it. If there is advantage on the side of the word *govern,* it is as a word of less precise and specific meaning; better by being merely less definitely committing—mere protective coloration. And even thus much of distinction I do not appreciate. What, for the interpretation of Marshall's thought, does the distinction mean to you? As far as I can find, you must make this out for yourself. You are left to infer what Marshall does not tell you, through reference to contexts that in turn do not tell. No matter what alluring vistas of possibility vagueness may leave open, never is it a nearer approach to explanation. At the best, it is merely a larger room in which to pursue your own search. It only baffles discussion or criticism, if you find no new meaning in this new word that is offered as some sort of enrichment or amelioration of *fix* or *determine.* For my own part, I don't get the new meaning, but only a new unprecision. *Govern* is not, to be sure, a vague word or an unexplaining word, but only, for the purposes of any relevant distinction, an unspecific word, and a word which, if it hides issues, does it only in the strict sense that it does hide them. If, in point of intention, it reports some clean-cut distinction, that distinction should be made precise, in order that the issues offered should become appropriate for examination. Here as elsewhere the first obligation of the reader is to understand. Wherefore the first obligation of the expositor is is to make his position clear. In any meaning that I can attach to *govern* in this connection it means *determine.* What particular distinguishable thing else does Marshall mean by it? All that he implies is that he does not mean *determine,* but just something else—oblivious of any obligation to tell exactly what else.

I fancy, however, that, as earlier, he may have in mind the "basement" level of approach. But this also means not much more than the obvious, until it gets over into a precise statement, as also until it arrives at a precise articulation with the process facts of enterpriser cost. He has in mind—as I infer—the fact that these "basement" data do somehow in their working get themselves focussed into terms of enterpriser costs. But explanation must amount here to telling *how.* As he leaves the analysis, his recourse to the general conditions of demand and supply reads not like support and supplementation of the enterpriser cost process, but rather as a displacing of it and a repudiation of it—a position that he didn't need to take, an erroneous position, as I hold, and also a position discrediting and abandoning the theoretical system that he has made it his task to justify and to defend.

And further, in so far as ever with him prices receive any explanation other than that of the general conditions of demand and supply, they get this explanation from cost of production, and from cost of production that is—at the latest step of it, at least—cost in the money sense. And he repeatedly recognizes price as dependent on marginal cost of production in the usual as also in the classical sense. For present purposes, therefore, it need not matter that, in the sense of the classical analysis, one may believe in the determination of price by money cost of production, and yet may definitely deny the determination—as a long-run and forward-looking computation—by *marginal* costs of production. Nearer the truth, as I hold, is Marshall's position in the following:

period is the normal firm of that period, the *representative* and the *normal* being for that time interconvertible terms. The price of that time is reported by Marshall to be equal to the marginal costs of

---

"... we must *go to the margin to study the action of those forces which govern* the value of the whole. ... Of course the withdrawal of (say) iron from any of its necessary uses would have just the same influence on its value as its withdrawal from its marginal uses ... iron, or any other agent of production, is not (under ordinary circumstances) thrown out of use except at points at which its use yields no clear surplus of profit; that is, it is thrown out from its marginal uses only." (p. 410)

But the purposes of the present discussion must be clearly held in mind. We are trying to find out precisely what in the normal period—presumably the true long-period normal—Marshall presents as the relations of the costs of production of the representative firm to price. Its marginal costs of production, it is clear, are reported to be commensurate with price. But what is to be made of the seeming insistence that not even the marginal costs of even the representative firm of these normal periods are to be understood either to determine or to govern prices? Does Marshall mean merely that the marginal cost and the marginal product of the representative firm bear on the price of the product in the sense and in the degree solely that the supra-marginal costs and items bear on it? Or is it his view that all these items of product have one and the same costs—all of them being marginal, and all being cost-determining, in the sense that any one of them is?

It is at any rate certain that the fact distinctive of the representative firm is that its *marginal* costs are commensurate with price. Possibly also they are held to *govern* the price, but to govern it in the sense solely of indicating or of recording, as items of cost in the enterpriser's cost process, the working of the underlying and ultimate causal influences. For it is clear that in general Marshall's analysis does attach to the marginal item of product a peculiar functional significance with respect to the price of the product. Of thus much the marginal-isolation procedure, by which he finds himself able to urge that true rents always—like quasi-rents temporarily—are price-determined or price-governed, the while that in normal periods all hires of cost-acquired goods and all hires of labor (some parts of extraordinary-ability hires being excluded) become price-determining or price-governing; may stand as the decisive proof. Never with him do true rents carry any price-causal significance, no matter what may or may not, by the "basement" approach, be the case with the lands themselves. Always true rents are made the results of price in a sense that not always are any other hires or outlays. True rents are held never to enter into those costs that influence prices. The hires that have this causal influence are the non-land hires, those hires that make part of the costs of production on marginal lands, or at the intensive margin of supra-marginal lands.

The tenability of this marginal-isolation procedure is not now in question. Only the fact of it is to the present purpose; and this fact is to the purpose solely as showing that non-land hires are presented by Marshall as price-explaining or price-causing in a sense that land hires are not. This position is plainly pivotal to classical doctrine in general and to any systematic defense of classical doctrine. Marshall takes it.

Moreover, Marshall's commitments are elsewhere many to the view that marginal costs of production—in the superficial and representative sense, it may well be—have the determining and functional bearings on price that traditionally in classical thought, as also among economists in general, they have been taken to have.

the representative, the normal, producer—and perhaps also to be determined by, or governed by, the marginal costs of that producer:

> Let us call to mind the "representative firm," whose economies of production, internal and external, are dependent on the aggregate volume of production of the commodity that it makes; and, postponing all further study of the nature of this dependence, let us assume that the normal supply price of any amount of that commodity may be taken to be its normal expenses of production . . . by that firm . . . the price the expectation of which will just suffice to maintain the existing aggregate amount of production. . . ." (pp. 342-43)

And thus it follows that there must be taken to be as many representative producers in this true long-time normal period as there are different products and therefore different cost-of-production schedules for these different products. For it is clear that each representative producer has his particular cost-of-production schedule reporting his unit costs or his marginal costs for his different volumes of output:

> Thus the history of the individual firm cannot be made into the history of an industry. . . . And yet . . . the aggregate production for a general market is the outcome of the motives which induce individual producers to expand or contract their production. It is just here that our device of a representative firm comes to our aid. We *imagine to ourselves* at *any* time a firm that has its fair share of those internal and external economies, which appertain to the aggregate scale of production in the industry to which it belongs. We recognize that the size of such a firm . . . is governed, other things being equal, by the general expansion of the industry. We regard the manager of it as reckoning up whether . . . he should introduce a certain new machine and so on. We regard him as treating the output which would result from that change more or less *as a unit,* and weighing in his mind the cost against the gain.
>
> This then is the *marginal* cost on which we fix our eyes . . . we . . . expect a gradual increase in demand to increase gradually the size and the efficiency of this representative firm. . . .
>
> . . . when making lists of supply prices (supply *schedules*) for long period in *these industries*. . . . (pp. 459-60)

> In a stationary state. . . There would be no distinction between long-period and short-period normal value . . . for the representative firm . . . always doing the same class of business . . . in the same way . . . its normal expenses by which the normal supply price *is governed* would be always

the same. The demand lists of prices would always·be the same, and so would the *supply lists.* . . . (pp. 367-68)

Wherefore it is clear that, at any other price for each commodity than that which is taken to be the actual normal price of it, another producer would be the normal representative producer:

And as with the growth of trees, so was it with the growth of businesses as a general rule before the great recent development of vast joint-stock companies. . . . Now that rule is far from universal . . . after a while, the guidance of the business falls into the hands of people with less energy and less creative genius. . . .
. . . the general character of our conclusions is not very much affected by the facts that many of these economies depend directly on the size of the individual establishments . . . and that in almost every trade there is a constant rise and fall of large businesses, at any one moment some firms being in the ascending phase and others in the descending. . . .

. . . We shall have to analyze carefully the normal cost of producing a commodity, relatively to a given aggregate of production; and for this purpose we shall have to study *the expenses of a representative producer* for that aggregate volume. . . . (pp. 316-17; italics Marshall's)

And it must also be clear that with each commodity there are an indefinite number of non-representative and, in this sense therefore, non-normal producers in the normal time:

At any particular moment some businesses will be rising and others falling. . . . Any particular increase of production may be due to some new manufacturer who is struggling against difficulties . . . in the hope that he may gradually build up a good business. . . . (p. 378)

In the normal time, therefore, it seems, the representative firm may be the sole fully adjusted firm—a non-equilibrated time. The representative firm is that one among the various producers of each particular commodity whose marginal cost is commensurate with the market price. It is not, then, as of necessity, a firm marginal as a unit, either in the long or in the short time, but only the firm whose *marginal* cost at *that time* is identical with the going market price:

. . . if nature is offering a sturdy resistance . . . the supply price will rise; but if the volume of production were greater, it would perhaps be profitable to substitute largely machine work for hand work and steam power for muscular force; and the increase in the volume of production would have diminished the expenses of production of the commodity of our representative firm. . . . (pp. 344-45)

The representative position or function is then not likely to be held long by any particular producer. Stability in the particular price means therefore the stability of marginal costs with changing representative producers; and thus it permits, and indeed requires, the shifting of representativeness from one firm to another:

. . . the growth of his [the able man's] business brings with it similar economies of specialized machines and plant of all kinds. . . . The increase in the scale of his business increases rapidly the advantages which he has over his competitors, and lowers the price at which he can afford to sell. This process . . . if it could endure for a hundred years, he and one or two others like him would divide between them the whole of that branch of industry. . . .

But here we may read a lesson from the young trees of the forest as they struggle upwards through the benumbing shade of their older rivals . . . those few become stronger with every year, they get a larger share of light and air . . . they tower above their neighbours, and seem as though they would grow on forever. . . . But they do not . . . sooner or later age tells on them all . . . and one after another they give place to others. . . . (pp. 315-16)

. . . it will suffice to suppose that firms rise and fall, but that the "representative" firm remains always of about the same size, as does the representative tree of a virgin forest. . . . (p. 367)

. . . Thus the rise and fall of individual firms may be frequent, while a great industry is . . . moving steadily forward; as the leaves of a tree . . . grow to maturity, reach equilibrium, and decay many times, while the tree is steadily growing upwards year by year. (p. 457)

But at this normal time, then, the money cost of the representative firm—a changing firm, but with the aggregate output of it and of the industry remaining unchanged—appears to fix or govern, on the supply side, the price of product. Changing prices would modify the product, or changing product the prices. But the firm that is representative is nevertheless a changing firm.

This normal situation is, of course, one that remains alive, with competition actively going on within it, and with the waxing and waning of individual fortunes—just as the forest or the stream may be a changeless total made up of swiftly changing units; or as the merchant may maintain his stock of goods intact, although particular units are constantly being replaced by others. Recall merely that this true long-period normal is simply the *terminus-ad-quem,* the conceptual goal at which things would arrive, if the processes of change were only suspended long enough to allow a complete equilibration to be reached. It is a point—that is, it would be a point—where all distinctions between prime and supplementary costs must be taken to have been erased, and where all hires—excepting true rents—must have shifted into price-determining influences.

It seems, nevertheless, that there are short-period normal values —possibly for one particular commodity. Marshall says (p. 367): "In a stationary state. . . .There would be no distinction between long-period and short-period normal value. . . ." Nowhere, however, it seems, is there asserted for any normal period—true long-time or any other—any normal buyer or consumer, nor, securely, any normal seller—a serious and even a disastrous theoretical lack, unless these normal data are, by assumption, taken to be conceptually provided; for normal demands are assumed, though seemingly attaching to no one in particular—along with normal supplies. Perhaps there are also normal price-offer schedules, or even a representative price-offerer or a representative price-offer schedule. But as we have earlier noted, Marshall recognizes with the normal analysis the schedule nature of both the demand and the supply facts. And he indicates clearly that in the stationary state the representative firm of that time would have a supply schedule. It is in fact representative in normal times by the test that the market price is identical with the marginal cost of its aggregate production.

It is, then, safely to be asserted that what is normal in any period is representative in that period, and that any normal period connotes at least one representative producer in that period.

But what about representative firms, and other representatives, in all of the various and different short-period normals? Representativeness, it is clear, may accrue long before any true long-period normal can have arrived, either conceptually or objectively. The representative producer of any time is seemingly that producer whose marginal costs, in view of his product at that time, are identical with the market prices of that time:

. . . the normal cost of producing a commodity, relatively to a given aggregate volume of production . . . *the expenses of a representative producer* for that aggregate volume. . . . (p. 317)

. . . The normal price for any given daily supply of fish . . . is the price which will *quickly* call into the fishing trade capital and labour enough to obtain that supply in a day's fishing of average good fortune. . . . (p. 370)

Precisely what *flows* with demand and with supply may mean for price theory deserves attention in this connection. Not some one price, certainly, but rather a series of prices must be implied. Each point or item in the series must report an equilibrium at the particular time between the two funds summing up at the time in two stocks accumulated from the flows. For consumption must also be conceived as a flow. For price purposes the funds exist only after account is taken of the deductions through the collateral flow of consumption. The goods-offer schedule equating at any particular time against the price-offer schedule of that time affords the particular price resultant of that time. Each price in the time series of prices has therefore been arrived at as the equating point between two funds that are, for the purpose, not themselves flows but the funds provided by the flows. As a price series the graphical presentation must trace an irregular line of adjustment from left to right dividing into equal parts a ribbon area of demands and supplies schedules. *Flows* permit of no one price but only of a series of prices, a price flow. Wherefore accurately there can be no one normal price for a period, excepting in the sense of some sort of representative price as the mean or mode or median of a price series.

But no single price in the series is a stable price. It is by mathematical processes solely that any one normal price can be arrived at, and this as a center of oscillation and not as a factual price for the period, or securely for any one time during the period. But, differing only in degree, any time or period, month, year or millenium, becomes by these mathematical procedures a normal period. Stability as the essential trait of normality disappears:

. . . some commodities . . . conform pretty closely to the law of constant return. . . . In such a case the normal level about which the market price fluctuates will be this definite and fixed (money) cost of production. . . . . . . if a person chooses to neglect market fluctuations . . . then he may be excused for . . . speaking of (normal) price as governed by *cost of production*. . . . (p. 349)

No criticism is intended here of the concept of flows. The purpose is solely to make clear what they mean for price analysis. The dynamic view of prices never discredits or displaces, but only supplements, the static view. The significance of any change is reported only through one static analysis for the beginning and another for the end of the period of change—dynamic processes not processes in limitless space, but processes with terminals.

And in the *short-period* normal situation, what about the relation of the costs of the representative firm of that time to the market prices of that time? It appears—but not securely—to be a relation of the representative firm or firms to the price of but one commodity, or, possibly, to one group of commodities. As in the true long-period normal there may be several representative producers of one particular good, so, it seems, there may be in this less normal—but still normal—time, several different producers of that particular good with reference to which the time is a normal time.

Therefore with any one particular good a normal price in the short-run sense should, it seems, imply the disappearance of any distinctions between prime and supplementary costs. But this appears not to be the Marshall doctrine:

Thus, although nothing but prime cost enters *necessarily and directly* into the supply price for short periods, it is yet true that supplementary costs also exert some influence indirectly. . . . (p. 376)

This quotation may not, however, refer to short-period normals; though it occurs in the course of normal-price discussions, and in a chapter entitled *Equilibrium of Normal Demand and Supply . . . with Reference to Long and Short Periods.*

There is, then, in the short-period normal a representative pro
ducer for at least one particular good. And he is representative by
the test that his marginal costs are commensurate with the price
of the particular good. There should, indeed, be representative pro
ducers at all times for all commodities, irrespective of whether the
several prices are or are not normal. But, if there are, the particular
traits or indicia of recognition are not clear. Recognition is, however
always possible, though mistakes are possible, and perhaps probable,
in arriving at a judgment of representativeness—not merely in
ordinary times or in short-period normal times, but even also in
true long-period normals:

. . . a Representative firm is that particular sort of average firm, at which
we need to look in order to see how far the economies, *internal* and
external, of production on a large scale have extended generally *in the
industry* and country in question. We cannot see this by looking at one
or two firms taken at random: but we can see it fairly well by selecting,
after a broad survey, a firm . . . (or better still, more than one) that
represents, to the best of our judgment, this particular average. (p. 318)

As we have earlier seen, forecasts of normality may readily
be discredited by eventualities. And these present judgments may
also be erroneous; and many of them admittedly are so. But when
they are right, by what criteria are they right? Just what is a normal
firm or, at a normal period, a representative firm?

How many representative producers there may be in any one
trade is not yet clear. The analysis thus far, however, would seem
to make room for several, or even many, though different forecasters
or observers might variously select them. But what man or firm
among the different entrants to a trade will turn out to be representative? One at least in any normal time there will be, and perhaps in
any time; and thereby, when a long-period normality should arrive,
the marginal costs of this representative firm will govern the price
of the product.

Suppose now that some one entrant into the trade has it in mind
to become a representative producer in the trade; though why he
should so decide, or why hope so much or so little, we are not
informed. But is it a far goal? That must presumably depend on

what particular kind or grade of normality he expects and intends. It might be decades or even generations ahead. Some sort of normality, however, he may expect to achieve early—if he tries—or perhaps equally well if he does not try. But how far ahead in point of time is he to look? And on what facts must his reasonable expectation be conditioned?

. . . anyone proposing to start a new business in any trade. . . . If himself a man of *normal* capacity for that *class of work,* he may look forward *ere long* to his business being a representative one . . . with its *fair share* of the economies of production on a large scale. . . . (p. 377)

But he will not, it seems, harbor this hope or this expectation unless he regards himself as a man of normal capacity for his class of work. Men are not, it is true, always self-appraising in just this sort, or always thus modest in their self-appraisals. Nor commonly does a man enter a business with this moderate enthusiasm for its prospects or for his prospects in it.

But taking himself to be a man of normal capacity for this sort of work, what considerations will persuade him to enter the trade? And, in turn, what considerations will be similarly persuasive with a man self-appraised as of lower capacity; or of higher capacity?

. . . If the net earnings of such a representative business seem likely to be greater than he could get by similar investments in other trades to which he has access, he will choose this trade. . . . (p. 377)

Take it, then, that this man, self-appraised as of normal capacity, does or may decide after this sort. But would not any man, whatever his capacity or his appraisal of it, be equally prone to make his decision by precisely this same test? Assume some particular man to be, or to believe himself to be, (a) a fairly low-grade individual; or (b) a man of exceptionally brilliant prospects: in either case it would equally hold that "if the net earnings of such a representative business seem likely to be greater than he could get by similar investments in other trades to which he has access, he will choose this trade." We have, then, no need of normal men as entrants; no need of their regarding themselves as normal; nor of any decision to enter that is special to any grade of entrant or to any grade of self-appraisal. Nor does it seem actual that a man who is considering various alternative fields of investment will have in thought with any one of them a firm or business representative or normal in that field; although he will certainly consider whether the trade in general is achieving relatively attractive gains and bids fair thus to continue.[5]

But assuming that this man were disposed to look for and to fix upon a representative firm, how would he go about it? Take it that he sets himself to select a firm or business that is, we will say, model; or average; or typical; or usual. Precisely what is a representative firm? What are the insignia?

. . . On the one hand we shall not want to select some new producer just struggling into business . . . nor on the other hand shall we want to take a firm which by exceptionally long-sustained ability and good fortune has got together a vast business. . . . But our representative firm must be one which has had a *fairly* long life, and *fair* success, which is managed with *normal* ability, and which has *normal* access to the economies, external *and internal,* which belong to *that aggregate* volume of production; account being taken of the class of goods produced, the conditions of marketing them and the economic environment generally. (p. 317)

These requirements are, then, that the firm must be of some particular, but in point of statement, unspecific, (1) age; (2) advantages; (3) profits; (4) past ability of management; (5) good fortune; (6) normal ability of current management; (7) normal access to external economies; (8) normal access to internal economies; (9); (10); (11); (12); (13); (14); (15); (16); (17); account taken of all these various specific conditions with reference to, (a) the class of goods, (b) the conditions of market-

---

[5] It is certain that from among the investor-entrants representatives cannot be declared as of the date of entry. Each of the investors is a marginal investor at his final unit of investment. But it is obviously from among these entrants that later a representative is to be selected. Those investors, however, if any there are, who look forward to becoming ere long representative investors, must most of them, and probably all of them, be disappointed by the event. Under this head Marshall quotes Leroy-Beaulieu to the effect that out of every one-hundred new businesses that are started twenty disappear almost at once, fifty or sixty vegetate neither rising nor falling, and only ten or fifteen are successful. It should again be noted that the distinguishing trait of representativeness is the reporting of that investment return adequate to induce enough entrant investment to maintain the stability of prices.

ing, and (c) the economic environment generally. Whether then, there are 34 or 51 or 68 or more different tests with which the representative firm must concurrently comply, may not be in justice clear; nor is it clear what *fair* and *normal* should in these connections be taken to mean. But take it that there are only 10 different lines of test; and that there is one chance in 50 that any particular firm will meet the requirement of, say, age; or size; and so on. Generously estimated, therefore, the chances are some billions to one against any particular firm fulfilling these cumulative requirements. The chance of picking the firm rightly are inconsiderable, even though there existed much of a chance of their being any to pick. It would not, for example, be especially difficult, were there available bases of information, to select a man of average height; or of average weight; or possibly of average proportions of limbs to one another; and of each of these to head; or to feet; or even of average complexion. But it would be an entirely safe adventure to kill the first man you should see meeting all of these requirements at once. And should there be any firm meeting these earlier multiple specifications, what warrant is there for holding that the marginal costs of this firm would be identical with the market price—unless, indeed, the marginal costs of every firm must be thus identical? Moreover, it would be ill should it turn out that in the very nature of the true long-period normal, there can be—or could be—no differentiated marginal costs. But this in its due time. It is, however, possible that in Marshall's thought all of these various and separate tests telescope —under normal conditions—into the one requirement of a median or average or modal gain, either in volume or in rate. On any other terms, the notion has seemingly to be one near to impossibility of attainment even in basically conceptual conditions—that is to say, in factually impossible conditions. But even so, the difficulties with regard to marginality would be not the less serious.

But it is promptly to be added that whether this selection can be made, or how securely made, or by what tests arrived at, cannot greatly matter. For no true long-period normal is in prospect. And at no pre-normal time are either money or real costs held to have, any determining relation to prices. The costs result from the prices that the general conditions of demand and supply purport to explain. Therefore nothing of importance turns on whether at these times there is any representative firm; or how many there may be; or how the one or more may be selected; or what are the insignia; or whether the selection is correct or incorrect. Only when quasi-rents and supplementary costs in general cease to be functionally differentiated from prime costs—in purely conceptual periods, that is—can any of these issues concern us; that is, never.

Marshall presents, however, the representative firm of any ordinary time as a descriptively objective fact—its marginal costs therefore identical with the actual price. But not the less are its costs price-determining, this fact being, indeed, the occasion for the appeal to the normal period—in which solely are prices to be found determined by costs—or, at all events, explained by costs.

But something further requires to be said if, in the short-period normal, there is a situation partaking in sufficient degree of the qualities of the true normal period so that all costs—other, of course, than true rents—become price-determining. And similarly, something further must be said if the meaning of a short-period normal is that, within a system of prices that are not normal, some one particular price becomes normal. For this would mean the price-determining function of the costs of that particular commodity, the while that the costs of other commodities continued to be price-determined—the rent of your mule, or the wages of many of your employees price-determined; while my mule and my employees must be getting hires that are price-determining.

Chapter XIII

COSTS IN GENERAL

UNLESS selling prices indemnify producers' costs, the goods will not get produced. This is, however, a generalization having rightly to do only with money costs, because it has to do only with money receipts. The reference is to costs from the point of view of the enterpriser-employer. It holds also that if his outlays do not afford a sufficient inducement to the payees, the individuals in the employee relation, for turning over to his control the agents of production, he must fail of attaining this control. And with the analysis pushed further stages back; if these payees in turn have to submit to money costs in providing productive agents, his payments to them must indemnify them for their costs of production, else the productive agents must ultimately cease to be forthcoming. The outlays of each employer are in turn the receipts of his employee-producers. This is not a recondite truth; what you collect from me I pay to you.

It is clear, then, that this regress method of accounting for some of the enterpriser's costs is a possible way. And if somewhere in the regress line, these money costs resolve into something else than money costs, and something explanatory of them, a most significant step will have been achieved. There is in this aspect, however, nothing significant in any regress from one purely money cost to another.

But no enterpriser's selling price needs at any particular time to indemnify the enterpriser for more than the immediate charges that the situation of the immediate time imposes on him. The outlay by him necessary at the time for control of any particular factor is its cost to him. It need not be an indemnity adequate to the covering of all the costs attaching to the factor in the regress aspect, but only enough to overcome the resistance at that time to his control of it at that time. His costs may, then, go along with losses to operators or investors earlier than himself in the regress series, either immediate or distant.

And if the enterpriser has been himself an investor in materials, in cost-produced equipment, in lands, or in business organization, the money debits that *now* the selling price must cover may fall indefinitely short of a full indemnity for his total of money costs, inclusive of those in the regress aspect. The credits now for whatever he produces now must be merely enough to justify now his choice to maintain, so far, his output.

The generalization, therefore, that the selling credits must indemnify the money debits in production holds only in a meaning appropriate to the particular time for which it speaks. Understood as covering more than the debits appropriate to that time, the error is manifest. As Professor Carver has pointed out, the crop will get harvested if only the price returns from it will be enough to cover the price burdens attaching to the mere harvesting. But the prospect of returns at this level will not induce a new crop. Or at cultivating time, the field will get cultivated if only the prospective prices promise to indemnify the price burdens reckoned forward from that date. But in the long run these returns must be inadequate. And similarly with the farm and the equipment and the family labor that are already committed: planting will take place, not as conditioned on an adequate investment return, but only on returns indemnifying the debits attending the making of the crop. But prospective returns at this low level must mean smaller stocks of equipment later, deteriorating farm buildings, starved lands, the diminished hiring of labor, and possibly also the partial or even the complete diversion of investment and of family effort from this line of production. Other crops may be substituted. The family may move to town.

But it does not follow that the farm will go unused. In fact, not all of the alternatives open to this cultivating owner have been noted. The ranking alternative policy that attaches a land cost to his own cultivation of the farm, or to part of it, or to his equipment goods and stock, or to part of either, may be the selling or the renting of them. His own labor also he may divert in part or entirely into teaching school or soliciting life insurance. Or he may shift into tenant farming or become the hired man of another cultivator. The rent that he could get by leasing his farm may as clearly be a cost to him as to another cultivator that should lease the farm. Similarly of his own property holdings or of his own labor. The distribution of proprietorships has no essential bearing on the analysis. Foregone incomes, "virtual outlays," may be costs along with outlays in the strict sense. Always it is the ranking price alternative that reports the price resistance and the indemnity level. It is easy to misapply the distinction between prime and supplementary costs. A supplementary cost to one operator may be a prime cost to another.

The principle that credits from sales must indemnify the entire series of debits that production imposes—that money costs fix market prices—holds only in the completely forward-looking view of costs. But it approximates the truth for any producer who buys or hires for his current productive undertaking any earlier produced productive agent. The individuals that have earlier produced the agent for hire or sale have no such assurance. But, as they may receive less than the return on the expectation of which their investments were conditioned, so, on the other hand, they may receive more. In the longer view, however, the flow of investment is the regulative influence to approximate the actual returns to the conditioning expectations. It is this forward-looking process as a long-time influence that justifies the generalization that cost of production determines prices, in the sense of an indemnity for the entire regress series of agents and inventories.

But in the sense of indemnifying current producers for their current outlays to command the intermediates of production, the broader generalization still holds; subject always, however, to the limitations imposed by the particular time venue, and to due allowances for the lags and unprecisions attaching especially to the shorter-time processes of adjustment.

It is, then, obvious that the prices appropriate to this shorter-time process may be notably above or notably below the prices toward which this longer-time process is tending—the prices which, were conditions sufficiently stable, the results of the process would finally approach; prices not, to be sure, such that they can be forecasted in precise terms, but only in some general approximation. With time enough, that is to say, the prices in a price system will adjust to one another into something approaching a stable system. The principle of adjustment is always the opportunity-cost principle, both on the supply and on the demand side of each price. Any price offer for any commodity is arrived at by reference to what the purchasing power will alternatively command. The price or hire of any cost good in one use must be not less than that at which a competing use will take it. Investment in indirect goods of any sort is conditioned on something better not elsewhere offering. This opportunity-cost principle is then the leading principle of these processes of systematic equilibrium, in buying, in producing, and in investing. In the sense, therefore, of illustrating this principle, each price and all prices have normals—in the sense of one point or of a system of points of stable equilibrium appropriate to any given set of fundamental conditions. In strict logic, also, as we have already seen, no one price could be a stable price excepting as all other prices had stabilized—a price system, a system of interdependent and interacting prices.

It is, then, solely after this sort that Marshall's account of normal price and of normal price systems must be interpreted so far as it is to be defended. And in this sense it is an entirely defensible account of the process. It must be noted, however, that while Marshall invokes normal or representative producers, and *a* normal or *the* normal demand, and *a* normal or *the* normal supply—both as quantitative totals—he finds nowhere a representative item of demand or a representative item of supply, but only a representative or normal producer. Nor anywhere does he find to his purpose a representative or normal buyer, or middleman, or laborer, or lender, or borrower, or investor. With none of these does he find occasion for means or modes or medians. Nor anywhere by the test of the objective facts does the economic process, descriptively presented, make call for any assumptions or devices of this generally representative sort. It is, indeed, the especial significance of the familiar marginal analysis, wherever it is in place, that it has been effective to set economics free from the need of any average or economic men, or of representative lands or machines or landlords or buyers or sellers or consumers. Nowhere, in fact, is there room for normals excepting in the sense of setting limits on the working of the descriptively objective processes. Nor is there more need anywhere for normals or representatives with the machine processes of industry than with other acquisitive—and in this sense productive—activities of professional men or merchants or transporters or speculators. A representative *chose in action* or lawsuit or research staff is as much in place as a representative worker or factory or manufacturer. It is doubtless true that no observer can more securely select a marginal producer, or the marginal item of any producer's product, than he can select a representative producer. But in the actual process there are these margins; they are descriptive and not merely conceptual facts. There are no representative producers and no representative items of output in the aggregate product in society or in any one industry. Economic men or representative activities or situations are devices of analytical indolence and vagueness, only one degree less pernicious for competitive problems than is the collective or the organic approach. Even if and when the competitive process should have equilibrated, there could be no representative items in the still on-going competitive processes. Because this competitive process is, in the very nature of it, a completely individualized process, all accounts of it in terms of organism or of representatives or averages or norms are not merely gratuitous; they are unfaithful to the objective facts. They are not in the process. And even equilibrium conditions are implicit in the process only in the sense of trend, as something that under stable conditions, long enough continued, will in the nature of the process become actual. The representative firm is a concept adapted to excuse the economist from formulating generalizations that will cover the actual and individual character of all the real processes:

. . . the aggregate production for a general market is the outcome of the motives which induce individual producers to expand or contract their production. It is just here that our device of a representative firm comes to our aid. . . . We regard the manager of it as reckoning up whether it would be worth his while to add a certain new line to his undertakings; whether he should introduce a certain new machine and so on. We regard him as treating the output which would result from that change more or less [which asserts, at the most, only somewhat] as a unit. . . . (pp. 459-60)

Rightly arrived at and rightly employed for purposes of analysis, there are, then, no serious objections to be urged to these normals. Something in this general nature the business man employs in those forecasts of conditions in the light of which his plans and policies for the future have to be currently formulated. In view of things as they are, and of the possible or probable modifications of them, he must do his planning, in the conscious or implicit recognition of the opportunity-cost principle and of its application in the evening-up of things.

It is, therefore, not so much against Marshall's interpretation of normals, of their nature or of the methods of their arrival, as against the doctrinal significance of them, present and future, that criticism is to be directed. Assuming that they will come, or may come, what about them when they do come? What doctrinal significance attaches at the present to the assumption—or will attach to normals when they have come, or would attach if they did come?

Their significance for Marshall' system of thought is both extra-ordinary and pivotal. For it is only in normal conditions—and these of not quite determinate sort—that in Marshall's view cost of production can come into a price-determining relation to prices. In pre-normal or interim periods, most costs of production derive, in his view, from prices—as always, it is to be noted, do true rent costs. It is thereby that normals come to be functionally of pivotal significance. What earlier were results, come now to take on a price-influencing or determining or governing relation to prices. The directions of flow in the cause-and-result sequence are reversed—what was result becomes now cause. Prices now derive from costs, while earlier they derived solely from the general conditions of demand and supply, in a sense that for explanatory purposes makes no account of costs. True, the normal period is—or better, will be—or best, would be—a period of persisting competitive activities in neither greater nor less degree or kind than before it was. But the systematic analysis becomes a new one. The processes that persist fall into new functional categories. The analysis that before held, holds no longer. What was never before true—that costs of production explain or determine prices—comes now into its new time and rights of truth. Thereby the classical doctrine still stands, to be sure, unquestioned—but only for those times that objectively never are. Economic situations are merely always tending toward times at which the classical account will, or would, hold. Its truth is that of trend solely—not accurately toward prospects that are merely remote, the far-off divine events that creation is to achieve; but only toward conditions that are of mere logical or conceptual validity, or of that golden time when the traveller's journey is done and the years have passed away. For any ordinary time and conditions, it is certain that classical doctrine does not hold. The truth that is in it belongs solely with the normal period.

It is not, then, in Marshall's view, because of the readjustments that are constantly taking place, or even of the modification in fundamental conditions that may be gradually going on; and not because of the retardations and unprecisions in the influence of costs on prices, that the classical explanation of the prices of ordinary times is inadequate. Nor is it merely that—in Marshall's view—it confuses the causal relations. It is worse than this: it precisely reverses in its account the sequences that are held to be actual. It interprets as cause that which is effect. By functional tests it is error, *during these interim* periods. The residual of truth that is in it is, therefore, only for normal conditions. It would, however, always hold, if only these long-time processes of adaptation and readjustment were purely logical and timeless in their working. Solely, then, in this long-time logical view does the classical doctrine make its case.[1]

[1] It must be obvious that this interpretation of Marshall attributes to him the view that *in normal periods* all of the enterpriser's outlays in the hires of agents—other than land, of course—together with most or all of the incomes accruing to him from his investment in non-land agents, have a causal, that is to say, a price-

Commonly, however, in both ordinary and normal periods, demand is treated by Marshall, not as a self-warranting datum, but as itself requiring to be explained. And as somehow related to utility or to marginal utility it achieves its explanation. When so regarded and so explained, demand holds always the causal relation to price, never the result relation.

---

determining or price-governing, relation to the price of his products; and that in pre-normal periods the cause-and-result relation runs in the reverse direction.

It must, however, be pointed out that in at least one connection Marshall denies, or appears to deny, that ever any hire, even of cost-acquired agents, is price-determining—except, possibly, the hires of pure effort:

". . . Quasi-rent . . . is a necessary profit [capital return] in regard to those other (supplementary) costs which must be incurred in the long run in addition to prime costs; and which in some industries . . . are very much more important than prime costs. *It is no part of cost under any conditions:* but the confident expectation of coming quasi-rents is a necessary condition for the investment of capital in machinery, and for the incurring of supplementary costs generally." (p. 424, note)

It is possible that Marshall has in mind here that not the hire of an agent, but the mere existence of it, is the fact of ultimate bearing on price—the "basement" level of approach. If so, however, this is to place machinery and land as, at the time, on the same level of causal status; and should deny equally the causal bearing of most effort hires and of raw-material prices, all these being equally existent as productive facts; and it even puts in question the causal status of pure-effort hires, excepting possibly at their minimum of requirement. There is support for this interpretation in the fact that the note refers to a paragraph on the same page that reads as follows:

"In this connection it may be noted that the opinion that the existence of inferior land, or other agents of production, tends to raise the rents of the better agents is not merely untrue. It is the reverse of the truth. For, if the bad land were to be flooded and rendered incapable of producing anything at all, the cultivation of other land would need be more intensive; and therefore the price of the product would be higher, and rents generally would be higher. . . ." (p. 424)

On the whole, however, I take language of this note to indicate merely that Marshall is here using the word *cost* in a meaning unusual with him; that he intends not money cost but *real cost,* and is speaking in the regress emphasis. If, however, his position here is neither carelessness in terms; nor shift in level of analysis, with error at that; nor repudiation of his general position—it must follow merely that I have systematically erred in my interpretation of his general position.

The only generalization in the classical account of the price process that for those pre-normal periods Marshall leaves unquestioned is that of the derivation of price through demand and supply—the general conditions of them. It must, however, remain clear that these, as the sole explanation offered by Marshall for prices in ordinary times, are not to be understood to be discredited by him for normal times. Prices in that time are also to be accounted for through demand and supply. But only then is cost of production to be invoked as the explanation for supply. Up to that time, supply is just supply, accounting for itself, or not requiring to be accounted for, or perhaps, impossible of being accounted for.

Occasionally, doubtless, defective demand and supply terminology, reinforced, to be sure, by Marshall's indifference to precision in terms, leads him, in point purely of definition, to report demand and supply in terms of a price either achieved or assumed; as, for example, with the larger demand attending a falling price, or with the demand or the supply *at a price.* So long, however, as he holds firmly by the schedule interpretation, his ultimate position receives its due and clear formulation. For never, in fact, does Marshall intend to leave it in doubt that demand and supply account in the causal sense for price. Sometimes even, as notably in the present connection, he appears to rest content with an analysis going no further back than the general conditions of demand and supply. Always, nevertheless, demand is taken to derive somehow from utility as the ultimate fact.

But what, in turn, about supply and about the relation of it to cost of production. For it is not the functional bearing of demand and supply on price, but only the functional bearing of cost of production on supply, that concerns the present discussion. Is always cost of production causal with reference to supply, and through supply causal for price? Or is somehow cost of production a mere derivative from a price that demand and supply have together determined?

It is Marshall's view that, while supply is not, for the purpose, necessarily to be taken as an ultimate term in the price-causal sequence, it must, nevertheless, for all non-normal periods, be accorded a position prior to that of cost of production. Costs of production, indeed, during all pre-normal periods appear only as the final term in the causal sequence, as the results of a price that demand and supply have independently established. Up to the point of the arrival of normal conditions, costs of production are held, therefore, to carry no price-determining functions. They are, instead, presented as price-determined items. Not securely, however, is this to be asserted for pure-effort incomes. In the large, at any rate, supply is accounted for by Marshall only through recourse to the general conditions of it. It is in normal conditions solely that supply is accounted for by cost of production. It is in these conditions solely that costs of production are causal.

But were there for Marshall any doctrinal necessities imposing this recourse to normal periods and leading him to his denial of the causal bearing of cost on prices in ordinary times, and as well to to affirmation of it in normal times?

There clearly were. For Marshall's fundamental thesis is, as we have earlier seen, the ultimate determination of relative prices by relative real costs. During such periods, therefore, as relative money costs determine prices, relative real costs must account for relative money costs. This continuing proportion does not, it is obvious, hold for periods in which the distinction between prime and supplementary costs appears to demand recognition. At any particular time many of these money costs were incurred for items of investment commitment in earlier periods. The demand and supply conditions of any time often make slight account of these money costs in the field of equipment goods and organization, as also of abilities cost-acquired through training. If the costs of the current time are taken as determinants of current prices, these costs must be in great part made up of hires that are indefinitely out of line with their money costs in the regress emphasis. Even more, therefore, may they be out of line with whatever real costs were in the background of the earlier investor commitments in money terms. Not only, then, must this real-cost account of relative prices speak for a time when prices could be found proportional with the full total of money costs in the regress emphasis, but also for a time when these money costs could be found proportional with the real costs assumed to be in the background of the money costs. Only a period in which in general investors' money commitments should find themselves justified by those returns in the expectation of which the investor commitments were conditioned, would meet this primary requirement that relative prices must be proportional with relative money costs in the regress sense. The normal-equilibrium period—the true long-period normal, one thinks—must be the only situation meeting these doctrinal specifications. For no other time would it be possible to urge the proportionality of prices with money costs, excepting in a sense entirely out of touch with returns to the original investors—a short-time money-cost account of supplies, with all the circuities and superficialities appropriate to it. Ultimately it explains nothing; as also it ties up with nothing that from the classical point of view could find acceptance as explanation. At the best, its affiliations must be with a cross-section view of the underlying situation, the "basement" approach, without reference to any historical or genetic connections; the approach to which—when nothing better offers—Marshall appears, in a tentative and insecure way, to have recourse.

And thus it is, in part, that Marshall comes to repudiate the view that in any pre-normal period prices are determined by the enterpriser-money costs of that period. This would be to commit himself to a cost determination quite manifestly out of line with real costs, because out of line with even the total of money costs. It would be a view affording slight or no room for the price-determining function of supplementary costs. No renting or hiring enterpriser concerns himself with the costs that are supplementary from the point of view solely of the original investor-proprietor's regress costs. The enterpriser's is fairly consistently a cross-section view of costs. For the most part, the costs that are supplementary from the regress point of view are prime for him. It is only in the forward-looking and long-time view that these supplementary costs come to be indistinguishable from prime costs—this forecast view erasing or absorbing the distinction, and pointing to prices that are, in point of trend, inclusive of investment costs. It is, we may note in passing, on this line of distinction that the problem of the functional bearing of interest charges on prices must be resolved.

Moreover, it is only in the long-time view and in the investment-flow emphasis that the classical account of the relation of land rent to prices makes either an intelligible or plausible case. Interpreted as turning on the test of costs in origin, the bounty-of-nature view, it requires the exclusion equally of fertility and of spatial rents from costs—the factors responsive to investment influences and the factors that are not responsive. But this position requires in turn, in point of genesis, a distinction between cost-acquired fertility and original fertility, a distinction only conceptually practicable. But with this distinction abandoned, fertility rents and equipment rents become, for every doctrinal and functional purpose, indistinguishable. If the device of marginal isolation applies to either, it applies to both. Moreover, if any functional distinction could be urged between the position rent of land and the hires of ordinary instrumental goods, it must stand as a distinction of degree having reference to the flexibility of stocks. It becomes, therefore, a distinction of responsiveness to investment influences, a distinction that, presumably, as excluding land from price-determining costs because of its permanent unresponsiveness, must therewith exclude all other hires for the period of the unresponsiveness of each particular factor. Hence, Marshall's doctrine of quasi-rents. But the exclusion of the hires of those goods originating in money-cost outlays—and presumably, therefore, of real-cost origins—led again to the necessity either of admitting land rents for a time to the price-determining function along with other rents, or of excluding all, for the respective periods of the unresponsiveness of the factors.

And thus it is that another angle of analysis has appeared to advise the selection of the period of equilibrium between investment anticipations and investment returns as the sole period in which it is possible to defend the view that relative total costs of production determine relative prices. And thus it is that still the earlier difficulty holds over of eliminating land rents from the price-determining function, the while that equipment rents and training rents and native ability rents are included. And thus the earlier discredited device of marginal isolation has again to be invoked. But not now, be it noted, is this device made to turn solely on distinctions by degrees of responsiveness. Instead it becomes also a distinction of function that, turning on degree of responsiveness, shall somehow apply to exclude from the price-determining rôle that factor solely that is taken to be at the extreme point of unreponsiveness. It is therefore a distinction that either holds the functional antithesis of cause to effect as itself a matter of degree, or presents the distinction of degree as one that comes into bearing only at the point of the extreme case of degree—so that results can report no differences of degree.

In its nature, however, marginal isolation takes no account either of degrees or of times. If it applies at all, it applies completely. If ever it did or will apply, it applies now; or, applying now, it must apply at any other time. Moreover, if it is to be applied to land, it calls imperatively to be applied to equipment goods, as eliminating the rents of both from the price-determining function. It is purely a cross-section analysis in view of the various stocks of factors as they are. The degree of responsiveness of the various stocks of factors to their respective hires has obviously nothing to say for their functional relations in the fixation of prices, and especially nothing to say for the functional bearing of their marginal uses on prices. It is seemingly this confusion of responsiveness with functional significance that leads Marshall—albeit hesitatingly and in not quite full commitment—to exclude from the causal bearing on prices, even in normal periods, the hires of extraordinary native ability. The substitutionary relation for productive purposes between land and the other productive factors—and therefore for cost purposes between land hires and other hires—has already been sufficiently stressed as outlawing any distinctions of functional bearing on prices between the factors or their hires. This argument need not here be further stressed; nor the equal unit cost at the marginal use with the other uses, if and when the right proportion of factors has been achieved—the equal application, that is, of the law of the right proportions of factors, and of the law of diminishing returns; nor the indistinguishability of fertility from positional productivity; nor the equal applicability of the principle of opportunity cost to land uses with other uses; nor the identity of land with capital from the point of view of competitive enterprise; nor the equal standing of land investment with other investment from the point of view of competitive enterprise, and therefore of the equal standing of land with other agents of production in the fixation of the right proportioning of factors by each enterpriser, in view of his individual situation and of the relative costs attaching to the various factors; nor the entire irrelevancy of any of these different bases of distinction from the point of view of the cost computations of the different competing enterprisers.

Instead, the particular point of emphasis at present is that the marginal-isolation procedure breaks down for the normal-time analysis as hopelessly as for any other time. Moreover, to admit true rents to the function of price determination along with other rents is to abandon the ultimate purpose of this choice of the normal period, wherein solely cost of production, exclusive of rents, is to come into the price-determining function—this function being denied it in all other periods. But to exclude at normal periods true rents from the price-determining function is also to exclude equipment rents, along also with ability rents and with pretty much the entire range of returns on investment commitments. We are back again at the point of prices explained solely through true-effort costs, along with, albeit dubiously, raw material costs; or again, at the point of faring forth anew in the search of such explanations as an examination of the general conditions of demand and supply may finally discover.

But how now does the case stand with real costs and with their proportionality with money costs? For this also is a doctrine that with Marshall comes into its rights only in normal periods. It is a position that purports to find its justification through the regress analysis, wherein, supposedly, money costs and real costs become equal by title of their ultimate coalescence. For it need not be here repeated that the money-cost regress, so far as it is no other or no better than this, is not logically superior to no regress at all, since it is merely an arrest at the original stage of money costs. To explain A's money outlays to B through B's money outlays to C, and C's to D, and so on back, arrives at its limit only with the original investors' money outlays. And as we have seen, Marshall's account of this regress is in the main that purely of a money-cost regress.

Such, however, is clearly not the purpose of it. Implicit with Marshall in this regress procedure is the argument, or the assumption, that at each step in the regress there are money payments to be made not solely as adequate money indemnities to command the equipment goods deriving from earlier items of money outlay, but also as indemnities for current effort and waiting costs. At every stage in the regress therefore price returns on labor of one sort or another, or on waiting—no matter whether of the recipients of the hires or of the enterpriser himself—get into the cost process. These labor and waiting returns, viewed both as outlays and as receipts, are held to go back ultimately to real-cost explanations— price costs underlaid by real costs. Even where the labor itself, or the efficiency of it in production, is mainly due to money maintenance costs, or to investment outlays in the acquisition of skill, the regress method is relied on somewhere to uncover real-cost explanations of the money-cost facts. Ultimately, then, all money costs for raw materials and wages and interest and equipment goods or hires —but not for lands or their hires—find real-cost explanations at the point where original investment takes place, the point of the adoption of investor policies in the employment of the continually maturing volume of investment capital—funds. This point is the terminal situation of investment expectation that, moving into stable adjustment with a later situation of realization, proclaims this later period to be a normal period. A normal period is such, one thinks, by precisely this test. This appears, at all events, to interpret Marshall's position at its best of theoretical appeal.

It is, then, at this point in the regress analysis that Marshall's position has finally to be tested. And what then about these investor funds? They are themselves price items, made up of mere money units, precisely as the food and training are—mostly at least—price items. By what warrant at this end of the regress, this terminus-a-quo, are these price items to be each accepted as reporting units of discomfort cost in either labor or waiting or in some combination of the two?

A new regress from this point is in fact imperative. These funds for investment derive from earlier processes. They are funds diverted from consumption. They must, then, trace back somewhere to human effort, and to effort involving, at the margin at least, discomfort units for the different producers that are equal unit for unit. Or, so far as they are returns of capital, they must also uncover, somewhere back, their origins in human efforts, in discomfort units on which, as base, further real costs of waiting may accrue as additions. These original effort discomforts along with

the compounding of the discomforts of abstinence, but debited
with all the derivative units of satisfaction that have accrued and
been consumed, must at the time of the investment in industrial
equipment, account in terms of interchangeable discomfort units
for the interchangeable capital units that have come to be seeking
investment at the present, as against their consumption use at present.

Whether all this seems credible or not, take it nevertheless for
the time being as unquestioned, so far as the real costs of effort
are concerned. But what about these waiting costs inter-individually,
dollar for dollar, with all these different investors? Are they unit
for unit equal?

It may seem obvious that they are not. On the face of it, however,
even thus much in the negative may appear to be unknowable—
only the affirmative being certainly unsafe of assertion. But not
rarely, though we may not know in any particular case what thing
is true, we may be certain of some things about it that are not
true. I do not, for example know where you, my reader, may be.
But I do seem to know of some places where you are not—say,
under my table or in my pocket—taking it, that is, that you are
somewhere, which perhaps I ought not to assume. It does, at any
rate, seem probable that the dollar savings of Mr. Rockefeller are
not equally grievous with those of the ordinary day laborer, assuming thus much for the quantitative inter-individual comparability of
human experiences.

But at the margins? For away from all margins there are inexhaustible areas of the unknown. These margins are, in fact, hair
lines of actuality between infinities of speculation. So what about
the savings margins of these two men in point of the quantitative
inter-individual equality of their real costs? The possibility of
any clear proof of the quantitative inequality of Mr. Rockefeller's
marginal real costs per dollar of saving with those of the day
laborer falls still something short of being complete. But this much
is certain; margins report not quantities but only ratios between
quantities. The margin for the laborer is one of approximate indifference between buying at present, say, a loaf of bread and

buying something in the future with his dime—increased of course, it may be, through its accumulations. With Mr. Rockefeller the margin is also one of indifference between some present buying and some later buying. We can know nothing certainly—though we may believe much—as to the quantitative aspects of the terms in either of these purely individual ratios. But there can be no proof, and there is no basis for the belief, that there are any inter-individual equalities of feeling quantities in the case. The dollars of price offer are doubtless interchangeable dollars. But dollars also are merely terms in value ratios—price merely one instance of value; values never quantitative. Only the terms in the ratios are quantities. The ratios between them are not quantities. Marshall's doctrine goes to pieces, therefore, not so much for its defective value analysis as for its forgetfulness of the very nature of the value problem.

Wherefore, logically, Marshall appears to come into the need of a representative investor, though, so far as can be made out, he has none. And if he had, this representative investor must, in order to be adequate for the purpose, be quantitatively representative in both terms of his saving ratio.

And we have now further to note that similar difficulties present themselves with regard to the real costs of effort. Inter-individual and interchangeable units of labor discomfort must be established for all of those labor incomes that were saved.

In addition also the effort discomforts and the savings discomforts of each of the individual investors must for each be summed up into a total of real costs, to be set over against the summed-up real costs of every other of the investing individuals; in such sort that these aggregate individual discomforts, that command interchangeable dollars to be spent or saved, shall be indistinguishable in point of the respective individual real costs behind them. It is evident therefore that representative laborers, had Marshall invoked them as going along at this stage of the regress with the representative savers that also he might have invoked, must still fall short of meeting all of the requirements of his analysis. There would need be also a representative individual as an effort-and-saving investor.

Marshall has left, it seems, only one possible exit from these cumulative perplexities. He must have a *representative dollar*. And at an early step in the development of Marshall's argument provision against this requirement was carefully, though mainly by inference, made. And this fact was at that time for later purposes duly noted in these discussions. Buyers' dollars were, it will be remembered, there made representatives of utility and, in addition, measures of utility or of marginal utility. This is Marshall's method of getting along without a representative buyer or consumer, or a representative demand schedule. With equal and essentially similar justification and cogency, the representative and measure function attributed by Marshall to dollars with respect to the satisfaction of desires in demand and consumption aspects, may be extended to cover the discomforts of effort in the supply aspect. The next and obvious step would be to apply it to waitings. And no greater difficulties need be met in applying it to efforts and waitings combined.

If thus much, then, can be accomplished for the terminus-a-quo, the way has become fairly clear for the application of the same procedure to the situation at the terminus-ad-quem—the point at which, by the aid of the concept of a normal, the discomforts of the earlier time, being measured and reported in money terms in that price system, come also to be equilibrated with the discomfort costs of the later time, as summed up in the measuring dollars of that later time. This normal time is in turn, by assumption, the time of a system of prices thoroughly equilibrated with one another—in such sense that all of the money costs that are representative of discomforts are marginally equated against the utilities represented and measured in price offers. Dollars that are the prices in the earlier time, being the dollars that get invested, report an equality between discomforts and utilities in that time. These invested dollars function as items of cost in the later time. At this time, then, the dollar costs that are representative of discomforts in both the earlier and the later time, equate in the exchange processes of the later time in such sort that the dollars of marginal discomfort costs are equal to the dollars of demand utility: A is equal in point of feeling magnitude to B; A and B are both equal to C; C is equal to

D; wherefore A and D must be equal. And all of this gets accomplished through the ascription of the measure function to money —a long series of equalities in feeling quantities deduced from the mere fact of exchange equalities through the money intermediate. And thus does the case for the discomfort theory of relative prices become complete.

But at or during just what period? There are in a time series an indefinitely large number of normals shading off one into another. To which one or to which ones in the series shall this equilibrium between investors' expectations and investors' realizations, with derivative all-round equalities of discomforts with utilities, be taken as appropriate? Marshall's analysis appears to provide no reply to this not unreasonable query. But perhaps there is no need. If this measure function of both discomforts and utilities always and everywhere attaches to money, with the mere fact of an exchange at a price the certification of an equality between discomforts and utilities, these desiderated equalities belong to all times and conditions, whether normal or other. And especially must these equalities go along with production directed by hiring or buying enterprisers, where regress complications of proprietorships do not complicate the situation—where, that is to say, all the costs of production are taken to be prime with respect to the producers. In such sense as ever prices conform to costs, always prices conform to prime costs in this interpretation of them—to all costs of producers with whom all costs are prime. For it is costs in the regress procedure that involve the notion of supplementary costs and impose the distinctions of proprietorships—notions and distinctions that are cancelled by absorption in any completely forward-looking view of costs.

Since only in this completely forward-looking cost analysis do prices purport to be dependent on these fixed-charge, or supplementary-cost, items, Marshall comes to hold that, for the period of their independence, costs do not account for prices at all. But prime costs do so account—in the times when and for the producers for whom the costs are prime. The supplementary-cost distinction mixes questions of proprietorships into issues of costs. It is this distinction of proprietorships that may have dictated to Marshall the quasi-rent classification of factors and their price-determined hires. And it is the exclusion of these hires in ordinary times from any causal bearing on prices that appears to have imposed with Marshall the conceptual device of the normal period. And thereby, though perhaps not inescapably, the normal period imposes the representative producer.

It is, moreover, only at this normal period that the real-cost explanation of relative prices attains seeming credibility. This explanation turns out, however, to require not merely representatives and normals all round the circle, but also representative dollars completely equipped with the measure function.

It is manifestly hazardous to attempt an account of the processes of another's thought; it being difficult enough to become precisely certain of what he thinks, to say nothing of why he thinks it or of how he came to think it. It seems clear, nevertheless, that Marshall's quasi-rent doctrine gets its place in his system of thought through two different lines of analysis, each of them directly connected, to be sure, with his labor-cost theory of value.

These two lines of thought have already been independently examined:—

(1) The view, just now under discussion, that solely in a hypothetical period of complete equilibrium, are the prices of products accurately proportional with their cumulative price costs, dating forward from the period of original investment in equipment goods and organization—there being thus a background provided for the proportionality of prices with real costs. Always this normal period serves as denoting the direction of price trends. It is a view that negatives for any period other than the normal the fixation of prices by enterprisers' money costs or by real costs. This view asserts instead, for all pre-normal times, the price-determined nature of the hires of practically all of the agents of production—the quasi-rent doctrine. It is a view that articulates with the explanation of the costs, and thus of the prices, of these normal times through the investment of the constantly maturing volumes of capital funds

in aids to later production, accordingly as the best prospective returns may advise. This assumption of the arrival of a period of
normal adjustment has appeared not only to justify at that time
the inclusion of the hires of all cost-acquired agents among price-
determining costs—along with the rents of natural fertility—but
also, by the aid of the marginal-isolation analysis, to continue un-
disturbed the exclusion of the rents of land from price-determining
costs.

(2) A view equally clearly deriving from the labor-cost theory
of relative prices, and equally clearly requiring the exclusion of
land rents from any causal bearing through costs on prices. But
this view, while also a regress view in point of its emphasis on
costs in origin, has no necessary connection with the flow of investment funds or with any hypothetical period of ultimate price
equilibration. It is a view directly and simply of classical derivation.
By an analysis earlier traced, it imposes also the distinction between
land and capital. It presents land rents as always price-determined,
but as over against the rents of cost-acquired agents taken as always
price-determining. It holds prices to be everywhere and always
determined, on the level of the enterpriser analysis, by money costs,
with land rents always the sole price-determined hires. In its
consistently cost-origin view, it takes fertility rents to be functionally
indistinguishable from spatial-extension rents. Distinctions based
on degrees of responsiveness of the different stocks of agents to
their hires are not admitted. The sole reliance in this aspect of
the analysis is at all times the device of isolation at the margin of
the utilization of land, with this device conceived to be exclusively
applicable to land and its hires—the quasi-rent doctrine getting,
therefore, no recognition. Marshall, however, found the quasi-rent
doctrine necessary in connection with the impossibility of distinguishing between cost-acquired and original fertility.

Nevertheless, as we have seen, the first of these two views,
through its assumption of the normal-equilibrium period, arrives
at an analysis that for that period is in substantial harmony with
that of the view affirming for all times the price-determined status
of the hires of the spatial-extension aspects of land. And the two

views concur also in relying on the device of marginal isolation for establishing the determination of land hires by prices.

All consistently classical renderings of systematic economic doctrine concur, it must be noted, in this marginal-isolation analysis as peculiar in final and functional aspects to whatever is held to be land, or land capital, and to the hires of it. By this test, therefore, the various systems of economic thought are to be recognized as classical or not classical. Only by the test of this isolation procedure are the various formulations of the land capital issue essentially to the purpose; as also only by this test are the various lines of analysis distinguishing land from capital, with reference to price, essentially to the purpose. And by this test also, and only by the degree or method of applying the marginal-isolation procedure, can it for the purpose matter whether and how the distinction between land and capital, or between land capital and other capital, is arrived at or urged. Everywhere and always, in whatever guise presented, this denial of the functional bearing of the hire of land on prices is the ultimate characteristic of the classical economics. All other issues—and there are many of them, as has already become clear—are subordinate and tributary issues. This rent-cost doctrine, as the necessary supplement of the labor-cost account of relative prices, is the pivotal position in the classical system of thought.

The arrival of normal-price conditions means, as we have seen, a completely achieved response by such of those agents of production as are susceptible of response, to the hires to be had for them; as also a completely achieved response of these hires to the costs conditioning the forthcoming of the agents. At the normal time, then, the price of each product is presented by Marshall as commensurate with the marginal cost of production of the representative producer in that trade—this producing individual or firm being representative both of the producers and of the conditions of production in that trade. The different conditions, producers inclusive, in the different fields of production get summed up in the situation of the respective respresentative producers. Each representative producer is therewith taken to be representative in point of his marginal cost—price costs, obviously, as commensurate with the market price.

We have, then, to examine somewhat narrowly the significance of marginal cost of production in normal periods.

Always under ordinary conditions the enterpriser must take account in initiating his program, of all sorts of possible or probable changes not only in the price of his product, but in the prices at which different volumes of product will find purchasers. Also he must take account of changes in the prices or the hires of his cost good; and further again, of the changes in the size of the under-taking best adapted to these varying conditions in the prices of his cost goods and in the market conditions for his product. The prospect of widening markets or of higher prices may advise the installation of a large industrial unit, along with higher fixed-capital charges and a generally increased overhead, or may advise even a division of his resources placing greater emphasis on the fixed-charge aspect of his undertaking. So long as the prospect is for less favorable markets, smaller fixed commitments promise the better rate of return on his total investment, as well as the lower total unit costs, and even possibly the lower prime costs.

In point of fact, as he is well aware, the future will recurrently present to him both favorable and unfavorable conditions, say, for example, with a growing or again a diminishing vogue for his products. In what lines relatively, and in what volume as a total, shall he plan his undertakings? How may he best adapt himself to the ups and downs that are inevitably ahead? Even had he some near-monopoly in his field, his problems must remain the same in kind, differing only in degree. Style changes in some industries are a constantly increasing hazard as well as a constant lure. Technology changes are the same. Competing products enter the market. He will have to make such best guess as he may, in view of his resources and his assumed abilities—always, however, in the certainty that whatever will be a good fit for one set of conditions must turn out an ill fit for another. Both the size and the make-up of his undertaking he must project as a compromise, that best adjustment that he can find practicable to the longer-run course of things. The high ratio of fixed-capital outlays in many or most industries will make prompt readjustments impossible. The pro-

398 THE ECONOMICS OF ALFRED MARSHALL

portion of factors best for him with one set of conditions may be the worst for another. Most of the time he must be either under-equipped or over-equipped for each particular condition—the situation rarely one to which his plant is optimally adapted; his actual output either too great or too small for the highest rate of earnings per unit of output, or even for the lowest prime costs per unit of product. His problem in times of brisk markets will be how intensively to operate the plant in view of his rising incremental costs of production; at another time how small an output will be consistent with even meagre earnings, or will involve, in a longer-time view, the minimum of loss. He must guess; and his guess has to be one as to the best compromise in view of shifting debit and credit in the outlook. Continually therefore in view of the changing conditions, he will have changing problems of marginal costs. And even were he, in some long-time view, or at any particular instant of the actual industrial process, a representative producer, and were aware of that fact, his general range of problems would be these same problems.

But what, then, about his marginal costs in this hypothetical normal time—this merely conceptual, might-be time, this time that can come to be a process fact only in the sense of direction of trend and of limit of trend, for so long as the underlying conditions remain unchanged?

It seems clear that if and when, in view of stable conditions of product and of cost prices, each and every enterprise has achieved it optimal size and the optimal relation among its constituent parts, its costs must be the same for all of the different units in its total product. Marginal costs mean nothing. As the enterprise has one selling price for its products, so it must have one unit cost. Differential costs for increments of product connote a bad proportion of factors for the current market conditions in point of selling prices and of cost prices.

The various enterprisers in the particular trade are selling at the same prices. Even had each his own differential incremental cost, all of the enterprisers would have the same marginal costs, since all are selling at one price. But when each has arrived at his optimal size and his optimal proportion of factors, there is no room for differences among enterprisers even in point of unit costs. Each enterpriser is producing up to the limit of costs set by the stable market prices open to all. And if it is also true that for each producer there is one cost for all his different items of product, the situation arrived at is surprisingly simple—as also almost incredible. All the competitors in each particular industry have access to the same hiring as well as selling methods and prices. All borrow at the same rates of interest. Equipment for all is at that price and that rent affording to investors in general a return adequate to the maintenance of stocks.

I am most dubious both of this interpretation and of the inferences from it. The conclusions seem to follow, however, from the assumption that the normal period obliterates the distinction between prime and supplementary costs. And this conviction is strongly supported also by Marshall's doctrine that human beings are factors of production that are cost-provided through investment motivations. Implicit in this interpretation and these inferences is the view that the distribution of proprietorships is irrelevant to computations of costs and to the determination of prices.

The perplexities attach mainly to making certain just what the assumption of a normal period is taken to include. If all enterprisers in each particular industry have equally participated in the opportunity to attain right proportion of factors, under conditions of equal interest charges, equal hires of productive equipment, equal control of credit facilities, with one selling price for output, there can be room for neither intensive margins in costs of production nor differences of costs with different producers:

. . . with regard to the great bulk of manufacturing industries, the connection between supply price and amount shows a fundamentally different character for short periods and for long.

For short periods, the difficulties of adjusting the internal and external organization of a business to rapid changes in output are so great that the supply price must generally be taken to rise with an increase, and to fall with a diminution in the amount produced.

But in long periods both the internal and the external economies of production on a large scale have time to develop themselves. The marginal supply price is not the expenses of production of any particular bale of goods; but it is the whole expenses (including insurance, and gross earnings of management) of a marginal increment in the aggregate process of production and marketing. (pp. 501-2)

. . . In a stationary state the income earned by every appliance of production being truly anticipated beforehand, would represent the normal measure of the efforts and sacrifices required to call it into existence.

The aggregate expenses of production might then be found either by multiplying these marginal expenses by the number of units of the commodity; or by adding together all the actual expenses of production of its several parts. . . . The aggregate expenses of production being determined . . . the average expenses could be deduced by dividing out by the amount of the commodity. . . .

. . . .

. . . in a stationary state, but only there . . . every particular thing bears its proper share of supplementary costs; and it would not ever be worth while for a producer to accept a particular order at a price other than the total cost, in which is to be reckoned a charge for the task of building up the trade connection and external organization of a representative firm. . . . (p. 810)

Seemingly, however, there will be differences in volumes of resources, in managerial ability, and in the size of the business units —differences, therefore, it may be, in unnecessary profits per unit of product and in total unnecessary profits, and in total margins of gain—and possibly also in the rates of return on the investment of capital:

Returning to those central difficulties of the equilibrium of normal demand and supply which are connected with the element of time. . . .

When different producers have different advantages for producing a thing, its price must be sufficient to cover the expenses of production of those producers who have no special and exceptional facilities. . . . When . . . the thing is being sold at a price which covers these expenses, there remains a surplus beyond their expenses for those who have the assistance of any exceptional advantages. . . . (p. 499)

It is Marshall's assumption of the complete irrelevance of the distinction between prime and supplementary costs that is perplexing, especially with reference to the enterpriser's individual return on his personal efforts:

... We shall have to analyze carefully the normal cost of producing a
a commodity, relatively to a given aggregate volume of production [for
the representative firm, like other firms, has a supply schedule]; and for
this purpose we shall have to study *the expenses of a representative producer* for that aggregate volume . . . not . . . some new producer just
struggling into business . . . under many disadvantages . . . content for a
time with little or no profits . . . establishing a connection and taking the
first steps towards building up a successful business; nor on the other
hand . . . a firm which . . . has got together a vast business. . . . But . . .
one which has had a fairly long life, and fair success. . . . (p. 317)

. . . the general character of our conclusions is not very much affected by
the facts that many of these economies depend directly on the size of the
individual establishments . . . and that in almost every trade there is a
constant rise and fall of large businesses, at any moment some firms being
in the ascending phase and others in the descending. For in *times of
average prosperity* decay in one direction is sure to be more than balanced
by growth in another. (pp. 316-17)

It must at any rate be clear that if all the factors of production,
inclusive of individual capacities, are for each producer rightly
proportional, with the prices of products stable—as the Stationary
State assumes—there can remain no place for prime costs or for
differential costs among the items of product of that producer:

Of course we might assume that in our stationary state *every business*
remained always of the same size, and with the same trade connection.
But . . . it will suffice to suppose that firms rise and fall, but that the
"representative" firm remains always of about the same size, as does the
representative tree of a virgin forest . . . the economies resulting from
its own resources . . . constant: and since the aggregate volume of production is constant, so also are those economies resulting from subsidiary
industries in the neighborhood, etc. . . .

In a stationary state. . . .There would be . . . no fundamental difference
between the immediate and the later effects of economic causes. There
would be no distinction between long-period and short-period normal
value, at all events if we supposed that in that monotonous world the
harvests themselves were uniform: for the representative firm being
always of the same size, and always doing the same class of business to
the same extent and in the same way, with no slack times, and no specially
busy times. . . . The demand lists of prices would always be the same,
and so would the supply lists; and normal price would never vary. (pp.
367-68)

The emergence of distinctions between prime and supplementary costs, with differential marginal costs as inevitably attendant, assumes that investments in equipment goods or in human productive capacities have been either overdone or underdone relatively to the prime-cost outlays in production—outlays in the total wrongly distributed; the stationary, and seemingly the normal, state incompletely realized; the real costs of effort and the real costs of waiting have still to be equilibrated to the most desirable outcomes:

> In a rigidly stationary state in which supply could be perfectly adjusted to demand in every particular, the normal expenses of production, the marginal expenses, and the average expenses (*rent being counted in*) would be one and the same thing, for long periods and for short. . . . (p. 497).

Marshall appears, however, not to conceive of his normal as a world become so far monotonous that the harvests themselves are uniform. And always, presumably, there must be non-representative producers. With them, then, it must be true, or with some of them, that the distinction between prime and supplementary costs is holding over. And with disturbances like bad harvests, proportions of factors which are temporarily bad must be general. Either enduringly or temporarily—or both—the situation is one of incomplete equilibrium. Marshall is quite correct in saying (p. 497) that "the language both of professed writers on economics and of men of business shows much elasticity in the use of the term Normal when applied to the causes that determine value."

But, as we have seen, Marshall makes room in this normal period not only for the coming in of new firms and for their growing power and efficiency, but also for their declining power and final disappearance. Thus the representative position shifts from firm to firm, remaining not long with any one. Only the size is constant. And at any one time there may be several. Non-representative and non-normal firms belong with the normal time to which normal prices are appropriate. These are prices commensurate with the marginal costs of the representative firms of the different industries. But representative, then, of *what?* For this is a period that somewhat

approximates, but does not attain, the complete equilibrium of the
Stationary State; and yet still is in point of degree, near enough
to it so that its prices are *normal*—with all the functional and
causal transformations thereunto appertaining. The solution is not,
it seems, to be found through taking the representative firm to
be some mode or average of all the different competitors in each
particular industry—as that one firm that is representative of the
general achievement in approaching the best proportioning of fac-
ors and in adjusting size to take advantage of the economies in
production possible in view of the aggregate absorptive capacity
of the market; for this would assume the adjustment to conditions
to be everywhere incomplete—the representative firm representa-
ive only of this general incompleteness, not itself faultless by this
est, and not even the least faulty among them all. It will not be,
we recall, either the best or the worst of them. And there may
be several representative firms in one industry. Few of the competitor firms, therefore, and seemingly no one of them, could at
any particular time be free of the distinction between prime and
supplementary costs.

Or may the representative firm be one that has achieved, both
in size and in proportion of factors, whatever advantages the situa-
ion offers—the while that the others are still in the process of
adjustment, but are not yet completely adjusted? If so, however,
he representative firm would be representative merely of the situa-
ion, and not of the firms competing within it. For all of these
problems of prime and supplementary costs, as well as of size,
would obviously persist. For it is only in the Stationary State—
he extreme of the never-to-be achieved—that in Marshall's view
he equilibration becomes complete. Different periods are normal
only through their differing degrees of distance from this complete equilibrium. It can, then, be only in degree that the distinc-
ion between prime and secondary has been absorbed. There can
be marginal costs for the representative firm—but this solely by
he title of the incomplete normality of even itself. Inasmuch,
however, as all the other producers are in the same case, we have

still to seek the distinctive traits of the representative firm of any non-stationary period. The representative firm of any mere normal time must be representative of non-normality.

It seems at all events clear that not even the true long-period normal can offer more than a near approach to the conditions in which there is nothing left of the distinction between prime and secondary, and in which therefore differential marginal costs disappear from the scene.

But with what sort of normal periods, and by title of what degree of normality, under this test of remoteness from the complete equilibrium, does Marshall attribute to the firm representative at that time those differential marginal costs that are commensurate with normal market prices? Can it be that in any of these periods cost of production takes on—through the grace of the representative firm of that time—a causal and determining relation to prices? But this is to make mish-mash of the entire functional distinction; with normality a matter of degree, costs become causal as matter of degree. Often, however, Marshall does appear to hold that to even the various short-time normals the larger generalizations of normality apply:

The general drift of the term normal supply price is always the same whether the period to which it refers is short or long. . . . In every case the price is that the expectation of which is sufficient and only just sufficient to make it worth while for people to set themselves to produce that aggregate amount; in every case the cost of production is marginal. . . . (p. 373)

But the discussion here seems to refer to only one price, and to have in mind only a price stably appropriate to a set of conditions, given but changing. And perhaps these short-time normals never afford more than instances of definite trend toward the period when the doctrinal requirements for true normality will be fulfilled —or, possibly, no normal ever actual, excepting as an actual movement toward a conceptual limit of trend:

. . . It is to the persistence of the influences considered, and the time allowed for them to work out their effects that we refer when contrasting

Market and Normal price, and again when contrasting the narrower and the broader use of the term Normal price. (p. 348)

Take it, then, that the winter-underclothing industry will have its ups and downs of activity, and that market gardening will not, over the entire year and successive years, run on an even keel of price offers, or of cost, or of output, or of prices. There must, then, be periods of over-equipment and periods of under-equipment; and therefore periods when the distinction between prime and supplementary costs remains significant. Only in degree, then, can any cost be price-determining or any cost price-determined.

But these difficulties of degree hag-ride the analysis everywhere. The central doctrine of normality is one of trend. There are no discontinuities in the process, but, instead, a degree-by-degree movement from pre-normal to normal conditions by virtue of the readjustments working out through investors' policies. The reversal of the functional relation of costs to prices from the price-determined to the price-determining status must arrive, if ever it is to arrive, at the point when the processes of readjustment are complete, at the incredible and purely conceptual period of the Stationary State. There is no better case of asserting it at any one of these mid-process normals than at any pre-normal time. If, then, it can be asserted neither for any ordinary time nor for any one of these mid-process normals, but only for the complete adjustment of the Stationary State; it can never actually arrive. Never can prices be fixed by costs. Instead, costs must always be in some indefinite part price-determining, and in some other indefinite and residual part price-determined.

Not rarely Marshall appears to mean by a normal, not some one price that is for the period stable, an equilibrating point, and not any actual price at all, but only an average of the changing prices of a period that is conceived to be a normal period—as when,

. . . a person well acquainted with the woollen trade sets himself to inquire what would be the normal supply price of a certain number of millions of yards annually of a particular kind of cloth. . . .

Let us suppose a list of supply prices (or a supply schedule) made on a similar plan to that of our list of demand prices: the supply price of each amount of the commodity in a year, or any other unit of time, being written against that amount. As the flow, or (annual) amount of the commodity increases, the supply price may either increase or diminish; or it may even alternately increase and diminish. . . . (p. 343)

. . . in his estimate of the amount of work that could be got out of the machinery, etc. under normal conditions, he would probably reckon for minor interruptions from trade disputes such as are continually occurring, and are therefore to be regarded as belonging to the regular course of events, that is as not abnormal. (p. 365)

The unit of time may be chosen according to the circumstances of each particular problem: it may be a day, a month, a year, or even a generation: but in every case it must be short relatively to the period of the market under discussion. . . . (p. 342)

There are indeed not many occasions on which the calculations of a business man for practical purposes need . . . extend the range of the term Normal over a whole generation: but in the broader applications of economic science it is sometimes necessary to extend the range even further, and to take account of the slow changes that in the course of centuries affect the supply price of the labour of each industrial grade. (p. 365, note)

The period therefore that is for the purposes itself normal is normal by reference to its setting relatively to the periods before and after. The thought, moreover, has obviously to do with a normal supply *flow* and a normal demand *flow,* both of approximate constancy in the large, but with room for variations from season to season, and for variations from year to year in the quality of the seasons: excesses or shortages of heat or moisture, wind and flood, abundant harvests and famine, ups and downs of prices—all without derogation from the normality of each particular price of meat, grain or fruit or garden truck.

It is possible that the following is not intended to report Marshall's own position:

. . . This is the real drift of that much quoted, and much-misunderstood doctrine of Adam Smith and other economists that the normal, or "natural" value of a commodity is that which economic forces tend to bring about *in the long run.* It is the average value which economic forces would bring about if the general conditions of life were stationary for a run of time long enough to enable them all to work out their full effect.

But . . . the existing tendencies may be modified before they have had time to accomplish what appears now to be their full and complete work. . . . (p. 347)

Which fact it precisely is that appears to make call for Marshall's concept of normals. In the main, at any rate, Marshall's normal price in the normal period is neither the mean nor the mode:

. . . the conditions which are normal to any one set of sales are not likely to be exactly those which are normal to the others: and therefore it is only by accident that an average price will be a normal price; that is, the price which any one set of conditions tends to produce. . . . (p. 372)

The notion is instead that of a price that is the center of oscillation for the time in question:

When demand and supply are in stable equilibrium, if any accident should move the scale of production from its equilibrium position, there will be instantly brought into play forces tending to push it back to that position; just as, if a stone hanging by a string is displaced from its equilibrium position, the force of gravity will at once tend to bring it back to its equilibrium position. The movements of the scale of production about its position of equilibrium will be of a somewhat similar kind. (p. 346)

. . . the value of a thing, though it tends to equal its normal (money) cost of production, does not coincide with it at any particular time, save by accident. . . . (p. 401)

On a stock exchange, for example, or a board of trade, there is a ceaseless up and down of prices, even on a particular day. *The* price of the day might, then, be taken to be an average, weighted or unweighted, of the different trades; or the median quotation, weighted or unweighted.

The important thing here is to arrive at a secure interpretation of the meaning of the *normals* with which we have to deal. For present purposes, however, this is important solely by virtue of the functional significance attributed by Marshall to them. For to the arrival of these normals—that may never become exemplified in even one quotation—Marshall attaches the potency of reversing the preceding direction of the causal sequence between cost of production and price. Excepting for these functional transformations, we need have no serious quarrel with normals—or any great concern with them.[2]

It must be noted that neither with representative nor non-representative producers does Marshall take any account of opportunity cost. Even, however, when a large investment has already been made, there may still be important alternative openings. A farmer, for example, may be irrevocably committed to his investment in his farm. But he has still choices of different crops. The ranking resistance to a particular crop is commonly some alternative crop. It does not suffice to reduce all crops to terms of corn. His best alternative against wheat may, it is true, be maize. But it may equally well be oranges or grapes. Or he may plow up his vines or cut down his trees and shift over into stock or dairy farming. Or he may turn to truck farming or chickens. Or again he may rent out part of his land—or, for that matter, all of it—and move to town. Or he may sell off part of his cattle or his equipment. So again he may divide his own working time between farming and teaching school, or soliciting fire or life insurance, or organizing granges. Never is cost rightly presented until the ranking resistance is recognized.

Even a great railroad system may have alternative possibilities—freight as against passenger traffic, for example; or the sale of some

[2] We ask for distinctions that are functionally defensible. If, for example, in the long-time adjustment, the $100 rent on a cost-provided machine will be then a price-determining cost, why is not also the $100 rent that is being paid on a machine that is already in existence? Or, say, its $50 or its $137.50 rent? Will at that distant time the price-determining rent be $100 for all machines of this particular grade of efficiency, when once the new machines have begun to come in? Promptly? Or just after, or just before? Or will it be $100 for these new ones, and nothing for the earlier? Will there be an instantaneous change from nothing up to $100? Or from the actual $50 up to $100? Or from the actual $137.50 down to $100?

If there are actually to be changes that are quantitatively of this sort, and that also are *functional* changes, the distinctions that report them are defensible. But still there is suspicion attaching to the view that costs of hiring machines now have no cost-bearing on prices now; or that nothing can be price-determining now that later will not be in the same degree and continuously so; or that anything is a cost now only in the degree that, whether more or less than now, it will sometime come to be a cost; or that in order to be a cost once a thing must first have been a cost twice; or that anything must be a cost now at less than what you pay for it, because later you will get it for less; or that it has to be a cost now, if a cost at all, at more than you now pay for it, because later you will have to pay more.

of its feeding or connecting lines, or of some part of its rolling stock; or the leasing partly or entirely of its properties. Within fairly flexible limits, also, the steel trust may redistribute its lines of output as market conditions may advise.

Nor does it suffice to reply that to sell a farm is not to modify land stocks but merely to redistribute proprietorships. Similarly is it with labor and wages; to dismiss men is not to increase or to decrease the population. Considerations of this sort belong solely to the "basement" approach to price problems, not to the approach through enterprisers' money costs. These last are significant mainly as adjusting and equalizing processes. Even when the farmer moves to town, that is not a fact either of birth or death; and in moving he is rather adapting himself to prices than changing prices, although his reaction on prices is still actual. And so in the main his shift from grapes to oranges is a result of price conditions that are only infinitesimally affected by him—the output of grapes less, and that of oranges more; but neither the more nor the less of land.

It thus becomes clear that no firm can be representative through the equality of its costs with the market price, unless and until due account has been taken of its situation with respect to displacement costs—representativeness a more complicated matter than, even on the face of it, it appears to be.

Some further attention has now to be directed to the significance of the marginal costs of production of whatever may be the representative firm. Take it for good measure that the period is one of complete equilibrium, the Stationary State; that the demand schedules of all the different commodities are normal; all producers normal; all alternative openings normal; all prices of cost goods, all wages, all rents and all consumer goods completely adjusted relatively to one another. Assume further that all the prices are stabilized against changes in demand from seasonal influences, as also against climatic variations—flood, famine and drought included—so that no complications of periods of under- or over-pressure on plant or organization may be present to trouble us; no attendant problems of prime against supplementary costs remaining over to make us afraid. These changes of seasonal and unseasonal weather are not, it is true, to be cured by edict. Factually speaking they must be there. But while we are about it, we may as well make over the weather as make over human beings into freedom from all abnormalities. All this is within the powers of concept, hypothesis and axiom; for these are limited solely by the requirement of lack of internal contradiction. They can do pretty much anything—short of assuming a three-year old colt to be made in a minute.

Take it, then, that a particular producer is representative in point of every aspect of cost; that he has continuously the right proportion of factors, in view of their stable costs, and in view of the stable market prices of his products, and of all other products; and that he has also the right proportion of factors in view of his own resources and capacities and of his disposition to put forth productive effort. Can he have differential marginal costs?

It seems that he can, unless he is himself a constant in point of health, strength, industriousness and desires. His margins may not, to be sure, be discomfort margins as distinguished from margins of displaced recreation or amusement. But effort margins he still may have. Crusoe, for example, will carry his rising real costs to the point of equation with his falling utilities of products. Nor need it matter that his provision of equipment goods has been made ideal relatively to one another and to his own productive effort. Unless he were a constant in ability and in disposition to labor, his equipment would be recurrently excessive and scant and effort margins would present themselves. Labor is a cost to the producer in the degree that it enters into his necessary return, precisely as is true of outlay costs or of foregone returns.

But when investment is large, effort may be a negligible aspect of cost. And especially is this the case when an enterprise is marginal as a unit against an alternative opening, the problem not one of the extension of the first enterprise but of the shifting out of it into another. The Rockefeller or the Marshall Field margin is one of policies in the extension of investment or in choices of enterprises rather than in the strain and stress of more intensive effort.

And so much effort being justified in any case, the farmer's problem is what choice to make in utilizing his efforts and resources —how to distribute them in a particular enterprise, or whether in part or entirely to shift one or both into some alternative field. And thus if this farmer is taken to be the representative producer, the normal period can have arrived only with his best proportioning of factors, himself included, and with his best distribution of resources in point of fields of production.

None the less may effort enter as a prime cost into the marginal cost, if the proportioning of factors is defective, or if the enterpriser is not himself a constant in effort aspects. And thus it is that the distribution of proprietorships is at some times and in some degree relevant to the cost analysis, if only in point of risk charges. It does not matter for the purpose whether the worker is a slave or a free man, and whether he works for himself or for another. Nor does it cancel the distinction to think of him as his own capital and of his labor income as interest on his wealth in himself.

The truth is that in the enterpriser analysis the distinction between the employer and the employee point of view is impossible of a complete working out—a distinction that is essentially one of proprietorships still holding over; and thereby a remnant of the difficulty with prime and supplementary costs still present.

Everything is clear enough, however, so far as the two points of view can in practice be effectively differentiated. Your own labor in your own direct service has discomfort-cost elements and therefore may present intensive margins. Your employees, as sometimes you may allow yourself to suspect, have also theirs. But theirs are essentially their own affairs, not yours. Your concern is with your money costs in getting their services in your undertaking. The discomforts are their costs in getting from you your wage payments to them. Their discomforts are not your costs of getting their work from them. There are no discomfort margins here from your point of view in your productive process, but only from that of the laborers, who, in turn, have no part in the enterpriser costs. You are not adding their discomfort costs to your equipment and organization and free-capital costs, but only the wages that you pay. From your point of view, for either money-cost or real-cost purposes, there is no distinction between the laborers with their hires and mules with theirs, or machines with theirs, or lands with theirs. You are consistently in the employer point of view. All these expenses of yours—rewards they are from the other point of view —are just your expenses.

You don't view yourself that way, to be sure. You are able to distinguish yourself from any other. Most of us are—a distinction without which the competitive process could not get on, and with which ethics hardly can. It is an actual distinction—for both purposes. And it is precisely the distinction that makes the competitive economic process difficult to fit into economic generalizations.

But adopt, nevertheless, a completely consistent employer point of view, and the case is not so forbidding. Just assume the corporate organization, where even the executives are all in the employee relation, along with all the other workers that are hired and with the properties that are either owned or hired. Take further a completely forward-looking point of view. Or regard the corporation as strictly a hiring and buying producer, in a cross-section view of the process.

No violence, it is clear, is done to Marshall's doctrinal procedure anywhere, nor even any strain made upon it, through the adoption of an entirely forward-looking point of view with costs, and of this rigorously exclusive employer analysis of them. Precisely this is the logic of Marshall's reliance on the processes of the original investors—and especially in view of his insistence that not only the gain-achieving abilities of human being but the human beings themselves, must be regarded as items of productive capacity deriving from these investor policies, the parents being the investors. Thus, at that extreme limit of Marshall's analysis that intends the cancellation of the distinction between prime and supplementary costs, the discomfort costs of the enterpriser must in any case go out of the setting. In this aspect, therefore, the representative firm must be admitted to be preferable to the representative enterpriser.

But with all these conditions met, there is no place left anywhere in the normal period for marginal costs of production; nor safely, it may be, for marginal real costs of production anywhere.

There is, to be sure, nothing in all this to deny that the method of arriving at the right proportions of factors may be the experimental and tentative methods of incremental investment; but these only as intermediates in the process of arriving at the limit achievement in unit costs. Doubtless all of the hired agents of production will be used up to an intensive margin with each—but this as merely the method of best proportioning them to one another, in view, of course, of their respective costs. The diagrams that indicate a declining scale of productivity for each factor, those trapezoids of accomplishment for each, make for obscuring the fact that all the units of productivity are equally paid, being interchangeable units—a quadrilateral and not a trapezoid of achievement, as it is also for distributive shares. The trapezoid form includes a surplus of payments that provide the material for the quadrilaterals of receipts for the cooperating factors. Always it is implicit in these curves and areas that equal money payments attach to units of price-productive service.

The curve reporting the declining incremental return to units of expense applied to land (whether valued or not) is the curve that makes room for wages and machine hires. The same diagrammatic device with the machine will report the room for wages and land rents. All of the various expense costs being included, there is the same cost for each unit of product. It is only enterpriser efforts and enterpriser returns that give the appearance of differences in costs.[3]

---

[3] ". . . Of course the return to this last dose [of capital and labor to land] cannot be separated from the others; but we ascribe to it all of that part of the produce which we believe would not have been produced if the farmer had decided against the extra hoeing.

Since the return to the dose on the margin of cultivation just remunerates the cultivator, it follows that he will be just remunerated for the whole of his capital and labour by as many times the marginal return as he has applied doses in all. Whatever he gets in excess of this is the *surplus produce* of the land. This surplus is retained by the cultivator if he owns the land himself." (pp. 154-55)

All of the doses are, to be sure, equally productive—the supra-marginal with

The fact is that many of the traditional diagrams lead to incorrect analyses. The usual reports of the costs of production in agriculture through curves inclining upward need to be interpreted as curves of incremental prime cost, in view of a land commitment earlier made and now taken to be definitive; and are almost always wrong at that. As a curve of incremental prime or unit costs it should fall in its very early stages; while as a curve of unit prime costs it should fall steeply in its earlier stages and should turn upwards only in its later reaches, the curve of incremental prime costs rising the more rapidly. In the usual curve, the land is being regarded as a supplementary-cost good. It is an agent the hires of which are not now being ranked as costs, because now no money has to be disbursed, or because now the hires have no bearing to determine what further costs remain now worth while. Dated as of now rather than from an earlier and consistently forward-looking standpoint, only those costs that now enter into the present choice as to the making of the crop have now to be considered—are now, that is to say, prime costs.

But the curves that indicate costs with industries traditionally regarded as affording increasing returns, the industries to which are attributed the falling curves of cost, need inspection in this connection. For if these are really curves of declining incremental

---

the marginal dose. But Marshall's ascription of the increased output to the increased labor, while tenable purely as matter of physical causation, is not securely to be carried over into the distributive analysis. There are here two steps: (a) the change in the distribuendum, (b) the change in the terms of its distribution. The accuracy of the productivity theory of distribution is at issue.

Assume that on free land there are 100 units of labor applied, at an aggregate price output of 100, with a wage of 1 per unit of labor. With 100 further units of labor applied, under conditions imposing the emergence of rent, a product of 180, reduced by, say, 20 for rent, allots a wage not of .90 but of .80. Some part of the product causally to be ascribed to the increased labor has been distributively imputed to the land. Causally speaking, the change was a labor change; its result an 80 increment of product. The distributive process allots only 60/80 of this product to the factor causally accounting for it. To assert that the land produced 20 of the second outcome of product is to deduce from the distributive fact the causal inference—the theory established by assuming its thesis.

This I take to be a valid refutation of the logic of this particular argument in support of this productivity analysis; not, however, as earlier it has seemed to me, a valid objection to the theory itself. The added labor may, for example, have spaded up underlying layers of fertile humus. The effort that releases a spring is not safely to be accounted the cause of all resultant phenomena.

prime cost, rather than of declining unit costs, they have little bearing on either output or price, except, perhaps, to indicate the course of action and of prices to which unrestricted competition may sometimes lead, those prices which will spell insolvency—the prices, for example, that railroad wars did once occasionally bring about, and that wrecked most old investors and discouraged all new—pure prime-cost prices, or less. Curves of cost taking account of supplementary charges would look still further different—both in incremental and in unit aspects.

But in view of the fact that farming is pretty plainly now a capitalistic enterprise along with most of the others—no matter whether ever earlier it were other—it is a dangerous analytical procedure that affirms one line of doctrine and one set of curves appropriate for agriculture, and another line of doctrine and another set of curves for other industries. And even further worse is a doctrine that conceives of agriculture as just one industry and of manufacturing as an indefinite number of other industries. It is safe to say that if ever a unit cost situation is found in manufacturing, it is also to be found in agriculture. Rising or falling unit costs are equally appropriate to both. A curve of declining costs in any particular enterprise, through changes in the size of the business unit, may point to advantages either a) in incremental prime costs, or b) in total unit costs. Or the curve may point to an industry over-equipped for market conditions, where the volume of product may be expanded either a) at declining incremental prime costs, or b) at declining total unit costs. Curves of rising costs may point either a) to rising incremental prime costs, or b) to rising total unit costs, through too small a business unit under the market conditions. Or they may point to a) rising incremental prime costs, or b) to rising total units costs, through a bad proportion of factors, in view of their respective rents or prices.

No one of these cases is of exclusive application to extractive or manufacturing or merchandising industries; although it is true that the especial inelasticity of the land factors with most agricultural products—in view of the checker-boarding of land holdings—makes these agricultural industries in peculiar degree illustrative of disadvantages from the unfavorable size of the business unit, as also from the bad proportioning of it.

It may again be noted that, rightly drawn, most of these curves—those of prime as well as those of total costs, both incremental and unit—would change in shape, some of them radically, when further extended, especially to the left. Moreover, these curves must differ for different lines of product—say, for fruit farming as against chickens or bees, or for garden truck as against milk farming, or for milch cattle as against meat cattle. Of the different curves appropriate in point of principle to the various aspects of merchandising, and especially to the advertising aspects, I have only the dimmest notion. But it is clear that in the main the traditional curves will not serve.

And what then about it all, especially as far as Marshall's analysis is concerned? I don't accurately see. But I suspect that these problems of marginal cost are not, for this particular purpose, adequately to be handled until they are made free of proprietorship complications and of enterpriser labor costs; and that only the corporate approach can serve for avoiding these perplexities. Nor am I able to make out what part in this normal-period situation to ascribe to the opportunity costs of the enterpriser. Recognition of either his effort or his opportunity costs must, I think, necessitate the reinstatement of marginal costs. Not so, however, I think, in the logic of Marshall's thought. For, so far as labor returns are concerned, with their earlier exclusion as quasi-rents from price-determining costs, and their later inclusion in the normal period, there is no way of getting on with Marshall's argument, excepting to regard all human beings as investment items, and therewith to dispose of them similarly with machinery and mules, with no real costs attaching to them anywhere for enterpriser purposes.

This would no doubt go along with Marshall's similar disposal of machine and labor hires. But it would do this only by attaching what I take to be incredible motivations as explanation for the forthcoming of human beings. It would, moreover, negative his title to talk of *marginal* costs of production in the differential sense. It would also outlaw the use of discomfort costs anywhere in these normal times—despite the fact that this normal-time recourse was, so far as I can make out, contrived for the purpose of reducing money costs to real-cost terms, thereby establishing relative prices as proportional with relative real costs.

For obviously, if men are to get hires as equipment goods get their hires, as items of return on capital investments, these men can not also be paid proportionally with the discomfort costs in the current putting forth of their efforts; the hires cannot be the sum of these separate claims. Marshall must choose; and either choice is as devastating as the other for his ultimate thesis. Investment items, if they could get paid according to their current pains of operation —as in the nature of the employer point of view they not readily could—could not be getting paid according to the investor require-ments. If the hire is enough for the sum of the original real costs of production plus the real costs of the waiting, and no more, there is no balance for the men, more than for the machines, for the burdens of any present functioning. And if the investors were in their time aware that before they, or any one else, could collect anything as interest, an adequate payment must be deducted for the dis-comforts of the worker, never a baby could be allowed to be born.

Moreover, the case is worse yet. For if, through the marginal-isolation procedure, the ordinary quasi-rent properties cease to be price-determining in their hires, all returns to laborers, as cost-derived items of productive power, must also be denied any causal bearing on price. The fundamental proportion thesis goes to wreck.

On the other hand, if, in this normal time, the marginal-isolation procedure ceases somehow to apply to exclude the hires of equip-ment goods from the price-determining function, a similar reversal will suffice to reinstate the hires of labor as price-determining costs. But forthwith, and by equal title, the hire of land must enter. No more, therefore, in normal than in pre-normal times, in either the cross-section or the regress aspect, can prices be proportional with real costs. The fundamental thesis is again, and hopelessly, in insolvency.

Chapter XIV

LAWS OF RETURN

NEITHER Marshall's discussion of the laws of return nor his analysis of the interest problem presents issues that are necessarily and crucially connected with his general system of thought. For the most part, each is an independent topic for examination, significant rather against the background of classical thought in general than against that of Marshall's particular presentation of it. Whether, therefore, we shall interpret Marshall as committed to the device of marginal isolation equally for all of the factors of production, or as disclaiming its application to any one of them, will have little to do with his particular discussions of the laws of return. Not much in his general analysis stands or falls with these laws as he presents them.

His provisional formulation of the tendency to diminishing return runs, not in terms of any investment in land, with land conceived as a value fact, or of money debits for wages, equipment goods, fertilizers, seed and the like, but rather of quantities of labor and of capital—efforts and waitings—applied to some particular area of land, to the end of achieving an amount, and not a price total, of produce:

An increase in the capital and labour applied in the cultivation of land causes *in general* a less than proportionate increase in the amount of produce raised. . . .
. . . every agriculturist . . . desires to have the use of a good deal of land; . . . when he cannot get it *freely,* he will *pay* for it, if he has the means. If he thought that he would get as good *results* by applying all his capital and labour to a very small *piece,* he would not pay for any but a very small piece.

When land that requires no clearing is to be had for nothing . . . cultivation is "extensive," not "intensive." He does not aim at getting many bushels of corn from any one acre, for then he would cultivate only a few acres. His purpose is to get as large a total *crop* as possible with a given *expenditure of seed and labour;* and therefore he sows as many

acres [of land, note, that is free] as he can manage to bring under a light
cultivation. . . . (p. 150)

And forthwith we make our first acquaintance with Increasing
Returns: it arrives as a larger rate of return through a more intensive cultivation—the enterprise affording better results in
produce through the combination of more labor and capital with
each *acre* of land:

> . . . he may go too far: he may spread his *work* over so large an area that
> he would gain by concentrating his *capital and labour* on a smaller *space;*
> and under these circumstances . . . the land would give him an *Increasing
> Return;* that is, an extra return larger in proportion than it gives to his
> present expenditure. . . . (pp. 150-51)

And thus we come to a new angle on the principle of *diminishing
return.* It records, by the test of a return in produce, something
short of what the enterpriser could achieve by apportioning more
wisely the amounts of labor and of capital—*combined*—to this
area of land. When he moves to good results, through the application of more labor and capital to a given area of land, he experiences
Increasing Returns. But when he moves toward bad results (still in
terms of produce, note) with the application of more labor and
capital to the area of land, he is experiencing *Diminishing Returns:*

> . . . But if . . . he is using just so much ground as will give him the
> highest return . . . he would lose by concentrating his capital and labour
> on a smaller area. If he . . . were to apply more to his present land, he
> would gain less than . . . by taking up more land [free land still]; he
> would get a *Diminishing Return.* . . . (p. 151)

It appears thus far, then, that these two laws of return do not
formulate two principles, but merely report the antithetical applications of one principle, viz., that the best results are achieved
by that combination of factors that is best; the results from moving
toward it recording, therefore, increasing returns; and, from moving
away from it, diminishing returns. The case is similar to that with
soda biscuits—the principle one of ratio. If they come out yellow
and dry, the fault of course was too much saleratus, or too little
flour; the right thing, indifferently less of the one or more of the
other. With either fixed, it is for the other to get changed, the

rightness solely with the ratio. And similarly, when one has the capital and the labor, or both, and land is free, the remedy for a bad ratio is ready through adding, or, it may be, through subtracting land. Or more may be added of the labor or of the capital or of both—if already these two are rightly related to each other. If, however, the mixture is already made—say, the saleratus in the flour or the flour in the saleratus—with subtractions impossible, the remedy has obviously to be through the addition of whatever is ratio-wise short.

The practical application of this principle of rightness turns, therefore, on what thing you start with as the fixed thing, the thing to which the adaptations have to be made. It would, no doubt, have been physically possible to start with the saleratus, and dose it with the flour. Actually, however, the start would have been the other way about. But whatever you have or choose as the inelastic thing, that thing you dose the other into. And by the test of the ratio principle, the successive doses have almost inevitably a declining unit significance with relation to the ultimate rightness, as a limit point. Progressively better biscuits are not to be had through endlessly repeated doses of the originally short factor. There is a law of diminishing return. But it is a derivative from the ratio principle. There is a limit—something like the valencies of chemistry. And this limit that is implicit in the ratio fact decrees a diminishing significance for the successive stages in the approach to it. The doses must, to be sure, be of a size, or even of changing sizes, appropriate to the situation. Unless you are going entirely to fence your pasture, you may as well not fence at all. Your getting any steam from your boiler is conditioned on fuel enough for a temperature of 212 degrees Fahrenheit.

And still the term that is usual for the case may seem a strange one. To be moving away from the right ratio, rather than toward it, you might expect to find called the law of *diminishing* return, despite the fact that this must be the case of a process becoming *increasingly* bad. But for the additions of the saleratus for salvaging, not only what was earlier put in, but as well the entire investment of flour—why this term of disparagement? The thought, however, is merely of process that, while it is doubtless good for so far as it can be carried, discloses, nevertheless, its ill quality of an early running down, precisely because it faces the bad certainty of its sometime running out. It is analogous to the principle of utility declining toward a zero limit.

Actually, moreover, the economists have never called the antithetical process, that of going wrong and of getting increasingly worse, one of decreasing return. As soon as this good thing—that is nevertheless good at a diminishing rate—is in this aspect thought of as a case of *decline,* there is no room left, in this ratio aspect of the case, for *increasing* returns. And when utility gets on the further side of zero it is called disutility: just as when return falls below nothing it is called loss. There is in this connection no place for increasing returns, if diminishing returns are not to be abandoned. And the principle of diminishing return has its warrant of traditional and established use. If, then, you should turn out to have carried the process of dosing with the saleratus too far—beyond the balance that is wisdom—there is nothing for it but to embark on another and further curative program of dosing with the other ingredient or ingredients. No dosing policy ever leads to anything else than diminishing returns—or ever is anything other than an illustration of it.

This central and unifying principle of ratio should now be clear, along with the two possible ways of violating it in the foregoing case; and as well with the two possible ways of honoring it—by focussing your activities on either one of the two factors involved.

And now we get the general drift of Marshall's provisional formulation. It is the principle of the declining service and the limited efficiency of the dosing regimen. He says (p. 156, note) that "the law of diminishing return bears a close analogy to the law of demand. The return which land gives to a dose of capital and labour may be regarded as the price which land offers for that dose." But Marshall goes on to say that if you start with a bad ratio, as practically always you do, and move thence toward a better, through applying more "expenditure" of capital and labor to less land, where before you had too much, you are illustrating the law of increasing return; while if you started with just enough to go with the capital and labor—or just enough labor and capital to go with the land—and then made an increase on either side—but none on the other—you would have placed yourself within the realm of diminishing return in its bad working: Increasing Return, either of the two ways of getting yourself right with this one ratio principle; Diminishing Return, either of the two ways of getting yourself wrong with this same one ratio principle—in all, therefore, four methods, two directions, one principle. The naming speaks neither for the four different ways, nor for the one principle, but for the two directions.

The immediate issue does not, then, concern the difficulty of getting land and capital, as concrete items employed in agricultural processes, into one sum, or of totaling this composite aggregate with a land area, or of arriving at a sum of all of these for comparison with a volume of corn or grass. Instead, the issue is more narrowly one of definition—of such choice of terms as shall lead away from, rather than into, ambiguity or confusion of thought. For Marshall points to this law of diminishing return as the key to the scatterings or the migrations of peoples. But he is not talking of dispersions or migrations due to the unwise handling of land resources in point of the other factors applied—bad husbandry, the derogatory sense of Diminishing Return—or of these populations having carried their dosings of other things to the land up to the precise point of the right combination, and no further—the law as a commendatory pronouncement, in the meaning just now attached by Marshall to increasing returns—but is only asserting that, in view of the numbers, no tolerable per capita return is to be had from the land. He is talking of the land shortage that crowding means and imposes, without reference to the skill of the culture in general, or to the particular wisdom of the combining of factors. It is just a bad situation:

. . . As his sons [a cultivator's] grow up . . . [with] more capital and labour . . . they will want to cultivate more land. But perhaps by this time all the neighbouring land is already taken up, and in order to get more they must buy it or pay a rent for the use of it, or migrate where they can get it for nothing.

This tendency . . . was the cause of Abraham's parting from Lot, and of most of the migrations of which history tells. And wherever the right to cultivate land is much in request, we may be sure that the tendency to a diminishing return is in full operation. . . . (p. 151)

But this is obviously a social situation rather than any question of rightness or error in individual policies of husbandry. It raises no issues of any individual application of something or other to land, within a situation that has developed landlords and has discovered land rents—all to the outcome that somehow the volume of produce accruing to the cultivator is inadequate, by whatever test he applies. But by the test of a pecuniary accounting, were this in point, the returns from any particular tract of land may be generous exceedingly, especially for the landlord. There is no menace of the land not getting cultivated, though men may leave it, or many leave the country. Nor is the problem one of prices or of wages, but only of the per-capita command of extractive products, mainly food—the difficulty for most individuals of getting enough to eat—not a question of price profits or of land rents; not, that is, a problem of distribution, but solely the fact of a scant distribuendum—the fact of famine, which is nothing but most people hungry most of the time—diminishing returns from the social point of view, and these in terms of nutriment. Socially speaking, and then only in the disparaging emphasis, this is the law of diminishing return. It has no correlate of increasing returns.

But in Marshall's next sentence the individual bearing of the situation is invoked—the way in which, if only over-population had not translated itself into a per-capita inadequacy of land, an individual would act. And in conformity with this individual interpretation of the situation, the analysis reverts to capital and interest, to enterpriser's efforts, to rents, and to a summary of results in which rents, gain margins, interest, and *quantities* of *produce* and of land stand all in one line in a joint appearance:

. . . wherever the right to cultivate land is much in request, we may be sure that the tendency to a diminishing return is in full operation. Were it not for this tendency every farmer could save nearly the whole of his *rent* by giving up all but a small *piece* of his land, and bestowing all his capital and labour on that. If all the *capital* and *labour* which he would in that case apply to it, gave as good a return in proportion [to what?] as that which he now applies to it, he would get from that plot as large a *produce* as he now gets from his whole farm; and he would make a net *gain* of all of his rent, save that of the little *plot* that he retained. (p. 151)

And thus, following the thread of the individual undertaking, with labor and capital as discrete quantities applied to land as an area, and rendering quantity returns, from which nevertheless somehow rents get deduced, the discussion continues:

. . . almost every great authority on agriculture . . . when they tell a farmer that he would gain by applying his capital and labour to a smaller area, they do not necessarily mean that he would get a larger gross produce. It is sufficient . . . that the saving in *rent* would more than counterbalance any probable diminution of the total *returns* that he got from the land. . . . (p. 152)

But there can be no question that in its inception "the great classical Law of Diminishing Return" was public rather than private in interest and application. Malthus was stressing the menace of famine through over-population. The law ran in terms of a declining per-capita product in the extractive industries, and especially in the food industries, with an increasing population. It was presumably through observation of the commonplace facts of competitive farming that the law was formulated. But still it was formulated in its public and national applications—"its chief application, not to any one particular crop, but to all the chief food crops":

. . . It refers to a country the whole land of which is already in the hands of active business men . . . and asserts that an increase in the total amount of *capital* applied to agriculture in that country will yield diminishing returns of *produce* in general. This statement is akin to, but yet quite distinct from, the statement that if any farmer makes a bad distribution of his resources between different plans of cultivation, he will get a markedly diminishing return from those elements of expenditure which he has driven to excess. (p. 408)

Promptly, nevertheless, the law took on individual, competitive and price aspects, leading ultimately, to be sure, to a widely inclusive principle, but first to that of the margin of cultivation of land—an analysis serviceable for explaining the emergence of the hires of land, but leading easily to the specious method of marginal isolation for the exclusion of these hires from the cost-causal relation to price; thereby an indispensable succour to the labor theory of value; and following therefrom, a century-long weariness of mystery, muddle and mischief.

For it is evident that the easiest and most obvious illustrations of the law of diminishing return are in these agricultural processes. In the lack of any clear recognition of the analogous generalization of the diminishing incremental utility of all direct goods, the declining incremental significance for price purposes of all indirect goods other than land escaped formulation. The marginal analysis at large was yet to be developed. Even marginal cost of production was in the main associated with the margin of cultivation. In the large, it is clear, the marginal law remained a land law—the margin of production, a land margin. It had to do with the extractive industries. And just this for most of Marshall's analyses it still remains. Still with economists at large the general law finds illustration mainly in agricultural processes. And this, as we have seen, the doctrinal necessities of the classical analysis imperatively required.

But never, after all, in its formulation or application, has the law remained consistently a public or national law. Always—and almost by necessity—it has appealed for illustration to private enterprise and to price processes. Its later applications have been mainly to the price analysis. But the trail of its origin is nevertheless still over national problems. Marshall says (p. 339, note): "The expenses of production of any amount of a raw commodity may best be estimated with reference to the 'margin of production' at which no rent is paid." It is this absorption in the land aspects of the law that dictates the conviction that there is one analysis for cost of production in agriculture and another for cost in other industries.

Marshall continues: "But this method of speaking has great difficulties with regard to commodities that obey the law of increasing return"—whatever that may later turn out to be. The prevailingly public bearing of diminishing returns is also manifest in the following:

But when the older economists spoke of the Law of Diminishing Return they were looking at the problems of agriculture not only from the point of view of the individual cultivator but also from that of the nation as a whole. Now if the nation *as a whole* finds its stock of planing machines or ploughs inappropriately large or inappropriately small, it can redistribute its resources. It can obtain more of that in which it is deficient . . . *but it cannot do that in regard to land:* it can cultivate its land more intensively, but it cannot get any more. . . . (p. 170)

But obviously it can, as far as fertility is concerned; and by transportation many nations can increase their stock of available land with regard to area. Moreover, the stock of land for any one product is elastic through the substitution of one use for another. Agriculture has its different products, as well as manufacturing. Hides, fibres, cotton, wool, lumber and rubber are not to be reduced, along with meat and cereals, to a homogeneity of nutritive content. Nor are even items of spice or flavor, like radishes, celery and pepper, or even most of the fruits that are lacking in any significant nutritive quality, to be reduced for purposes of the rent analysis or for relative prices at large, to terms of corn.[1]

An approximately equal degree of inelasticity with that land, even as area, attaches for a generation to the stock, or stocks, of human beings. In any case, there is in the business world no point in talking about what nations do or do not do, or about what they could or could not do, were they to try. We are not engaged in generalizing any of those collective processes that are actual—still less those that might be, but are not; or those that can never be.

But with the later recognition that the law of diminishing return applies in the competitive sense to equipment goods equally with land, no room was left for any special significance for price purposes

---

[1] ". . . consider the competition between various branches of agriculture for the same land. This case is simpler than that of urban land, because farming is a single business so far as the main crops are concerned; though the rearing of choice trees (including vines), flowers, vegetables etc. affords scope for various kinds of specialized business ability. The classical economists were therefore justified in provisionally supposing that all kinds of agricultural produce can be regarded as equivalent to certain quantities of corn; and that all the land will be used for agricultural purposes, with the exception of building sites which are a small and nearly fixed part of the whole. But when we concentrate our attention on any one product, as for instance, hops, it may seem that a new principle is introduced. That is however not the case." (pp. 434-35)

in the appeal to the margin of cultivation, or to the device of marginal isolation, as peculiarly appropriate either to land or to agricultural enterprises, or as valid for any purposes of the distinction between price-determining and price-determined costs. And especially for Marshall, in view of his derivation of human beings from pecuniary investment, along with the ordinary sorts of equipment goods, the necessity became imperative either to abandon the recourse to the marginal uses of indirect goods for the segregation of price-determining money costs, or to abandon the entire doctrine of the determination of relative prices by relative costs of production. Either the device was indefensible with lands, or it must be extended to implement goods—to say nothing of the productive capacities of human beings.

But Marshall's choice was of an intermediate position—not, for all periods, the abandonment of either money costs or the money-cost aspects of efforts and waitings as explanatory of price, but only the abandonment for ordinary periods, pre-normal periods, and the retention for normal periods—the bearing not for all times denied, but merely postponed to times that never will be—at the most a doctrine of trend. Only, then, in the normal period can land hires and other hires come into their own in point of functional relations to the fixation of prices. The marginal analysis, taken by Marshall to be valid during ordinary periods for the exclusion of all hires of indirect goods from price-determining costs, seems to him to permit in normal periods the inclusion of all of them excepting the hires of the spatial-extension aspects of land—the marginal-isolation procedure becoming in these normal times selective, as earlier it was not, and all of this through some virtue attaching to the investment process at its earlier time, the time of the terminus-a-quo, and lasting over into the later time as a functional distinction that attaches to equipment hires and to labor hires a causal bearing on prices that is denied to land hires. The marginal analysis applies equally at all times to all; but marginal isolation, in normal periods, only to land. The argument against this view does not need to be repeated. Only the affiliations of the view with the law of diminishing return are here to be made manifest. It becomes evident, then, that with Marshall there must remain a sense in which the law of diminishing return with reference to land has aspects peculiar to it, not only in social, but in competitive problems.

But is it as the source of raw commodities that these peculiar aspects of the law attach to land? The distinction here in mind is not, it seems, a mere reformulation of the distinction between the extractive and the non-extractive industries, else mining would go along rather with agriculture than with manufacturing, with mining royalties excluded along with land rents from any causal bearing on prices. This distinction of function comes back again to one of responsiveness—not of the appropriateness of the law of diminishing return or of the device of marginal isolation—and thus fertility rents go along with machine rents and mining royalties, with the rents of land, as spatial extension, on the other side. Buildings also, it is clear, are capital; but the principle of diminishing return applies to them:

... Buildings tower up towards the sky; ... and for this expenditure there is a return of extra convenience, but it is a diminishing return ... a limit is at least reached after which it is better to pay more ground rent for a larger area than to go on piling up storey on storey any further; just as the farmer finds that at last a stage is reached at which more intensive cultivation will not pay its expenses, and it is better to pay more rent for extra land ... the theory of ground rents is substantially the same as that of farm rents. ... (p. 168)

And the law applies, moreover, much more widely:

And what is true of building land is true of many other things. If a manufacturer has, say, three planing machines there is a certain amount of work which he can get out of them easily. If he wants to get more work from them he must laboriously economize every minute of their time during the ordinary hours, and perhaps work overtime. Thus after they are once well employed, every successive application of effort to them brings him a diminishing return. At last ... he finds it cheaper to buy a fourth machine. ... (p. 168)

And as we have earlier seen, the law applies to plows. But it is obviously now a somewhat far cry to the further position taken by Marshall:

. . . It [the law of diminishing return] refers to a country . . . and asserts that an increase in the total amount of capital applied to agriculture in that country will yield diminishing returns of produce in general. This statement is akin to, but yet quite distinct from, the statement that if any farmer makes a bad distribution of his resources between different plans of cultivation, he will get a markedly diminishing return from those elements of expenditure which he has driven to excess. (p. 408)

The distinction between prime and supplementary costs appears to apply to every case of over-equipment in totals or in the specific factors of an undertaking, presenting thus a situation of maladjustment or of misproportion of factors, and permitting of differential incremental costs. It applies, then, to land commitments equally with others:

If a manufacturer expends an inappropriately large amount of his resources on machinery . . . or on his office staff, so that he has to employ some of them on work that it is not worth what it costs; then his excessive expenditure in that particular direction . . . may be said to yield him a "diminishing return." . . . (p. 169)

But it is still clear that Marshall preserves the distinction between the land law and the law in other connections; and it now becomes also clear that this distinction is ultimately one of responsiveness. For the discussion continues:

. . . But this use of the phrase, though strictly correct is apt to mislead unless used with caution. For when the tendency to a diminishing return from increased labour and capital applied to land is regarded as a special instance of the general tendency to diminishing return from any agent of production . . . one is apt to take it for granted that the supply of the other factors can be increased . . . to deny . . . the fixedness of the whole stock of cultivable land in an old country—which was the main foundation of those great classical discussions of the law of diminishing return, which we have just been considering. Even the individual farmer may not always be able to get an additional ten or fifty acres adjoining his own farm, just when he wants them, save at a prohibitive price. And in that respect land differs from *most other* agents of production even from the individual point of view. This difference may indeed be regarded as of little account in regard to the individual farmer. But from the social point of view, . . . it is vital. . . . (p. 169)

For the purposes of the individual farmer, the distinction that turns on the difficulty of getting more land just when he wants it, may not impress him as against repairs from town, or another reaper or engineer or horse. Such distinctions as are valid here have probably more to do with the length or irrevocability of the commitment. In any case, however, Marshall is now reducing the law to a wide one of the wise proportion of factors, with the application of it to land merely a special case that may be looked at either in its collective or its competitive aspects. And it becomes further obvious that the law cannot stand as distinguishable in its relation to land through any special application of the marginal analysis to land uses; or from any defensible application of the device of marginal isolation to it; or from any exclusion of land from the generalization that advantage for gain always attends the right proportion of factors, and harm the wrong. Even, indeed, with the law in its social formulation, the principle is the same, only that in the competitive and individual sense the disadvantage is due either to the error of the individual or to his inadequate resources, while in the social sense the deficiency attaches to Destiny or to Divine Ordinance—responsiveness tied up with origins. Equally in either case the principle is one of proportions, in view of whatever are the terms of modification. But Marshall still insists that—

. . . though there is some analogy between all these various tendencies to diminishing return, they yet are not identical. Thus the diminishing return which arises from an ill-proportioned application of the various agents of production into a particular task has little in common with that broad tendency to the pressure of a crowded and growing population on the means of subsistence. The great classical Law of Diminishing Return has its chief application, not to any one particular crop, but to all the chief food crops . . . and asserts that an increase in the total amount of capital applied to agriculture in that country will yield diminishing returns of produce in general. . . . (p. 408)

But not the less in Marshall's view is there the law, or a law, of diminishing return in the individual and gain-seeking sense. Thus the proportions in a total investment may be improved through a final dose of building charges or equally well through a final dose of ground charges:

We may apply the phrase *the margin of building* to that accommodation which it is only just worth while to get from a given site . . . suppose
this accommodation to be given by the top floor of the building.

By erecting this floor, instead of spreading the building over more
ground, a saving in the cost of land is effected. . . . The accommodation
. . . is only just enough to be worth what it costs without allowing anything for the rent of land. . . .

Suppose, for instance, that a person is planning a hotel or a factory;
and considering how much land to take for the purpose. If land is cheap
he will take much of it; if it is dear he will take less and build high. . . .
(pp. 447-48).

And again; just as the men in the factory may be too many, at
their wage, for the space provided, at the charge for it, so the space
may be unwisely large for the men. Or there may be not idle space
or men, but idle machines:

. . . the efficiency of specialized machinery or specialized skill is but one
condition of its economic use; the other is that sufficient work should be
found to keep it well employed. . . .
. . . so far as the economy of production goes, men and machines stand
on much the same footing. . . . (pp. 264-65)

. . . On the margin of indifference between hand-power and horse-
power their prices must be proportionate to their efficiency. . . .

.   .   .   .

. . . We have noticed . . . how the proportion of hops and malt in ale
can be varied . . . the extra price which can be got for ale by increasing
the quantity of hops in it. . . .
The notion of the marginal employment of any agent of production
implies a possible tendency to diminishing return from its increased employment.
Excessive applications of any means to the attainment of any end are
indeed sure to yield diminishing returns in every branch of business; and,
one may say, in all the affairs of life. . . . (pp. 406-7)

. . . the return . . . just sufficient to repay his [an owner-cultivator's]
outlay and reward him for his own work . . . will be the dose on the
margin of cultivation, whether it happens to be applied to rich or to
poor land. . . . (p. 630)

Marshall's seeming indifference to whether diminishing returns
—inclusive of one meaning of increasing returns—shall run in
terms of doses of labor or of wage outlays, waiting or interest, land-

use alienated or land rent disbursed, product as quantity or product as price income, has already been incidentally noted. It is, nevertheless, shortly to be stressed that the law of diminishing return, and along with it the laws of increasing and of constant return, appear to be indicated mainly by the test of their bearing on prices. Or, perhaps more accurately, each of these laws is a law of prices through unit costs. When the situation is one to which rising money costs, marginal or unit, are appropriate to greater output, the law is that of diminishing return—a diminishing quantum of product per unit of money cost. Constant returns report costs unchanging as volume of output changes—neither more nor less goods per unit of cost. Increasing returns report unit costs falling with expanding product—more goods per unit of cost.

We seem to be dealing, therefore, with combinations of non-commensurable quantity facts, both of process and of product, that work out into divergent price results, and that emerge finally in functional classifications, finding their bases in price outcomes, either as test or as evidence. Actually, however, in Marshall's view, is this law of diminishing return to be interpreted to formulate considerations of quantity as distinguished from considerations of price, or, possibly, to formulate relations between quantities as process facts and prices as outcome facts? The following quotations, for example, appear to run consistently in terms of quantities of capital and of labor, somehow totaled, as over against quantities of produce, but without any assured reference to individual undertakings for gain:

Thus various then are the parts which man plays in aiding nature to raise the different kinds of agricultural produce. In each case he works on till the extra *return* got by extra capital and labour has so far *diminished* that it will no longer remunerate him for applying them. . . . We are thus brought to consider the law of diminishing return.

It is important to note that the return to capital and labour now under discussion is measured by the *amount* of the produce raised independently of any changes that may meanwhile take place in the exchange value or price of produce . . . the law itself . . . has to do not with the value of the produce raised, but only with its amount. (pp. 148-49)

. . . much land . . . could be made to give more than double its present gross produce if twice the present capital and labour were applied to it skilfully. Very likely . . . if all English farmers were as able, wise and energetic as the best are, they might profitably apply twice the capital and labour that is now applied. Assuming rent to be one-fourth of the present *produce,* they might get seven hundredweight of produce for every four that they now get. . . . But . . . taking farmers as they are . . . there is not open to them a short road to riches by giving up a great part of their land, by concentrating all their capital and labour on the remainder, and saving for their own pockets the rent of all but that remainder. . . . (p. 152)

But earlier on the same page Marshall indicates nothing more for the present purpose than, possibly, his indifference to the particular line of our present inquiry. The case is, however, quite definitely presented as one of individual pecuniary enterprise:

. . . If a farmer pays a fourth of his produce as rent, he would gain by concentrating his capital and labour on less land, provided the extra capital and labour applied to each acre gave anything more than three-fourths as good a return in proportion, as he got from his earlier expenditure. (p. 152)

Again, as a "final statement":

Although an improvement in the arts of agriculture may raise the *rate* of *return* which land generally affords to any given *amount* of capital and labour . . . a continued increase in the application of capital and labour to land must ultimately result in a diminution of the extra *produce* which can be obtained by a given extra amount of capital and labour. (p. 153)

Increasing Returns

We have already noted Marshall's report of increasing returns as indicating merely the course of approach to the right proportion of factors—with diminishing returns interpreted as a movement in the reverse direction. This, however, is to make increasing returns bear the meaning commonly attached to diminishing returns, the meaning, moreover, commonly attached to the term by Marshall himself. He does not, however, long abide by this view; though in essentials it again is presented in a note on page 151: "Increasing return . . . is also partly due to the fact that where land is very slightly cultivated the farmer's crops are apt to be smothered by nature's crops of weeds,"—more labor applied to the care of the crop making for better results. But nowhere else, it seems, does Marshall so interpret the term.

We have earlier noted his selection of rising unit costs or rising incremental costs as indicating the presence of diminishing returns, or, it may be, as declaring the ultimate meaning of the law. Falling unit costs in turn mark the law of increasing return. But those influences making for higher costs and higher prices may be offset by these other influences making for falling prices. When in their bearing on costs and prices these two sets of influences are equilibrated, the law of constant return emerges. Taken together, then, these three laws of return register all of the possibilities for price with changing aggregates of output: the price will stay constant, or will rise, or will fall—constant, diminishing and increasing returns:

We have seen that an increase in normal demand, while leading in every case to an increased production, will in some cases raise and in others lower prices. But now we are to see that increased facilities for supply (causing the supply schedule to be lowered) will always lower the normal price at the same time that it leads to an increase in the amount produced. For so long as the normal demand remains unchanged an increased supply can be sold only at a diminished price; but the fall of price . . . will be much greater in some cases than in others. It will be small if the commodity obeys the law of diminishing return; because then the difficulties attendant on an increased production will tend to counteract the new facilities of supply. On the other hand, if the commodity obeys the law of increasing return, the increased production will bring with it increased facilities . . . and the two together will enable a great increase in production and consequent fall in price to be attained before the fall of the supply price [schedule] is overtaken by the fall of the demand price [the price at which the more will be purchased]. . . . (pp. 465-66)

. . . we say broadly that while the part which nature plays in production shows a tendency to diminishing return, the part which man plays shows a tendency to increasing return. . . . (p. 318)

The thought with increasing returns has presumably to do with the advance in the productive efficiency of men, through science in its bearing on technology, through tools and machines, and through methods and organization. Many of these advances, however, are significant for agriculture and for the extractive industries in general; and for mining as notably as for manufacturing. But Mar-

shall's inclination to think of the principle of diminishing return
as in some peculiar sense a land law, and as having some peculiar
association with the extractive industries in general, the while that
the principle of increasing return is taken to apply to manufacturing
and transportation—and perhaps also to merchandising—is evident in the foregoing, as also in the following quotation:

... in those industries which are not engaged in raising raw produce an
increase of labour and capital generally gives a return increased more
than in proportion [to what?] ; and further this improved organization
tends to diminish or even override any increased resistance which nature
may offer to raising increased amounts of raw produce. If the actions of
the laws of increasing and diminishing return are balanced we have *the
law of constant return,* and an increased produce is obtained by labour
and sacrifice increased just in proportion.

For the two tendencies towards increasing and diminishing return
press constantly against one another. . . . In a country . . . in which the
blanket trade is but slightly developed . . . it may happen that an increase
in the aggregate production of blankets diminishes the proportionate
difficulty of manufacturing by just as much as it increases that of raising
the raw material. In that case the actions of the laws of diminishing
and of increasing return would just neutralize one another; and blankets
would conform to the law of constant return. . . . (pp. 318-19)

... The *law of increasing return* may be worded thus:—An increase of
labour and capital leads generally to improved organization, which increases the efficiency of the *work of labour* and *capital.* (p. 318)

This formal wording of the law of increasing return makes
room, it must be noted, for the significance of human development
only in the aspect of improving organization—not precisely the
relation of the size of the industrial or business unit to its effectiveness for amount of produce, or for rate or amount of pecuniary
gain, but for effectiveness of that better internal structure that is
made possible by the change in size. Moreover, Marshall elsewhere
makes it clear that increasing returns may apply also in agriculture
—the truth being, it seems, in Marshall's view, merely that relatively rarely does agriculture illustrate in the large, or in any
particular undertaking, this trend toward falling unit costs to which
the better organization with better size may open the way. Factually,
no doubt, this position is becoming less secure. Even with the

ordinary lines of farming the trend toward the larger unit is marked. Rubber and fruit plantations, forestry undertakings, mines and fisheries, and the enormous wheat farms of the Soviets deserve attention in this regard. But it is the logic rather than the purely factual basis of Marshall's analysis that at present interests us. Not even in the national or social aspect are these generalizations of Marshall's safe. In no competitive and individual sense, at any rate, can these two laws of return be set over against each other by the types of industry to which they apply. The law of proportions and the law of size, or of organization made possible by size, may be illustrated at the same time in the same undertaking:

. . . parallel cases can be found of a diminishing return to particular resources when applied in undue proportion, even in industries which yield an increasing return to increased applications of capital and labour when appropriately distributed. (p. 409)

An industry may be well off in point of proportions and badly off in point of size, or the other way about.

Of these three laws, then, only that of constant return appears to be essentially nothing but a price-record law, a mere declaration of price outcomes. The others purport to refer to causes. In any case, however, whether they are more than mere price affirmations, they arrive somehow at summations in price terms; prices rising, prices falling, prices neither rising nor falling. Whatever, then, may be the causal influences invoked by these laws, they must be influences accounted for in price terms, precisely because these laws report them as emerging in these differentiating price outcomes—the laws so formulated as to fix the discussion, in point both of causes and of results, in the price field. What, then, are the functional relations and connections between land areas—not land values or land rents —and the prices of agricultural produce? Do these laws of return tie up with efforts or only with the wages of efforts? With waiting, or only with interest? Or with things in general, or only with the hires of the things? What for the purposes does *produce* mean? Is it a mere quantum of output or is it a price sum? Precisely what is capital, and what the dose of it that gets applied? Is it machinery? A dose of fertilizer or of seed as a quantity might fall short of being relevant; but it would be intelligible. But what is a dose of building or of threshing machine or of combined harvester? Is capital being thought of as mechanical appliances, equipment goods, or as funds for all sorts of buying and hiring? And what, in turn, is labor? And how get it and capital together for the getting dosed into a land area—to the end of a price outcome?

We have already made incidental reference to some of Marshall's ambiguities in this regard that no specific reference to the national or the private formulation of the particular law would unravel. But so, in turn, has Marshall noted them:

It is true that when the tendency to diminishing return is generalized, the return [but nothing said about the debits] is apt to be expressed in terms of value, and not of quantity. It must however be conceded that the older method of measuring return in terms of quantity often jostled against the difficulty of rightly interpreting a dose of labour and capital without the aid of a money measure: and that, though helpful for a broad preliminary survey, it cannot be carried very far.

But . . . if we want to bring to a common standard *the productiveness of lands* in distant times or places . . . it is probably best to take as a common standard a day's unskilled labour of given efficiency. . . .

A similar difficulty is found in comparing the returns obtained by labour and capital applied under different circumstances. So long as the crops are of the same kind, the quantity of one return can be measured off against that of another; but, when they are of different kinds, they cannot be compared till they are reduced to a common measure of value. . . . (p. 171)

But this is only a part of the difficulty. The produce of different lands can be compared only when reduced to a price statement. But, to be significant for comparison, both of these crops that are severally priced must be set over against the price debits incurred in obtaining them. What Marshall intends to offer for this is not clear. He continues:

. . . When, for instance, it is said that land [as mere tract?] would give better returns to the capital and labour expended on it [and in it?] with one crop or rotation of crops than with another, the statement must be understood to hold only on the basis of the prices at the time [what prices?]. In such a case we must take the whole period of rotation together . . . counting on the one hand all the labour and capital applied during the whole period, and on the other the aggregate returns of all the crops. (pp. 171-72)

Assuming, however, that Marshall intends completely to reduce to price terms this law of diminishing return in its competitive aspect, it remains entirely clear that he does not intend any such thing with the law of increasing return, though it is not so clear why he should not:

Increasing Return is a relation between a quantity of effort and sacrifice on the one hand, and a quantity of product on the other. . . . To measure outlay and output in terms of money is a tempting, but a dangerous resource: for a comparison of money outlay with money returns is apt to slide into an estimate of the rate of profit on capital. (pp. 319-20)

But no matter how clear may be Marshall's intentions in this respect, he does not succeed. He falls inadvertently into the price morass. It is especially with the law of constant return—a good-for-nothing law anyway, one thinks, as pronouncing nothing more than a mathematical truism—that the misadventure occurs. For, at the equating point of a constant of price, this purely quantity law of increasing returns comes into balance against the influence of the law of diminishing returns as a purely price law—in point, at least, of the produce. On the side of increasing return, therefore, there is a trend toward a smaller *quantity* of *effort* and sacrifice per unit of *produce*. This trend is taken to offset in point of degree the trend under diminishing return toward a result smaller in terms of price per unit of unskilled labor. Marshall says (p. 318): "If the actions of the laws of increasing and diminishing return are balanced we have the *law of constant return.* . . . " The effort does not promise success. Almost as well attempt to equate the rush of a half dozen stallions with the dogma of the Invisible Church.

Chapter XV

INTEREST

IN a price society all individual incomes, with the exception of mere windfalls, arrive either from efforts or from possessions. Effort is compensated either through wages or through profits in the restricted sense. Property incomes arrive either as the rents of particular items of goods or as interest on loan contracts. Dividends are a composite of effort and property incomes. In the competitive pecuniary process all these individual incomes are awarded through the price mechanism. Either as things commanding a selling price or as things retained on reservation terms they fall within the price system. Free goods are not in this sense income. The price analysis is therefore appropriate to everything falling within the income concept—in principle a price return that reports an equating point between demand and supply schedules.

In the widest sense of the term *interest,* all incomes from wealth are included—land rents, house rents, piano rents, automobile rents, as well as the incomes from equipment goods. These last it is that Marshall calls quasi-rents, since they bear for a time, as he holds, a functional relation to the fixation of prices similar to that of land rent. Equally well, perhaps, they might have been termed quasi-interest, in view of their similarity to interest in its narrower technical sense.

For Marshall rightly recognizes that in the usages of the market place interest is merely one among the many different property incomes. Interest in the business world is a money return on loaned money or on wealth reported in money terms—a return computed as a rate on a money base, a per cent, per-dollar, per-period return. That capital with which interest has to do is quite other than capital in the sense of a factor of production, an equipment good in a mechanical process, or than any sort of durable direct good. Instead, it is a money sum that is loaned. Or it is a property computed or

439

regarded as a money sum—interest and income reported in terms of a dollar-time unit. It is analogous to the ton-mile unit with freights.

In this aspect it is instructive to note that the common law recognizes two sorts of rental contracts: leases of realty and bailments of personalty. The charges that are rents in the inclusive sense of that term are also interest in the inclusive sense of the term interest—returns from wealth, incomes from capital. In the narrower and technical sense, however, interest is a term inappropriate to lease and bailment contracts. These last provide for the return of the specific property covered by the contract. It is no part of the purpose of the interest contract that a specific return be made. Never is such a return stipulated. The interest contract has to do solely with money loans. And, like leases and bailments, it is a double-obligation contract; an undertaking with regard to the property parted with and another undertaking covering the time charge for it. With the interest contract there is a principal sum to be liquidated through a money payment; and along with it there is a time charge, which also is stipulated to be in the form of money as a per cent of the principal sum.

The interest contract, that is to say, has to do with the exchange intermediate, with the standard thing. Only when an investment or a rental contract is stated, not in terms of a specific thing, e.g., a farm, but of the price of it, e.g., a $10,000 farm, with the time charge set, not in particular things, for example hay or sheep, but as a percentage of return computed on a money appraisal of the land as base, does the essential interest relation take on the technical interest statement. And even were the subject of a loan hay or sheep —free, however, of any obligation to return the specific property lent, and with a time charge computed as a percentage agio in hay or sheep—this intermediate sort of contract would be of the interest rather than of the bailment type, with hay and sheep appointed as the deferred-payment standard for the case.

Rent and interest, therefore, when each term is used in its most inclusive sense are loose and over-lapping designations. It is solely with interest in its narrow and technical sense that precision with terms is achieved; interest pointing thus to a field of phenomena exclusively its own and to problems and analyses peculiar to it. What account is to be given of the rates of return on money loans?

When any particular thing, as a house, a piano, or a sewing machine is lent out, the payment for it is often called *Rent*. . . . But we cannot properly speak of the interest yielded by a machine. If we use the term "interest" at all, it must be in relation not to the machine itself, but to its money *value*. . . . (p. 74)

Rent is therefore an amount of return from an item of wealth purely as such. But this is not to deny that the owners of lands or horses or machines get returns on them that are essentially interest returns. These returns can obviously be carried over into the interest form of report, as a percentage return on a money-valued investment. But the problems of rent and of interest are separate problems in point both of reasons and of processes. Rent is a mere sum, an amount, whether of money or of something else. Commonly it is a hire apportioned to a factor in a productive process. Its explanations are distributive. Interest is not an amount but a rate. It accrues not from a thing but from a money loan. There is no obvious or necessary connection between the two types of return. Rents may bear on interest rates; but they are not interest rates; nor are they safely to be invoked to explain interest rates. In fact, interest is not conditioned on processes of production taking place anywhere, excepting, to be sure, in the long run as a condition of human existence. Moreover, the sum that shall be invested in any item of property, or the money value to be ascribed to it, is commonly to be arrived at only on the basis of an interest factor already given. A farm commanding a rent of $500 annually will be worth not far from $5000 where interest rates run near to 10 per cent, but will be worth near $10,000 if interest rates run in general only half so high. That you can buy for $1000 a tract of pasture land or a dwelling or a machine that will net you upwards of $50 annually may decide you to offer a five per cent rate for funds— seemingly, therefore, so far, an explanation for the interest phenomenon. Only how account for the prices at which you can buy?

Such essentially is Marshall's report of interest and of the capital base of it:

> The payment . . . for the use of a loan . . . expressed as the ratio which that payment bears to the loan . . . is called *interest*. And this term is also used more broadly to represent the money equivalent of the whole income which is derived from capital. It is commonly expressed as a certain percentage on the "capital" sum of the loan. Whenever this is done the capital must not be regarded as a stock of things in general. It must be regarded as a stock of one particular thing, money, which is taken to represent them. . . .
>
> The command over goods to a given money value, which can be applied to any purpose, is often described as "free" or "floating" capital. (p. 73)
>
> Thus the rate of interest is a ratio: and the two things which it connects are both sums of money. So long as capital is "free," and the sum of money or general purchasing power over which it gives command is known, the net money income, expected to be derived from it, can be represented at once as bearing a given ratio . . . to that sum. But when the free capital has been invested in a particular thing, its money value cannot as a rule be ascertained except by capitalizing the net income which it will yield: and therefore the causes which govern it are likely to be akin in a greater or less degree to those which govern rents. (p. 412)

It may be taken, then, as clear that—

(1) The capital with which the interest contract has to do, the capital on which interest runs as a percentage of a money obligation as principal, is money capital—free or general or floating capital.

(2) Capital in any other form commands, not interest, but hires that are of the general nature of rents.

Therefore capital, as that for the control of which interest is paid, has never any direct connection, and no necessary connection, either direct or indirect, with capital as industrial goods or even as any sort of production or consumption good either durable or temporary.

The interest problem as Marshall presents it lends itself readily to the ordinary demand and supply analysis. And thus when once the various demands for each particular sort of capital funds are accounted for, and when also therewith the supplies of these funds, the theory of interest becomes complete. The task is, then, on the demand side to explain the price-offer schedules for funds; and on the supply side to explain the funds-offer schedules. Thus and only thus can interest be analyzed.

Precisely in line with the foregoing is Marshall's admirable formulation of the interest problem. Interest as a rate per cent per dollar per period is presented as the point of adjustment between a rate-schedule of demands for funds as over against a rate-schedule of offers of funds:

. . . the demand for the loan of capital is the aggregate of the demands of all individuals in all trades; and it obeys a law similar to that which holds for the sale of commodities: just as there is a certain amount of a commodity which can find purchasers at any given price. When the price rises the amount that can be sold diminishes, and so it is with regard to the use of capital. (p. 521)

. . . a quasi-rent . . . in the long run . . . is expected to . . . yield a normal rate of interest . . . on the free capital, represented by a definite sum of money that was invested in producing it. By definition the rate of interest is a percentage; that is a relation between two numbers (see above, p. 412). A machine is not a number. . . . (p. 424, note)

Further extremely significant similarities between the rental and the interest contract have now to be noted. Both contracts have to do with wealth in its time aspect—with hires that attach through lapse of time. A lease, for instance for a year, is the sale of a year's control of a particular item of property. The rent is the difference between what the farm is worth from now on and what it is worth from a year hence on; the lease the alienation of the first year's term of service out of the total of services attaching to the complete ownership of the farm—the sale of a first-year segment from eternity.

Precisely similar in principle is the loan of a sum of money or currency—the interest payment the agreed differential between a sum of money now and the same sum of money a year hence. Interest at 5 per cent per annum means that a dollar now is of equal worth with $1.05 a year hence—the control for the first-year segment out of eternity being transferred at a five-cent charge. Interest is a hire or an agio attaching with lapsing time to the control of money, a time charge reported as so many units per hundred loaned. It merely formulates differently the same fact to define interest as a rate of premium in favor of present money in the exchange relation between present money and future money. But whatever the form of statement, the five per cent of interest means that $5 is the stipulated charge between lender and borrower attaching to a year's control of $100 of purchasing power.

Rent and interest are then alike thus far: with both there is a double agreement; a principal thing lent and to be returned, and a time-charge payment. With both there is a lender's abstaining. With both there is a borrower's payment for a time control. With both the relation is one of an exchange of a present control for a future control; 100 now, for example, for 105 then—the rent or the interest the agreed boot to reinstate the equality disturbed by the lapse of time. Equally, therefore, rent and interest are time differentials, which is merely another way of asserting that they are equally time-control charges. Equally these contracts report in money terms the preference for having now as against having later. Equally they are sales of time segments of property. Equally, therefore, as reporting the price of this control or of this property segment, they must appeal to the same ultimate principles of explanation. It need not for the purpose matter that farms and renters being widely different, and slaves, mules, horses and workmen not interchangeable items out of great stocks, there can be no such large fluid and fully competitive market as that which attends the demand for and supply of funds. These are rather issues of process or of precision than of ultimate principle.

Nothing in the foregoing appears to be controversial from the point of view of Marshall's analysis of interest. If there are issues they lie further ahead. His demand and supply setting of the problem of the hire of loan-fund capital admirably formulates the problem. Only therefore in point of the adequacy of his account of the derivation of these demands and supplies schedules can there be occasion for criticism or controversy.

We may now set out in greater detail the analysis of the demand for funds:

Everyone is aware that no payment would be offered for the use of capital unless some gain were expected from that use; and further that these gains are of many kinds. Some borrow to meet a pressing need, real or imaginary. . . . Some borrow to obtain machinery, and other "intermediate" goods . . . some to obtain hotels, theatres and other things which yield their services directly, but are yet a source of profit to those who control them. Some borrow houses for themselves to live in, or else the means wherewith to buy or build their own houses; and the absorption of the resources of the country in such things as houses increases, other things being equal, with every increase in those resources and every consequent fall in the rate of interest. . . . (pp. 580-81)

It is not, to be sure, quite clear in what meaning Marshall is here using the term *capital*. In a preceding paragraph Marshall uses capital as the correlative of labor in the factor sense, and as relevant to the problem of the distribution of a jointly produced product:

The relations between demand and supply cannot be studied by themselves in the case of capital any more than they could in the case of labour. All the elements of the great central problem of distribution and exchange mutually govern one another. . . . (p. 580)

The quotation with which we started opens consistently with this concrete capital notion. But with the some that "borrow to meet a pressing need . . . and pay others to sacrifice the present to the future," the thought almost certainly shifts over to the funds concept of capital. Note also the borrowing of houses or "the means wherewith to buy or build their own houses." This must certainly carry the meaning of funds—excepting for "the absorption of the resources of the country" that the building entails, and for the increased construction of houses that goes on "with every increase in those resources and every consequent fall in the rate of interest." *Capital* appears here to shift its meaning over from concrete items of wealth or of product to *funds*—and thence back to the wealth and the resources—but all the while without reference to the notion of capital as a factor of production and a claimant in the distributive process. And even though it may have been securely left to the reader to make due allowances for shifts in the meaning of the term, it is still true that the movement of the analysis leaves room for but one meaning. With two meanings for the term the analysis becomes not only puzzling but incoherent. With the concrete or factor notion it is worse. With the funds meaning it is intelligible though inconsistent. Presumably Marshall is in the main thinking of funds—general, free or floating capital—since he has elsewhere definitely committed himself to the funds meaning of capital for purposes of the interest problem. Is he, however, quite definitely discussing interest? So one infers; and the chapter specifically deals with *Interest of Capital*. The paragraph ends with his mention of "the demand for durable stone houses in place of wood houses which . . . indicates that a country is growing in wealth, and that capital is to be had at a lower rate of interest; and it acts on the market for capital and on the rate of interest in the same way as would a demand for new factories or railways." Moreover, it seems clearly to be funds that are the subject of discussion in the next paragraph:

. . . people will not lend gratis as a rule; because, even if they have not themselves some good use to which to turn the capital *or its equivalent,* they are sure to be able to find others to whom its use would be of benefit, and who would pay for the loan of it. . . . (p. 581)

It is in addition fairly certain that in the first few lines of the following paragraph capital means funds; though it is not at all so clear for the remainder of the paragraph:

. . . few, even among the Anglo-Saxon and other steadfast and self-disciplined races, care to save a large part of their incomes . . . many openings have been made for the use of capital in recent times . . . and thus everyone understands generally the causes which have kept the supply of accumulated *wealth* so small relatively to the *demand for its use,* that that use is on the balance a source of gain, and can therefore require a payment when loaned. . . . (p. 581)

But in the next paragraph the meaning must be clearly that of wealth or resources or factor goods—all three, it seems—excepting to be sure, for the one word *income:*

. . . The chief task of economics then as regards capital is to set out in order and in their mutual relations, all the forces which operate in the *production* and accumulation *of wealth* and the *distribution of income;* so that as regards both capital and *other agents of production* they may be seen *mutually governing* one another. (p. 582)

But it is nevertheless clear that Marshall's analysis of interest has actually to do with capital in the sense of loanable funds. With nothing else, indeed, could there be rate schedules as distinguished from price schedules, or an emergent rate of interest instead of a price:

. . . Scholastic writers argued . . . that he who lent out a house or a horse [or a tract of land without a house?] might charge for its use, because he gave up the enjoyment of a thing that was directly productive of benefit. But . . . interest on money: that, they said, was wrong. . . .
. . . The doctrine . . . really implied . . . that . . . the loan of money, *i.e.* of command over things in general, is not a sacrifice on the part of the lender and a benefit to the borrower, of the same kind as the loan of a particular commodity: they obscured the fact that he who borrows money can buy, for instance, a young horse, whose services he can use, and which he can sell, when the loan has to be returned . . . there is no substantial difference between the loan of the purchase price of a horse and the loan of a horse. (pp. 585-86)

. . . though he [Böhm-Bawerk] excludes houses and hotels, and indeed everything that is not strictly speaking an intermediate good, from his definition of capital, yet the demand for the use of goods, that are not intermediate, acts as directly on the rate of interest, as does that for capital as defined by him. . . . (p. 583, note)

When we come to discuss the Money Market we shall have to study the causes which render the supply of capital for immediate use much larger at some times than at others; and which at certain times make bankers and others contented with an extremely low rate of interest, provided the security be good and they can get their *money back* into their own hands quickly in case of need. . . . (pp. 591-92)

It may however be well to carry a little further our illustration of the nature of the demand for capital for any use; and to observe the way in which the aggregate demand for it is made up of the demands for many different uses.
. . . Suppose that the rate of interest is 4 per cent . . . and that the hat-making trade absorbs a capital of one million pounds . . . they would pay 4 per cent per annum *net* for the use of it rather than go without any of it . . . they must have not only some food, clothing, and house room, but also some circulating capital. . . .
A rise in the rate of interest would diminish their use of machinery; for they would avoid the use of all that did not give a net annual surplus of more than 4 per cent on its value. . . . (pp. 519-20)

We must defer to a later stage our study of the marvellously efficient organization of the modern money market by which capital is transferred from one place . . . to another . . . or from one trade . . . to another. . . . (p. 591)[1]

Taking it, however, as entirely clear that Marshall's account of capital as related to the interest problem is intended to run, and does actually run, in terms of free or fluid or general or floating capital—funds available for loan at interest—it is fairly to be said that his interest analysis is not, as of strict necessity, the worse through whatever may be his collateral inaccuracies and ambiguities of terminology. So long, therefore, as his analysis on the demand side of the problem runs consistently in the loan-fund tenor, no criticism will here be offered. Recurrently, nevertheless, he is on the dangerous verge of slipping into a quite different theoretical approach. While, then, it is presumably not to be charged that his inaccuracies of expression parallel similar indefinitenesses in his actual thought, it is safely to be said that they make inevitably for confusion and misunderstanding with the reader or critic. Of so much, indeed, the present discussion may be an outstanding illustration.

For the present, however, it suffices to say that with capital consistently interpreted in this loan-fund sense, and with the demand for capital understood to take account of all the different occasions and motivations making for the borrowing of these capital funds: consumption borrowing; industry and industrial equipment; transportation; merchandising; advertising; the buying of cars, furniture, radios, lands; fiscal deficits; tax-farming; promotion; bribery; wars; dives; gambling; adulteration; scandal journals; theaters, decent and indecent; high art and pornography; rum-running; piracy of all sorts; gainfully organized murder—all the ways of doing all the things that occasion borrower offers of interest rates for funds—

---

[1] It would be possible, but hardly seems necessary here, to point out in much greater detail Marshall's shifts of meaning, even in his discussions of interest, from the funds concept of capital—to which his interest analysis is appropriate—over to the concrete-capital concept which is relevant solely to the hires of things and which may, or may not, have thereby distributive bearings, but which is impossible for the purposes of any account of interest as a rate arrived at in the capital-loan market.

when these conditions are met, the demand aspect of the interest problem, *on the strictly schedule level,* is rightly and adequately presented. Precisely this, in a fair interpretation, appears to be in substance Marshall's position.[2]

But Marshall's analysis of the supply side, the funds-offer side, of the interest problem commands a much less ready acceptance. Assuming then that the demand aspect of the loan-fund and interest problem has received its due report, something remains to be said of this supply aspect. For it must be clear that only when all the demands for funds have been catalogued and explained, and all the funds for loan at their respective rates of offer have been catalogued and explained, has a complete theory of interest been presented. What, then, about the sources of loanable funds?

It is on the face of it strange that the traditional answer—Marshall's answer also—has been *savings,* and savings only. Not everything that is saved is capital in the sense of something available for lending at interest rather than, it may be, for rent. Houses, factories, roads, fertility, furniture—these are all provision against the future. Commonly their existence traces back to an earlier decision to get them through one's money rather than to spend it on goods of early consumption. This was to save. But through the sale of wealth of this sort for money one comes into the holding of loan-fund capital. No new waiting comes in thereby, but only waiting with reference to a different article of wealth. Equally well, however, the sale of lands may provide one with capital funds. For from the individual point of view one can be a saver and waiter with natural bounty as well as with any other good. Moreover, the leasing of land is as clearly a case of waiting as the lending of the money from the sale of it:

[2] See *Principles,* 580-81, *ante.* But to be debited against this statement is, for example, the following:

". . . But there is a clear tradition that we should speak of Capital when considering things as agents of production; . . . of Wealth . . . as results of production, as subjects of consumption and as yielding pleasures of possession. Thus the chief *demand* for capital arises from its productiveness, from the services which it renders, for instance, in enabling wool to be spun and woven more easily than by the unaided hand, or in causing water to flow freely . . . instead of being carried laboriously in pails; (though there are other uses of capital, as for instance when it is lent to a spendthrift, which cannot easily be brought under this head). . . ." (p. 81)

. . . there is no substantial difference between the loan of the purchase price of a horse and the loan of a horse. (pp. 585-86)

It matters not for our immediate purpose whether the power over the enjoyment for which the person waits, was earned by him directly by labour, which is the original source of nearly all enjoyment; or was acquired by him from others, by exchange or by inheritance, by legitimate trade or by unscrupulous forms of speculation, by spoliation or by fraud: the only points with which we are just now concerned are that the growth of wealth involves in general a deliberate waiting for a pleasure which a person has (rightly or wrongly) the power of commanding in the immediate present, and that his willingness so to wait depends on his habit of vividly realizing the future and providing for it. (pp. 233-34)

But it is clear also that the direct holding or the leasing or the bailment of any item of wealth is for the individual owner a saving of it. In the sense of the term *waiting* used in all these discussions, he is waiting for it—albeit getting meanwhile an income from it. Whatever one owns and keeps imposes either saving or waiting or both. The lending or the leasing of an item of wealth is merely a way of waiting alternative to the owner's direct exploitation. Whatever the form of the time income, it is the reward of the saving-waiting.

It is, however, solely with the waiting that is connected with the medium of exchange and with the lending of it that the interest contract is concerned. In every case of this sort there is, to be sure, a waiting—but this in no sense more significant than that whenever you lend realty or bailment goods or money to some one else, you go without meantime. You forego selling or keeping for yourself. *Ipso verbo,* lending is waiting. But even so, if you collect a hire, you are not in essentials going without. You are enjoying your preferred form of income from the property in question; a case of one particular income displacing any alternative.

Say that I lend you $100: I might have used it for current expenses—not waiting. Or I might have purchased an income-rendering property. That would be waiting. I lend it to you as my preferred form of investment. I wait in the sense solely that all uses of my money excepting to spend it, and all ownership of anything in place of selling and spending, must equally be waiting.

I might have bought stocks or bonds or working cattle or lands or apartments—waiting again. To lend to you is merely that particular sort of waiting that I have chosen as my preferred method of getting an income out of my property. Any one of these methods as alternative to spending must be a case of saving-waiting. All wealth exists for the individual through waiting—the loan to you one case of it, among a number of alternative waitings.

Marshall, however, appears to regard the saver of funds to lend, and the lender of the funds that he has saved, as in some peculiar and especially significant sense a saver, or a waiter, or both, as over against the mere owner of wealth, or the lessor or bailor of it. And it is in this emphasis that Marshall arrives at the generalization that the limiting influence on the volume of loan capital—and so far a decisive influence on the interest terms at which it will be loaned—is the waiting that is implicit in the very fact of the saving that is inseparable from the having of any wealth for keeping or lending. The fact is, nevertheless, that the loan fund and the lending of it connote—as far as the analysis has yet gone—merely one particular line of choice among various openings to an individual —income possibilities attaching to ownership, to the mere fact of saving-waiting.

In any case, Marshall prefers *waiting* rather than *abstinence* as accurately descriptive of the accumulation and the retaining of any sort of wealth:

The sacrifice of present pleasure for the sake of future, has been called *abstinence* by economists. . . . Since, however, the term is liable to be misunderstood, we may with advantage avoid its use, and say that the accumulation of wealth is generally the result of a postponement of enjoyment, or of a *waiting* for it. . . . (pp. 232-33)

. . . the *supply* of capital is controlled by the fact that, in order to accumulate it, men must act prospectively: they must "wait" and "save," they must sacrifice the present to the future. (p. 81)

. . . the general fund of capital is the product of labour and waiting. . . . (p. 534)

. . . The interest of which we speak when we say that interest is the earnings of capital simply, or the reward of waiting simply, is *Net* interest. . . . (p. 588)

We are not yet ready for an issue in the background of the supplies schedule in the interest problem—Marshall's final appeal to real-cost explanations of interest rates, his asserted proportionality of the hires of funds to the underlying real costs of waiting. Thus far no criticism has been urged against *waiting* as the determining influence on the volume of loan capital—excepting for the essential meaninglessness of the term; or, perhaps better, the sheer repetitiveness of it. True, all individual wealth, since it continues to exist, is conditioned on saving. For the individual, this holds equally for land. No item of wealth, whether funds or concrete things, could be lent, had it not come into existence and did it not continue to exist—or so at least, it seems at present. But the lending of it is of a piece with the waiting that has preceded; it is a continuation of the same waiting. Waiting is everywhere where there is wealth, funds or other. It is implicit in the very fact of lending; or is merely another name for it. No added thought goes with the assertion that a lender is a waiter. Similarly, a seller is a forever-waiter. Interest is no more a reward of waiting than are the various instances of rents, ground or other; or than the selling price of a good is the pay for the forever-waiting for it—the present worth of the never-ending time series of waiting indemnities. Explanation should be something better than a mere linguistic sleight-of-hand. Moreover, what would the waiting explanation make of a contract of deferred money payment, with interest maturities provided for —covering, say a singer's concert fee, or a lawyer's trial fee, or the prize of a victor in a race? An earlier saving? But there is waiting at any rate—for one's pay.

It is not, however, true that savings are the sole source of lending power. Saved funds are, to be sure, capital. But the functional distinctions between different sorts of capital are not to be erased by saying that one will buy the other. To attribute to the funds themselves whatever manner of productivity or gainfulness attaches to whatever the money may buy or is actually used to buy, applies, for example, to invoke land rents to explain interest; or house rents; or touring-car rents; or speculative or merchandising gains. The distinction between equipment capital and fund capital cannot so disappear. As well reduce all intermediate goods and all durable direct goods to money capital through the fact that all may be traded over into money. Some sources of gain are still industrial while others are not. To assert that money gives milk because one can buy with the money something that will give milk merely confuses the analysis—though not necessarily to wrong conclusions.

More and more, at any rate, the world's lending is being done, in the first instance at least, in the great commercial banking centers and by the commercial banking institutions. If you or I were seeking a loan, or were our grocer or haberdasher needing to borrow, it would commonly be with a bank that the loan application would be made. And similarly with the great merchandisers and manufacturers. The money market is characteristically a bank-funds market, though often, no doubt, it is in part only temporarily so. The markets where interest rates on lending and borrowing trans-actions are in the main fixed, and are to be studied for the explaining of interest and of the ups and downs in the various rates, are the commercial banking markets. The lending by banks is not char-acteristically of money, but of deposit credit. The commercial bank does not—as does the savings bank—lend the deposits of its clients. Instead, it creates them for its customers as the proceeds of their bills and notes. This is the significance of reserve and deposit-credit banking. The reserves are not there for lending and do not get lent.

Assume that the proprietors' investment in a bank does derive from savings—is waited-for wealth. The commercial deposit-banking miracle declares itself in the lending by the banking system of several fold the liquidating worth of the banks in it and from ten to twenty-fold their holdings of money. The bankers are manu-facturers of circulating media on cost-of-production terms and at a charge that is computed as interest rate. Their accommodations to borrowers are worked out on terms of assuming liabilities rather than of advancing anything that they, or any others, may have saved. Banks are not savers of funds but creators of them, through the discounting process and at a charge. They are essentially underwriters of the credit of borrowers. Or, again, they may be described as institutions engaged in diluting the circulating medium for the particular benefit of their borrowers. Banker and customer exchange promises, the customer getting thereby cash rights that are in some respects even more serviceable than actual money. But just how the exchanging of a bank's demand promise for a customer's term or call promise involves the sort of saving that solely is supposed to provide loan material, it is not easy to make out. At any rate, the bankers are there and are supply factors along with the savers for the making of loans. And were it not for both the legal and the practical necessity for reserves—could the banks meet the demands of depositors through the further issue of their promises in the form of demand notes—there would be no assignable limit to their lending activities. Practically such was the situation in the European countries engaged in the great war; whereby interest rates were held low for years; but therewith the currencies were diluted through the expanding volumes of bank credit with disastrous inflations of prices. Measurably in all of the warring countries and almost exclusively in some of them, budgetary necessities were met through the bank-created output of funds.

These larger meanings of the commercial banking process for interest theory are practically beyond the range of Marshall's treatment of the interest problem—a calamitous gap. For it is clear that, with loan-fund capital the subject matter of the interest contract, the commercial banks account, especially in the short run, for the largest and most variable share of these loan-fund grants; and, as the main supply-changing influence, account in the main for the ups and downs of interest rates. In the main also, it is these short-run fluctuations and trends that are of practical importance. It is not strange that for the business man within his horizons of observed fact the traditional theories of interest are not especially instructive or impressive.

In this connection, nevertheless, occasional references to the banking process are to be noted in Marshall's discussions:

We must defer to a later stage our study of the marvellously efficient organization of the modern money market by which capital is transferred

from one place where it is superabundant to another where it is wanted;
or from one trade that is in the process of contraction to another which
is being expanded. . . .

. . . .

When we come to discuss the Money Market we shall have to study
the causes which render the supply of capital for immediate use much
larger at some times than at others; and which at certain times make
bankers and others contented with an extremely low rate of interest. . . .
(pp. 591-92)

. . . In these or in other ways he [the ordinary workman] may increase
his capital till he can start a small workshop, or factory. Once having
made a good beginning he will find the banks eager to give him generous
credit. . . . (p. 309)

. . . there is a much more rapid increase in the amount of capital which
is owned by people who do not want to use it themselves, and are so
eager to lend it out that they will accept a constantly lower and lower
rate of interest for it. Much of this capital passes into the hands of
bankers who promptly lend it to anyone of whose business ability and
honesty they are convinced. . . . (p. 308)

. . . The great classical Law of Diminishing Return . . . refers to a
country the whole land of which is already in the hands of active business men, who can supplement their own capital by loans from banks. . . .
(p. 408)

Again it is to be noted that in most connections Marshall applies
the law of diminishing return to his analysis of the rates of interest
on loan-fund capital. But there is no law of diminishing return for
funds or even securely for factor capital, provided that the investor
uses his funds wisely, making an all-round and proportionate
expansion of his undertaking. In Marshall's usual analysis of the
distributive process, indeed, smaller rather than greater unit costs
are indicated as likely to be achieved as capital goods get more
abundant—with attendant higher net gains as a total, and not rarely
also with higher rates of gain on the total investment. And seemingly this holds both competitively and socially. But the tacit
assumption by which solely to justify this view is that the land
investment, or the land holding, is unchanged; or that the aggregate
of land stocks is fixed; or that the particular enterpriser cannot, or
will not, enlarge his enterprise proportionately. But Marshall makes

it clear that often the enterpriser does use his funds in the purchase of more land as well as of more equipment goods; or again, in hiring more labor, or even in doing more advertising. And whether these purchases be of land or of machinery, Marshall thinks it meaningless—or worse—to deny that either is capital to the exclusion of the other. His sole distinction is that, in point of the price bearing of the hires, the returns on the equipment goods are quasi-rents rather than true rents or, in strictness, interest rates.

It should, then, follow that purchased land is capital, and the returns on it interest, in that broader sense that includes quasi-rents.

Earlier citations have indicated Marshall's usual view that capital for the purposes of the interest analysis is fund capital. If so, however, the attempt to apply to it the law of diminishing return must require a complete re-orienting of the entire discussion. But other quotations have been submitted to indicate that not rarely his analysis of diminishing return with respect to interest rates conceives capital, not as funds, but as factors of production utilized in the industrial process of turning out, not more price product, but more goods, and somehow thereby invoking the principle of the due proportioning of factors.

The temptation is doubtless strong in connection with the theory of interest to conceive of capital as concrete equipment goods, and as in this sense the subject matter of the dosing process. Thereby there is worked out a marginal productivity theory in the explanation of instrument *rents* as somehow tributary to the explanation of interest *rates*—fund capital commanding these rates by virtue of the concrete capital commanding, through the distributive process, these rents. You can, at price so or so, buy a thing that earns in the industrial process thus much rent. It returns you therefore a particular *rate of return* on your outlay. Only, whence the price at which you were able to buy? On occasion Marshall indicates his full appreciation of this difficulty and admirably exposes the circuitous reasoning seemingly involved in this doctrinal procedure:

> . . . The values of the stone and of the machine alike would be reached by capitalizing the income which they were capable of earning. . . .
> . . . to say that the purchaser expected normal interest on the price which

represented the capitalized value of the services, would be a circular statement that the value of the services rendered by stones is governed by the value of those very services.

Such circular reasonings . . . always tend to overlay and hide the real issues. . . . (pp. 416-17 and note)

. . . If the investors of capital [funds clearly] push it into every occupation in which it seems likely to gain a high reward; and if, after this has been done and equilibrium has been found, it still pays and only just pays to employ this machinery, we can infer . . . the yearly rate of interest. . . . But illustrations of this kind merely indicate part of the action of the great causes which govern value. They cannot be made into a theory of interest . . . without reasoning in a circle. (p. 519)

It is true that an interest factor has to be used in getting a present worth for these prospective rents. To escape the circuity, however, it suffices that the interest factor is not conditioned on the particular rents in question. Instead, each of the trading individuals already has a rate, or rates, peculiar to himself. Thereby, in view of the prospect for him from his control of a unit of the factor in question, he arrives at his particular bid or reservation price. The goods offers may, it is true, derive from costs rather than from this individual capitalization process. Always, however, whatever capitalization takes place, takes place as preceding the bid and leading up to it. There is no one interest rate or one promise of earnings for all. Marshall's loan-fund approach, with the different bases of bids for it and with the different bids, should have been extended in principle to the process of arriving at present-worth prices of income-controlling goods. The assumption of one prospective series of incomes for everybody and one interest rate for everybody in the capitalization process misconceives the factual setting of the process.

Moreover, Marshall's adoption of the funds concept of capital for his interest analysis, should have attached the same meaning to it in his dosing analysis—"a dose of labour and capital" meaning merely a dose of money outlay distributed among the various lines of costs under the principle of right proportions in view of the enterpriser's individual situation and judgment. Just this clearly does Marshall some of the time mean. At other times, however, a dose of capital connotes merely a quantum of concrete industrial goods—presumably, nevertheless, priced goods.

If, however, instead of countless different uses behind the individual demands for capital funds, there were only one use, and that for a particular kind of indirect good, a dose of fund capital would become interchangeable with a dose of capital goods. The ordinary productivity theory of interest as appealing to the marginal price significance of concrete capital goods in the industrial process would then afford an adequate explanation of interest. If, for example, $1000 would secure the production of, say, a ditching machine of a $50 net annual earning power, there would be explained the disposition to borrow funds at a rate of interest approximately as high as 5 per cent. The money loan to finance the money costs would afford the basis for a rate. The only defect in this as an actual explanation of interest rates is that the assumed condition is indefinitely far from the actual fact.

Not only, however, are there actually a wide variety of industrial factors to be combined in the capital dose, but there are countless demands for funds for applications that are not industrial—as for the purchase of durable direct goods, like dwellings or building lots. Nor does it greatly matter whether the item of property is reproducible or not. In either case it absorbs funds for lending. Doubtless the result may be merely to redistribute proprietorships and purchasing power; that is to say, there need be neither more nor less media of exchange. But a redistribution of purchasing power through borrowing, especially if no allowance is made for the banking process, is all that the absorption of loan-fund capital means. When purchasing power moves from the hands of those individuals disposed to lend it at available rates of interest instead of otherwise investing it or of spending it, and into the hands of individuals of the counter disposition, it ceases to function as loan fund. Items of media become loan fund or cease to be loan fund according to the attitudes of the successive holders with regard to lending.

Not only therefore with durable indirect goods are all of the perplexities of distributive theory commonly involved in arriving at the mere rents of the goods, but also the marginal analysis for fund capital involves indefinitely more than the outlay of these funds for capital goods of the equipment sort. With only capital goods, however, to absorb funds, and with only one kind of capital goods, units of fund capital would command interest rates derived directly from rents. Nor would any circuity be involved. The cost method of accounting for prices would be adequate, as equally the capitalization method—stocks determining rents and rents determining interest rates. Actually, however, merchandising in its various aspects of inventories, salesmanship, advertising and customer credits, absorbs alone a far greater volume of short-time funds than the factory processes of production. Moreover, the sales departments of industrial enterprises probably call for larger volumes of funds than are required for raw materials and the industrial processes. Installment selling, fiscal deficits and war finance might also be mentioned.

It is obvious, then, that contract interest, the interest phenomenon of the market place competitively fixed as a rate per cent, reports merely the time hire of purchasing power in terms of the medium of exchange—interest as presented in the contract of deferred payment of the standard, under the influence of all the various demands for it, with the marginal principle applying to all these demands. Marshall's ultimate position is therefore in its demand aspect admirable—on the purely money level—tied up, that is to say, with no "realities" of the underlying utility sort. Not so much can be said for the supply side of the analysis even irrespective of the real-cost supplementation shortly to be examined. To omit commercial banking was to omit the better half of the play.

But it is the transcendent merit of Marshall's capital-fund approach that it arrives, as we have seen, at a rent or a rate of interest that need not, on the demand side, derive from any one specific return on anything, but from the rate-offers of numbers of bidders for funds for all the different motivating purposes and uses. When on the supply side of the case lower costs of production provide a larger volume of any particular agent, these lower unit costs and this larger volume lower the unit rents of the agents, and thereby in turn, through the capitalization process, lower the market price of the agents. Cost and capitalization are not opposing but articulating and supplementary explanations of price. Even were the equipment-goods demand the sole basis for the demand for capital funds, there need be no seeming of circuity where these demands and supplies schedules are made up of different price-bidding and different price-holding dispositions. The only necessity, indeed, is to arrive, under a system of exchange through an intermediate, at a capitalization process that is not derived exclusively from the returns of the good to be capitalized. If, for example, 18th century rocking chairs were the only durable good to be had for money, the holders of the chairs wanting money and the seekers of them able to command it through borrowing, an exchange price would get allotted to the chairs. Or take even a Crusoe situation—the construction of a canoe under consideration. The grade of it will be fixed at a point where the prospective services from it are equated against the sacrifices of production.

It is, then, again to be urged that Marshall's recognition of capital funds—not machines, or raw materials, or present consumables, or any particular sort of direct or indirect goods—affords the guiding thread to any tenable interest analysis in the actual modern situation. Most interest theories have erred, on the demand side of the analysis, mainly through stressing some one or other aspect of the entire truth. Marshall's doctrine, at its best, makes room on the demand side for all of the contributions of truth from these less inclusive theories.

But, in the absence of other demands for funds, might not the stress for funds for the buying of immediate consumption goods be adequate for the explanation of a rate of interest on funds? Assuredly so, if only the volume of savings were not great enough to more than saturate this consumption demand. And would not interest rates be lower if, other things remaining equal, the indisposition to save were less marked? It is past denial that the volume of savings has something to do with interest rates. And savings might be, but are not, the sole source of funds for loan. And in the absence of other gain-seeking demands for funds, might not technological needs furnish an interest-supporting demand? Clearly enough so. Or in the absence of other gain-seeking demands for funds, might not merchandising, or promoting, or speculative ventures in general—say, town-lot enterprises—provide an interest-supporting demand? Undoubtedly it might thus be. And in the absence of other demands for loans, might not the house-building industry or the touring-car industry—durable direct goods—maintain an interest rate? Equally plainly so. Or in the absence of other demands for funds, might not borrowing to buy farms or pasture lands or forests or mines or town-lots or franchises explain an interest rate? There can rightly be no denial.

And in a society in which no productive activities were taking place; in which there were no parasitisms or predations; in which there were neither long-time direct nor long-time indirect goods to be bought; in which again there were only immediately consumable goods, and these provided recurrently by divine or other bounty —to reservation Indians or university students, for example— might not borrowing demands for funds present themselves and get supplied on interest terms? Some of us have seen precisely this.

And in a society in which no savings for loans were actual, excepting in that Pickwickian sort presented in banking, might not banking provide lending power for which interest-paying demands would be extended and on which interest charges would be collected? Banking funds are forthcoming only on cost of production terms. The same basis for interest on bank funds would exist as, without banking, there would be for saved funds.

There is, then, occasion to be impatient with most interest theories only on the side of their errors of exclusiveness, their lack of catholicity, their non-eclectic character—in sum, for their disloyalty to the time-out-of-mind principle that a market adjustment is explained only when a full account of both demand and supply influences has been rendered.

Marshall's analysis of the capitalization process, also, is defective only for the lack of that full individualization to which his funds approach is especially appropriate.

The supply side of Marshall's analysis—on this purely money-cost level—does not, as we have seen, command an equal degree of approval. We have now, however, further to examine Marshall's account of the real costs of *waiting* as the offered explanation of the volume of loan funds.

Interest we have seen as the terms of exchange of present dollars against future dollars. When 100 present dollars will buy 105 dollars a year from date, the rate of interest is thereby declared to be 5 per cent per annum. An individual's bid for funds at this rate reports his willingness to forego what 105 dollars will buy then in order to have what 100 dollars will buy now. And so a lender's funds offer at this rate declares his willingness to forego what 100 dollars will buy now in order to have what 105 dollars will buy a year hence. Accurately, then, interest is not, as Marshall defines it, an exchange premium in favor of the present goods, but a premium in favor of present dollars—with only the explaining motives in the goods—so long as the motivations on each side have to do with consumption goods. Our borrower chooses the present services against the future; the lender, the future services against the present.

But when it is necessary to pay any one a premium in dollars to get him to wait, in what sense is this waiting a real cost—in a sense to *explain* his requirement of this premium? If in the present I exchange, say, my plums for your peaches, is what I must pay to you in plums to get you to transfer to me the peaches a report of the real costs to you of the peaches—the displaced utility to you of the peaches a real cost determining how much I must pay to you in plums? Does real cost mean in this connection no more than what must be paid to get the thing done—the selling or the lending? If so, this appeal to real costs as underlying and explaining production or selling or lending is gratuitous. The real cost declares itself in the very fact of the transaction, and in the very terms of it —implicit in it. The prima donna must be paid thus much to sing; what is the real cost to her of her singing? We know by knowing how much must be paid to get her to sing. This is entirely simple in more than one meaning of the word.

And the real costs of a lender of funds? He may insist on a 5

per cent return from you because he could make these funds pay
him thus much directly in his own use of them. Five per cent is
therefore his *real* cost in lending the funds to you?

Or one must have a certain rent from one's land, else he will
retain it for his own direct use. Does the rent that you must pay
him report the real costs to him of leasing the land to you—this
rent being the amount that he must have to induce him to lease the
land? Or perhaps he will not let you have it for less because he can
get thus much from some one else. This foregone rent is, then,
the real cost to him of leasing the land to you?

Or an owner can make his land pay him $100 under his own
cultivation, or can get $110 rent from you—this not as a choice for
him between present consumption and future consumption, or
between present money and future money, but a choice merely
between alternative sums of future money. Is this saving? And
waiting? And what is his real cost in the case? He earlier bought
the land; or he inherited it; or he stole it—it not, as Marshall agrees,
mattering which. At any rate, he could now sell it. But actually
he does not. He leases it to you for a year—a sale to you of a one
year's use of the land. His money cost is obviously $100—assuming
this to be his ranking alternative to leasing. But you had to—at least,
you did—pay him $110. Under this had-to view the $110 must be
the real cost to him of leasing the land to you, as also its money
cost to you.

But if so, real costs decline into meaninglessness. They turn out
to mean either the actual quid-pro-quo or the minimum quid-pro-
quo; or the purchase price; or, possibly, the foregone use or price.

We recall now Marshall's occasional preference for *sacrifice*
instead of *waiting* and our earlier perplexities with regard to it;
did it mean just waiting or something further? And we recall also
our recent great discovery that every lease, loan, bailment or sale
is also, *ipso verbo,* a waiting. In this sense, the waiting theory of
interest may turn out to be merely one variety of the productivity
theory. For so long as wealth—land or a house or an equipment
good—is productive of a price-product with passing time, or con-
tributes to gain, or affords to its owner valuable services, there must

be interest on the funds with which to buy the income-rendering thing. There must be a *sacrifice* in making over the use. There must be a payment to induce this sacrifice, this *waiting*. Or there must be a deferring of the opportunity to consume—a choice of consumption times; real-cost aspects a-plenty.

Therefore waiting declines also into meaninglessness—waiting inevitably implicit in your letting anything go, whether for a time or always—real costs thus implicit in whatever you must be paid for doing it. But the sum that any borrower or lessee or bailee or buyer pays you is at the same time his own *money* cost. Inasmuch nevertheless, as by paying to you he gets the thing, for a period or for ever, his payment to you displacing for you the gratifications from consumption within your reach by selling the good or refusing to loan—his payment to you reports the real cost in the transaction *to you*.

But does Marshall arrive at anything like these positions so far as in the contract of deferred payment real costs are concerned. What in this connection do the real costs of waiting mean to him?

To the *pains* or discomforts *of abstinence* he wisely declines to commit himself. That with both toothache and hunger you have two pains is clear. But if you bear both of these pains in order to get yourself some whiskey when you shall get to town, you do not, it seems, come under a third pain—one more than if you had no money. Moreover, even when *abstinence* is taken in a sense free from any ascription of pain, Marshall finds it to assert, or to connote or suggest, over much:

. . . this term has been misunderstood: for the greatest accumulators of wealth are very rich persons, some of whom live in luxury, and certainly do not practise abstinence in that sense of the term in which it is convertible with abstemiousness . . . we may with advantage avoid its use, and say that the accumulation of wealth is *generally* the result of a postponement of enjoyment, or of a *waiting* for it. . . .

. . . The extra pleasure which a peasant who has built a weatherproof hut derives from its usance . . . is the price earned by his working and waiting . . . similar in all fundamental respects to the interest which the retired physician derives from the capital he has lent to a factory or a mine to enable it to improve its machinery. . . . (pp. 232-33)

Of course, one may have so great an income that the consumption of it would be an intolerable burden, or even an impossibility—unless giving were accounted a consumption or a spending, displacing thus the else inevitable *waiting*—assuming, to be sure, that this no-choice not-spending were *waiting,* in the intended sense of carrying with it those real costs that attach to postponed consumption:

Karl Marx and his followers have found much amusement in contemplating the accumulations of wealth which result from the abstinence of Baron Rothschild, which they contrast with the extravagance of a labourer who feeds a family of seven on seven shillings a week; and who, living up to his full income, practises no economic abstinence at all. The argument that it is Waiting rather than Abstinence, which is rewarded by Interest and is a factor of production, was given by Macvane in the Harvard *Journal of Economics* for July, 1887. (p. 233, note)

So far as one can make out, this position of Professor Macvane is cited by Marshall in full approval, and is presented as his own position. Perhaps the phenomenon of waiting is taken to present only the marginal fact, as being there subject always to real costs. But Marshall says:

There are indeed some who find an intense pleasure in seeing their hoards of wealth grow up under their hands, with scarcely any thought for the happiness that may be got from its use by themselves or by others. . . . But were it not for the family affections, many who now work hard and save carefully would not exert themselves. . . . (p. 228)

At any rate (p. 234), "the higher the rate of interest the higher his reward for saving"—seemingly a mere tautology. And (p. 232) "human nature being what it is, we are justified in speaking of the interest on capital as the reward of the sacrifice involved in the waiting for the enjoyment of material resources, because few people would save much without reward . . ." It seems, then, that the sacrifice involved in waiting, the real cost of it, is just the waiting—the principle inclusive of leases, bailments and sales as well as of money loans.

. . . the *supply* of capital is controlled by the fact that, in order to accumulate it, men must act prospectively: they must "wait" and "save," they must sacrifice the present to the future. (p. 81)

... the accumulation of wealth is held in check, and the rate of interest so far sustained, by the preference which the great mass of humanity have for present over deferred gratifications, or, in other words, by their unwillingness to "wait." ... (p. 581)

It is, then, merely the preference that some individuals clearly have, and that the majority of individuals are assumed to have, for present gratifications over future gratifications, that constitutes the real cost of waiting—not accurately that explains it, but that actually it is, and that provides "*the* supply price" of funds for lending. And thus it appears that to choose the more distant of two pleasures, where the later is also the greater, connotes the undergoing of a real cost explanatory of the limited volume of funds, and, so far, of interest commanded by them—every lease, bailment or sale, therefore, a real-cost phenomenon on both sides. It should follow also that if, through your real-cost efforts, you can produce either commodity A or commodity B, your cost of, say, A, is your effort cost plus the pleasure that B might have afforded you.

In fact, however, as Marshall notes, what you have to pay to get an owner to lend to you does not turn so much on what you must pay him to induce him to save, as on what he can gain from the direct use of his funds, or can derive from purchases of farms or dwellings or stocks, or can get some one other than you to pay him as interest. That is to say, interest as what has to be paid to get the loan turns out to be a waiting cost, a real cost, only in the sense of the displacement of the ranking alternative for gain:

Everyone knows that people will not lend gratis as a rule; because, even if they have not themselves some good use to which to turn the capital or its equivalent, they are sure to be able to find others to whom its use would be of benefit, and who would pay for the loan of it: and they stand out for the best market. (p. 581)

By the test of this logic, rents of land, as well as of cost-produced or cost-acquired equipment goods, are interest, or at all events, are costs. If nothing else goes wrong for Marshall here—and it is not clear that anything else does—quasi-rents become costs by the same title and at the same times as interest in the technical sense.

Recall, moreover, the theoretical bearing attached to real costs. Relative prices are to be explained—in normal times, at least—by relative real costs. Wages and interest are the money costs that have to be proportioned to real costs, land rents being excluded from the determination of prices through the device of marginal isolation. Not only, then, must wages be proportional with the discomforts of effort, and interest with the discomforts of waiting, but these discomforts of effort and of waiting must be homogeneous—since wages and interest are homogeneous in terms of units of money costs—in such sort that prices that are proportional with their respective money costs may also be proportional with the respective underlying real costs, as aggregates of effort discomforts and waiting discomforts. But wages were not presented as real costs by the simple quantity test of the wage, as merely the money compensation necessary to command the labor. It was the discomfort of the effort that was to explain *why* the wage must be paid. But it has now come to be clear with regard to interest that the real costs of waiting amount to nothing more than is implicit in the mere fact that interest has to be paid to get that waiting done that is itself nothing more than the mere lending.

The plain fact appears, then, to be that Marshall's analysis of interest amounts to a refutation of the central thesis of classical economics—which is also Marshall's ultimate thesis.

Note on Waiting

No important issues turn on Marshall's recurrent assertion that waiting is itself a factor of production: not the plow productive, but the waiting that, it is assumed, conditions its presence, or, perhaps, that is the plow; you eat not the fish but the fishing; wear not the coat but the making; fertilize not with the manure but with the hay and grass that the cow ate, along with the waiting, the fencing and the herding of which she was the subject—the productivity of capital goods not the attribute of them but of the waiting of which they are the subject. This is not as unusual a view as it seems to me it should be:
". . . capital itself is the product of labour and waiting: and therefore the spinning is the product of labour of many kinds, and of waiting. . . ."
(p. 587)

". . . There is a real and effective competition between labour in general and waiting in general. . . ." (p. 541)

With Adolphe Landry (*L'Interest du Capital, Paris, 1924*), this view appears to be pushed one step further. He carries his "renonciation" doctrine to the extreme point of conceiving capital, not in terms of anything that is, but instead of something that has failed ever to be. It *is* the foregone marginal utilities that its creation involved—ultimately neither the loan fund that has come to be available, nor, still more securely, the equipment goods that are in stock, but the consumption goods that, because of the providing of the funds or of the equipment goods, never came to be. The foregoing or the abstinence or the waiting is no longer conceived as the influence, or as one of the influences, limiting the capital quantum, as the cost resistance to its emergence; instead, the capital itself is taken to consist of those things that actually are not, having been foregone, and that still somehow function as the capital fact that actually is. Essentially, therefore, the thing borrowed is *waiting* —a conceptual reality of the extreme Platonic category, like most abstract nouns. Such, at all events, is my understanding of him.

To return to Marshall:

". . . Everyone is aware that the accumulation of wealth is held in check, and the rate of interest so far sustained, by the preference which the great mass of humanity have for present over deferred gratifications, or, in other words, by their unwillingness to 'wait.' . . .

. . . .

"Next it [economics] has to analyze the influences which sway men in their choice between present and deferred gratifications, including leisure and opportunities for forms of activity that are their own reward. But here the post of honour lies with mental science. . . ." (pp. 581-82)

This has some flavor of the impatience or perspective theory of interest. But just when did mental science or experimental method assure the economists of "the preference which the great mass of humanity have for present over deferred gratifications"? How go about to prove it? Some people appear to have it, and others equally clear have it not. At any rate of interest that is actual, there is obviously as much disposition to lend as there is to borrow. But even this may be explained by differences in wealth and income. Always there are these differences. Never are all of the borrowers consumer borrowers, and never are all of the lenders individuals who would prefer the present gratification to the future— or vice versa—were no increment promised. How go about it to prove what would happen in the absence of the interest rates that are always present? Presumably, no doubt, were the rate lower the decisions to borrow would be more and the lending less. But this proves nothing as to what would happen were there no increment to be had anywhere. All of these decisions have to be made within a long-established situation of interest rates and in the presence of a wide range of interest openings. There must, in fact, be interest rates on funds that will buy machines and lands and houses, so long as more wheat can be had with land than without, or more cloth with machines than with no machines, or more shelter within a dwelling than out of doors. The price productivities or valuable uses of things in time will continue as long as there is time, and will attach interest to the funds that will command the things—unless, indeed, the prices of the things shall go to infinity. As long as one would prefer a house to live in from now on rather than for a year from now on, there will be interest on the funds that will buy the house. The year's rent on the house, as a ratio to the price of the house, will provide a rate of interest on the funds for buying the house. More savings may affect the volume of machines, and thus the rent and therefore the price-rate, but cannot cancel it as long as it is pecuniarily preferable to have the things to use during the year than to wait for them to the end of the year. The time-rents on the things will motivate the hiring of the funds. And savings, in turn, can affect the rate only (1) as by bringing more things into existence, the rents on them are lowered, or (2) by raising the present-worthed price of the things. There is, then, no fault in the theory of interest that appeals for the *rate* to the price-efficiencies or valuable services of things in time, excepting that there are other influences motivating the demands for funds. Erring still worse in exclusiveness is the restriction of demands to industrial-equipment purposes exclusively. Similarly inadequate is the time-perspective theory, with consumption goods. All of the borrowing motivations have to do with the rate, precisely because they absorb funds. Nor can any of these influences be accorded finality by first allowing for the subtractions of funds worked by the others. Always this residual type of procedure involves fallacy.

Just now, however, we are concerned with the validity of the real-cost explanation of the limited stocks of funds for loan—waiving for the present explanation of the limited stocks of funds for loan and waiving for the present the bearing of commercial banking in the case. Is there, in the balance with human beings, a disinclination to postpone the consumption of goods—an abstinence or impatience protest, or a time-preference attitude—to explain the fact that the stocks of funds do not overwhelm or saturate the demands for them, to the disappearance of time premiums on funds? The issue, is, then, to be formulated as follows: What would be the prevailing attitude toward dollars now as against dollars a year from now, if there were nothing to rent, or no rents for what things there were; and no price increment anywhere attaching to the borrowers' controls of funds?

The issue has never been submitted to the test of experience—and never can be. Always there have been gain-motivated borrowings to compete with consumption borrowings. What would be charged consumption borrowers if there were no others, we have no experience to indicate. None of us will lend to these cheaply when the others will pay us better. But what if there were none of these others? Will analysis tell us?

The logic of the case must obviously be with the present-preference view as necessary to interest; for were all individuals at all times taken to be willing indefinitely to postpone their consumption, there could then be no limit on loans controlling goods but the limit on products—and no demand for loans at all. And still worse than this; nothing would get produced excepting for the mere fun of the productive process. The direct goods that one cares never to consume—is always willing to hold —are undesired goods, no goods.

The fact has to be, however, that each individual has a life over which to distribute his consumption. Precisely as there is, for men in general, an average expectation of life—the probable life at each age, some dying earlier and some later—so, as a matter solely of his individual preferences, each man would have his some-time point that would divide his prospective consumption into equal parts. Where would the average man draw this division line—thus reporting the mass attitude with reference to present holding as against present spending—in view always of course of the danger of dying, his own consumption thereby defeated? Most men, it is probable—but with interest collections entering into their choices—continue somewhat to accumulate all of their lives, inventorying in the average, more wealth at sixty years of age than at thirty. But it is of course to be said that they have the hazards of old-age need to consider, along with a falling off in the personal ability to earn. And they desire, many of them, to make provision for heirs and legatees.

There are always both emphases of preference. Men are severally at all points along the life-duration line, each with his own individual problem of distributing in his time his individual consumption. But with the average expectation of life constant, and with the age constitution of the population constant, how would the distribution of consumption take place in the assumed absence of all influences other than those of the pure time-preference?

For by taking all expectations of life to be equal, or so far equal as to cancel out through the constant age constitution of the population, and by a similar disposition of problems of sickness and old-age provision, of death, of care of dependents, of changes in productive efficiency, of opposing changes in powers of enjoyment, and of dangers of moth and rust and decay, and hazards of debtor defaults—we seem to have nothing further to rule out of our problem but opportunities for gainful investment or for the buying of durable items of valuable service.

Rule these out also; and having nothing left to compare but alternative satisfactions equal and interchangeable in all respects but those of the times of enjoyment—one, say, now and one a year hence—what would be the exchange relations between present dollars and future dollars? Would one hundred dollars now buy more than one hundred dollars a year hence? It could not be less, if only the dollars could be safely held over—no safety-deposit charges, for example.

With the bees and the ants, we are assured, there are instinctive urges to save. But with them also there are seasons of dearth to follow seasons of plenty. We human beings, however—as often we are told—have no instincts of this sort, but only reason and intelligent foresight to guide us; wherefore it comes to belong to us to prefer the present merely as the present. It is, it seems, just in us—*rationally* in us—to prefer the *now* to the *then*. Or perhaps it is irrationally in us, after all, since reason and intelligence ought always to guide us, but do not always. If such are the facts about our instinctive equipment, or such the more or less rational, but actual, ways of human choosing—and such doubtless the facts may be —how have we securely gone about it to find these things so? Or how now go about it? Experimentation? None adequate as yet. We must then resort to mental science.

But about this *impatience* or *disinclination:* shall you decide now to consume now or to consume a year later? To be disinclined to wait looks very much like wanting the satisfaction now. You don't want to wait for a thing that you want to have now. We seem to be discovering that we are disinclined now not to have what we want now; that the objection to lending is the not having now what we want now; and that one objects to waiting because one has a disinclination toward it.

But there may be more in the analysis. Just what is this *disinclination* to do that thing which lending means doing?

Disinclination may have two meanings: one simply quantitative, the other relatively quantitative. One may be tall or relatively tall; a thing may be digestible or relatively digestible; or digestible but relatively indigestible; or beautiful or relatively beautiful; or heavy or relatively heavy. And so one may be inclined or disinclined to things, either unrelationally or relationally. One may desire a particular thing—be inclined to have it or be disinclined to go without it. Or you may desire two things; and be more disinclined to go without one than the other—your two desires comparative in their strength, relative in their appeal in point of the desiring. Or the issue may regard the disposition to be made of a particular thing; whether it is desired the more for use now than for use a year hence—each use being recognized as having to displace the other—disinclination not to have being greater with the earlier use than with the later use. Disinclination means here more than mere desire; it connotes the relating of different desires.

In the non-relational sense, disinclination not to eat is merely disinclination to go hungry; is inclination to eat; is just desire for food, the utility that is mere desiredness. In the relational sense, the disinclination not to eat—which is the inclination, or the desire, to eat—pronounces against the displacement of eating by something else; let not this but the other desire go frustrate, satisfaction of both being out of the reckoning. Which will you have? The meaning of waiting is commonly of this relational sort; it is the making of a use of a thing *then* take precedence of the use *now*—saving apples for winter, or ice for summer, or food to a time of less plenty—the time of the relatively great need.

But the presence of a medium of exchange, the money intermediate—and especially the need of language to go along with it—further beclouds the precise meanings of words or the thinking behind the words. Is there any indisposition to save money? And if so, what is it and why is it? A non-relational desire for the intermediate now is really for something that the intermediate will buy now—only that, being money, its use in buying any one thing can arrive only after relating to one another, the different things purchasable with it. But among all these possible things, that one that is first in your appraisal is the one with which your issue of waiting is concerned. You are, say, disinclined to wait. But more now is implicit in the situation than the mere fact that you place this thing at the head of the list of all the things before you now from which to choose. Your desire for some later good or goods purchasable with your money is involved—that alternative thing, specific or as yet indefinite, that the immediate use will displace and defeat. Each of the two *money* uses, present and future, is desired only as intermediate, derivative, representative of a commodity use. Similarly of the future money uses. The inclination to spend now, the disinclination to wait till later to spend, reports merely the precedence of the thing of proposed immediate purchase over any later alternative purchase. And this is all that the disinclination to wait, to have money, can mean. Waiting, the preferred spending at the later time, derives from a comparison of the leading lure to spend at one time with that of another and later time. You just prefer the later use.

To introduce, then, into the problem of a deferred money outlay in the choice of alternative things the third factor of an independent indisposition to wait is a delirium of terminology, or a self-hocus-pocusing with words, or a sleight-of-hand in thought—to go along with the famous dictum that the sedative puts to sleep through its dormitive virtue. The real costs of waiting are no better than the abstinence pains that they replace. They are merely the harder to pin down to a definite meaning; defense by vagueness, the doctrine always something else, a perpetual change of venue defeating trial, the revolutionary generalship of

Washington, the Fabian strategy of retreat to previously prepared positions—in the woods. The independent actuality of waiting, along with the real costs of it, appears to illustrate the old perplexity of hunting in a dark room for a black cat that isn't there.

Nothing of this, however, denies that often with many individuals—and perhaps sometimes with all—the remoteness in time of a need or of a satisfaction may subtract from its present appeal, absolutely as well as relatively to another that is nearer. Often it does. And with you, for example, when it does, a dollar may make equal appeal today with the dollar and five cents of a year hence. But the reverse case also would presumably be commonplacely observed, were it not that other influences hide this separate working. From this source there is, no doubt, room for the emergence of interest rates, were only the prevalence of it factually clear. Ice gets saved to times of thirst; money for rainy days.

But what, now, not about the *disinclination* attending the displacement of a present satisfaction—or the delaying of it—but about the *waiting* itself? The lender is said to wait and to be paid for his waiting. But this is no more than to assert that he is paid for lending. This is once more to get in another word, supposedly carrying with it another thought and offering an explanation of something, but actually saying nothing not already said. *Lending* is one with *waiting*—waiting implicit in every lending. Goethe wisely noted that "Men often think, if only words they hear, that therewith goes material for thinking." For obviously, what for a time you let another have you go without till he returns it. To lend is to wait to get back what you lend. Solemnly to assert, then, that the lender is a waiter is solemnly to assert essentially nothing—not even a truism, but an identity by definition, something out of the dictionary.

But the confusion of thought implicit in this word-play has extended even to the notion that this waiting fact is peculiar to money loans as against leases or bailments. Lessors are not in the same sense waiters; they merely let some particular thing out for a year and then get back that same thing. Is abstinence or impatience to stand as a real cost behind land rents to explain or to justify them, or to rank them along with other costs like wages and interest?

And yet why all this sympathy for lenders of funds and none for sellers of goods, land or other? Instead of being disinclined to sell, they appear to be full of that inclination. But the leasing of land equally with the lending of money for a term is the alienating of one slice, the first one, out of a property eternity. A perpetual lease without rent is an integral legal title—waiting forever a real cost behind a sale. But somehow we seem to contrast the lenders of money and their griefs with the vendors of property and their joys. No one thinks of the lot of these last as an unhappy one, or of the lessors' case as grievous.

The truth appears to be that Marshall's preoccupation with real costs gratuitously confuses his interest analysis, but confuses it, as such, to no great harm. Were it not for the rôle of commercial banking in the case, with its *money* costs in its discounting process of providing funds, the notion of a *real* cost in the lending of capital funds, while making no difficulties for the factual processes of *money* costs, would be an important step toward the real-cost explanation of relative prices.

But still it is for us to note at present that sometimes borrowing on interest terms is done to get the funds with which to pay land rents, or to buy land—interest payments to the lender displacing rent obligations to the landlord. He now, in turn, may lend out his funds and collect interest in place of rent. If rent may change into an interest cost, rent itself should be a cost whenever interest is.

By this back-door entrance, rent appears likely to get into costs on the same terms with wage costs and with costs in general. You might, for that matter, buy the land, not by applying to a lender of funds, but by getting credit from the vendor himself—giving him your purchase-money note, secured, it may be, by mortgage on the purchased property, or on other property; perhaps a note in your favor against some third person; a mortgage or other note; or a corporation note—a bond; or a bank note; or a government note—these obligations, mostly interest-bearing, displacing your rent-paying obligation; just as you might buy a dwelling or furniture on the installment plan. These funds that lenders advance to borrowers go out into all directions of cost in the process of production: to meet payrolls, to buy raw materials, to pay taxes, or even to meet accruing interest obligations.

All this leads, however, to the question of whose *waiting* it is that is the ultimate test and significance of real costs in the borrowing relation. When you hire a dwelling, it is your landlord that is extending you credit—irrespective of how often he makes his collections. Part also of what you pay is ground rent. But suppose that you borrow the funds to buy the dwelling; or buy just a vacant lot. Marshall recognizes that the borrowing demand for funds to buy houses or to have them built for you is a transaction that absorbs "free capital," and along with all other borrowing of funds affects interest rates. So again with docks—and presumably so, therefore, with the water-frontage underlying the docks, or with land supporting the dwelling. But still there may be room to say that when you borrow to buy a tract of pasture land or a vacant town lot or a stone quarry—are borrowing, that is, to buy something that having neither effort costs behind its existence nor waiting conditioning its preservation—you have, to be sure, incurred a money cost of your own, but still a money cost that has no basis in real costs; therefore a money cost that is a price-determined cost. Just to buy something does not impose a real cost on you, along with the purchase price. Land rent does not change from a price-determined to a price-determining cost by the mere fact that for yourself you have got it over into the form of an interest cost.

There are three individuals to consider in the case. A lender to you, as also, it may be, a lessor to you, *waits.* You as investor *wait* for your return in an undertaking in which *land* is one investment item. But the man who sold the natural bounty to you bought it from the man next back in the chain of title to the preemptor or owner by prescriptive title, or possibly by legalized squatter claim. Your vendor also may have borrowed the funds on interest terms to buy the land. But, whether or no, he had his interest costs of carrying, and perhaps taxes. Is he also a waiter? In no ordinary sense has he any waiting costs relatively to you, through the mere fact of selling to you. He did not wait on you but sold for cash to you. To think of him as waiting on you, because he sold you the property, never to get it back, seems farcical for the purpose. Nor does it in any sort matter for the actual purpose what his earlier waitings may or may not have been.

As for you, you are, it is true, an investor hopefully awaiting your expected returns. But you are not a waiter, either with or without interest —interest being payable not to you but by you.

But the man who lends to you? There is no issue possible about his *waiting,* since it is just another word for *lending.* If there are real costs in the interest relation, his are those real costs. They will not, however, be the less or the more by what you expect to do or turn out to do with the borrowed money, or by how the person to whom you pay it became earlier possessed of what he turns over to you—land or potatoes or machines—or by what service he provides in your behalf—*e.g.,* house occupancy or pasture use, or labor performed for you.

Moreover, if the lender's lending is a real-cost sort of waiting, it is again to be stressed that the lessor's leasing is equally also a waiting— the seller's selling a supreme case of waiting. And if this looks like fudge —as it is—along with it as fudge must go the entire real-cost aspect of the lending process.

Taking it, then, as past knowing whether, free from all the complications from which in human experience it is never free, the mere preference for present satisfactions over future satisfactions would in the balance attach a real cost to the waiting that is implicit in the fact of lending funds—we console ourselves with the fact that, excepting for whatever importance may attach to real-cost explanations of money costs, there is no need to know. There are influences enough in actual affairs adequate to the explanation of interest rates, irrespective of any assumed fundamental preferences of the real-cost quality: demands for industrial equipment, socially beneficial or other, inclusive of lands and agricultural machinery; for labor and raw materials; for equipment goods in clearly predatory enterprises; for merchandising, inclusive of equipment; for durable consumption goods. There is nothing to indicate that with in-dustrial borrowing solely—in the lack of any consumption borrowing wise and unwise; of fiscal deficits in general; and of war bonds—there could be no lending for interest. Nor does Marshall so hold. He does not accept the consumption perspective theory of interest; nor, even though often he appears to attribute interest to the marginal efficiency of equipment goods, does his funds capital permit in principle this view; or even an appeal to the marginal efficiency of funds in the gain process; but only to the marginal inducement to borrow for no matter what pur-pose. As a borrowing of funds, it makes gratuitous and even impossible the resort to any marginal isolation other than that implicit in the marginal borrowing of capital funds.

And further, the implicit position that borrowing to buy land affords a demand for funds, and thus that land rents may transform themselves into interest charges; that land is interest-paying as soon as its returns are presented as a rate per cent on its market value; and that lands get valued through the capitalizing of their prospective returns into a present worth of price—these positions suffice to commit him to the view that capital is any durable, objective and valued source of valuable private income, a private possession affording income; and interest that income computed in the dollar-time unit. But these are views that it was the essential thesis in Marshall's undertaking to refute. For they divorce interest as a money cost from dependence on any original real cost of saving—and this entirely irrespective of whether the homogeneity of interest dollars is anywhere paralleled by a homogeneity of real-cost savings; entirely irrespective also of whether banking loans have behind them any real costs at all. And if all property, no matter whence derived, and all hires of the property, articulate with waiting in the purely indi-vidual sense, real costs go out of the reckoning, by the test of the original theoretical bearing of them.

INDEX

INDEX

Abstinence; in Senior's theory, 13
  See also Waiting
Austrian School, 17, 71, 116
Averages, misuse of in utility analysis, 89 ff.

Banking; as source of loan funds, 453-455
  See also Capital, Interest, Money

Cairnes, J. E., 5, 109, 111
Capital, 140-164
  in classical economics, 9, 11 ff.
  definition of, 144, 145, 152 ff., 207 ff.
  See also Interest, Land, Land capital, Saving, Waiting
Classical economics; elements of value theory, 69 ff., 165 ff.
  outline of system, 5-14
Constant return, 432, 435, 436, 438
Consumers' surplus, note on, 101-106
Costs; Austrian treatment of, 116 ff.
  capital, 11 ff., 138, 140 ff.
    See also Interest
  employee, *see* Costs (real)
  functional relation to supply and price, 107-139, 375-417
  land, *see also* Land capital, Opportunity costs, Rents
  marginal, in relation to normal price, 398, 409 ff.
    See also Marginal isolation
  money, 107 ff.
    in classical economics, 6 ff.
    in neo-classical economics, 19, 23
    in relation to current prices, 126 ff.
    in relation to normal periods, 388 ff.
    in relation to real costs, 388 ff.
  price-determined and price-determining, 27, 108, 131 ff., 140 ff.
    See also Quasi-rents
  prime, 287, 377, 400 ff., 411, 429
  real, 107 ff., 249-252, 324, 388 ff., 462 ff.
    in classical economics, 6 ff., 11 ff.

in neo-classical economics, 18, 20, 22, 23
regress analysis of, 126 ff., 261 ff.
relative, 112
social, 227
supplementary, 257, 377, 393, 400 ff., 411, 429
waiting, *see* Waiting
  See also Opportunity costs
Cost of production, *see* Costs
Cost of reproduction, 114

Definitions, notes on Marshall's use of, 152-164, 207-214
Demand; curves or schedules, 40 ff.
  in neo-classical economics, 15 ff.
  reciprocal, 37
  relation of utility to, 69-101
  See also Demand and Supply, Marginal utility, Price offers
Demand and Supply, 37
  general conditions of, 20, 28, 132, 253, 283
  mechanics of, 37-46, 355 ff.
Diminishing return, law of, 418-438
Distribution, theory of; productivity, 296
  use of marginal isolation in, 181 ff.
  See also Earnings of management, Interest, Land rents, Marginal isolation, Wages
Dosing, *see* Marginal isolation

Earnings of management, 319-327
  normal earnings, 320 ff.
  as quasi-rents, 278 ff., 319 ff.
Economics; note on Marshall's definition of, 29-35
  See also Classical economics, Neo-classical economics, Institutional economics
Economics of Distribution, The, by J. A. Hobson, 184n.
Equilibrium; moving, of prices, 21
  normal, 25
  See also Normal
Fertility, *see* Land capital, Rents

479